JOSEPH J. PLAUD, Ph.D.
DEPARTMENT OF PSYCHOLOGY
UNIVERSITY OF NORTH DAKOTA
POST OFFICE BOX 8380
GRAND FORKS, ND 58202-8380

Behavior Analysis of Language and Cognition

D1566677

Behavior Analysis of Language and Cognition

The Fourth

International Institute on Verbal Relations

Editors:
Steven C. Hayes
Linda J. Hayes
Masaya Sato
Koichi Ono

Behavior Analysis of Language and Cognition / edited by Steven C. Hayes, Linda J. Hayes, Masaya Sato, and Koichi Ono

320 pp.   Paperback. ISBN 1-878978-17-9

Hardback. ISBN 1-878978-18-7

© 1994 CONTEXT PRESS
933 Gear Street, Reno, NV 89503-2729

Printed in the United States of America

About the Conference Series

The International Institute on Verbal Relations is a series of week-long working meetings on the analysis of language and related issues, primarily but not exclusively from a behavioral point of view. Each Institute involves formal presentations as well as formal and informal discussions among a small, select group of international participants. The Institutes are held in relatively isolated locations so as to create an intensive, distraction-free discussion.

There have been four Institutes, held in Bad Kreuznach, West Germany in June of 1986, Tequesquitengo, Mexico in June 1987, Aguas de Lindoia, Brazil in January 1989, and Mt. Fuji, Japan in July 1992. The proceedings of the International Institutes are published by CONTEXT PRESS. The proceedings of the First Institute were published as *Dialogues on Verbal Behavior*, edited by Linda J. Hayes and Philip N. Chase, in 1991; the proceedings of the Second and Third Institutes appeared as *Understanding Verbal Relations*, edited by Steven C. Hayes and Linda J. Hayes, in 1992. *Behavior Analysis of Language and Cognition* represents the proceedings from the Fourth International Institute on Verbal Relations.

Table of Contents

Section 1
Stimulus Relations and the
Nature and Acquisition of Verbal Events

Section 2
Cognition and the Impact of Verbal Events

Acknowledgements

This volume is the proceedings of the Fourth International Institute on Verbal Relations, which was held at the the Fujizakuroso Hotel at the foot of Mt. Fuji July 10 through 15, 1992. The conference was a working meeting of the authors in this book, plus a small number of discussion leaders not in this book, including Iver Iverson and Makiko Naka. We thank them for their efforts.

The IIVR 4 was supported by grants from the National Science Foundation (#INT-9117055) and by the Japan Society for the Promotion of Science. We thank them for their support.

There is no more important area of research for behavior analysis than language and cognition. We hope the contributions in this volume will advance the work that needs to be done.

Steven C. Hayes
Linda J. Hayes
Masaya Sato
Koichi Ono

March, 1994

Chapter 1

Relational Frame Theory: A Functional Approach to Verbal Events

Steven C. Hayes

University of Nevada

For the past several years I and my colleagues have been developing a new behavior analytic perspective on verbal events, which we term Relational Frame Theory (RFT). This approach is housed firmly in the behavior analytic tradition but my experiences in presenting the model suggest that some proponents of that tradition are uncertain about or even worried about Relational Frame Theory. This chapter is about that worry.

Goals for this Chapter

My purposes in this chapter are threefold. First, I want to walk through an operant explanation of derived stimulus relations as learned behavior, and to lay out some of the research that is supportive of this approach. Whether or not one wishes to adopt the trappings of the RFT analysis, behavior analysts need to face this somewhat more general question. It is unseemly not to try first to make existing behavioral principles work in the area of derived stimulus relations.

Second, I want to describe how RFT can be part of a more general approach to verbal behavior, spanning the range from word-referent relations to the scientific analysis of the natural world.

Third, I want briefly to show that even though RFT greatly undermines Skinner's specific theory of verbal events, his sensitivities have a place in the overall view of verbal events RFT produces. Relational and direct contingency accounts are largely speaking about different things, and if you delimit their respective domains, many of the contradictions between them are reduced or disappear.

A Brief Summary of Relational Frame Theory

Relational Frame Theory has been discussed in detail elsewhere (e.g., Hayes, 1991; Hayes & Hayes, 1989, 1992; Hayes & Wilson, 1993), but a brief summary seems necessary for the reader unfamiliar with the approach. I have three central things to say about relational frames.

Relational Frames have Three Primary Characteristics

Behavior analytic researchers can be mislead by concentrating too much on stimulus equivalence as an example of relational phenomenon. The very word "equivalence" suggests that the important issue is how classes of similar events form, how sets of stimuli can be created, how these sets differ from functional stimulus classes, and so on. Much is unknown about these questions, and years of important research will be done on them. Some of the other chapters in this book lay out ways to proceed. But it is equally, if not more important to focus on the *relational* issues inherent in stimulus equivalence. Sidman's definition of stimulus equivalence (Sidman & Tailby, 1982) puts the emphasis there, because reflexivity, symmetry, and transitivity are all relational terms. These properties *result* in classes of stimuli in the case of stimulus equivalence, but if the relational phenomena are more general than equivalence, they may *not* result in classes of stimuli in other cases.

For example, suppose a person learns to select B given A, and C given B (for simplicity sake we will ignore the awkward language of conditional discriminations, but this is what we mean). Now B is paired with a shock. We know that A and C will produce physiological arousal as a result (Augustson, Dougher, & Markham, 1993). If we focus only on this fact, the important question seems to be "why are all three stimuli in the same class?" Such a question is worthwhile, but is not the most challenging issue in such effects.

To see this, imagine a slight twist in this experiment. The subject has been pre-trained to relate events differently. The subject may have been given a history of selecting a comparison that *comes shortly after* the sample in the presence of certain contextual cues. Perhaps an alarm clock is a sample, and a picture of waking up is one of the comparisons. After an extensive history of this kind, this same person learns (in the presence of these contextual cues) to select B given A, and C given B (where A, B, and C are now arbitrary stimuli). B is then paired with a shock. The question is this: what effects will A and C now have? It seems highly likely to me, based on quite similar work that we and others have done, that A will produce arousal, but C will produce more calm even than a novel stimulus. The issue is no longer a simple issue of class composition. We cannot say, for example, that A and B are in a class, but C is not, because the effects of C are also based upon its relation to B. A, B, and C are not in a class—they are in a *relation*. This issue is inherently more challenging to behavior analysts, and more important.

What kind of relation are were speaking about? A psychological relation exists if the stimulus functions of one event depend upon the stimulus functions of another event. Stimulus relations, so defined, can be directly trained or derived, and can be based on formal properties or arbitrary. Classical conditioning, modeling, or operant conditioning all involve stimulus relations in a psychological sense.

RFT defines a specific subset of psychological stimulus relations: those in which the relation involved is arbitrarily applicable, derived, learned, and controlled by context. Such arbitrarily applicable relational responding is said to involve the following three properties:

Mutual Entailment. In a given context, if A is directly related to B, then, in that context, a derived relation between B and A is mutually entailed. More technically, if by direct training the stimulus functions of B depends upon A, then by derivation those of A depend upon B. The specific derived relation depends upon that which was trained. For example, if B is better than A, then A is worse that B. Mutual entailment is the generic case of what is termed "symmetry" in the equivalence literature.

Combinatorial Entailment. In a given context, if A is directly related to B, and B is directly related to C, then, in that context, a derived relation between A and C is mutually entailed. Combinatorial entailment is the generic case of what are termed "transitivity" or "equivalence" in the equivalence literature.

Transformation of Stimulus Function. In a given context, if there is a mutual relation between A and B, and A has some additional psychological function, then, in a context that selects that function as relevant, the stimulus functions of B may be transformed consistent with its mutual relation to A.

These are the defining characteristics of arbitrarily applicable stimulus relations. RFT asks the question: where do such psychological relations come from? Is stimulus equivalence the only example? If not, what other kinds are there? What impact do they have on human functioning?

Relational Frames Can be Learned

RFT begins with the supposition that organisms can learn to respond relationally to any stimulus event, and that performances such as stimulus equivalence, some forms of exclusion, and verbal behavior itself can be analyzed as generalized instances of such responding. The idea of relational learning is hardly new. It has been shown hundreds of times with non-arbitrary stimulus sets. For example, mammals, birds, and even insects can readily be trained to select such stimuli as "the dimmest" of several options (Reese, 1968). Non-arbitrary relations, however, are defined by the formal properties of the related events themselves. Given a choice of two or more objects of different brightness, one will indeed be "dimmest" and that status is established by the formal properties of the event relative to the formal properties of a set of stimuli.

RFT adds a very simple idea: at least some organisms can learn to respond relationally to an event where this relational response occurs because of contextual cues other than simply the direct and formal properties of the event relative to the formal properties of a set of stimuli. Read this sentence: A is smaller than A. Based on formal properties, the letter A is larger than the letter A, but the relational response of treating one event as larger than another is contextually controlled in normal adults and can be applied to any set of events regardless of their formal relations. In other words, as a verbal relation, what is crucial is not the formal properties of A versus A, but rather a history of reinforcement for the application of a particular relational response controlled by cues such as "is larger than" or ">."

We call such responses "relational frames" (or, to keep it as a verb, "framing relationally"). The word "frame" is used to connote a response that can involve any stimulus event, just as a picture frame can contain any picture (the same connotation that led Skinner to speak of "grammatical frames" and "autoclitic frames"). Because relational frames are controlled by context rather than exclusively by the direct properties of the related events themselves, they are said to be arbitrarily applicable. Relational frames are specific kinds of *learned arbitrarily applicable relational responses*.

Just as relational learning is not new, the idea of overarching behavioral classes that contain virtually unlimited numbers of members is familiar to behavior analysts. Generalized imitation is perhaps the classic example. An unlimited variety of response topographies can be substituted for the topographies used in the initial training not because imitation is entirely unlearned because what is learned is an overarching behavioral class of do-what-others-do behavior (e.g., Baer, Peterson, & Sherman, 1967; Gewirtz & Stengle, 1968). Learned arbitrarily applicable relational responses are conceived to be such overarching classes.

Relational Frames are the Defining Characteristic of Verbal Events

Several researchers have suggested that stimulus equivalence provides a good working model of sematic meaning. RFT takes this idea one step further. If stimulus equivalence is just the most basic example of a relational frame, then perhaps relational frames are a defining characteristic of verbal events (Hayes & Hayes, 1989). This claim is in some senses not empirical because "defining characteristics" are inherently terminological matters. But there are many arguments, both logical and data-based, to be made. For example: a) the obvious features of verbal events as defined in lay language (e.g., indirectness, conventionality, specificity, and so on) are readily understandable in terms of arbitrarily applicable relational responding (see Hayes & Hayes, 1992; Hayes & Wilson, 1993), b) language abilities covary with relational abilities at least to a degree (Devany, Hayes, & Nelson, 1986), c) procedures used to train or test derived relational responding can also be used to train reading, or other verbal performances (e.g., de Rose, de Souza, Rossito, & de Rose, 1992) and d) the meaning of terms like "symbol," "reference," and so on seem to require bidirectional stimulus relations in lay language (in that regard it is interesting that the very word "relation" comes from the same root as the term "reference"). Other logical arguments can be made (e.g., see Hayes & Hayes, 1989), but presenting these is not the purpose of this chapter.

Contextualists such as myself cannot get too excited about definitional matters in the abstract because scientific categories are always only useful fictions at best. If RFT is "true" it will only be so in the sense that it is useful. It should stand or fall by whether it leads to applied and basic advances in the area of verbal relations.

The theory is fairly specific in its implications in some areas, which makes the workability of the approach testable. The many studies we have already done in the area have been tests of that workability, and so far the approach has worked well. But there are many other kinds of research waiting to be done. For example, RFT suggests that extensive training in underlying abstract relations should increase the flexibility and sophistication of verbal performances in children. We should literally be able to train equivalencing (and "opposing" or "differenting") as behaviors, and improvement in these areas should lead to improvements in the use of language. If this key idea is not the case, RFT should be put aside as an approach to verbal behavior.

Let me give a brief example of what RFT might lead applied researchers to do. If we were to develop language training methods based on RFT they would emphasize the acquisition of basic relations (same, opposite, different, greater than, before, etc.), the establishment of flexible contextual control over these relations, the flexible combination of such responses into sets of relations, transformation of stimulus functions through these relational sets, control over such responding by subtle aspects of the natural environment, and the use of all of this to predict and manipulate the environment. The usual behavioral approaches to language training have been too caught up with content—with the training of specific words, or the acquisition of specific concepts applicable in the real world. These are important, but RFT suggests that the flexibility and development of the underlying behavioral process is equally important. I play games with my 5-year old son Charlie that give an example of what I mean by "flexibility." These games are designed to increase the arbitrary applicability of his relational responses. When driving about, I ask him questions such as "If I were you who would you be to me?" or "if green were red when should I stop?" or "If x is the opposite of y and y is the opposite of z, and I like x, which would I like, y or z?" Even young children can be taught such abstract relational responses—RFT suggests they are much more important than one might suppose.

There are other empirical ways to approach the connection between verbal behavior and relational frames. For example, some of the effects known to occur with verbal instruction ("insensitivity" to changing contingencies, increased ability to deal with delayed or probabilistic consequences, and so on) should also occur with relational stimuli. We could literally construct artificial languages using relational preparations to test this. Many other examples could be given, but my point is simply that this core assumption of RFT, even though it is a definitional assumption, is also testable to a degree.

To summarize, RFT leads to a view in which derived stimulus relations are a defining characteristic of verbal events; they have three dominant properties—mutual and combinatorial entailment and the transformation of stimulus functions; and they can be approached as learned behaviors. Those interested in equivalence or similar performances can reject the first two points, and still be interested in the third. Thus, I will present some data supportive of this position.

Deriving Stimulus Relations as Learned Behavior

What are the characteristics of discriminated operant behavior? There are several, but four properties seem particularly important: a) operants develop, b) operants are flexible and can be shaped, c) operants can come under stimulus control, and d) operants are controlled by their consequences. If deriving stimulus relations is learned behavior, all four of these characteristics should apply. Some evidence exists in each area, and in all cases the data are supportive.

Development

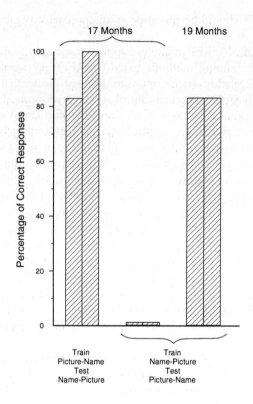

Figure 1. *The symmetrical performances of Charlie at age s 17 and 19 months*

Learning is an inherently developmental concept. As a result of experience with the contingent relationships between situations and actions, these actions evolve. If deriving arbitrary stimulus relations is operant behavior, it too should develop over time. Does it?

The question is a difficult one because in many areas the performances involved occur quite early, and thus this question must be asked with infants. Recent evidence from work with pinnipeds is encouraging, because it suggests that deriving arbitrary stimulus relations can be trained in nonhumans in a manner envisioned by RFT (Schusterman & Kastak, 1993). If so, this question of the development of derived relational responding will ultimately be thoroughly researched with nonhuman under controlled conditions. For now, however, the primary preparation in which to ask this question is in longitudinal human developmental research. This is difficult work to do because human infants are notoriously hard to study, and much of the work is necessarily naturalistic.

At least one such study exists. Lipkens, Hayes, and Hayes (1992) followed from 12 to 26 months the relational development of an infant boy named Charlie (the reader will not be surprised to learn that this remarkable boy's last name is "Hayes"). During that time Charlie showed several instances of relational development.

Figure 1, for example, shows the development of symmetry from 17 to 19 months. At 17 months Charlie showed Name - Object symmetry given Object - Name training, but not vice versa. By 19 months he showed Object - Name symmetry given Name - Object training.

It seems unlikely that this developmental effect was due to difficulties in oral behavior, because he could readily imitate orally, but if so Figure 2 should be more convincing. In this case Charlie showed mutual exclusion as early as 16 months, but

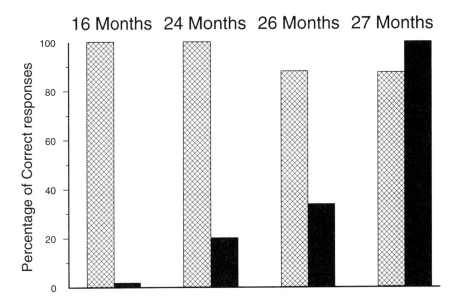

EXCLUSION

Exclusion and Resultant Derived Symmetry

Figure 2. A clear example of a developmental trend in Charlie's relational performances. The cross hatched bars show his exclusion of objects with known names given novel names. This performance was present as soon as we tested for it. The fill bars show the development of a symmetrical relation between the unknown name and the unknown object (a dervied, derived performance). He was over two years old

did not derive a symmetrical relation between the novel name and excluded object until much later. The developmental trend in this case cannot be explained by the acquisition of oral performances, since he showed that in another context by 19 months (see Figure 1).

There are other such data in Lipkens, et al., 1993, but the point is made. Derived relations seem to emerge over time in very young children. This does not prove that relational responding is an operant, but it makes that more plausible. The converse is also true: if there were no evidence of development it would prove that such responding is *not* learned behavior.

Establishing Different Response Forms

Operants can be shaped and therefore show a high degree of flexibility and variability in form. If stimulus equivalence is an example of a relational frame then it must not be the only example. Derived relations of many kinds should be establishable. They are.

In the study by Steele and Hayes (1991), for example, subjects were trained in the presence of three different contextual cues to select a comparison that was either different from, the same as, or opposite of the sample stimulus. For example, given the cue "O" (actually it was not an "O" but an arbitrary nonsense graphical form, but the letter "O" works here for expository purposes) and a short line, picking a long line was reinforced; or given the same cue and a few dots, selecting many was reinforced. Conversely, given cue "S" and a short line, picking a short line was reinforced; or given the same cue and a few dots, selecting a few dots was reinforced. Over time "O" came to control a opposite relations, "S" a same relation, and so on, as was shown by the perfect performances on new, non-arbitrarily related sets of stimuli. The pre-trained contextual cues were then used in an *arbitrary* matching-to-sample procedure. The trained network shown in the top of Figure 3 lead to the derived performances shown in the bottom of that figure.

For example, if in the presence of the "O" cue, subjects were trained to pick B3 and C3 given A1, and D1 given C3, subjects now picked B3 given D1 in the presence of an "O" cue, but *avoided* B3 given C3 and an "O" cue, selecting B3 only when an "S" cue was present. For the point of view of conditional equivalence classes this result makes no sense, but it does if the cue controlled relational responding. An opposite of an opposite of an opposite is opposite (D1 - B3), but an opposite of an opposite is the same (B3 - C3). Ongoing research in our laboratory and in Dermot Barnes llaboratory have used similar methods with even more complex relational network and with the same basic outcome. Either equivalence or non-equivalence can emerge from arbitrary matching to sample when cues are pre-trained to control various kinds of non-arbitrary relational responding. Importantly, three, four, or even more relations can be shown in the same individual at the same time. Similarly, even relations that are not strictly symmetrical (e.g., "larger than") can be used in this procedures and with the same outcome. These last two points are theoretically crucial because it becomes almost impossible to account simply for the results by mere combinations of equivalence and non-equivalence.

This shows that derived relational responding is quite flexible—stimulus equivalence is apparently but one example of an arbitrary derived stimulus relation. If derived relational responding is learned behavior, such flexibility and contextual

Trained Relations

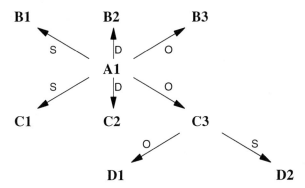

Basic Set of Tested Derived Relations

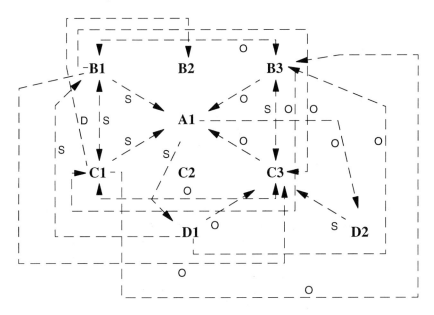

*Figure 3. The trained relations in the top panel produced the
derived relations in the bottom panel when the indicated pretrained relational cue
(represented by O, D, or S, for opposite, different, and same, respectively) was presented.*

control is as it should be. There seems to be no reason a priori that subjects could
learning a relation such as "same" without also being able to learn a relation such as
"bigger than" or "before" or "cause of" or an infinity of such relations.

Contextual Control

The data were have just described show that relational responding can come under stimulus control—as it should if it is learned behavior. Many other studies have shown this in the equivalence literature (e.g., Wulfert & Hayes, 1988).

Consequences

If relational responding is an operant and if this behavior is at the core of verbal events, then it is certainly an operant with a huge history. Behaviors with extraordinarily long histories can be less sensitive to consequential control by virtue of that history, but if relational responding is an operant it should be shown to be at least sensitive to its consequences. It has.

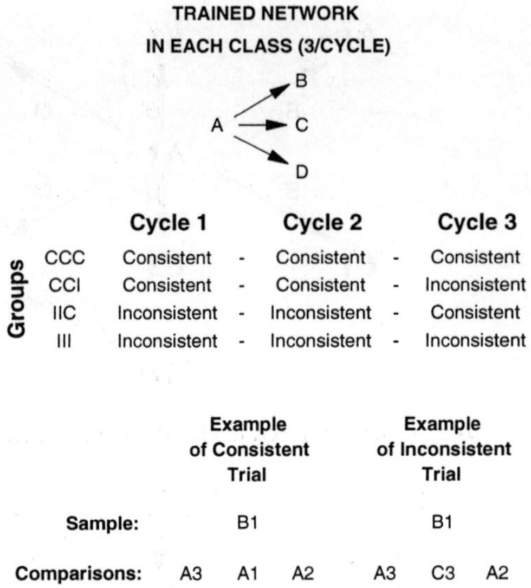

While the original consequence for relational responding is probably arbitrary and

**TRAINED NETWORK
IN EACH CLASS (3/CYCLE)**

```
            B
          ↗
A ←——▶ C
          ↘
            D
```

		Cycle 1		Cycle 2		Cycle 3
Groups	CCC	Consistent	-	Consistent	-	Consistent
	CCI	Consistent	-	Consistent	-	Inconsistent
	IIC	Inconsistent	-	Inconsistent	-	Consistent
	III	Inconsistent	-	Inconsistent	-	Inconsistent

	Example of Consistent Trial			Example of Inconsistent Trial		
Sample:	B1			B1		
Comparisons:	A3	A1	A2	A3	C3	A2

Figure 4. Training and testing used. Three separate sets of four-member equivalence classes were trained in each cycle.

social, as in earliest language training, over time such relational responding is probably maintained because it is so useful in dealing with the environment. Verbal behavior helps make sense of the world—to make it predictable and modifiable.

Based on this line of reasoning, we (Leonhard and Hayes, 1991) thought that specific forms of relational responding should be disrupted if conditions were arranged such that this responding did not help make sense of the world. In an Alice in Wonderland world, verbal relations should be relied upon less and less.

Figure 4 shows the procedure used. Subjects were given the conditional discriminations necessary to form three four-member equivalence classes, and were then tested on all three classes. This cycle was repeated three times, each time with a whole new set of stimuli. What was manipulated was the presence of inconsistent testing items. Some subjects received the all the usual equivalence testing items. Others received those same items but in addition were given an equal number of nonsensical testing items that could not be answered on the basis of equivalence (see bottom of Figure 4).

There were four conditions (see the middle of Figure 4). Subjects were either given a history of inconsistent testing, or consistent testing over the first two cycles.

Half of each were then given consistent or inconsistent testing in Cycle 3. The results are shown in Figure 5. Subject exposed to inconsistent testing in Cycle 3 showed lower equivalence responding on the items that could be answered based on equivalence (the two bars on the left of Figure 5 compared to the two on the right). This, however, could be explained by the possibility that inconsistent items led to new equivalence relations and thus class disorganization in Cycle 3. What is more crucial is that equivalence was disrupted in Cycle 3, even if all the testing items could be answered on the basis of equivalence, if the subjects had a *history* with other stimuli of inconsistent testing. Conversely, equivalence is disrupted less by inconsistent items in Cycle 3 provided that the subject has had a *history* of consistent testing with other classes. It appears as though the coherence of the test items themselves function as a consequence for derived relational responding. Equivalence can be weakened simply by arranging for equivalencing not to pay off for the subject in a more organized and simplified world.

Summary

Can we think of derived stimulus relations as the result of relational responding as an operant? By the criteria normally applied to operants, no data currently exist that would contradict such a view, and several kinds of data are actively supportive. This does not close the book on the matter, but there should be no reason to abandon a parsimonious solution in the absence of strong reasons to do so. Specific relational responses act like overarching operant classes.

The RFT view also explains data supposedly supportive of other approaches. For example, RFT provides a technical analysis of how verbal mediation works. Data showing that naming helps in the formation of relational networks can be explained on the basis of names as contextual cues for

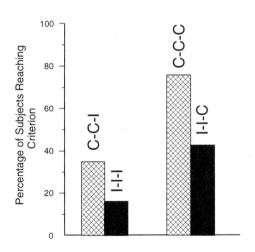

Effect of Testing History on the Derivation of Equivalence Relations in Cycle 3

Figure 5. Results for the equivalence testing items in Cycle 3. The bars on the left had inconsistent testing in Cycle 3; those on the right had consistent testing only. The solid bars had a history of inconsistent testing in other cycles; the hatched bars had a history of only consistent testing.

relational responses, and on the basis of derived relations formed to the names themselves. Using language to *explain* equivalence has other difficulties: a) equivalence forms so early (Lipkens, et al., 1993) that verbal mediation seems to be a weak explanation, and b) verbal mediation requires a technical behavioral analysis that does not itself appeal to derived stimulus relations. So far as I am aware, all such attempts end up imagining implausible training histories, appealing to strong effects for backward conditioning, or explaining derived relations by another form of derived relations. When added to the lack of parsimony these approaches produce, there seems to be little reason to recommend them at this point.

Why Not Approach Derived Relational Responding as Learned Behavior?

The concern about RFT may simply be because we have not yet spoken clearly enough and long enough to be understood. Other researchers are only now testing and extending RFT (e.g., a terrific series of studies out of Dermot Barnes' laboratory in Ireland) and it takes time for alternatives to become known and be seen clearly. Some of the ready objections from within the behavioral analytic camp (e.g., "this is a structural analysis" or "this is mentalistic") do not actually apply to RFT and it is not too difficult to remove these misunderstandings through explication of the theory. But there are other sources of difficulty.

The Unwarranted Dominance of *Verbal Behavior*

First and perhaps most importantly, RFT directly challenges B. F. Skinner's perspective on verbal events. Because of Skinner's intellectual dominance within behavior analysis, some people take his theory of verbal behavior to be *the* behavior analytic view of verbal events rather than *a* behavior analytic view of verbal events. RFT presents an anomaly to these persons: it is clearly antagonistic to Skinner's specific theory, and yet it purports to be a behavior analytic approach. A behavior analytic friend of mine, who is otherwise quite interested in RFT, once exclaimed during a conversation "Oh no! You are not going to take away *Verbal Behavior*, are you?"

Skinner's analysis, while brilliant and compelling, has many weaknesses, as some behavior analysts—including myself—have argued for some time. In this context I would like to mention one that behavior analysts should find most disturbing: it is not a truly functional analysis. A true functional analysis explains and categorizes behavior on the basis of distinct psychological functions. Distinct psychological functions are those functions that involve unique histories or behavioral processes from the point of view of the behaving organism. Skinner's analysis is not a functional analysis in these terms.

Imagine a situation: a rat presses a bar. Deflection of the bar is detected by an experimenter sitting outside the chamber. After about ten bar presses on average, the experimenter reaches into a bag of food pellets and drops a piece of food into a funnel leading to the rat's food dish. The bar press is clearly verbal behavior by Skinner's definition because reinforcement for it is mediated by another organism, and that organism requires special training to do so (Skinner recognized this explicitly, saying that the experimental animal and the experimenter form a "small but genuine verbal community," 1957, p. 108).

Now picture a situation that from the rat's point of view is the same in every detail. The rat pushes a bar and about every ten times food arrives in the food chamber. When we look outside the chamber, however, we see that the other end of the bar the rat is pressing has pierced a bag of food pellets. About ten presses is all it takes to jar loose a pellet, which falls neatly into the funnel and from there into the food dish. Although the situation is identical from the point of view of the rat, this now is *not* verbal behavior, because the bar press is not reinforced through the mediation of another organism. Unlike all other functional analyses accepted within behavior analysis, this so-called functional analysis of verbal behavior distinguishes "functions" from the point of view of an *observer* rather than from the point of view of the behaving organism. The "functional differences" have to do with the *literal* source of stimulation rather than the *psychological* source of stimulation.

Suppose a pigeon pecks a key light three times. In case one, the light comes from an electrically excited filament in a vacuum. In case two, it come from the sun. In case three from a wax candle. Imagine that the illumination is indistinguishable. To follow Skinner's logic, we would call the first peck "Edison-produced behavior," the second "fusion-produced behavior," and the third "bee-produced behavior." These are not functional categories in a psychological sense, because the psychological issue is not the source of the lighted object, but the source of the behavioral function of the light. Similarly, in the case of verbal behavior, it is not a functional analysis to suggest that the difference between verbal and nonverbal behavior comes from the source of the objects that might function as reinforcers. The psychological difference, if there is a difference, will be found in the nature of and sources of the actual behavioral functions involved.

In contrast, RFT creates a division between verbal and nonverbal behavior that is truly functional in a behavior analytic sense. Arbitrarily applicable relational responding is a category that refers to a particular source of behavioral functions. The historical differences are understandable entirely from the point of view of the behaving organism of interest–not from an observer perspective. The difference are not about the sources of objects, but of psychological functions. RFT may be true or false, but it is behavioral. Despite its hegemony within behavior analysis, Skinner's analysis is not in fact a behavioral analysis. It is inconsistent with Skinner's own metatheoretical and theoretical approach.

Choosing the Approach Versus Choosing the Outcome

The second major source of difficulty is that RFT alters fundamentally how we view many key behavioral concepts and principles when they are applied to verbal organisms. RFT is a very conservative position at the level of initial behavioral process. The key question in RFT is "can we think of deriving stimulus relations as operant behavior?" If the answer is "yes," however, there are dramatic behavioral implications. Here are just a few: a) equivalence is only one example of a infinitude of possible derived relations, b) new forms of stimulus control emerge from these behaviors, c) many important behavioral processes such as stimulus control or reinforcement control must be rethought in the practical world of verbal organisms, d) many of the cognitive criticisms of behavioral thinking end up having more substance to them than behaviorists would like to believe, and e) the psychological gulf between verbal and nonverbal organisms widens.

Here we have a paradox—an extremely conservative approach at the level of process seems to lead to troublesome outcome implications. This may in turn help explain another paradox. Some very careful and conservative behavior analysts seem attracted to extremely liberal accounts for relational phenomena at the level of behavioral process. No account is more dramatically liberal than the claim that equivalence is a primitive (Sidman, 1990), for example, because this means that the phenomenon cannot be analyzed into components that are known within existing behavior theory. Ironically, these liberal process accounts lead to much more limited outcome implications for behavior theory more generally—because they isolate stimulus equivalence as a special case and emphasize that relational phenomena are primarily just other ways to form stimulus classes. In my view, parsimony and conservatism should be a matter of process, not outcome. We must let the chips fall where they may.

Putting Derived Relational Responding in its Place

Relational responding is not the whole story of language development. As it stands it is most relevant to semantics. Semantics is a foundation for verbal events, but it is not the whole of it.

We can define some of the scope of the phenomena to be explained by considering two issues: how are stimulus functions acquired or modified, and how does social influence work. The first issue can be divided into two basic kinds of phenomena, as is shown in Figure 6.

Stimulus functions can either be acquired or modified directly or via derived means. The former is a nonverbal process. The latter is a verbal process. Consider, for example, the stimulus functions of the word "sick." Suppose I told a person they would feel sick shortly before I administered a nauseating and quick acting but nonlethal poison. With several administrations, the word "sick" would elicit aversive bodily sensations, even before the poison was delivered (see Figure 6). This is a direct stimulus function. It may also occur now to words that sounds like "sick" or to settings like the one in which the poison was administered. In this case the functions are indirect but are based on the actual formal properties of the experienced events.

Derived stimulus functions in turn can be arranged into three rough groupings: conditions in which a neutral stimulus acquires a function because it has been related to another event with a function; situations in which relational network is modified; and situations in which non-arbitrary events in the previously nonverbal world have their functions modified via participation in relational networks. These three kinds of events are not distinguishable at the level of psychological process and I am not

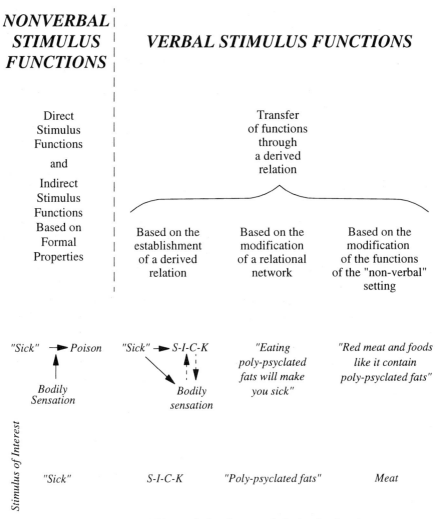

Figure 6. Distinguishing verbal and non-verbal stimulus functions.

suggesting them as fundamental categories for that reasons—rather they are increasingly complex forms of the acquisition or modification of stimulus functions through derived relational responding.

The transformation of stimulus functions has primarily been studied with equivalence relations, and are instances of the first grouping. Transfer has been shown with conditioned reinforcing functions (Hayes, Brownstein, Devany, Kohlenberg, & Shelby, 1987; Hayes, Kohlenberg, & Hayes, 1991), discriminative functions (Hayes, et al., 1987), elicited conditioned emotional responses (Augustson, et al., 1993) and extinction functions (Augustson, et al., 1993), among others. These kinds of effects expand the degree to which directly acquired stimulus functions are psychologically present though increasingly indirect means. To continue with the examples diagrammed in Figure 6, suppose that the oral word "sick" has been directly trained to go with the bodily sensations of feeling ill. The oral name has also been matched to the written name S -I - C - K. Under those circumstances an equivalence class may form between these three elements, and the functions of one of the elements may transfer to the others. The written word, for example, may now produce bodily sensations.

The second kind of phenomenon is more complex. In this case a set of derived stimulus relations are modified by virtue of a new relation. This is the kind of process involved in abstract reasoning. It is easy to give practical examples, but as of yet no behavior analyst has modeled these events using equivalence-like procedures rather than natural language preparations. Increasingly elaborated sets of relations are developed in which new relations occur in the context of a set of established relational actions. To continue with an example from Figure 6, the sentence "Eating poly-psychlated fats will make you sick" is a much more complex version of the process seen with simple equivalence classes. The sentence specifies an if ... then relation between an action and a consequence under certain stimulus conditions. The effects of the action can do some degree be present via a transformation of a set of relation even without directly experiencing the specified outcome. This is more like what we mean by "understanding a rule" that is the simple equivalence situation, although the process is the same.

The last level of complexity is one in which the stimulus functions of the natural world are altered by virtue of the application of a relational network. These increasingly elaborated sets of relational responses modify the stimulus functions of the environment so as to enable more effective commerce with it. At this level, formal properties in the environment act as a cue for relational activity and in turn are modified by those activities. In the example in Figure 6, the statement "Red meat and foods like it contain poly-psychlated fats." With the right history and credible rule givers, red meat may now literally look sickening, as many formally similar foods. The person may begin avoiding greasy french fries, for example, even though they have never been directly related to our imaginary "poly-psychlated fats."

Arbitrarily Applicable Does Not Mean Arbitrarily Applied

This last example begins to raise a tricky issue for RFT. The role of arbitrarily applicable relational responding in the understanding and modification of the natural world presents a seeming contradiction. On the one hand, relational frames are arbitrarily applicable. On the other, they are rarely arbitrarily applied. As is shown in Figure 7, we can think of this as a combination of two continua. As relational responding becomes freed from formal contextual control, it becomes more conventional and arbitrarily applicable and thus more flexibly subject to social regulation and social cues. This is the essence of verbal behavior. But the utility of verbal behavior is hardly purely conventional. Verbal relations allow us to break up and to recombine the properties of the natural world, and thus to interact more effectively with the verbal analyzed world. Thus, a behavior that is arbitrarily applicable comes more and more under the control of subtle formal properties and components of these properties as contextual cues for relational responding. In other words, while verbal relations are arbitrarily applicable they are rarely arbitrarily applied outside of symbolic logic, philosophy, or mathematics classes.

These two dimensions help explain why Skinner's analysis of verbal events relied so heavily on the regulatory effect of subtle formal properties over verbal behavior. When a relation is made between two events, formal properties can almost always be found to "explain" the relation. Only bare phenomena such as stimulus equivalence reveal the arbitrary qualities of the underlying activity.

Here is an experiment to make my point. Select two concrete nouns -- anything -- before reading the next sentence. Now, we will call the first noun "A" and the second "B." How are "A" and "B" alike? Different? Why is A better? How is A the father of B? My guess is that every one of these relational questions, or a myriad like them, will lead to a sensible answer justified by supposed formal properties of the related events. But often these same formal properties would hardly control the non-arbitrary relational capabilities of nonverbal organisms. In other words, the formal properties used to "justify" such relational activities are themselves abstracted as a result of these same relational abilities. If it is always possible to answer such questions we must either suppose that all objects are related in all ways to each other, or that such relations are arbitrarily applicable and that formal properties are context for such activities but not the source of them.

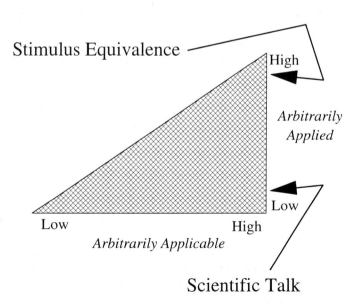

Figure 7. Distinguishing arbitrarily applicable from arbitrarily applied relations.

Communication

In addition to the transformation of stimulus functions involved in verbal reasoning, the second major use of verbal relations is as a method of social control. Communication can be either verbal or nonverbal, depending upon whether the social interchange is dependent upon relational frames or not, respectively. We will deal here only with verbal communication. The basic system is shown in Table 1.

The first two rows we have already dealt with in the context of the transformation of stimulus functions. The characteristic pattern at the third level (what I am calling here the level of persuasion) is that persons, whether speakers or listeners, are acting both with regard to a verbal relation between events (whether or not those events are purely verbal events or include stimuli in the natural environment) and with regard to another person. For example, I spend quite a bit of time telling things to my children: explaining the rules of baseball, showing how numbers work, pointing out the signs of spring, and so on. These verbal episodes involve both the verbal material and the listener. When explaining the rules of baseball, for example, I have learned to do it in small doses, not to expect immediate understanding, repeat material frequently, and to link my words to action on the field. These patterns are under the control of my 5 year old Charlie, because if I violate them he becomes agitated, withdraws, becomes confused, and so on. My verbal behavior in such circumstances is constantly under two sources of control constant control.

As a listener the same thing occurs when our listening is regulated both by specified and derived relations with the verbal content (again, whether the material is purely conceptual or includes events in the world), and by the psychological qualities of the speaker from the point of view of the listener. Naturally, I do not mean the speaker as an object when I speak of "the psychological qualities of the speaker from the point of view of the listener." The other may not exist at all in a literal sense, as when we mistake a sound in the kitchen for our mate and happy tell a story about our day only to find that the sound was the wind and our mate is not even yet home.

The fourth level is the level of verbal regulation. This is only a listener function, but the speaker and listener involved may be the same person. At this level, antecedents that have their functions because they participate in relational frames actually guide behavior—the behavior is rule-governed.

Understanding a rule requires that I have the requisite minimal verbal elements (the relational frames needed) and that I bring these to bear on the verbal material. Being socially persuaded involves all of this plus the psychological influence of the speaker. Following a rule requires contingencies that influence the correspondence between the rule and behavior.

We have distinguished three kinds of contingencies that produce rule-following (Hayes, Zettle, & Rosenfarb, 1989). Pliance is behavior due to a history of socially-mediated consequences for a formal correspondence between antecedent verbal stimuli and relevant behavior. Tracking is rule following due to a history of a formal correspondence between antecedent verbal stimuli and the contingencies contacted

Table 1

Levels of Verbal Social Communication

		Speaker	Listener
Miminal Verbal Elements	Relating	Deriving relations and transforming functions	Deriving relations and transforming functions
Verbally Dealing With Concepts and the World	Reasoning	Speaking with meaning (rule generation)	Listening with meaning (rule understanding)
Verbally Dealing With Concepts, the World and the Other	Persuading	Verbal communication (e.g., refering, explaining requesting)	Verbal influence (e.g., believing doubting, agreeing)
Verbally Guided Behavior Change	Regulating		Pliance Tracking Augmenting

by the form, frequency or situational sensitivity of the relevant behavior. Both tracks and the plys "describe contingencies." In pliance the correspondence between the rule and behavior alters the behavior of the verbal community; in the tracking the contingencies are not altered by the rule, or by the behavior it governs—rather, the form, frequency or situational sensitivity of the relevant behavior contact the contingencies regardless of whether or not the behavior is rule-governed. Augmenting is behavior due to antecedent verbal stimuli that alter the degree to which events function as consequences. *Motivative augmenting* is behavior due to antecedent verbal stimuli that temporarily alter the degree to which previously established consequences function as reinforcers or punishers, while *formative augmenting* is behavior due to antecedent verbal stimuli that establish given consequences as reinforcers or punishers. We have written frequently about this level of verbal behavior. It is fully verbal, in our sense of the term, because it is fully dependent upon relational frames.

Skinner's System and RFT

From a contemporary behavior analytic point of view, Skinner's system has theoretical and empirical flaws, but his sensitivities are often very useful. Many, but not all, of Skinner's verbal units have to do with the third level of verbal relations I have just described—issues that are essentially involved in language pragmatics. They are not the defining characteristics of verbal behavior, and trying to make them be so moved Skinner to adopt a nonfunctional definition of verbal events, but they are important distinctions nonetheless.

The tact combines two issues we have dealt with in RFT. First, Skinner tried to use it in place of our minimal verbal element of a relational frame of coordination. Frames of coordination establish equivalence classes and other derived relations of similarity or sameness. Skinner also used the tact, in part, to deal with (in our terms) situations in which a speaker refers a listener to a relation between an event and a verbal term. RFT rejects the first use of a tact because a tact relation is not a derived relation. The second issue, however, is embraced by RFT, and is reflected from the point of view of the listener in the technical category of tracking. We have not yet worked through the similar arrangement from the point of view of the speaker, but when we do I expect to find something there very much like the tact.

A mand is more obviously at the third level. What is important about mands, from the point of view of RFT, is the control over verbal events by the psychological functions of the listener for the speaker. This issue is dealt with from the point of view of the listener in the technical category of pliance. We have not yet worked through the similar arrangement from the point of view of the speaker, but when we do I expect to find something there very much like the mand.

There is also a great deal to do in analysis of verbal events from the point of view of RFT. We have made only the most feeble attempts to deal with grammar, for example (e.g., Wulfert & Hayes, 1988), or any of the more structuralistic matters within verbal behavior. Much of what needs to be done in territory fairly well worked over by Skinner—the field will have to work out how relational concepts such as equivalence or relational frames change how we much deal with these matter. Speaking from the vantage point of our research team, because we have been building this approach from the ground up we are not yet ready to deal with these issues fully, but it may still be possible to integrate the direct contingency analysis of Skinner with the present relational account. One major way has been suggested (Chase & Danforth, 1991; Hayes, 1991): Skinner did not specify the training that a listener actually needed to reinforce most speaker's verbal behavior. In the normal verbal community what seems to be needed is training sufficient to form a reasonable set of conventional contextually-controlled relational frames and a set of conventional stimulus relations formed through these frames.

Skinner's focus on trained social mediation reemerges from a focus on arbitrarily applicable relational responding. Framing relationally necessarily involves trained social mediation, precisely because it is arbitrarily applicable. Only the social/verbal community can arrange reinforcement for such activities because, at least initially, the activities are not based on the formal properties of the related events and the natural contingencies they engage–they are inherently conventional. Only a trained audience, themselves verbally competent, could or would teach such conventional and arbitrary relations. Relational frames, however, are functionally distinct psychological events from the point of view of the behaving organism. Actual social mediation is an observer concept that helps explain how these functionally distinct events are established.

Conclusion

RFT is an evolving approach, but its core concepts have been quite stable fore some time. I have tried to make the case in this chapter that it is an approach fully within the behavioral tradition. Skinner's theory is not *the* behavioral theory of verbal events–it is *a* theory, and it is one that is based entirely on concepts that are over 50 years old. If such a book were to be written now from a behavior analytic point of view, it would have to include relational phenomena as its core, and that fact alone would dramatically alter the approach. Metaphorically, as a field, behavioral psychology needs to begin to "write that book."

References

Augustson, E. M., Dougher, M. J., & Markham, M. R. (May, 1993). *The transfer of CER eliciting and extinction functions via stimulus equivalence classes.* Paper presented at the convention of the Association for Behavior Analysis, Chicago.

Baer, D. M., Peterson, R. F., and Sherman, J. A. (1967). The development of imitation by reinforcing behavioral similarity to a model. *Journal of the Experimental Analysis of Behavior, 10,* 405-416.

Barnes, D. & Keenan, M. (1993). A transfer of functions through derived arbitrary and non-arbitrary stimulus relations. *Journal of the Experimental Analysis of Behavior, 59,* 61-81.

Chase, P. N. & Danforth, J. S. (1991). The role of rules in concept learning. In L. J. Hayes & P. N. Chase (Eds.), *Dialogues on verbal behavior* (pp. 205-225). Reno, NV: Context Press.

de Rose, J. C., de Souza, D. G., Rossito, A. L., & De Rose, T. M. S. (1992). In S. C. Hayes & L. J. Hayes (Eds.), Understanding verbal relations (pp. 69-82). Reno, NV: Context Press.

Devany, J. M., Hayes, S. C., & Nelson, R. O. (1986). Equivalence class formation in language-able and language-disabled children. *Journal of the Experimental Analysis of Behavior, 46,* 243-257.

Gewirtz, J. L. & Stengle, K. G. (1968). Learning of generalized imitation as the basis for identification. *Psychological Review, 5,* 374-397.

Hayes, S. C. (1991). A relational control theory of stimulus equivalence. In L. J. Hayes & P. N. Chase (Eds.), *Dialogues on verbal behavior* (pp. 19-40). Reno, NV: Context Press.

Hayes, S. C., Brownstein, A. J., Devany, J. M., Kohlenberg, B. S., & Shelby, J. (1987). Stimulus equivalence and the symbolic control of behavior. *Mexican Journal of Behavior Analysis, 13,* 361-374.

Hayes, S. C. & Hayes, L. J. (1989). The verbal action of the listener as a basis for rule-governance. In S. C. Hayes (Ed.), *Rule-governed behavior: Cognition, contingencies, and instructional control.* (pp. 153-190). New York: Plenum.

Hayes, S. C. & Hayes, L. J. (1992) Verbal relations and the evolution of behavior analysis. *American Psychologist, 47,* 1383-1395.

Hayes, S. C., Kohlenberg, B. K., & Hayes, L. J. (1991). Transfer of consequential functions through simple and conditional equivalence classes. *Journal of the Experimental Analysis of Behavior, 56,* 119-137.

Hayes, S. C. & Wilson, K. G. (1993). Some applied implications of a contemporary behavior-analytic account of verbal events. *The Behavior Analyst, 16,* 283-301.

Hayes, S. C., Zettle, R. D., & Rosenfarb, I. (1989). Rule following. In S. C. Hayes (Ed.), *Rule-governed behavior: Cognition, contingencies, and instructional control.* (pp. 191-220). New York: Plenum.

Kohlenberg, B. S., Hayes, S. C. & Hayes, L. J. (1991). The transfer of contextual control over equivalence classes through equivalence classes: A possible model of social stereotyping. *Journal of the Experimental Analysis of Behavior, 56,* 505-518.

Leonhard, C. & Hayes, S. C. (May 1991). *Prior inconsistent testing affects equivalence responding.* Paper presented at the meeting of the Association for Behavior Analysis, Altanta.

Lipkens, G., Hayes, S. C., & Hayes, L. J. (in press). Longitudinal study of derived stimulus relations in an infant. *Journal of Experimental Child Psychology.*

Reese, H. W. (1968). *The perception of stimulus relations: Discrimination learning and transposition.* New York: Academic Press.

Schusterman, R. J. & Kastak, D. (1993). A California seal lion (Zalophus Californianus) is capable of forming equivalence relations. *The Psychological Record, 43,* 823-839.

Skinner, B. F. (1957). *Verbal Behavior.* Englewood Cliffs, NJ: Prentice Hall.

Sidman, M. (1990). Equivalence relations: Where do they come from? In D. E. Blackman & H. Lejeune (Eds.), *Behaviour analysis in theory and practice: Contributions and controversies* (pp. 93-114). Hillsdale, NJ: Erlbaum.

Sidman, M. & Tailby, W. (1982). Conditional discrimination vs. matching to sample: An expansion of the testing paradigm. *Journal of the Experimental Analysis of Behavior, 37,* 5-22.

Steele, D. L. & Hayes, S. C. (1991). Stimulus equivalence and arbitrarily applicable relational responding. *Journal of the Experimental Analysis of Behavior, 56,* 519-555.

Wulfert, E. & Hayes, S. C. (1988). The transfer of conditional sequencing through conditional equivalence classes. *Journal of the Experimental Analysis of Behavior, 50,* 125-144.

Chapter 2

The Natural and Artificial Selection of Verbal Behavior

A. Charles Catania
University of Maryland Baltimore County

Selection has gradually displaced association as the fundamental paradigm for the analysis of behavior. The following citation from *Science and Human Behavior* is a significant marker of the transition from a treatment of behavior that takes physics as its reference science (as in Skinner, 1938) to one that emphasizes behavior as a fundamental part of the subject matter of biology:

> In both operant conditioning and the evolutionary selection of behavioral characteristics, consequences alter future probability. Reflexes and other innate patterns of behavior evolve because they increase the chances of survival of the *species*. Operants grow strong because they are followed by important consequences in the life of the *individual* (Skinner, 1953, p. 90).

This quotation is one of Skinner's earliest references to the analogy between phylogenic and ontogenic selection.

The Varieties of Selection

In his interpretations of human behavior, and of verbal behavior in particular, Skinner (1981) appealed to three varieties of selection: phylogenic selection, corresponding to Darwinian natural selection; ontogenic selection, corresponding to operant selection or the selection of behavior by its consequences; and cultural selection, corresponding to the selection of behavior as it passes from one individual to another (although the phrase *selection by consequences* sometimes seems to refer only to the second or operant variety of selection, Skinner used it to refer to all three varieties of selection).

Each of these three varieties of selection involves some kind of variation that provides the source materials upon which it operates, and each has some basis for selecting what survives. Verbal behavior is an especially significant antecedent and consequence of cultural selection, and a major concern of the present account is how this third variety of selection may be relevant to an analysis of verbal behavior. One objective is to make the case that selection at this level is not simply reducible to selection at the other levels.

In the historical development that established Darwinian natural selection as the primary account of biological evolution, the distinction between natural selection and artificial selection played a crucial role. Artificial selection was well known; the question was whether natural contingencies of selection were similarly effective in producing changes in populations of organisms. The distinction between natural and artificial selection may also be significant at other levels of selection. A second major concern of the present account is to explore some implications of the distinction between natural and artificial selection, with special emphasis on its relevance to cultural selection and verbal behavior. But first it is necessary for us to review some properties of selection, starting with phylogenic selection.

Phylogenic Selection

In the Darwinian account of evolution in terms of the differential survival and reproduction of the members of a population (Darwin, 1859), the environment selects the individuals who pass their characteristics on from one generation to the next and thereby shapes the characteristics of those in later populations. Evolution by natural selection requires variations within populations; these variations are the stuff upon which phylogenic selection works.

The theories of evolution that competed with Darwin's were not about whether contemporary species were descended from the very different ancestors found in the geologic record. They all took that for granted, but they differed in what they had to say about the way evolution came about. Selection was well known even before Darwin, but it was the sort used by humans in horticulture and animal husbandry. People knew how to breed plants or livestock selectively for various characteristics (e.g., workhorses for strength and racehorses for speed). Part of Darwin's insight was that a similar kind of selection occurred in nature, without human intervention. There was no argument with artificial selection in Darwin's day; natural selection was the problem (for more detailed accounts, see Bowler, 1983; Catania,1987; Dawkins, 1986).

The evolution of the horse provides striking evidence for natural selection. Over the 50 million years or so since the dawn horse, *Eohippus*, the individuals in the populations from which modern horses are descended gradually increased in size and speed (Simpson, 1951). Many descendants of *Eohippus* were the fastest of their kind in their time, but none like them exist any longer. When selection operates on some relative property, such as speed relative to the mean for a population, the mean for the population changes. For example, after capture by predators has repeatedly selected faster escape, few descendants of the originally slow runners will be left even if that slower running speed had provided a selective advantage at a much earlier time when it was fast relative to the population mean (a similar kind of selection operates on the speed of the predators, because the slowest of those are less likely to catch their prey than the fastest). As *Eohippus* demonstrates, it is inappropriate to assume that examples of ancestral forms will be found within current populations.

In this account, the source of selection is in the environment (the environments of predators include their prey and the environments of prey include their predators). Selection both creates and maintains the features of organisms. For example, the ancestors of whales were once land mammals. After they moved back to the sea, the evolutionary contingencies that made legs advantageous no longer selected for well-formed legs. Instead, selection began to favor limbs that were effective for movement through water. The legs of the ancestors of whales gradually disappeared; in a sense they had extinguished or become extinct (cf. Skinner, 1988, p. 73).

Consider another example. In environments that include tall trees with edible leaves, long necks may be advantageous, especially if shorter trees are scarce or if their leaves are often depleted by competitors. Giraffes arose through the natural selection of relatively long necks. Such selection could not occur in environments that lacked tall trees (just as a discriminative stimulus sets the occasion for the selection of operant behavior, the tall trees set the occasion for the selection of long necks: cf. Skinner, 1988, p. 73). But the selection also depended on available variations. In one species variations among individuals might allow the selection of those with longer necks; in another they might allow the selection of those who climb trees more efficiently. The environment selects from populations of organisms, but that selection can only operate on the variations available within those populations (compare the behavioral principle that a response cannot be reinforced unless it is emitted).

Selection can operate on different features in different populations, and not every feature that seems adaptive is necessarily a product of phylogenic selection. Selectionist accounts demand more than just a plausible story about how some property of an organism might be advantageous. The same is true of selectionist accounts of behavior (to say that a response has been reinforced, it is not enough to know that it occurs often).

Ontogenic Selection

In the Darwinian account, natural selection operates upon successive populations of organisms, but selection can also operate on successive populations of responses within the lifetime of an individual organism (parallels between phylogenic and ontogenic selection have been explored in considerable detail: e.g., Catania, 1978, 1987; Catania & Harnad, 1988; Skinner, 1975, 1981, 1988; Smith, 1986). In ontogenic or operant selection, responses are affected by their consequences within the lifetime of the individual organism.

The procedure called *shaping* produces changes in behavior by arranging consequences for some responses but not others. If only the strongest forces exerted by a food-deprived lever-pressing rat produce food, stronger presses occur more often and weaker ones less often, and over time the rat's presses increase in force. Although such selection is ontogenic rather than phylogenic, its properties parallel the kind of selection relative to a population mean that were illustrated by the evolution of the horse. In this example, the opportunity to eat is the consequence that selects some responses and not others; responses within the class that produces food survive, while those outside the class extinguish.

Let us now recall the role of artificial selection in the Darwinian account. As already noted, artificial selection was familiar in Darwin's time; what was questioned was whether such selection could operate naturally. Shaping provides the ontogenic parallel. It is typically an artificial selection procedure, as when an experimenter shapes a pigeon's clockwise turns or as when a behavior therapist shapes the vocalizations of a nonverbal institutionalized child. The effectiveness of shaping is self-evident; what is questioned is whether it also operates naturally to produce the varied patterns of behavior seen in everyday life.

Ontogenic selection involves more manageable time spans than phylogenic selection, but still it can be difficult to observe natural selection in action. Typically only outcomes are available, after the natural contingencies have already done their work. For example, ontogenic selection is presumably involved in shaping the skill with which grizzly bears catch salmon in the rivers of the Pacific Northwest, but all that is usually seen are differences between the inefficient performances of young novices and the well-coordinated actions of experienced adults; it is not feasible to record the details of shaping in such environments (the phylogenic analogy is in the incompleteness of the fossil record).

Consider now the parents who always wait a while before attending to a crying child. They may not notice that they have gradually shaped louder and more annoying cries. The attention strengthens the crying and annoying cries are, by definition, those most likely to get attention. If one watches what a parent does when a child throws tantrums, it is usually easy to guess how the tantrums might have arisen through the natural selection of behavior by its consequences. The contingencies that produce such problem behavior seldom occur in isolation, so other behavior or other reinforcers may eventually displace it. Its spontaneous disappearance might be taken as evidence that the problem behavior had a source independent of shaping. Yet it would be as inappropriate to draw such a conclusion in this ontogenic case as it would be to deny that dinosaurs were a product of natural selection on the grounds that some catastrophe such as the impact of a comet caused their extinction.

Shaping can be demonstrated over minutes rather than over days or years or millenia. Anyone who has mastered the art of shaping knows that five or ten minutes is plenty of time for the shaping of a single response. If contingencies that are deliberately arranged over relatively short periods of time can change behavior so much, it is reasonable to assume that those that occur naturally over substantial periods throughout an organism's lifetime will also do so. Many contingencies may take hold of behavior over the course of months or years in the life of a young child. Some may produce desirable behavior; others may do the opposite. The self-injurious behavior of an institutionalized nine-year-old may seem resistant to change, but nine years is a very long exposure to selective contingencies. This does not mean all such behavior is produced solely by ontogenic contingencies, but it is certainly safer to be alert for their effects than to assume they do not exist.

The issue has been particularly controversial with respect to the acquisition of verbal behavior in children, and only limited data are available to demonstrate the role of contingencies (e.g., Moerk, 1983; Whitehurst & Valdez-Menchaca, 1988). Now consider a child who sleeps, eats, and performs other functions for sixteen hours of the day. Let accidental contingencies work more slowly, in the everyday verbal interactions between parent and child, so that an hour or so must be allowed for each new word. That is still eight words per day, which means that the child can acquire several thousand words in a year. That is not too far from the vocabulary of a five-year-old. Why is it then that some linguists claim that learning processes are irrelevant to the acquisition of vocabulary? Whether or not children are phylogenically predisposed to master some of the properties of human language, they will be unable to engage in the verbal behavior of their native communities unless appropriate vocabularies are selected by their verbal environments.

Cultural Selection

The third variety of selection, cultural selection, occurs when behavior can be passed on from one organism to another. The behavior an organism acquires within its own lifetime is eventually lost if the organism cannot pass it on to others. Through cultural selection, however, behavior can survive the death of the organism that acquired it. The behavior then survives in what others do.

In phylogenic selection and ontogenic selection, evolution and shaping depend upon variable populations on which selection can operate. Similar constraints exist at the level of cultural selection. For example, cultural practices that favor ethnic diversity may have advantages over ones that do not simply because they allow such variability.

The conclusion that behavior is a product of cultural selection demands more than the observation that the behavior is shared by the members of a group. The shared behavior may instead simply be the product of common phylogenic or ontogenic variables that have operated independently on the behavior of each individual. Somehow the behavior had to get from one individual to another, and one issue is the sense in which behavior can do so (clearly the behavior must be characterized in terms of classes of responses rather than in terms of specific instances: cf. Skinner, 1935).

The third variety of selection includes observational learning, imitation, and the survival of cultural practices; it manifests itself perhaps most significantly in verbal behavior. For example, what someone has said or written can survive that person's death if it is passed on to and repeated by others (Darwin's discussion of natural selection in the evolution of human languages is completely consistent with such an account: Darwin, 1871, Chapter 3). The verbal behavior that has survived within and been shared among the members of a group is part of the culture of that group, but shared in this way it need not be correlated with genetic relatedness (e.g., it is not necessary to be closely related to Darwin to be able to repeat some of his words appropriately). Verbal behavior may have created special problems for behavior analysis because it is part of this different domain.

Much of what any of us knows has been taught, either in the informal context of interactions between family members or in the formal context of educational institutions (the selection of educational systems can be thought of as the selection of methods for artificial selection). We may think of imitation and observational learning as commonplace because they so often enter into human behavior. But it is not clear how often they occur even among nonhuman warm-blooded vertebrates, although their occurrence is well-established among primates (e.g., Hikami, Hasegawa & Matsuzawa, 1990; Itani, 1958; Kawamura, 1959; Mineka, Davidson, Cook & Keir, 1984; Yamada, 1957). Human cultures, however, depend on the selection that occurs as behavior is passed on from one individual to another (e.g., Harris, 1977; see also Dawkins, 1976, on *memes*). Certain ways of raising children, of obtaining and preparing food, of building shelters, and of dealing with group members and with outsiders survive over successive generations.

Consider patterns of child rearing. Suppose that children reared according to most patterns are as likely as adults to rear their own children according to one pattern as according to any other. But suppose also that a very few patterns work so that when the children become adults they are likely to rear their own children in the same way as their parents had reared them; these might be called self-replicating patterns of child rearing. In a large population, whenever one of the self-replicating patterns happens to be used by some parents it will be used again in the next generation, but the other patterns will come and go. Little by little, over many generations, the self-replicating patterns will displace the ones that are not self-replicating. Once traditional patterns of child rearing originate in this way, they are likely to survive for very long periods of time.

In cultural selection, behavior is selected and maintained by a social environment. Not only must individuals be able to acquire behavior by observing the behavior of others; they must be able to do so selectively. In early human history, those who could learn by observation how to make stone tools or fire or garments probably had survival advantages over those who could not (in every variety of selection, the selection operates at the level of the survival of individual members and not at the level of the survival of the group). Perhaps behavior acquired through cultural selection is then simply maintained by reinforcement contingencies. But this might not be the case.

Let us return to the child rearing example. Suppose some patterns of child abuse are more likely to be repeated over generations than other more benign varieties of child rearing, in that an abused child is more likely to become an abusive parent. Such abusive patterns might be less likely than others to be maintained by reinforcement contingencies, and might also reduce the probability that children of abusing parents will survive to maturity. If these patterns are more strongly self-replicating than the others, however, they may nevertheless become dominant in the population even though their selection is opposed by phylogenic and ontogenic contingencies.

This is why the domain of cultural selection may require different kinds of analyses. For example, an analysis of reinforcing effectiveness at the individual level may not be consistent with the effects of cultural selection at the level of the population, as when behavior that is transmitted from one individual to another only with difficulty is displaced by competing behavior that is less likely to be reinforced but is more easily transmitted. Patterns of behavior that depend on the survival of certain types of verbal behavior among the members of a group (perhaps including celibacy, suicide, and modern war) need not be consistent with phylogenic and ontogenic contingencies. These potential difficulties will not be resolved here, but in the face of them it is appropriate to consider the phylogenic contingencies that may have selected the social environments within which cultural selection could operate.

The Phylogenic Origins of Cultural Selection

Discriminating the behavior of other organisms, whether of one's own or of other species, has clear selective advantages. The discriminative stimuli provided by other organisms are often more important than those provided by inanimate objects and events. For example, parental investment in offspring may be wasted if the parent cannot discriminate between its own offspring and the offspring of others; potential mates must be distinguished from potential competitors, and among the potential mates the receptive must be distinguished from the unreceptive, and so on.

As an additional example, consider the relation between predator and prey. A predator that can distinguish whether or not it has been noticed by its prey has a distinct advantage over one that has not; an advantage also accrues to a prey that can distinguish whether or not it has been noticed by its predator. Over an extensive phylogenic history, selection has presumably operated on both attention to the behavior of prey in the evolution of predators and attention to the behavior of predators in the evolution of prey. Following from such selection, discriminations of social behavior may have become so important that they often override other types of discriminations.

Discriminations of the behavior of others are at the heart of our human concept of intentionality (cf. Dennett, 1987): we say we understand someone's intentions when our discriminations of the various properties of that person's past and current behavior enable us to act appropriately with respect to what that person will do in the future. Judgments of the intentions of others are, above all, social judgments, and it takes no special assumptions about the phylogenic contingencies that must have operated on social behavior both within and across species to see that such contingencies could shape well-prepared capacities for social discriminations.

Discriminations of the behavior of others are prerequisites for imitation and observational learning (Zentall & Galef, 1988; see also Catania, 1992, Chapter 10). Problems to be addressed in accounts of their phylogenic origins include constraints on the imitative class (e.g., imitation must be limited by those instances, such as imitating another organism that has just injured itself, in which imitation has aversive consequences) and the different dimensions of stimuli for the observed and observing organisms (e.g., in imitation of a posture, the felt position of the organism's own limbs must correspond to the seen position of the other's).

Not all following is imitative. Under natural conditions, young animals may learn to behave like their parents as a consequence of following parents to sources of food. But when one organism leads another to food, the proximity of that organism may acquire reinforcing properties. Following then emerges as behavior shaped by natural contingencies (cf. Miller & Dollard, 1941).

Sometimes the behavior of one organism allows another to act on the basis of stimuli that are available only to the first organism, as when a vocal call from one monkey allows another monkey to escape from a predator it had not seen. In monkeys, for example, predator calls can vary with kinds of predator, and the response to the call can depend on who the caller is and who the listener is (e.g., Gouzoules, Gouzoules & Marler, 1984; Seyfarth, Cheney & Marler, 1980). Presumably elicited cries produced by the attack of a predator on a group member provided the starting point on which phylogenic and ontogenic contingencies could work to select such behavior. A phylogenic account of such behavior must deal with the evolution of the behavior of both the caller and the listener (a plausible account of language origins must be able to deal simultaneously with the behavior both of speakers and of listeners, because verbal behavior cannot occur if speakers exist without listeners or listeners without speakers).

The Social Origins of Language

We can learn from each other through verbal behavior; for example, we can be told about contingencies instead of observing them. But verbal behavior cannot have originated in that way, because descriptions of contingencies require sentences and the earliest forms of language must have begun with single words (see Catania, 1991, for a more detailed account).

The primary function of language is simpler than communication. Language is an efficient way in which one individual can change the behavior of another. What is transmitted is the verbal behavior itself, and its primary function is to getting another organism to do something. Verbal behavior allows one to do things via the mediation of another organism. This behavior is quintessentially social and can emerge only in organisms whose behavior is already sensitive to social contingencies.

The argument for the primacy of this function is that other functions gain their significance only through it. The argument does not question whether transmitting information or describing feelings are functions of language; rather, it is that these secondary functions can become important only if they sometimes make a difference, by changing the behavior of others. Language could not have evolved for the communication of emotions (cf. Darwin, 1872), because that function was already served in other ways (it is easy to tell when a gorilla is angry). What other social function could then have provided the selective contingencies under which human language evolved?

Let us now briefly consider a scenario for the evolution of human language. In the geologic time scale, the 4 million years or so since our hominid ancestors began walking upright is very short. Even shorter, however, is the time since the emergence of our own species. Our human genealogy can be sketched only roughly, because the lines that separate different hominid populations are often hard to define (Conroy, 1990; Richards, 1987). The genus *Homo* appeared roughly 2.5 million years ago, in the hominid species called *Homo habilis*, at about the same time as the earliest evidence of tool use. The appearance of *Homo erectus* and the use of fire has been dated at about 1.7 million years ago, in eastern Africa. The appearance of *Homo sapiens* has been dated at about 250,00 years ago. The expansion of some groups, such as the Cro-magnons, was accompanied by the extinction of others, such as the Neanderthals. Anatomically modern humans emerged about 40,000 years ago; that is also a plausible date for the origin of human language.

But let us start earlier, with a band of preverbal hominids in which a minimal repertory of fixed action patterns elicited by vocal releasers is already established. Assume now that, as releasers, the calls of the hominid leader reliably determined some of the behavior of members of its band. At first the vocabulary of releasers was limited to just a few calls, not yet qualifying as verbal behavior but with relatively simple effects (e.g., corresponding to those of words such as *come* or *go* or *stop*). Over millenia, a more extensive repertory of more varied calls was differentiated. This vocal control presumably gave the group a competitive edge relative to other similar groups: keeping the group together during movement; coordinating aggression or flight in encounters with other groups; etc. Other kinds of vocal control presumably also evolved in interactions between mothers and their offspring, between mates, and within various subgroups of the hominid social unit.

If the details of these calls became weakly determined phylogenically, or could vary in properties that were orthogonal to those that made them effective as releasers, this rudimentary vocal control could later be supplemented by ontogenic contingencies. For example, a dominant speaker might learn to attack a listener who does not respond to a call, thereby punishing disobedience (many contemporary contingencies maintain the effectiveness of verbal control by reinforcing the following of instructions and punishing deviations from it).

Once vocal behavior had expanded to an extensive repertory including arbitrary as well as phylogenically determined calls, idiosyncratic repertories developed by particular leaders would ordinarily be lost to later generations until some ways of reproducing this behavior in the leaders' successors had evolved. Thus, the next critical step in this evolution was the repetition by the follower of the leader's verbal behavior (see also Jaynes, 1976, for an alternative scenario). This is the key to the cultural selection of verbal behavior. Once some individuals begin repeating what others say, verbal behavior becomes a kind of behavior that can survive within the behavior of the group; it can then be maintained by cultural contingencies as well as or instead of by ontogenic ones.

Repetition by the listener became especially critical as verbal behavior became more complex. By initiating relevant vocal behavior in those who were to become the leader's successors, it became a way in which that behavior could replicate itself. To the extent that control may sometimes have transferred from the leader's verbal behavior to the listener's own repetition of it, the repetition of the leader's utterances may also have established conditions under which the leader could give instructions to be followed in the leader's absence, at later times and in other places. Such a precursor of rule-governed behavior could enhance the influence of the leader and allow coordination within human groups to expand beyond the range of the human voice. The stage would then be set for human verbal memory, for instruction following and educational systems, and for the rapid and wide dissemination of human cultural practices.

Finally, consider the implications of increases in the complexity of verbal control with the expansion of human groups. As a consequence of contact with different and conflicting speakers, it presumably became important for listeners to discriminate among the various sources of verbal control (particularly between group members and outsiders and, within the group, along the dimensions of dominance hierarchies). In particular, if direct verbal control of the listener by the speaker was at some point supplanted by indirect control via the listener's repetition of the speaker's utterance, listeners eventually must have learned to discriminate themselves from others as the sources of verbal behavior. Responding directly to what someone else has said differs from responding to one's own repetition of the other's utterance, which in turn differs from producing a novel utterance of one's own. Discrimination of such sources of verbal control may have marked the beginnings of those processes we speak of as consciousness or self-awareness (cf. Jaynes, 1976).

Selection and Verbal Behavior

We are now in a position to examine selective processes that may operate in the acquisition and maintenance of verbal behavior. We begin with echoic behavior (including the imitation of semantic and syntactic as well as phonetic properties), because it is such an obvious case of the replication of verbal behavior; we will close with a treatment of the selection of the vocabulary of private events. The earlier discussion of artificial and natural selection at the ontogenic level used the shaping of the vocalizations of a nonverbal institutionalized child as an example of artificial selection; let us now consider how echoic behavior might be selected by natural ontogenic contingencies.

The Selection of Echoic Behavior

In his account of verbal behavior, Skinner (1957, 1986) argued that a major event in the evolution of language was when the vocal apparatus came under operant control. The ontogenic contingencies that could operate on vocalizations in such circumstances were necessarily natural rather than artificial ones. What sorts of consequences, then, might shape consistencies in the properties of human vocalizations?

Imitation of some properties of vocal stimuli appears relatively early in human infants' acquisition of speech, in the class of verbal relations called *echoic*. When a parent says and the child repeats "mama," the child's response is echoic to the extent that it is occasioned by the parent's utterance and to the extent that the phonemes uttered by the child correspond to those uttered by the parent. This is not a simple relation. The stimulus is a complex sound pattern, and the response consists of complex articulations, the coordinated movements of lungs, vocal chords, tongue, lips and so on. The child who hears "mama" must make just those articulations that will produce sounds that the parents hear as equivalent.

Correspondences between one's own and another's vocalizations exist naturally in echoic behavior, because both have auditory consequences and therefore provide stimuli in the same modality. But in the imitation of body movements, the felt positions of the parts of one's own body must match the seen positions of the parts of the other's body. These respective visual and kinesthetic stimuli are in different modalities. It is unlikely that the latter correspondences are as easily established as those in echoic behavior. A corollary is that it is unlikely that human vocal language evolved from an earlier gestural one.

Echoic behavior depends at least in part on the shaping of articulations by their vocal consequences. Even before their own vocalizations begin to be differentiated, infants have learned some discriminations among aspects of the speech of others (e.g., Eimas, Siqueland, Jusczyk, and Vigorito, 1971). Their initial babbling includes a range of human speech sounds, but sounds of their native language are ordinarily retained in their spontaneous vocalizations whereas nonnative sounds gradually disappear as the babbling evolves to self-repetitions (echolalia speech: e.g., "ma-ma-ma-ma-ma") and then to repetitions of the speech of others (echoic speech). Children discriminate between sounds of their native language and sounds from unfamiliar foreign languages, but they do not readily discriminate between sounds from two unfamiliar foreign languages; furthermore, discriminations of speech sounds that are easily learned at an early age may be difficult to learn later (e.g., Werker, 1989). For example, the distinction between spoken r and l in English does not exist in Japanese, and it is much more easily learned by a Japanese child than by an adult Japanese speaker.

Vocalizations can be reinforced (Bloom, 1984, Poulson, 1983, 1984). The vocalizations of infants are engendered and maintained by what the infants hear themselves saying; without these auditory consequences (as in cases of hearing impairment), the behavior does not develop. Perhaps sounds of one's native language become reinforcing relative to sounds of other languages simply because they often accompany the activities of important caregivers in an infant's environment (cf. Trehub & Chang, 1977; DeCasper & Fifer, 1980). The articulation that produces something that sounds more or less like what caregivers say may be reinforced automatically by this correspondence between the infant's and the caregivers' utterances. This is consistent with the demonstration of generalized vocal imitation in infants (Poulson, Kymissis, Reeve, Andreatos & Reeve, 1991), although the difficulty of learning such discriminations later in life must also be taken into account in making judgments about phylogenic limitations on these processes.

Echoic behavior is not defined by acoustic correspondence; it is defined by correspondences of the phonetic units of a language. Voices differ in many respects: An adult voice is deeper than a child's; a woman's voice differs from a man's; and people speak with varying regional dialects. Differences in vocal quality and regional dialect are irrelevant to whether verbal behavior is echoic; the criterion for echoic behavior is the vocal correspondences of verbal units such as phonemes and words (thus, the duplication of human sound patterns by parrots and other birds does not qualify as echoic behavior because their duplications are acoustic rather than phonetic).

This analysis suggests how echoic behavior, which is sometimes selected artificially, may have been selected naturally. If the analysis is appropriate, natural selection may fail in many different ways: e.g., relevant reinforcers may be absent (perhaps as a result of neglect or abuse by caregivers), or motor disorders may constrain articulation, or neurological deficits may reduce the effectiveness of social stimuli.

An interesting contrast is in the behavior of transcription, which involves correspondences in written rather than vocal properties of verbal behavior. As with echoic behavior, stimuli must be distinguished from responses (the visual properties of written words differ from the movements that must be made to write them), and the units of transcription are verbal rather than visual (the pictorial copy of a text must look like the text, whereas a transcription, as from printed text to script, need not). But the written verbal behavior of transcription rarely emerges as a result of natural contingencies (though it must have at least once); it requires artificial selection.

The natural selective contingencies suggested for echoic behavior may also operate with respect to other properties of verbal behavior. For example, it is hard to imagine how children could learn vocabulary with any consistency if what they said was unaffected by its consequences or, in other words, if the verbal community failed to respond to their verbal behavior in any way. Perhaps the problem is with which consequences are thought to count as reinforcers. Praise or consumable reinforcers such as candy are relatively minor consequences in the acquisition of language. The significant consequences are probably more subtle: hearing oneself saying something similar to what one has heard others say, getting something one has asked for, hearing a remark relevant to something one had just said, and so on.

Some see cases in which vocabulary is acquired through observation or imitation as an embarrassment to an account in terms of consequences. Yet among the consequences of echoic speech are the correspondences between sounds one has heard and sounds one has produced oneself. It is not too great a leap to extend such correspondences to include semantic and syntactic properties of verbal behavior. It is presumably important to discover that the relations among words and between words and things in one's own behavior correspond to those relations in the behavior of others. In this view, the verbal community, simply by engaging in verbal behavior, provides the discriminative stimuli that create and maintain the consistency of the child's verbal behavior.

Selective Contingencies and Rule-Governed Behavior

Sometimes what people do depends on what they are told to do; people often follow instructions. Such behavior, mainly determined by verbal antecedents, has been called rule-governed behavior; its properties differ from those of contingency-governed behavior, behavior that has been shaped by its consequences (Catania, Matthews & Shimoff, 1990; Schlinger & Blakely, 1987; Skinner, 1969).

Contingencies operate for the following of instructions. Sometimes the relevant contingencies are social, as when someone follows orders because of the aversive consequences of not doing so, or as when someone grants a request to please someone else or to avoid hurting the other's feelings; sometimes the contingencies depend on the relation between verbal formulations and nonverbal contingencies, as when someone successfully makes a repair by following a service manual, or as when someone avoids injury by acting on a warning (cf. Zettle & Hayes, 1982, on the respective classes of pliance and tracking).

The verbal community shapes the behavior of following instructions across a substantial range of activities throughout a substantial portion of each individual's lifetime. This can happen only if the contingencies that maintain instruction following are more potent than the natural contingencies against which they are pitted (we seldom bother to ask people to do things they would do on their own anyway). Thus, instructions may begin to override natural contingencies; people then do things when told to do them that they would never do if only the natural contingencies operated.

For the present purposes, the point is that, as illustrated by the examples above (perhaps more so for pliance than for tracking), the ontogenic contingencies of selection that maintain rule-governed behavior may be inconsistent with the cultural ones. Cultural contingencies that maintain rule-following may displace behavior that otherwise would have been maintained by ontogenic contingencies. The analysis must consider the contingencies operating both on those whose rules are followed and those who follow the rules. Education and instruction are, by definition, techniques for the artificial selection of behavior. They presumably emerged through natural selection, but in doing so they enhanced the effectiveness of cultural selection relative to ontogenic selection. To the extent that the contingencies of ontogenic and cultural selection differ, it is important for us to consider the ways in which they may interact.

Discriminating Properties of One's Own Behavior

In the context of learning about others, we also learn to discriminate properties of our own behavior. The case is particularly obvious with verbal behavior, because we learn the language with which we describe our own behavior from others. Thus, what we know about ourselves is a social product.

Now consider a human verbal learning experiment involving three kinds of participants: learners who talk aloud while learning verbal items and then predict how well they will remember the items, listeners who hear what learners say and make similar predictions based on what they hear, and observers who make predictions based on how well learners did on past items without hearing what the learners say (Vesonder & Voss, 1985). Under these conditions, the predictions of learners and listeners are equivalent and are substantially better than those of observers. The public behavior of the learner, to which the listener also has access, is good enough; if learners do know private things to which the listeners have no access (e.g., levels of confidence), the learners' predictions are no better because of them. Just as we judge others on the basis of observations of their behavior, we judge ourselves on the basis of observations of our own behavior (cf. Bem, 1967; Nisbett & Bellows, 1977).

The capacity to discriminate properties of one's own behavior is important in many types of human behavior. For example, the student who cannot tell the difference between superficial and thorough readings of a text may stop studying too soon. The practical significance of discriminating private events should be obvious. For example, the drinker who is a good judge of blood alcohol levels should know when to hand the car keys over to someone else. In human behavior, such discriminations may sometimes be incidentally learned, but we are most likely to learn them when they are taught to us by others. In other words, discriminations of our own behavior typically originate in the context of social behavior. They are sometimes selected naturally, but they are more likely to be selected artificially.

Discriminations of one's own behavior are critical to complex verbal behavior. Propositional language would be impossible without such discriminations. Consider saying either *This is a book* or *This is not a book*. To utter *is* or *is not* appropriately, we must be able to discriminate between saying *book* when a book is present and saying it when one is not. This discriminative control by our own verbal behavior is the most important property of the verbal class called *autoclitic* (Skinner, 1957).

If discriminations of one's own behavior are necessarily involved even in such fundamental verbal constructions, then they must have become established early in the evolution of complex utterances. Given this implicit role of discrimination of one's own behavior, the capacity for such discrimination properties may be a prerequisite for natural language. It is consistent with this view that deictic expressions develop early in the language acquisition of children (e.g., Wales, 1986); deictic terms involve distinctions that are relative to the speaker, as in *here* versus *there* or *this* versus *that*, and they therefore also entail discriminations of properties of one's own behavior.

Selection of the Language of Private Events

Some stimuli to which we respond verbally are accessible only to the speaker, as when we say we have a headache. We learn to talk about our feelings, but the relevant vocabulary is taught to us by the same verbal community that teaches us all the other words of our language. Such teaching can be based only on what is publicly shared by the speakers and listeners of the language (see Wittgenstein, 1953, and Skinner, 1945, for discussions of the difficulties created by positing a language of private events not based on the public practices of the verbal community).

The problem is how the verbal community can create and maintain these responses when it does not have access to the stimuli. A parent can teach a child color names because the parent can see the colors that the child sees and therefore can respond differentially to the child's correct and incorrect color naming (as argued above with respect to echoic behavior, so many different consequences follow from color naming that it ordinarily does not matter whether the parent teaches the color names through explicit instruction or simply allows the appropriate discriminations to become established through casual day-to-day interactions; the acquisition of color naming by children does not usually require artificial selection).

With private events, the vocabulary can be taught only through extension from terms based upon events to which the verbal community has access (cf. Skinner, 1945). For example, the child may learn to report pain because the parents have access to overt manifestations such as the event that caused an injury or the child's crying or facial expression; if the child has learned the names of body parts, the two kinds of verbal responses may be extended to the report of pain in a particular place.

A toothache is a discriminable event, but the person with the toothache has a different kind of access to it than the dentist who is called upon to treat it. Both respond to the unsound tooth, but one does so by feeling the tooth, and the other by looking at it and probing it with instruments. Their contact with the tooth might be compared with the different ways a seeing and a sightless person make contact with a geometric solid if one tries to teach its name to the other; the seeing person does so by sight and the sightless person by touch. One kind of contact is not necessarily more reliable than the other (e.g., in the phenomenon of referred pain, a bad tooth in the lower jaw may be reported as a toothache in the upper jaw; in this case, the dentist is a better judge than the patient of where the pain really is). The verbal community has inconsistent access to the public correlates of private events, and therefore cannot consistently maintain relevant contingencies of selection for the vocabulary of these events.

In the context of natural and artificial selection, the language of private events provides a problem that is in some respects the inverse of that for echoic behavior. Artificial selection of echoic behavior is demonstrable, and the case to be made is how it can be produced by natural selection. With regard to the language of private events, however, even artificial selection seems to present a problem, because the inaccessibility of private events makes it difficult to discover and arrange appropriate contingencies. Yet the very existence of the language of private events implies its selection by natural contingencies. The solution to the problem is that any feasible account of the acquisition of the language of private events must appeal to the public accompaniments of those events. In other words, artificial as well as natural contingencies must be based on such public accompaniments.

Consider the vocabulary of remembering, forgetting, and never having known (cf. Johnson & Wellman, 1980; Kolers & Palef, 1976; Miyake & Norman, 1979; Wellman & Johnson, 1979). We can often report whether we have forgotten something or never knew it in the first place. The distinction is not ordinarily taught explicitly, and yet children learn it in the context of being asked questions and answering them. The natural contingencies are usually good enough.

It should not be very difficult to construct artificial contingencies that will also be effective. Imagine a child who one day is given some task such as learning names for a set of objects. The next day the child is shown both those objects and a few new ones and is asked to name them. For some objects, the child's naming is successful; for others, it is not. Appropriate differential reinforcement can now be arranged for three different verbal responses: given successful naming, "I remembered"; given one of the original objects and unsuccessful naming, "I forgot"; and given one of the new objects and, necessarily, unsuccessful naming, "I don't know." With this start, the vocabulary can easily be extended to other tasks.

It would be misleading to seek the controlling variables of such reports inside the organism, because the reports are established on the basis of the public events available to the verbal community. This does not mean that no private correlates exist (some technology for the scanning of brain activity may one day identify brain events correlated with these different verbal reports). But studies of such correlates do not make them appropriate substitutes for the public correlates upon which the relevant verbal behavior is based (similarly, studies of events in the visual areas of the brain do not replace studies of how contingencies establish the discriminative functions of visual stimuli).

Studies of the development of the language of private events (e.g., Wellman, 1990) have appealed to the child's evolving theory of mind rather than to the natural contingencies that select the vocabulary of private events. Such studies show orderly progressions in the sophistication of the relevant vocabularies over childhood development, but nothing about such progressions is inconsistent with an account in terms of natural contingencies of ontogenic and cultural selection.

As for the vocabulary of mind that accompanies these progressions, it too is presumably shaped by natural contingencies. But such contingencies can shape vocabularies of dragons, elves and unicorns as well as those of dinosaurs, elephants and giraffes. The child's theory of mind should be the object of study for an experimental analysis of the child's verbal behavior; it does not follow that it should be the theory that guides such study.

This survey of modes of selection and the varieties of verbal behavior upon which they may act has been all too brief. It may be useful to recall that this verbal behavior too is a product of cultural selection. Its survival will depend on the selective contingencies that act upon it, and its evolution will depend upon the variations that it makes available for future selection.

References

Bem, D. J. (1967). Self-perception: An alternative interpretation of cognitive phenomena. *Psychological Review, 74*, 183-200.

Bloom, K. (1984). Distinguishing between social reinforcement and social elicitation. *Journal of Experimental Child Psychology, 38*, 93-102.

Bowler, P. J. (1983). *The eclipse of Darwinism.* Baltimore: The Johns Hopkins University Press.

Catania, A. C. (1978). The psychology of learning: Some lessons from the Darwinian revolution. *Annals of the New York Academy of Sciences, 309*, 18-28.

Catania, A. C. (1987). Some Darwinian lessons for behavior analysis. A review of Peter J. Bowler's *The eclipse of Darwinism. Journal of the Experimental Analysis of Behavior, 47*, 249-257.

Catania, A. C. (1991). The phylogeny and ontogeny of language function. In N. A. Krasnegor, D. M. Rumbaugh, R. L. Schiefelbusch, & M. Studdert-Kennedy (Eds.). *Biological and behavioral determinants of language development* (pp. 263-285). Hillsdale, NJ: Erlbaum.

Catania, A. C. (1992). *Learning* (3rd ed.). Englewood Cliffs, NJ: Prentice Hall.

Catania, A. C., & Harnad, S. (1988). (Eds.). *The selection of behavior.* New York: Cambridge University Press.

Catania, A. C., Matthews, B. A., & Shimoff, E. H. (1990). Properties of rule-governed behaviour and their implications. In D. E. Blackman & H. Lejeune (Eds.), *Behaviour analysis in theory and practice* (pp. 215-230). Hillsdale, NJ: Erlbaum.

Conroy, G. C. (1990). *Primate evolution.* New York: Norton.

Darwin, C. (1859). *On the origin of species.* London: John Murray.

Darwin, C. (1871). *The descent of man.* London: John Murray.

Darwin, C. (1872). *The expression of the emotions in man and animals.* London: John Murray.

Dawkins, R. (1976). *The selfish gene.* New York: Oxford University Press.

Dawkins, R. (1986). *The blind watchmaker.* New York: Norton.

De Casper, A. J., & Fifer, W. P. (1980). Of human bonding: Newborns prefer their mothers' voices. *Science, 208*, 1174-1176.

Dennett, D. C. (1987). *The intentional stance.* Cambridge, MA: The MIT Press.

Eimas, P. D., Siqueland, E. R. Jusczyk, P., & Vigorito, J. (1971). Speech perception in early infancy. *Science, 171*, 303-306.

Gouzoules, S., Gouzoules, H., & Marler, P. (1984). Rhesus monkey (Macaca mulatta) screams: Representational signalling in the recruitment of agonistic aid. *Animal Behaviour, 32*, 182-193.

Hikami, K., Hasegawa, Y., & Matsuzawa, T. (1990). Social transmission of food preferences in Japanese monkeys (Macaca fuscata) after mere exposure or aversion training. *Journal of Comparative Psychology, 104*, 233-237.

Harris, M. (1977). *Cannibals and kings.* New York: Random House.

Itani, J. (1958). On the acquisition and propagation of a new food habit in the natural group of a Japanese monkey at Takasakiyama. *Primates, 1*, 84-98.

Jaynes, J. (1976). *The origin of consciousness in the breakdown of the bicameral mind.* Boston: Houghton Mifflin.

Johnson, C. N., & Wellman, H. M. (1980). Children's developing understanding of mental verbs: Remember, know, and guess. *Child Development, 51,* 1095-1102.

Kawamura, S. (1963). The process of sub-culture propagation among Japanese Macaques. *Primates, 2,* 43-60.

Kolers, P. A., & Palef, R. (1976). Knowing not. *Memory and Cognition, 4,* 553-558.

Miller, N. E., & Dollard, J. C. (1941). *Social learning and imitation.* New Haven: Yale University Press.

Mineka, S., Davidson, M., Cook, M., & Keir, R. (1984). Observational learning of snake fear in rhesus monkeys. *Journal of Abnormal Psychology, 93,* 355-372.

Miyake, N., & Norman, D. A. (1979). To ask a question, one must know enough to know what is not known. *Journal of Verbal Learning and Verbal Behavior, 18,* 357-364.

Moerk, E. L. (1983). A behavioral analysis of controversial topics in first language acquisition: Reinforcements, corrections, modeling, input frequencies, and the three-term contingency pattern. *Journal of Psycholinguistic Research, 12,* 129-155.

Nisbett, R. E., & Bellows, N. (1977). Verbal reports about causal influences on social judgments: Private access versus public theories. *Journal of Personality and Social Psychology, 35,* 613-624.

Poulson, C. L. (1983). Differential reinforcement of other-than-vocalization as a control procedure in the conditioning of infant vocalization rate. *Journal of Experimental Child Psychology, 36,* 471-489.

Poulson, C. L. (1984). Operant theory and methodology in infant vocal conditioning. *Journal of Experimental Child Psychology, 38,* 103-113.

Poulson, C. L., Kymissis, E., Reeve, K. F., Andreatos, M., & Reeve, L. (1991). Generalized vocal imitation in infants. *Journal of Experimental Child Psychology, 51,* 267-279.

Richards, G. (1987). *Human evolution.* London: Routledge & Kegan Paul.

Schlinger, H., & Blakely, E. (1987). Function-altering effects of contingency-specifying stimuli. *The Behavior Analyst, 10,* 41-45.

Seyfarth, R. M., Cheney, D. L., & Marler, P. (1980). Vervet monkey alarm calls: Semantic communication in a free-ranging primate. *Animal Behaviour, 28,* 1070-1094.

Simpson, G. G. (1951). *Horses.* New York: Oxford University Press.

Skinner, B. F. (1935). The generic nature of the concepts of stimulus and response. *Journal of General Psychology, 12,* 40-65.

Skinner, B. F. (1938). *The behavior of organisms.* New York: Appleton-Century-Crofts.

Skinner, B. F. (1945). The operational analysis of psychological terms. *Psychological Review, 42,* 270-277.

Skinner, B. F. (1953). *Science and human behavior.* New York: Macmillan.

Skinner, B. F. (1957). *Verbal behavior.* New York: Appleton-Century-Crofts.

Skinner, B. F. (1969). An operant analysis of problem solving. In B. F. Skinner, *Contingencies of reinforcement* (pp. 133-157). New York: Appleton-Century-Crofts.

Skinner, B. F. (1975). The shaping of phylogenic behavior. *Journal of the Experimental Analysis of Behavior, 24*, 117-120.

Skinner, B. F. (1981). Selection by consequences. *Science, 213*, 501-504.

Skinner, B. F. (1986). The evolution of verbal behavior. *Journal of the Experimental Analysis of Behavior, 45*, 115-122.

Skinner, B. F. (1988). Replies to commentators. In A. C. Catania & S. Harnad (Eds.), *The selection of behavior*. New York: Cambridge University Press.

Smith, T. L. (1986). Biology as allegory: A review of Elliott Sober's *The nature of selection. Journal of the Experimental Analysis of Behavior, 46*, 105-112.

Trehub, S. E., & Chang, H.-W. (1977). Speech as reinforcing stimulation for infants. *Developmental Psychology, 13*, 170-171.

Vesonder, G. T., & Voss, J. F. (1985). On the ability to predict one's own responses while learning. *Journal of Memory and Language, 24*, 363-376.

Wales, R. (1986). Deixis. In P. Fletcher & M. Garman (Eds.), *Language acquisition* (2nd ed.) (pp. 401-428). New York: Cambridge University Press.

Wellman, H. M. (1990). *The child's theory of mind*. Cambridge, Mass: The MIT Press.

Wellman, H. M., & Johnson, C. N. (1979). Understanding mental processes: A developmental study of *remember* and *forget. Child Development, 50*, 79-88.

Werker, J. F. (1989). Becoming a native listener. *American Scientist, 77*, 54-59.

Whitehurst, G. J., & Valdez-Menchaca, M. C. (1988). What is the role of reinforcement in early language acquisition? *Child Development, 59*, 430-440.

Wittgenstein, L. (1953). *Philosophical investigations*. New York: Macmillan.

Yamada, M. (1957). A case of acculturation in the subhuman society of Japanese monkeys. *Primates, 1*, 30-46.

Zentall, T. R., & Galef, B. G., Jr. (1988). *Social learning*. Hillsdale, NJ: Erlbaum.

Zettle, R. D., & Hayes, S. C. (1982). Rule-governed behavior: A potential theoretical framework for cognitive-behavioral therapy. *Advances in cognitive-behavioral research and therapy* (Volume 1, pp. 73-118). New York: Academic Press.

Chapter 3

Stimulus Generalization, Stimulus Equivalence, and Response Hierarchies

Marc N. Branch
University of Florida

Read the following word and then list (write down) what comes to mind. The word is:

SCHOOL

Now look at what you have written. Your list might look something like:

> learn
> teacher
> days
> books
> semester
> grades
> test
> of hard knocks
> college
> recess
> friends
> math
> go to

This chapter is aimed partly at trying to understand things about lists like this and what they might imply. To discuss the issue, the notion of a response hierarchy will be the organizing concept. I shall be concerned both with the possible origins of such lists and their structure. That is, this chapter will encompass issues that are usually of interest to behavior analysts (the origins and function of behavior) and to cognitive psychologists (the structure of behavior).

Response Hierarchies

Let me begin by trying to define what I mean by a response hierarchy. The list that you produced and the one above give us some hints, but we need to review some basic concepts about verbal behavior before we can proceed. The three concepts that are most relevant to the issues I am going to discuss are the mand, tact, and intraverbal, each of which is a type of verbal operant according to the classification offered by Skinner (1957). The power and elegance of Skinner's treatment of verbal behavior is that individual instances of verbal behavior can be conceptualized as exemplifying the outcome of experiencing three-term contingencies. That is, a single, fundamental behavioral process is all that is needed to explain many facts about talking. Mands, tacts, and intraverbals differ not in the basic processes needed to establish them, then, but rather differ with respect to specific details of the three-term contingencies.

The three parts of the three-term contingency have been dubbed the ABC's of behavior: A for antecedent condition, B for the behavior that occurs in the presence of the antecedent, and C for the consequence that follows the behavior. The rule is simply that if the behavior occurs in the presence of the antecedent and a particular consequence follows that behavior, then, if the consequence is of a certain sort (called a reinforcer), the probability increases that that behavior will occur next time the antecedent condition is experienced. Conversely, if the consequence is of another sort (called a punisher) the probability decreases that the behavior will occur the next time the antecedent is encountered.

For the mand, the antecedent conditions are the presence of an audience (someone to hear and react to your utterances) and a state of deprivation or need. A typical example is that you are thirsty (e.g., have been deprived of water or have eaten recently something especially salty; see Michael [1982] for a discussion of the "needs" that help define mands). If the vocal utterance you make, e.g., "Water, please." results in someone giving you water then in the future when you are thirsty (the antecedent condition) you are more likely to say "water, please," than you were before. One characteristic of mands is that they may be said to "name" their reinforcer; in this case we are considering presentation of the water is the key to establishing and maintaining the mand. Speaking colloquially, mands are verbal operants that get things for the speaker.

For the tact the antecedent conditions include an audience and an environmental event or state of affairs. The vocal behavior that is reinforced is such that it satisfies a conventional correspondence between the environmental state of affairs and the utterance. The reinforcing consequence for the tact is one of its most important characteristics. Instead of something that directly satisfies some deficit or need for the speaker, the consequence is what is called a generalized reinforcer. The essential characteristic of a generalized reinforcer is that its effectiveness is not dependent on any particular need the speaker has. Tacts, then, do not get the speaker something he/she needs. Instead they tell the listener something about the world.

For the intraverbal the key antecedent conditions are other verbal behavior by the speaker. For example, if you say "A penny saved is a penny..." it is very likely you next will say "earned." Your previous verbal behavior serves as the key antecedent that controls the saying of "earned." Intraverbals, like tacts may be established and maintained by generalized reinforcers as the consequence.

Now we can return to our lists and see how we might describe the things we wrote. Technically, all the things we wrote may be considered intraverbals; they are verbal responses occasioned by a verbal stimulus, "SCHOOL." However, one of our interests is in how they got into our verbal repertoires in the first place. Words like "teacher," "test," and "grades" all are environmental characteristics or features of schools and probably exist as tacts. Expressions like "of hard knocks" and "days" probably were established as intraverbals, and "go to" probably has been established as a mand. "Books" is interesting in that it most likely exists as both a tact and an intraverbal.

The point of this introductory material about what we have to say in the face of the printed word "SCHOOL" is that in any given environmental circumstance we may have a lot to say, and that much of what we have to say has been established by exposure to three-term contingencies. What I want to suggest is that it is worthwhile to consider what we have to say in any particular circumstance has constituting a hierarchy of verbal responses. These exist as potential behavior. These behavioral potentials have interesting structural characteristics that have been the source of much speculation and research by cognitive psychologists, and may be amenable to a functional analysis aimed at characterizing their origins and maintenance. In the remainder of the paper I shall describe a bit about what is known about the structure of such hierarchies, speculate on three sources that may contribute to their development and maintenance, and then try to justify the utility of the notion by offering an interpretation of how they may be involved in a favorite pastime of mine, trying to solve crossword puzzles.

What I want to discuss concerning the structure of potential-response hierarchies comes mainly from research that has centered around the concept of semantic networks. Before doing so, however, a possible source of confusion needs to be discussed, and that is the relationship between an operant class and a response hierarchy. As most readers will know, an operant is a class of responses evoked, because of a prior conditioning history, by a set of stimulus circumstances (Catania, 1973; Skinner, 1935, 1938). Similarly, a response hierarchy as intended here is a class of responses evoked by a set of stimulus circumstances. The difference is in their provenance. In an operant class, reinforcement of some forms of the class results in increased probability of emission of other forms in the class (for the "functional operant;" see Catania, 1973). In the response hierarchies that I shall be discussing each of the forms (i.e., different words or phrases) has been established directly by a reinforcement history. That is, a hierarchy is a collection of operants. For example, suppose that in the presence of a tree and an audience the hierarchy evoked includes "tree," "elm," "leaves," "trunk," etc. Each of these verbal operants presumably has an independent reinforcement history responsible for its current level of probability. I refer to them as operants to emphasize that there is variation in each emission, i.e., the phonological characteristics of "leaves" for example will vary from emission to emission, and any particular instance of "leaves" may be one that never has occurred or been reinforced before, thus illustrating the concept of the functional operant.

The situation gets a bit dicier when hierarchies include members that have become more probable through the establishment of stimulus equivalence classes (cf. Sidman, 1986). In that case, some members of a hierarchy will have been established without direct participation in a three-term contingency as described above, but rather in terms of four- (or more) term contingencies that will be described in more detail later. There is a sense in which equivalence classes share a property of operant classes; in each, establishment of one form (operant) or stimulus-control relationship (equivalence class) affects not only the probability of the explicitly established form but also the probability of other instances. In the case of the equivalence class, nevertheless, each of the responses under stimulus control has at some point been established via a three-term contingency. The fact that they enter into new stimulus-control arrangements because they enter into an equivalence relation does not mean that they should be confused with a simple operant class.

Semantic Networks

The concept of the semantic network has enjoyed a prominent place in cognitive psychology for the past two decades. Perusal of any modern text on cognitive psychology (e.g., Benjafield, 1992; Reed, 1992) will reveal a substantial section devoted to the idea. I'll try to give a behavioral description of what a semantic network implies. A semantic network is an attempt to characterize some aspects of the nature of a person's verbal repertoire, and it can be viewed as relevant to how we should view the organization of a response hierarchy. Cognitive psychologists speak of a mental lexicon which is a metaphor, based on the notion of a dictionary, for how particular circumstances lead to the saying of certain words. Interestingly, most of the data that bear on the concept of semantic networks are in terms of reaction times. How a word is related to other words that we can say is inferred from studies of how quickly certain responses can be made. A key technique employed to examine the nature of the mental lexicon is the lexical decision task. In its simplest form this procedure involves asking subjects to decide as quickly as possible if a string of letters is a word. The latencies to make the decisions are taken as evidence of how the lexicon can be characterized. For example, Swinney (1979) had subjects listen to sentences like "Tom saw several roaches, ants, and other bugs." Concurrently, subjects performed a lexical decision task. Words like "insect" were judged to be words faster than words like "spy" (note its relation to the word "bug") which were judged more quickly than unrelated words like "bath." The facilitation for words like "spy" lasted only about 100 ms, whereas the facilitation for "insect" lasted much longer. This study used a relatively complicated procedure to demonstrate what is called semantic priming. A simpler technique is just to present pairs of letter-strings in succession and have a lexical decision made for each one of the pair. In some pairs both strings are words. In those pairs if the words are related, e.g., "track" and "car," the decision to judge "car" as a word is faster than if the first of the two words is something like "butter." A related procedure is a semantic decision task (cf. Collins & Quillian, 1969). In it, subjects are asked to judge, as fast as they can, whether statements are true. For example, subjects have been asked to judge the truth of statements like "a canary can fly," or "a canary can sing." Usually the former takes longer to judge than the latter. Similarly, it usually takes longer to say that "a canary is an animal" is true than it does to verify that "a canary is a bird." Two kinds of inferences have been made on the basis of results like these. The first is illustrated in the Figure 1 which is a depiction of a semantic network. Based on the latencies taken to make certain semantic decisions, one can describe the hierarchical relations among the key terms. The hierarchies are arranged based on logical relations among the key words. The relation "is a" defines subordinates and superordinates, whereas the relations "has," "can," and "is" define features. Features are closer to main concepts and are revealed by faster reaction times than are superordinate -- subordinate relations.

   The second kind inference drawn from results of studies about semantic networks may be of more relevance to the major focus of this chapter. The priming effects in simple lexical decision tasks are said to illustrate "spreading activation" through the network. Seeing one word "activates" words that are close in the network, the closer the word in the network the greater the activation as revealed by the magnitude and persistence of the priming effect. Seeing a word makes related words more "accessible." Given the usual close relationship between response probability and response latency, one might suggest that the priming effect provides evidence that stimuli make changes in the probability of saying groups of words, and that the these words may be seen as having a hierarchical arrangement of probabilities.

   A problem with the semantic-network concept is that is relatively silent with respect to the origins of the hierarchical arrangements. Logical analyses sometimes fail; for example people generally can verify "a chimpanzee is an animal" more rapidly than they can judge that "a chimpanzee is a primate" is true, despite, as illustrated in Figure 1, that by the logic of the hierarchy the latencies should be reversed. Because logical and other sorts of rules do not specify the structure of the hierarchy, the semantic-net concept is explanatorily weak. The structure of the hier-

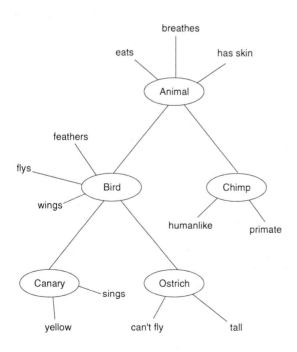

Figure 1. Example of a semantic network.

archy is determined by the latencies and therefore surely cannot explain them. There is no denying, however, that the latency effects are robust. There is a large literature testifying to the reliability of the phenomenon at the level of the individual subject (Collins & Loftus, 1975; Meyer & Schvaneveldt, 1976).

The evidence for the existence of a hierarchical character in a person's verbal repertoire is good, but an explanation for it does not yet exist. In addition, the fact that a given stimulus circumstance, e.g., the word "school," seems to "activate" such hierarchies does not tell us much about exactly what we say. In a particular circumstance we may have "a lot to say," but we do not say all that we can. When I see a school I do not usually say "learn," "grades," "hard knocks," and so on. Instead I probably just say "school." An important issue then, in addition to the origins of hierarchies, is how operants in them are actually "selected" for emission In the next section of this paper I discuss three processes, relatively well researched in the behavioral laboratory that may be involved in establishing hierarchical relationships in a verbal repertoire and in determining which of the operants in a hierarchy is actually emitted in a particular circumstance.. The three processes are (a) stimulus generalization, (b) relative frequency of reinforcement, and (c) stimulus equivalence.

Stimulus Control

Traditional views of stimulus generalization would lead one to question how this process could be involved in the production of response hierarchies and in their temporally local structure. A more recent, alternative view of stimulus generalization, however, may provide a basis (for a review, see Bickel & Etzel, 1985). A description of this view is most easily accomplished by describing experiments that led to the characterization. The seminal experiment in this realm was performed by Migler (1964). In his study food deprived rats were trained under a two-key interresponse-time-greater-than-t (IRT>t) schedule. Specifically, a press on key A illuminated a light behind key B, and a press on key B, if it occurred after a specified interval of time, was then reinforced by presentation of a food pellet. Presses on an unlit key B, i.e., before pressing key A, had no effect. Presses on key B before the time interval had elapsed turned off the illumination of key B, and then another key A press was required to start a new cycle. The final training procedure involved an auditory discrimination. Presses on key A not only illuminated key B, they also resulted in the onset of one of two auditory stimuli, clicks occurring at a rate of 2.5 per s or 45.8 per s. If the slow clicks were presented, key-B presses were reinforced if 6 s had elapsed since the press of key A; if the fast clicks were presented the required wait was 0 s. These contingencies resulted in sharply discriminated performance. The distribution of times between key-A and key-B presses was narrowly constrained about a value of about 2 s when the fast clicks were presented and sharply peaked at a value just longer than 6 s when slow clicks were presented. In preparation for generalization testing, 10 sessions were conducted with food pellets delivered after 50% of the correctly spaced key-B responses and a subsequent 20 sessions in which the probability of reinforcement of a correctly emitted key-B press was .33. In generalization-testing sessions every 10th cycle was a test. On a test cycle, a key A press was followed by illumination of key B and a click frequency in between 2.5 and 45.8 Hz. A plot of median time to switch between keys A and B over click produced orderly, seemingly continuous generalization gradients shown in Figure 2. A finer analysis of the data shown in Figure 3, however, revealed more clearly what happened in the generalization test. The left columns show simply how the basic discrimination held up during the generalization-testing sessions (there were 12 such sessions) by illustrating distributions of key-A to key-B times in the presence of the two training stimuli (numbered 1 and 8). The notable data are in the right column which displays the distributions of key-A to key-B times when the test stimuli were presented. It is clear that intermediate times rarely occurred. Instead different proportions of short and long key-to-key times were observed. In the presence of stimulus 7 (about 32 clicks per s) most A-to-B times were in the same range as when stimulus 8, the training stimulus for short key-to-key times, was presented. In the presence of stimulus 2 (about 3.5 clicks per s) most A-to-B times were like those seen when the training stimulus associated with the 6-s requirement was presented. Intermediate stimulus values were associated with mixtures of these two performances. In the test then, no new levels or types of responding were evident. Rather, only the established performances were observed and the relative probability of emission of either of the two was what was controlled.

In Migler's (1964) study, two performances were explicitly established and two performances predominated during stimulus generalization testing. Can the sort of analysis presented by Migler be extended to situations in which only one performance is established before generalization testing is conducted? I would like to describe two studies that suggest it is. The first is an under appreciated, but important study by Gray (1976). Her experiments are important not only from the perspective being emphasized here, but they also had importance for understanding the interactions between stimulus generalization and schedules of reinforcement. Gray studied stimulus generalization of behavior controlled by IRT>t schedules. Previous

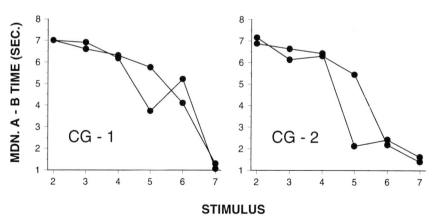

Figure 2. Median A to B time in the six test stimuli for both rats.

work on this issue (e.g., Hearst, Koresko, & Poppen, 1964) suggested that generalization gradients were quite flat after training with IRT>t schedules. This had led some (e.g., Hearst, 1965) to hypothesize that such gradients emerged because IRT schedules involve "interoceptive" stimulus control (e.g., by internal timing cues) that

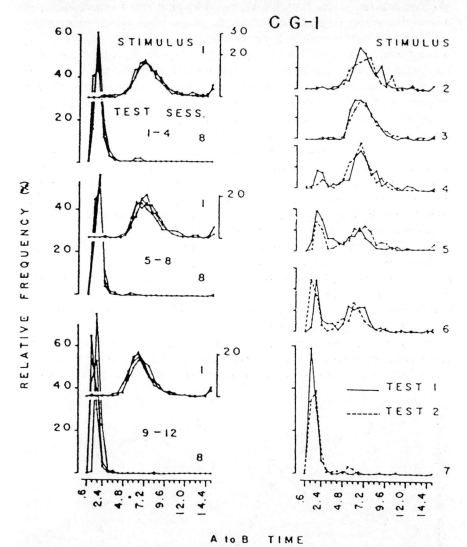

Figure 3. Rat CG - 1. Relative frequency distributions for performance during all 12 test sessions (two tests per test stimulus). The left-hand column of curves shows performance on the original training stimuli for the 12 sessions with the performance in Stimulus 1 displaced upward. The right-hand column of figures shows the performance (and its replication) in each of the six test stimuli.

blocks control by external stimuli. In Gray's (1976) experiment, pigeons were trained to peck a response key, illuminated by a 570-nm stimulus, under an IRT>8-s schedule of food presentation. The subjects were exposed to this procedure until behavior became stable from session to session (about 70, 90-min sessions). Next, generalization tests were performed where other wavelengths were presented, with no reinforcement possible, for 45-s periods. During the tests, IRTs were collected in 1-s class intervals (bins). For all subjects, many IRTs were less than 1 s, a finding not unusual with pigeons under IRT schedules. The key findings of the study are illustrated in Figure 4 which shows IRTs/opportunity (cf. Anger, 1956) over wavelength for each subject. The data have been separated by IRT class interval with gradients for short IRTs to the left and those for longer IRTs to the right. The rightmost three columns show data for IRTs that satisfied the schedule requirement. Particular attention should be paid to the results in the top three rows. Note that for IRTs that fall short of the criterion, gradients either are flat or inverted about the training stimulus, whereas IRTs that met the criterion reveal the sort of gradients one usually achieves with pecking as the response and wavelength as the stimulus dimension (cf. Rilling, 1977; Terrace, 1966). The gradients for *response rate* for these three pigeons were essentially flat, replicating earlier work. Gray's data reveal that excellent stimulus control can be established with IRT>*t* schedules. Previous investigator's had not seen the control because they failed to measure the operative response classes. Single-stimulus training with 570 nm produced two operative classes, IRTs less than the criterion and IRTs longer than the criterion. The stimuli in the generalization test controlled different mixtures of these two performances, much like the results of Migler's (1964) study.

The second study to be described was reported by Crites, Harris, Rosenquist, and Thomas (1967) who studied stimulus generalization in rats. Food-deprived rats were trained to press a lever under a variable-interval 60-s schedule of food presentation. Lever presses were reinforced when a 6.67 clicks-per-s sound was present and were not reinforced when the click rate was 20 per s. Periods of the two click rates alternated every 5 min in daily 90-min sessions. A 2-s period with no clicks separated the 5-min periods. Once 90% of lever presses occurred in the presence of the 6.67 clicks-per-s stimulus for two successive sessions, a one-hour generalization test was conducted during which click rates of 6.67, 10, 13, and 20 per s were presented. Interresponse times were collected during the tests separately for each click frequency. When IRT distributions were examined, the only differences in the distributions were evident in the longest class (IRTs longer than 10 s). Otherwise the distributions were indistinguishable, i.e., the IRT distributions obtained when the 6.67, 10, or 13 clicks-per-s stimuli were presented differed virtually not at all. That means that while the rats were responding during the tests, they responded in a manner consistent with that which had been established by reinforcement. The stimuli, however, did control how much of the time was devoted to responding. As the click frequency approached 20 per s (the stimulus correlated with extinction) subjects spent more time engaging in extinction-appropriate behavior, i.e., doing something besides pressing the lever. Figure 5 helps illustrate the key results. In it a

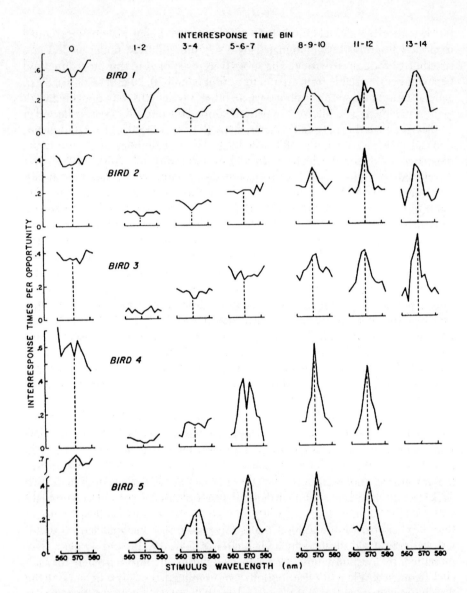

Figure 4. Generalization gradients of conditional response probabilities (IRTs/op) as a function of stimulus wavelength and IRT length. The dotted vertical line indicates the stimulus that was correlated with reinforcement during single-stimulus training and steady-state generalization. Data points based on fewer than 20 opportunities have been omitted.

plot of mean IRT (the reciprocal of average response rate) reveals a sloping generalization gradient, whereas a plot of *median* IRT reveals no change across stimuli.

As in the two studies described previously, the results reported by Crites et al. (1967) are consistent with the view that in stimulus generalization "what you reinforce is what you get." Generalization gradients are mixtures of established performances.

Lest one get the impression that such results are limited to non-humans consider an experiment by Cross and Lane (1962). In the study humans were instructed to hum at frequency of 147 Hz and 227 Hz (+ or - 2 Hz). Successful humming resulted in payment. A 500-Hz tone signaled when the subject was to hum. If that tone was presented at 74 dB then humming at 227 Hz was reinforced, if it was presented at 56 dB humming at the other frequency was reinforced. Once performance was established, a generalization test was conducted with other intensities. In the test, subjects emitted only the two frequencies that had been reinforced; no intermediate humming frequencies were observed.

Having argued that stimulus generalization reflects not some continuous change in behavior but instead reflects different probabilities of two (or perhaps more) response categories allows us to speculate about how stimuli control response hierarchies. The cases we have described may the thought of as the smallest of hierarchies, consisting of only two operants. The effects of presentation of stimuli intermediate to those under which the two operants that were established by the procedure illustrates what we might conceptualize as controlling the nature of the

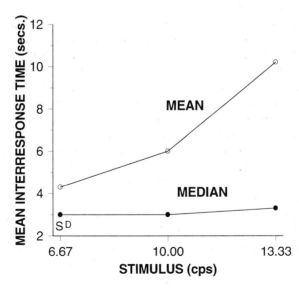

Figure 5. A comparison of mean and median measures of interresponse time during stimulus generalization.

hierarchy. The experimental situation is one in which all the available operants have some potential (or in cognitive jargon, are activated). The dimension-related stimuli merely adjust the probabilities of the behavior in the "activated" repertoire. The key feature being that previously established operants are what occur as stimulus conditions are varied.

The second type of process involved in the establishment of response hierarchies is direct reinforcement of the individual operants. This is the easiest of the processes to understand and one upon which Skinner (1957) relied most heavily to account for what I am referring to as response hierarchies. Take as a simple example the kind of experience with three-term contingencies in the presence of a ball. Figure 6 will aid in the discussion. In the presence of a ball a speaker may have experienced generalized reinforcement following saying "ball," "sphere," "round," "globe,", "orb," "throw," and "pelota" among other possibly reinforced utterances. We'll just pay attention to these seven. It seems reasonable to suppose that the various operants will have received different amounts of reinforcement. If that is so, they will exist at different strengths and thus can be considered to constitute a hierarchy. Seeing a ball, then, would make emitting each of the verbal operants more likely. The one actually emitted is usually argued to depend on other controlling factors (cf. Winokur, 1976).

A more likely scenario for some of the words related to ball, however, is not that reinforcement of uttering them has occurred in the presence of balls, but that reinforcement has occurred when some were said in the presence of other *words* about balls. (This would probably be the case for "pelota" if Spanish were a second language.) This scenario leads to the third route to a verbal hierarchy to be discussed, stimulus equivalence class formation.

Stimuli are said to be part of an equivalence class if they exhibit reflexivity, symmetry and transitivity in conditional discrimination procedures. Reflexivity means that two instances of a stimulus will be seen as identical. Symmetry means that either of two stimuli can be the conditional stimulus for selecting the other. Transitivity means that if stimulus A controls emission of a response to stimulus B and stimulus B controls a response to stimulus C, then stimulus A will also control a response to stimulus C. In this last example, if stimuli A, B, and C form an equivalence class, then it is true that stimulus C will control responses to stimulus B and to stimulus A via symmetry and transitivity. What equivalence implies is that, in a given context, the stimuli in the class are interchangeable.

How equivalence classes are established may have implications for the structure of response hierarchies. Suppose that the learning history took either of the two paths illustrated in Figure 7. In both cases the person first learns to say "ball" in the presence of a ball. Later, synonyms for ball are learned in the presence of the word "ball" or other synonyms. In the scenario on the left. Both "sphere" and "orb" are learned in the presence of the word "ball" and "globe" is learned in the presence of "orb." In the hypothetical history on the right the word "sphere" is learned in the presence of "ball," the word "orb" in the presence of "sphere," and the word "globe" in the presence of "orb." Both groupings will result in the formation of an equivalence class with a ball and the four synonyms as members. Let us focus,

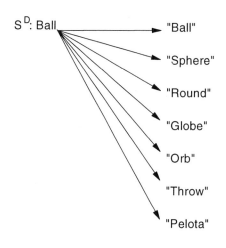

Figure 6. An example of a response hierarchy.

however, on learning of the word "globe" in these two arrangements. In both, it is learned in the presence of "orb," but the learning that precedes it is different. The concept of nodality (Fields, Verhave, & Fath, 1984) is useful in distinguishing the two cases. Nodes can be counted by enumerating the intervening discriminations that occur between members of the equivalence class. In the left-hand grouping there are two nodes between the ball and the word "globe," whereas in the right-hand set there are three nodes between the ball and "globe." It has been shown that number of intervening nodes influences the speed with which members of an equivalence class are recruited (e.g., Fields, Adams, Verhave, & Newman, 1990). Specifically, the rule seems to be that the more nodes between potential members of a class the slower those members are incorporated. To date, most research on the development of equivalence classes has focused simply on whether equivalence relations can be established. Relatively less research has been directed at the structure of those classes once they are established. For example, to my knowledge, no one yet has measured latencies in the conditional discrimination procedures that usually are employed. These, it seems to me, could be very interesting and might offer the possibility of direct ties to the research on semantic networks. Let me propose an experiment. Instead of the English words displayed

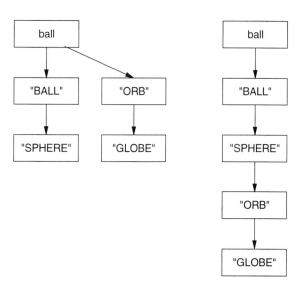

Figure 7. Two different equivalence classes structures.

in Figure 7, suppose arbitrary symbols were employed in the two training arrange-ments shown. Once the equivalence class was formed, one could actually arrange something like a lexical decision task and measure latencies to recognition that a symbol had or had not been part of the class. Stimuli could be presented in pairs as in a semantic priming task. My bet is that the network one would observe would (a) show "semantic" priming effects and (b) (more excitingly) that the priming effects, and therefore the inferred structure of the network, would depend on the training history. This would be a very important contribution to the study of semantic networks.

Word Recognition

The goal of all the foregoing has been to set a foundation for interpretations of what goes on when one tries to solve crossword puzzles. Before I get to that point, one other research area needs to be discussed, and that is the literature on word recognition in the study of reading. The study of reading has led to the discovery of some interesting relationships among behavioral activities and between behavior and physiology. For instance, at normal reading distance, the foveal image contains about 3 letters (Just & Carpenter, 1987). Since most words are longer than three letters it is clear that recognizing words depends not only on foveal images but on those from the visual periphery as well. The important part of the periphery is, for readers of English at least, is to the right because fixations on words tend to be at the left end (Rayner & Pollatsek, 1981). Bruner and O'Dowd (1958) have suggested that English words carry more information at the beginning than the end, so one would expect that we would learn to look more at the beginning of words than at the ends. The following illustrates the relative importance of letters at the beginning of words.

A. Final letters only: _he _____tion _f_____tions ___ies _n _____ing.

B. Initial letters only: T__ loca_____ o_ fixa_____ var_____ i_ read___.

Additional evidence that words are "read' from left to right, even though the eye does not move, is the existence of a serial position effect for reporting the letters in tachistoscopically presented words.

Even though only the images of three letters fall on the fovea at any one time, and even though fixations move from beginnings of words to beginnings of words, when reading the duration of fixation is controlled in an orderly way by the number of letters in the word. Fixations for a two-letter word average about 250 ms (this varies from individual to individual). Each additional letter prolongs the fixation by about 30 ms. Interestingly, this orderly relationship occurs only during reading of strings of words, not for the reading of individual words (Just & Carpenter, 1987). The finding that fixation time is closely related to word length implies that each letter controls behavior. As we shall see, single letters can play an important role in solving crossword puzzles. We should not be surprised that single letters control important behavior while we read (and solve crossword puzzles). Our earliest experience with reading involves three-term contingencies that incorporate single letters, and apparently this experience is manifested even after we become skilled readers. It seems likely that such control by individual letters is maintained at least partly by writing where we write one letter at a time and read as we write.

Reading and understanding words, not too surprisingly, is influenced by the context in which the reading occurs. The context most often considered by cognitive psychologists is the surrounding text. Take the following example in which context controls reading of a particular target word:

> The young man turned his back on the rock concert stage and looked across the resort lake. Tomorrow was the annual, one-day fishing contest, and fisherman would invade the place. Some of the best bass guitarists in the country would come to this spot. The usual routine would be disrupted by the festivities. (From Carpenter & Daneman, 1981).

If you are like most people you read the word "bass" to rhyme with "lass" rather than with "lace." This is a striking example of how local word context can influence what we say. This kind of effect was described by Skinner (1957) as a manifestation of supplemental sources of control.

Surprisingly, some formal aspects of written words seem to have little impact on word recognition. One might assume, for example, (especially after working on crossword puzzles) that the outline of a word, or the graphic features of short sequences of letters might be important sources of stimulus control. There is little convincing evidence that this is the case (Henderson, 1982). This is true despite the robustness of the "word superiority effect." In tachistoscopic word recognition tasks people are faster at recognizing words than non-words (something one would expect from a signal-detection view), even if the orthography is badly degraded.

Solving Crossword Puzzles

Now to crossword puzzles. In the remainder of the chapter I present examples from some recent attempts I have made to solve such puzzles, and as they are described I'll try to offer an interpretation based on the notions of response hierarchy and some of the other stimulus-control processes described earlier. The general interpretive scheme is that the clue for the word in the puzzle "activates" a hierarchy, i.e., makes a certain set of responses more probable. As letters are added via words that go across the word in question, additional stimuli involved in word recognition are added. Additions of these stimuli are a little like moving along a generalization gradient, and, as discussed earlier, different stimuli in a generalization gradient change the probabilities of previously conditioned operants (here words). As these operants are evoked they either are reinforced by fitting in the available space, or subjected to extinction because they do not. This whole interpretation, of course, is quite oversimplified and ignores several interesting behavioral phenomena such as the origin of being able to transcribe what one says to oneself. Also ignored in my interpretation are many of the direct problem-solving strategies involved in solving crossword puzzles. For example, many puzzles have themes that one can use to generate candidates for the correct answer for a particular clue. I am going to try focus mainly on what I see as interesting instances of stimulus control that may enter into solving crossword puzzles. Given these caveats let me proceed with some examples. I'll give the clue, then the constraints, and then relate how my behavior was controlled by the ensuing stimuli. The main goal here is to illustrate the types of stimulus control that seem to be operating so that one might speculate on the origins of that control. Some of the instances, I think , provide interesting challenges to anyone who cares to suggest how such control was established. One last apology, because it deals with an established behavioral repertoire, the interpretation is decidedly structuralistic. I hope you will all recall the preceding sections in which the histories that may have produced that repertoire were discussed.

Now to the examples. The first few illustrate the importance of early letters in a word as well as some other interesting characteristics. Let's take the first problem. The clue was "Note paper," and the response included 10 letters. Via words that went across I initially was able to get 3 letters as follows:

$$\_ \_ \_ \_ \underline{T} \_ \_ \_ \underline{S} \, \underline{I} \_$$

At this point I was still at a loss, until via another crossing word I got the first letter, so now the picture was:

$$\underline{S} \_ \_ \_ \underline{T} \_ \_ \_ \underline{S} \, \underline{I} \_$$

whereupon I solved it as SHEET MUSIC. Initially, as I suspect the puzzle maker intended, my behavior was mainly controlled by the non-musical meanings of "note." Getting the initial "S," however brought "sheet" to greater strength, and then the "SI" led to music. Perhaps a simpler example of how initial letters can control solutions is a problem where the clue was "House coat." Initially, I had that last of five letters:

$$\_ \_ \_ \_ T$$

and was at a complete loss. When I got the first letter so the problem became

$$P \_ \_ \_ T$$

I was immediately able to solve it as PAINT. Again, the puzzle maker tapped initially words related to a garment. Finding the initial letter gave rise to other words associated with house and thus resulted in a solution.

Mid-word letters also can be sources of stimulus control. A recent example in my experience was the clue "Future officers." Now the clue itself gave rise to "electees," and "candidates" and OCS (for officer candidate school). Unfortunately there were only six letters to be produced. I managed to get the first letter so the problem became

<u>C</u> _ _ _ _ _

but I still had no solution. Later I added a second letter so the picture became

<u>C</u> _ _ E _ _

Following which I immediately was able to produce the correct answer, CADETS. These kinds of solutions, where middle letters are crucial, are very common and reflect very interesting sorts of stimulus control. In this case, the E suggested a two-syllable word that helped in the solution.

Just as letters in the middle of words can be important sources of stimulus control so can ending letters. Consider the following two examples.

Clue	Spaces
Walkway	_ _ _ _
Canyon phenomenon	_ _ _ _

Both clues give rise to a number of possibilities, but none that were evoked in me were four letters long. But when I got the last letter of each as follows

_ _ _ <u>H</u>
_ _ _ <u>O</u>

the solutions, PATH and ECHO, came immediately. It is clear that control can exist at virtually any place in a word. Initial letters lead to more solutions than to later letters, but late letters can be important.

That ending letters can be important leads to a small aside about crossword puzzles that helps support the view that suffixes can exist as independent operants. Clues frequently will indicated that the word to be produced is plural, past tense, an adverb, or a gerund.. In these cases, I usually write in the "S," "ED," "LY," or "ING." Usually, of course, this provides no assistance in producing the root word (i.e., here are cases where ending letters provide no help). It does, however, provide letters for other words which go across and can, therefore, be quite useful. The fact that clues can lead directly to the emission of these grammatically important parts of words suggests that the parts exist as separable operants.

Despite what I have said so far about clues "activating" response hierarchies, there are times (many, in fact) in which, at least introspectively, the clue produces nothing. This happens, for example, when I have seen the clue word before, but cannot remember what it means, or the clue refers to some historical character, and I can't remember what the person did. In such cases, addition of letters seems to "jog" my memory so that I can solve the problem. An example of a clue that gave me no clue was "_ _ _ _ _ _ _ _ _ _ _ _ _ _ _ once in life." Fifteen letters comprised the answer.

As I worked through the puzzle I eventually got to the following state:

$$\_ \_ \underline{U} \_ \underline{N} \_ \_ \underline{G} \, \underline{O} \, \underline{A} \_ \_ \_ \_ \_$$

Here I was still stumped. I could generate just about nothing. "GOA" made me think of "goal" or "goad," but neither of them seemed any help. Finally, I got one more letter so I had

$$\_ \_ \underline{U} \_ \underline{N} \_ \underline{Y} \, \underline{G} \, \underline{O} \, \underline{A} \_ \_ \_ \_ \_$$

At that point I solved it. _ N _ Y was enough to make me say "only" which makes the series of letters in the middle "only go" which leads to the solution YOU ONLY GO AROUND. This, to me, is a particularly striking example how part of a stimulus coupled with the context of the clue can bring verbal behavior to the level of emission.

The kinds of stimulus control built into crossword puzzles also allow demonstrations of other kinds of interactions between parts of our repertoires. Let me describe one that illustrates how rule governance and these types of presumably contingency-shaped stimulus-control processes can interact. This example has to do with successive clues. In this puzzle, the preceding clue was "Lesion." That word has a special history for me because of one of my professors while I was a graduate student. He made sure that all of us understood that the word lesion is a noun, not a verb, despite the fact that many physiological psychologists treat it as a verb. We all received instruction that made us write or say things like "a lesion was made in the hypothalamus" rather than "we lesioned the hypothalamus." This is a lesson that has stayed with me, so that whenever I see the word lesion I am reminded not only of wounds but that the word is a noun. The very next clue was "Falls," and I was having a devil of a time with it. After a few runs through the puzzle the first two iterations were

$$\_ \_ \_ \_ \_ \_ \underline{S}$$
$$\_ \_ \_ \_ \underline{M} \_ \underline{S}$$

At this point I was working on words like succumbs, plombs, and the like. Then I got the next letter so I had

$$\_ \_ \underline{T} \_ \underline{M} \_ \underline{S}$$

I was still stumped, and remember, every time I look at this clue I notice "lesion" above it and pat myself on the back for remembering that it is a noun. Not until I got the letter that led to solution did I break out of the verb mold. Only when the puzzle became

$$\underline{A} \_ \underline{T} \_ \underline{M} \_ \underline{S}$$

did I stop trying verbs and switch to one of the noun meanings of Falls, namely AUTUMNS.

This episode helps to illustrate how tightly controlled my response to "lesion" was. I kept telling myself it was a noun, yet I kept treating the very next clue as if it were a verb, which it was not.

So ends my short treatise on verbal repertoires and how they may come to be involved and exemplified in solving crossword puzzles. The notion of experience producing potential behavior is a straightforward way to conceptualize what traditionally has been called learning. Potential behavior has the same status as potential energy in physics. Just as raising a mass to the top of a ramp and creating potential energy does not put anything into the mass, exposing a subject to contingencies creates a potential for behavior that does not require us to put anything into the organism. The notion of potential behavior carries none of the excess meaning that words like "representations," "expectations," "knowledge," and "memory stores" do.

This chapter has promoted the view of response hierarchies as a way to characterize the structure of potential verbal behavior. I have speculated not only on the resulting structure of behavior, but also on possible origins of such structure. If what I have written makes even a modicum of sense it provides another example of how a behavior-analytic approach to verbal (and other) behavior can deal with complex behavioral issues.

Preparation of this chapter was supported by USPHS Grant. No. DA-04074.

References

Anger, D. (1956) The dependence of interresponse times upon the relative reinforcement of different interresponse times. *Journal of Experimental Psychology, 52*, 145-161.

Benjafield, J. G. (1992) *Cognition.* Englewood Cliffs, NJ: Prentice-Hall.

Bickel, W. K., & Etzel, B. C. (1985) The quantal nature of controlling stimulus-response relations as measured in tests of stimulus generalization. *Journal of the Experimental Analysis of Behavior, 44*, 245-270.

Bruner, J. S., & O'Dowd, D. (1958) A note on the informativeness of parts of words. *Language and Speech, 1*, 98-101.

Carpenter, P. A., & Daneman, M. (1981) Lexical retrieval and error recovery in reading: A model based on eye fixations. *Journal of Verbal Learning and Verbal Behavior,20*, 137-160.

Catania, A. C. (1973) The concept of the operant in the analysis of behavior. *Behaviorism, 1*, 103-116.

Collins, A. M., & Loftus, E. F. (1975) A spreading activation theory of semantic processing. *Psychological Review, 82*, 407-428.

Crites, R. J., Harris, R. T., Rosenquist, H., & Thomas, D. R. (1967) Response patterning during stimulus generalization in the rat. *Journal of the Experimental Analysis of Behavior, 10*, 165-168.

Cross, D. V., & Lane, H. L. (1962) On the discriminative control of concurrent responses: The relations among response frequency, latency, and topography in auditory generalization.*Journal of the Experimental Analysis of Behavior, 5*, 487-496.

Fields, L., Adams, B. J., Verhave, T., & Newman, S. (1990) The effects of nodality on the formation of equivalence classes. *Journal of the Experimental Analysis of Behavior, 53*, 345-358.

Fields, L., Verhave, T., & Fath, S. (1984) Stimulus equivalence and transitive associations: A methodological analysis. *Journal of the Experimental Analysis of Behavior, 42*, 143-158.

Gray, V. A. (1976) Stimulus control of differential-reinforcement-of-low-rate responding. *Journal of the Experimental Analysis of Behavior, 25*, 199-207.

Hearst, E. (1965) Approach, avoidance, and stimulus generalization. In D. I. Mostofsky (Ed.) *Stimulus generalization* (pp. 331-355). Stanford: Stanford University Press.

Hearst, E., Koresko, M. B., & Poppen, R. (1964) Stimulus generalization and the response-reinforcement contingency. *Journal of the Experimental Analysis of Behavior, 7*, 369-380.

Henderson, L. (1982) *Orthography and word recognition in reading.* London: Academic Press.

Just, M. A., & Carpenter, P. A. (1987) *The psychology of reading and language comprehension.* Newton, Massachusetts: Allyn and Bacon, Inc.

Michael, J. (1982) Distinguishing between discriminative and motivational functions of stimuli. *Journal of the Experimental Analysis of Behavior, 37*, 149-155.

Migler, B. (1964) Effects of averaging data during stimulus generalization.*Journal of the Experimental Analsysis of Behavior, 7*, 303-307.

Rayner, K., & Pollatsek, A. (1981) Eye movement control during reading: Evidence for direct control. *Quarterly Journal of Experimental Psychology, 33A*, 351-373.

Rilling, M. (1977) Stimulus control and inhibitory processes. In W. K. Honig & J. E. R. Staddon (Eds.) *Handbook of operant behavior* (pp. 432-480). Englewoood Cliffs, New Jersey: Prentice Hall.

Reed, S. K. (1992) *Cognition (3rd edition).* Pacific Grove, California: Brooks/Cole.

Sidman, M. (1986) Functional analysis of emergent verbal classes. In T. Thompson & M. D. Zeiler (Eds.) *Analysis and intergration of behavioral units* (pp. 213-245). Hillsdale, New Jersey: Erlbaum.

Skinner, B. F. (1935) The generic nature of the concepts of stimulus and response. *Journal of General Psychology, 12*, 40-65.

Skinner, B. F. (1938) *The behavior of organisms: An experimental analysis.* New York: Appleton-Century-Crofts.

Skinner, B. F. (1957) *Verbal behavior.* New York: Appleton-Century-Crofts.

Terrace, H. S. (1966) Stimulus control. In W. K. Honig (Ed.) *Operant behavior: Areas of research and application* (pp. 271-344). New York: Appleton-Century-Crofts.

Winokur, S. (1976) *A primer of verbal behavior: an operant view.* Englewood Cliffs, New Jersey: Prentice-Hall.

Chapter 4

Stimulus Equivalence, Functional Equivalence and the Transfer of Function

Michael J. Dougher and Michael R. Markham
University of New Mexico

Stimulus equivalence continues to attract a good deal of interest among behavior analysts. Although some have suggested that equivalence may be the newest "fad" among behavioral researchers (Harzem, 1992, Malatt, 1991), others see equivalence as having clear implications for our understanding of complex behavior including symbolic behavior, language, (Hayes, 1989; 1991, Hayes & Hayes, 1989; Sidman, 1986; 1990) and the ability to behave appropriately in novel situations (Spradlin and Saunders, 1984). Moreover, some argue that stimulus equivalence constitutes a challenge to the traditional three-term contingency as the basic unit of analysis and is, therefore, interesting in its own right (Hayes, 1991, this volume; Sidman, 1986).

One of the most interesting aspects of stimulus equivalence research is what has been called the transfer of function through equivalence classes. Transfer of function refers to the acquisition of a psychological function via participation in an equivalence class. That is, once an equivalence class is formed, a function given to one member of the class generally transfers to other members of the class. This is a particularly interesting finding because it appears to be a process by which stimuli can acquire control over behavior in the absence of direct training. More generally it provides the framework for a behavior analytic response to the challenge from more cognitively oriented psychologists and psycholinguists to account for new behavior that has no apparent reinforcement history and is not attributable to simple generalization.

Although research on stimulus equivalence and the transfer of function seems both inherently interesting and promising, several fundamental questions and issues remain unresolved. For example, we have not yet adequately explained stimulus equivalence. That is, we have neither identified the prerequisites for equivalence nor do we have a fully developed and empirically supported conceptual account of it. As of yet, we have not reached an understanding of the relation between stimulus equivalence and related behavioral phenomena such as functional classes and functional equivalence. To the extent that we do not yet fully understand stimulus equivalence, neither do we understand the transfer of function through equivalence classes. It is not even clear that we are justified in using the term transfer through equivalence classes. It may very well be begging the question. For all we know, the relation could be reversed. That is, equivalence might be a result not the cause of function transfer. Alternatively, both might be a function of other behavioral processes. Issues such as these must be addressed before we can be said to have an understanding of equivalence and the behavioral phenomena that are said to result from it.

The purpose of the present paper is to address these concerns. In particular, existing accounts of equivalence, transfer of function, and the relation between stimulus equivalence and functional equivalence will be critically examined both conceptually and in the context of recent data collected at the University of New Mexico and other labs concerned with these issues. The goal of the paper is to challenge existing thinking and to suggest some alternative approaches to these issues. Let us be clear from the onset, however, that a fully articulated and empirically supported account of stimulus equivalence, functional equivalence and the transfer of function will not result from the present effort. These are extraordinarily difficult issues, and the data are simply not available to accommodate such a goal. Moreover, what is offered is done so rather tentatively and with the hope of facilitating discussion rather than offering a definitive account.

Some Definitions

In an attempt to minimize misunderstanding due to inconsistent terminology and to lay the groundwork for the arguments that follow, we will define a few key terms, at least as they will be used in the present paper.

Stimulus Equivalence

Few terms have received as much attention as stimulus equivalence. Yet some disagreement remains (Hayes, 1989; McIntire, Cleary & Thompson, 1989; Saunders, 1989; Vaughan, 1989). For present purposes stimulus equivalence refers to the derived stimulus relations of relexivity, symmetry and transitivity. While reflexivity, symmetry and transitivity have been defined repeatedly (e.g., Sidman, 1986; Sidman & Tailby, 1982; and virtually every published article on stimulus equivalence), the disagreement over the term stimulus equivalence seems to be focused on the requirement that these relations be derived or untrained. Part of the problem stems from Sidman's original attempt to define equivalence in mathematical and logical terms rather than in behavioral terms. As Vaughan (1989) points out, there is no logical requirement that equivalence relations must be derived. However, what is behaviorally interesting about equivalence is precisely that the relations are derived. Accordingly, untrained reflexivity, symmetry and transitivity is what is meant by stimulus equivalence in the present paper.

Stimulus Classes

Functional stimulus classes are comprised of stimuli that share a common stimulus function. That is, they all exert the same functional control over a specific class of behavior (Goldiamond, 1962, 1966; Skinner, 1935). More recently, Dube,

McDonald, and McIlvane (1991) have included a second defining criterion of functional classes which is that any variable applied to one class member will affect the others without direct training. That is, stimulus classes are also defined by a transfer of function criterion. Although these authors cite both Goldiamond and Skinner as incorporating both criteria in their definitions of stimulus classes, our own reading of these sources failed to identify the inclusion of the second criterion in their respective definitions. Actually, the first criterion appears to be definitional, while the second seems to be an assertion of the effects of an operation or manipulation; an assertion for which there appears to be relatively little empirical data. While it may very well be true that an operation performed on functional classes will result in the kind of transfer of function asserted in the second criterion, what would happen if the operation performed on one member did not transfer to the other members? Would we say that the stimuli were not part of a functional class even though they share a particular function? The two criteria seem to be logically distinct. The first pertains to the common function of the stimuli in the class, the second to the processes by which functions of the class members are modified. Moreover, there is evidence indicating that the two criteria are empirically distinct. For example, Rhatt & Wasserman (1989) report that the creation of discriminative stimulus classes with pigeons did not result in functional equivalence. Therefore, for purposes of the present paper, the two criteria will be considered separately. Only the former criterion will be used to define functional stimulus classes. Stimulus classes that meet both criterion will be defined as functional equivalence classes.

Functional Equivalence Classes

When a variable applied to one member of a functional stimulus class affects the other members in the absence of direct training, that set of stimuli is defined as a functional equivalence class, and the stimuli contained in the set are said to be functionally equivalent. Stimuli are functionally equivalent then, to the extent that they have similar functions and to the extent that a variable applied to one similarly affects the others. Like stimulus equivalence, functional equivalence refers to a set of relations among stimuli. It is defined by shared function and transfer of function.

Transfer of Function

Transfer of function is the test for functional equivalence. It refers to the acquisition of a stimulus function by a member of a functional stimulus class resulting from a variable applied to a different member of that class.

Stimulus Equivalence and Functional Equivalence

There is a growing body of evidence that psychological functions will transfer through stimulus equivalence classes. That is, experimental procedures that result in stimulus equivalence often result in functional equivalence. The general methodology typically employed in transfer of function studies is as follows. First, some number of equivalence classes are trained using match to sample or conditional discrimination training procedures. Subsequent to this training, which may or may not include tests for equivalence relations, a member of one of the classes is selected and given some psychological function. Then, the other members of the classes are tested to see if they have acquired the function. If the function is acquired by the other members of the class from which the stimulus was selected, but not by the members of the other classes, the function is said to have transferred through the equivalence class.

As an example, a recent study in our lab at the University of New Mexico investigated whether eliciting functions would transfer through equivalence classes. Using eight college students as subjects, we first trained three four-member equivalence classes using conditional discrimination procedures. Then, a member of one of the classes was selected as a CS+ and was repeatedly paired with mild shock in a respondent conditioning paradigm. A member of another class was selected as a CS- and was never paired shock. Stimuli from the third class were never presented during respondent conditioning and were used only to balance the conditional discrimination procedures. Following conditioning, all of the stimuli in the CS+ and CS- classes were presented individually to the subjects. Skin conductance was used to measure both conditioning and the transfer of function. Six of the eight subjects showed clear evidence for the transfer of the respondent eliciting function (Augustson & Dougher, 1992).

A variety of other stimulus functions have also been reported to transfer through equivalence classes. Lazar (1977) and Lazar & Kotlarchyk (1986) have demonstrated the transfer of discriminative stimulus control, Wulfert and Hayes (1989) have demonstrated the transfer of conditional stimulus control, Gatch and Osborne (1989) and Kohlenberg, Hayes and Hayes (1991) have reported the transfer of contextual control, and the transfer of both conditioned reinforcement and punishment has been shown by Hayes, Kohlenberg and Hayes (1991), and Greenway, Dougher, and Wulfert (1991). The only function that has not yet been demonstrated to transfer is that of establishing operations or establishing stimuli, and that research is currently underway.

Although these studies have been described as demonstrating the transfer of function through stimulus equivalence classes, there are reasons why this description may be unfounded. One problem has to do with the terminology, which is a bit odd from a behavior analytic perspective. The term transfer of function through equivalence classes implies that stimulus equivalence is a mechanism or process which mediates the transfer of some psychological function. It is as if a function travels along the symmetrical and transitive connections among members of an equivalence class. But this mediational and mechanistic language is more in line with methodological behaviorism than behavior analysis. When behavior analysts speak of respondent conditioning no mention is made of the transfer of function from the US to the CS. The CS simply acquires its function by virtue of its spatial and temporal relation to the US. This is a kind of functional equivalence that results from the contiguous arrangement of the two stimuli. Likewise, it may be more useful to speak of transfer of function as a particular type of functional equivalence that results from the procedures and operations that also produce stimulus equivalence.

A second problem is that it is not at all clear in these studies whether stimulus equivalence is necessary for the transfer of function to occur. One of the few studies to control for the effects of equivalence training was Hayes, Kohlenberg, and Hayes (1991), who showed that subjects who did not undergo the training procedures did not demonstrate transfer. However, all that can confidently be said here is that the training procedures, not necessarily stimulus equivalence, resulted in the transfer of function. Moreover, some of the subjects who did receive equivalence training did not undergo tests for equivalence relations before the transfer effects were tested (see also Wulfert & Hayes, 1989). This was a clever way of determining whether the testing itself was responsible for the transfer. But, while the answer was clearly no, omitting the testing raises serious questions about whether stimulus equivalence even "formed" before the transfer was tested. Some have suggested that the very tests for equivalence relations may be necessary for equivalence classes to form (Sidman, Kirk, & Wilson-Morris, 1985; Sidman, 1990). Ignoring for the moment the epistemological problems posed by talk of the "formation" or "existence" of stimulus equivalence classes (see McIlvane & Dube, 1990 for a discussion of this issue), the problem is that, by definition, we can not know if stimulus equivalence classes exist in the absence of the tests for equivalence relations. To use the transfer of function as the evidence for their existence begs the question, because the transfer is ostensibly due to the existence of stimulus equivalence classes. Unless we change the definition of stimulus equivalence to that of transfer of function or functional equivalence, we are stuck with the tests for reflexivity, symmetry, and transitivity to determine the existence of stimulus equivalence classes. What the Kohlenberg, et al. study did show was that interrelated conditional discrimination training resulted in both stimulus equivalence and functional equivalence. It did not and probably could not show that transfer occurred as a result of equivalence. That is true of all of the studies concerned with stimulus equivalence and the transfer of function.

Another problem concerns our relative lack of understanding of the exact relationship between stimulus equivalence and functional equivalence. One could very well argue, for example, that functional equivalence does not result from stimulus equivalence, rather stimulus equivalence results from functional equivalence. Consider the relations that define stimulus equivalence and the context within which they are trained and tested. According to Sidman (1986), stimulus equivalence results when some subjects are exposed to interrelated conditional discrimination arrangements. In his terminology, the sample stimuli in these arrangements function as conditional stimuli in that they determine the conditions under which the available comparison stimuli will function as discriminative stimuli for subjects' selections. A reinforcer is given for "correct" selections. Thus, we have a four term contingency. Now, in the tests for equivalence relations, (ignoring tests for relexivity) we take what was a discriminative stimulus, a comparison, and place it in the role of the conditional stimulus, the sample, and we take what was a conditional stimulus, a sample, and place it in the role of a discriminative stimulus, a comparison. When this is done with most languageable humans, the stimuli immediately exert the kind of stimulus control that we label symmetry and transitivity. That is, what was once the conditional stimulus for a particular discriminative stimulus is now the discriminative stimulus under the conditional control of what was the discriminative stimulus. The functions have transferred; there is a functional equivalence among them. According to Sidman's four-term contingency description, stimulus equivalence would appear to be a kind of functional equivalence. However, there is some reason to question the four-term or hierarchical account of stimulus equivalence, and this issue will be discussed in greater detail below. Before that, the literature directly concerned with the relation between functional stimulus classes, functional equivalence and stimulus equivalence will be addressed.

The Relation Between Functional Classes, Functional Equivalence, and Stimulus Equivalence

Apart from the studies described above concerning stimulus equivalence and the transfer of function, the relation between functional classes, functional equivalence and stimulus equivalence has been discussed directly. For example, Sidman, Wynne, Maguire and Barnes (1989) investigated the opposite question from that addressed in the transfer of function studies. That is, rather than asking if stimulus equivalence leads to functional classes, they asked if functional classes lead to stimulus equivalence relations. They used Vaughan's (1988) continuous reversal procedure to establish two functional stimulus classes with one normal and two mentally retarded adults. They then tested to see whether reflexive, symmetrical, and transitive relations emerged among the functional class members. Because one of the retarded subjects failed to show derived equivalence relations, the investigators concluded that while functional and equivalence classes can coexist, they appear to be independent processes. Dube, McDonald & McIlvane (1991) came to a similar conclusion regarding functional equivalence classes (they called them functional stimulus classes) and stimulus equivalence classes when one of their two subjects failed to show evidence of functional equivalence on a simple discriminative task after stimulus equivalence had been established.

While these investigators' conclusion that functional classes and stimulus equivalence classes are independent is certainly reasonable, an alternative account might be that the functional equivalence resulting from certain experimental procedures can, but does not necessarily, generalize to all functions. In other words, the specific functions that transfer through functional equivalence classes are themselves subject to stimulus control. There are some data which pertain to this question.

Wulfert and Hayes (1989) showed that the functional equivalence of discriminative control over a sequencing response could be brought under conditional stimulus control. In a recent study in our lab, Chiasson and Dougher (1992) showed that functional equivalence can be brought under direct contextual control. After training two four member equivalence classes, transfer of discriminative control over a sequencing task was reinforced in one context and punished in a different context. The contexts were different color backgrounds on the computer monitor. The color backgrounds came to exert contextual control over functional equivalence in subsequent tests for transfer.

Another piece of evidence was obtained in a study by Greenway, Dougher, and Wulfert (1992) who investigated whether functional equivalence of conditioned reinforcement and punishment would generalize to a new task. Replicating Hayes, Kohlenberg and Hayes (1991), we found the transfer of conditioned reinforcement and punishment with virtually all subjects when transfer was tested in a task similar to training. However, when transfer effects were tested in a different task, functional equivalence obtained for only half the subjects. Clearly, context exerts a considerable influence over functional equivalence.

The relation between functional stimulus classes and stimulus equivalence was also addressed by Hayes (1989) in his response to Vaughan's (1988) claim that stimulus equivalence had been demonstrated in animals. Briefly, Vaughan taught pigeons to peck at any of a set of slides arbitrarily defined as S+ and to refrain from pecking any of a set slides defined as S-. After repeatedly reversing the discriminations, he observed that the pigeons changed their response to all of the stimuli after experiencing the reversed contingency with just a few. Vaughan argued that the pigeons had effectively partitioned the stimuli into two sets which implies mathematical equivalence. Hayes' response was that Vaughan showed the existence of functional stimulus classes but not stimulus equivalence classes. He argued that it is the derived nature of stimulus equivalence relations that sets them apart from functional classes, and since the birds had direct training experiences with every member of each set, the control exerted over the birds' behavior could not be derived. Moreover, Hayes argued that derived relations would not be possible with functional classes. His argument is as follows. If stimulus A and B share a function (Y) so that they are both members of class X, and then A is given a new function (P) so that it is now a member of class Q, this does not mean that X and Q are equal. By equal, we assume Hayes means equivalent. That is, he would not predict that members of X will now evoke P and members of Q will now evoke Y. Hayes goes on to say that this would be impossible because it would end up with all classes combining into one.

However, recent evidence seems to refute this assertion. Wasserman and DeVolder (1992; see also Wasserman, DeVolder & Coppage, in press) reported the following category learning experiment with pigeons. They used four sets of stimulus categories (people, flowers, cars and chairs), each consisting of 12 individual examples. Slides of the individual samples from the four categories, C1, C2, C3, and C4, were projected on a screen in the experimental chamber. A peck to the screen lit two "report" keys, R1 and R2. Choice of R1 was reinforced if the slide was from C1 or C2, and extinguished if the slide was from C3 or C4. Choice of R2 was reinforced if the slide was from C3 or C4, and extinguished if the slide was from C1 or C2. Subsequent to this, "reassignment" training began, wherein C1 and C3 were reassigned to two new report keys, R3 and R4, respectively. That is, choices of R3 were reinforced if the slide was from C1 and extinguished if the slide was from C3, while choices of R4 were reinforced if the slide was from C3 and extinguished if from C1. Finally, the test phase presented slides from C2 and C4 and choices of R3 and R4. The results showed that the pigeons chose R3 in response to slides from C2 and R4 in response to slides from C4. These results suggest quite clearly that functional equivalence classes can result from the training of functional stimulus classes.

Hayes' point, however, that if this were to continue eventually the world would be one functional class is a good one and needs to be addressed. It would be similar to a situation where a single discriminative stimulus is given multiple behavioral functions. On any given trial, it might be impossible to predict which response would be evoked. Hayes has argued that this is unlikely to happen with stimulus equivalence because the context would determine which equivalence classes are in effect. But, it is not hard to imagine a situation where there are no specific contextual stimuli associated with equivalence classes. That is, there could be multiple equivalence classes with no contextual cues. In such a situation, the last response and its consequence might serve a contextual function. This is likely what occurred in the Vaughan (1988) study. The pigeons' last response plus its consequence was the contextual stimulus for the next trial. This would keep the classes from merging. At this point it is hard to know what can and would serve a contextual function, and the issue deserves more empirical investigation. In this regard, however, McIlvane, Dube, Kledaras, and de Rose's (1992) recent paper reports some non-human animal experiments which suggest that consequences enter into the controlling relation in conditional discrimination studies. That is, when one changes the specific reinforcer that has reliably followed a response in a conditional discrimination arrangement, it seriously disrupts conditional discriminative control. The point is that there are a variety of stimulus events that can and do exert contextual control, and this is likely to be true of functional equivalence.

If it is the case that functional equivalence can and does come under contextual control in much the same way that stimulus equivalence does, it is possible that stimulus equivalence and functional equivalence are not independent processes but simply reflect the transfer of different functions. The basic assertion here is that stimulus equivalence may be a kind of functional equivalence. In particular, functional equivalence occurs whenever there is a sharing or interchangeability of function. Stimulus equivalence occurs when this interchangeability of function occurs in a conditional discrimination arrangement. That is, stimulus equivalence results when there is a functional equivalence of conditional and discriminative stimulus control. All of this assumes that Sidman's four-term contingency or hierarchical model of stimulus equivalence is correct. However, while that account is certainly plausible, we will report some recently collected data which calls it into question.

Compound Stimuli in Emergent Stimulus Relations

The studies described below were not originally intended to investigate the adequacy of the hierarchical four-term contingency model of stimulus equivalence. Rather, they grew from our concern that, as they are generally conducted, stimulus equivalence studies may have limited relevance for our understanding of complex human behavior occurring in natural environments. The limitation of particular concern is that stimulus equivalence studies generally have been restricted to the dyadic relations among unitary stimuli. That is, unitary stimulus A is related to unitary stimulus B and then to unitary stimulus C, after which the requisite derived relations among these unitary stimuli are tested.

Stimulus relations in the natural environment often involve compounds and configurations of two or more stimuli, and it is the particular combination of stimuli which determines their particular effects or functions. This is illustrated by instances where the meaning of words within a sentence are a function of the relations of the words to each other. Consider the statement, "The bat landed by the pitcher." Here the meanings of the words bat and pitcher are unclear. The word "bat" could refer to a flying mammal or a baseball bat, and "pitcher" could refer to a container for pouring liquids or a person who throws a baseball. However, the meaning of these words is clearer in the statements, "The bat drowned in the pitcher" and "The pitcher swung the bat." In these examples, it is compounds of stimuli which determine their particular effects within each statement. If stimulus equivalence is to be a useful analogue of language, as it is purported to be, then it should address the issue of complex stimulus control. Moreover, it may be that the inclusion of compound stimuli in conditional discrimination paradigms would lead to the emergence of relations other than reflexivity, symmetry, and transitivity. This in itself might suggest alternative perspective on stimulus equivalence.

To date, only two reported studies (Stommer & Strommer, 1990a and 1990b) have used compound stimuli in conditional discrimination training procedures. In the first study, they trained relations of the form AB-D and AC-E, then tested for emergent relations among all possible pairs of unitary stimuli (e.g., A-B, D-B, B-C, B-E, and D-E). In the second, they trained the relations A-C, B-D and AB-E, then tested for relations among all possible pairs of stimuli (e.g., AA-D, B-C, C-E, and D-E). The results indicated that humans can learn conditional discriminations using compound sample stimuli and respond in testing to elements of the compound samples used in training. However, the results only demonstrated the emergence of standard equivalence relations when subjects were trained to match unitary comparisons to compound samples. Other possible emergent relations were not tested.

In the studies described below, we also used trained subjects to match unitary comparisons to compound samples, but our aim was to provide a context within which relations other than reflexivity, symmetry and transitivity could emerge.

The general method for the studies described below is as follows. Subjects were introductory psychology students who participated in the experiment for course credit. The experiment was run in a small room equipped with a chair and table upon

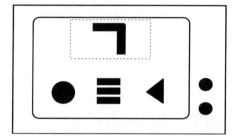

Figure 1. Depictions of computer presentations of compound sample and unitary comparisons (upper) and unitary sample and unitary comparisons (lower).

which was a 13 in. monochrome monitor, an IBM compatible PC, and a keyboard. All stimuli were presented on the computer monitor, and the computer controlled the presentation of the stimuli and recorded subjects' responses. Training trials consisted of a compound sample stimulus and three unitary comparison stimuli presented as depicted in Figure 1. Subjects selected one of the comparison stimuli by pressing the 1, 2, or 3 key on the computer keyboard. During baseline training, correct choices were followed by the word "Correct" presented at the center of the screen while incorrect choices were followed by the word "Wrong." Once subjects reached criterion on the

training trials, twenty additional trials were presented during which feedback was gradually faded (e.g., Correc., Corr..., C......, ...,...) in an attempt to ease the transition to testing trials where feedback was not given.

In all of the experiments the nine AB-C relations depicted in the top three rows of Figure 2 were trained. In some of the experiments the three C-D relations depicted in the bottom row of Figure 2 were trained. The comparison array, which is not pictured in Figure 2, always consisted of the same stimuli, C1, C2, and C3 or D1, D2, and D3, depending on the relations being trained. Trained relations were presented in blocks of nine or 12 trials consisting of one trial of each relation. Note that the nine AB-C trained rela-

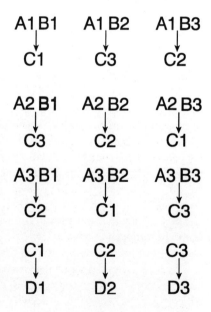

Figure 2. Depiction of 9 trained AB-C relations and 3 trained C-D relations.

tions are such that no stimulus was ever associated exclusively with any other. Thus, the design prevented subjects from responding to only one of the elements of the compounds. For example, if subjects were to correctly respond to the training relation A1B1-C1 based only on the presence of B1, then when presented with A2B1 they would likely choose C1 which would be incorrect. When B1 is compounded with A2, the correct choice is C3.

This training arrangement allows for the testing of a number of untrained relations, a subset of which is presented in Figure 3. The nine trained AB-C relations in combination with the three C-D relations allows for the emergence of nine symmetrical relations of the form C-AB, nine transitive relations of the form AB-D, nine equivalence relations of the form D-AB, 18 "associative" relations of the form AC-B, and 18 "associative equivalence" relations of the form AB-B. Figure 3 also illustrates the specific relations which can be tested after training A1B3-C2 then C2-D2.

The term "associative" relations was chosen with some reluctance given the problems resulting from original definition of stimulus equivalence in mathematical terms (Saunders & Green, 1991). Nevertheless, the term is illustrative of the relations that can emerge from the type of training described above. Essentially they are of the form: $(A+B)+C=A+(B+C)=(A+C)+B$. Associative equivalence in this case simply refers to the interchangeability of the D and C stimuli. To be sure, there are a variety of other relations that could be (and were) tested given the present training (e.g., A1B3-A2B3 and A1C2-A2C1), but these are beyond the scope of the present paper.

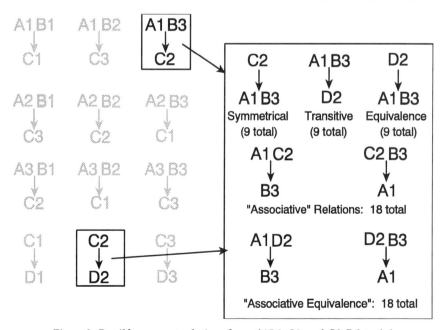

Figure 3. Possible emergent relations from A1B3-C2 and C2-D2 training.

The reason for testing the symmetrical and transitive relations that could emerge from the training described above was to determine whether stimulus equivalence does in fact emerge in these contexts. To summarize briefly the results of two studies, 11 of 12 subjects demonstrated the emergence of stimulus equivalence among the unitary and compound stimuli used in training as defined in Figure 3. More pertinent to the present discussion is the emergence of the so-called associative relations. Eleven subjects participated in the study and received training in the nine AB-C relations (as described above) until they reached a criterion of 98 correct out of 100 consecutive trials. Subjects were then tested for the emergence of the nine AC-B and nine CB-A relations described in Figure 3. Twenty blocks of 18 trials each were presented for a total of 360 testing trials.

The results of testing for all subjects plotted as percent correct over the 18-trial blocks are presented in Figure 4.

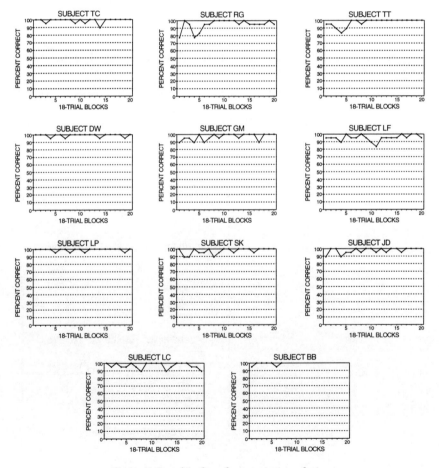

Figure 4. Results of test for associative relations.

All subjects attained and maintained a high level of correct responding across all trials. Subject BB terminated her participation after completing seven blocks of trials (126 trials), but performed at near perfect accuracy during testing. These results clearly indicate the emergence of what are here defined as associative relations. Before discussing these results, the results of a subsequent study testing for associative equivalence will be presented.

Five subjects participated in this experiment. The received training on nine AB-C relations and three C-D relations until they reached a criterion of 70 correct out of 72 consecutive trials. Subjects were then tested for nine simple equivalence relations (D-AB and 18 associative equivalence (nine AD-B and nine DB-A)

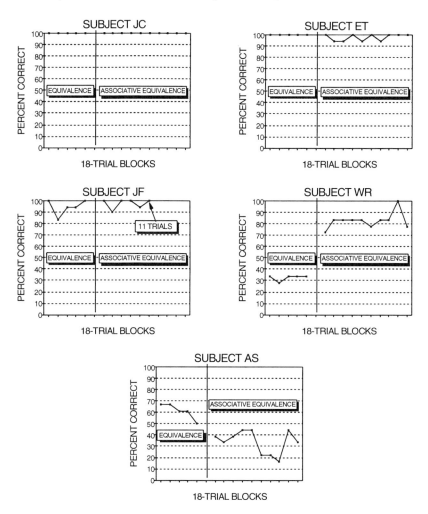

Figure 5. Results of tests for equivalence and associative equivalence relations.

relations. For simple equivalence, subjects received 10 blocks of nine trials, and for associative equivalence they received 10 blocks of 18 trials.

The results for the five subjects, plotted as percent correct over 18 trial blocks, are presented in Figure 5. Three subjects (JC, ET, and JF) clearly demonstrated the emergence of both equivalence and associative equivalence relations. Subject WR failed to demonstrate equivalence but did show evidence of associative equivalence. Subject AS showed no evidence for either equivalence or associative equivalence.

The results of these two studies suggest two conclusions. First, the use of compound stimuli in conditional match to sample arrangements allows for the emergence of stimulus relations beyond those reported in stimulus equivalence studies using unitary stimuli. That is, the relations can not be accounted for simply by appeal to reflexivity, symmetry, and transitivity. Second, the elements of the compound stimuli and the unitary stimuli related to them acquire some measure of stimulus control in relation to each other. That is, they appear to be interchangeable. If AB is related to C, then AC is related to B, and BC is related to A. This raises the question of their functional relation to each other. How should we describe this relation? We might consider one of the elements of the compound to function as a contextual stimulus (Sidman, 1986, Lynch & Greene, 1991, Wulfert & Hayes, 1989) for the conditional control exerted by the other over the discriminative control exerted by the unitary sample. But which of the elements is the contextual stimulus and which is the conditional stimulus? (See also Thomas & Schmidt, 1989 for a discussion of the difficulty in determining the respective functions of stimuli in certain kinds of conditional discrimination arrangements.) It appears that the elements of the compound exert a reciprocal influence on each other and on the unitary sample stimulus which putatively functions as a discriminative stimulus for subjects' choices.

Another question raised by these data is why all of the stimuli used in training did not collapse into one large equivalence class (see also Serna, 1991)? As an inspection of Figure 2 reveals, all of the stimuli used in the study were related to each other either directly or through symmetry and transitivity. However, the subjects' behavior suggests quite clearly that something prevented this collapse. One possibility is that the result of training was the formation of stimulus compounds comprised of the elements of the compound samples and the unitary comparisons related to them. This suggests that the comparisons exerted some reciprocal influence over the compounds, so that all or some critical number of the elements of the compounds together with the comparisons had to be present in order to evoke a response. Continuing with this line of thought, one is led to the possibility that the elements of the compounds in combination with the related comparisons functioned as a compound discriminative stimulus for the subjects' choice behavior. This account is similar to the one suggested by Strommer, McIlvane and Serna (1992), who argue that what are called conditional discriminations in match to sample arrangements may actually be an example of simple discriminative control by compound stimuli with separable and substitutable elements. The present findings lend some support to this account. As well, they call into question Sidman's notion of a unidirectional, hierarchical arrangement of function in conditional discrimination tasks.

The issue of compound stimulus control in stimulus equivalence has been addressed directly by Sidman (1986) and others before him (e.g., Berryman, Cumming, Cohen & Johnson, 1965; and Cumming & Berryman, 1965), who have argued cogently against it. The essence of Sidman's argument is that compounding of the sample and comparison stimuli in conditional discrimination tasks would preclude the emergence of transitivity and, therefore, stimulus equivalence. Moreover, he argues that the independence of the conditional and discriminative functions of the sample and comparison stimuli, respectively, can be demonstrated by relating a new stimulus to a member of an existing equivalence class and then testing for conditional control of the other members over the discriminative function of the new member, and vice versa (see also Bush, Sidman & de Rose, 1989; and Lynch & Green, 1991 for an extension of this argument to higher-order equivalence).

There appears, however, to be a critical difference between Sidman's treatment of compound stimuli and that of Strommer et al. Whereas Sidman describes compounds as unitary stimuli, Strommer et al. see compounds, at least in some conditional discrimination arrangements, as comprised of separable and substituable or interchangeable elements. If the elements of compounds are separable and substitutable, and the data reported above seems to indicate that they are, then Sidman's four-term contingency description of conditional discrimination arrangements may be a plausible but unnecessary construction. That is, it may not be necessary for the sample and comparison stimuli to function as conditional and discriminative stimuli, respectively, for stimulus equivalence to occur. For example, if A is conditionally related to B, then to C, and C is then related to D, A will exert what appears to be conditional control over the discriminative function of D if A is the sample and B is one of the comparisons in a match to sample arrangement. Thus, as Sidman argues, because A and D have never been directly related they could not function as a unitary compound and the independent conditional function of A is demonstrated. However, if we see this training as creating a stimulus compound consisting of the separable and substitutable elements A, B, C, and D, the presence of the compound or some critical subset of it "occasions a response to whichever element of the compound is displayed as a comparison stimulus" (Strommer et al., 1992, p. 6). Thus, rather than the result of a four-term contingency, conditional discriminations, and stimulus equivalence may be the result of a three-term contingency where the discriminative stimulus is a compound comprised of separable and substitutable elements. As Stommer et al. argue, what is defining in stimulus equivalence is not the hierarchical relationship among the stimulus elements but the separability and substitutability of the elements of the compound.

If we embrace the separable-and-substitutable-element compound discriminative stimulus account of stimulus equivalence (and it is clear the this is a move one makes quite tentatively given the paucity of data), we are left with at least two tasks. The first is to explain how the elements of a stimulus compound come to be separable and substitutable. The second gets back to the original objective of the present paper, and that is to relate this account of stimulus equivalence to the transfer of function or functional equivalence. At the risk of getting ahead of ourselves, we will argue below that the substitutability of the elements of a compound is a kind of functional equivalence. So we will address first just the issue of separability.

It is certainly not hard to imagine a training procedure that would result in stimulus control by the elements of a stimulus compound, and it is certainly not difficult to identify real-world examples of this kind of training. One could simply present a stimulus compound and reinforce discriminations of some identified set of elements. This is clearly what is entailed in many of the educational tasks and games we impose on children. Reading, for example, requires the discrimination of elements within a complex of words, and spelling requires discrimination of a smaller set of elements (letters) from within the set of stimulus compounds we call words. When children are given an n by n array of letters and asked to find the hidden words, they are being specifically trained to identify the elements of a stimulus compound. The fact that the inability or diminished ability to discriminate the separable elements of stimulus compounds has been associated with autism and severe mental retardation (e.g., Lovaas, Koegel & Schreibman, 1979; Lovaas, Schreibman, Koegel & Rehm, 1971) suggests that this ability may even be critical to normal human functioning.

With respect to the role this kind of discrimination might play in stimulus equivalence, a recent study by Wulfert, Dougher and Greenway (1991) is suggestive. These authors specifically trained subjects to combine two stimuli to form unitary compounds before exposing them to conditional discrimination training and equivalence tests. The results clearly showed that this training substantially interfered with the subjects' performance in tests for transitivity and, therefore, the emergence of equivalence. Although the authors argued that the results supported Sidman's position that stimulus equivalence can not result when the sample and comparison stimuli function as a unitary compound discriminative stimulus, an alternative account is equally plausible. One could argue that the training procedures taught the subjects to ignore the individual elements of the compounds, thereby interfering with any influence The compounds, then, were not functionally comprised of separable elements, and this precluded responding in a way that satisfied the criteria for stimulus equivalence.

Regarding the second issue, as stated above, it is our contention that the substitutability or interchangeability of the elements in a compound is a kind of functional equivalence. The question is what kind of function? As the data from the studies described above suggest, the elements can be seen as exerting a reciprocal influence on each other in such a way that then some critical combination of them occurs, it evokes a response. Thus, it doesn't matter, whether AB is the sample and C is the comparison or whether AC is the sample and B is the comparison. The combination of the elements in a particular way evokes a response to whichever element is presented as a comparison stimulus. The functional equivalence is seen in the derived control of AC-B and BC-A given training in AB-C. It is perhaps more clearly seen when, after training in AB-C and C-D, D acquires whatever function C has and, therefore, becomes interchangeable with A, B, and C. The argument holds for stimulus equivalence relations emerging from procedures using unitary stimuli as well. The function might be described as an enabling one in that all of the elements or some "critical" number must be present in order for the compound to evoke a response. Critical, in this case, is defined by the specific training and testing requirements. If, for example, training consists of AB-C and then C-D, it is not now necessary that all four elements be present to evoke a response; any three will do if the testing procedures require the selection of a unitary comparison in the presence of a compound sample. Similarly, if training consists of A-B and A-C, any two elements will evoke a response to the comparison stimulus.

The essential argument here is that regardless of whether stimulus equivalence is seen as the result of interchaneability within a hierarchical, conditional stimulus control arrangement or as resulting from interchangeability within a separable-compound discriminative stimulus control arrangement, it is a kind of functional equivalence. If we can assume this to be true, the critical issue then becomes one of explaining functional equivalence. Because of the relative dearth of data relevant to this issue, any attempt to account for functional equivalence at this point seems wildly speculative. Accordingly, it may be best to simply conclude by suggesting that future research efforts on this issue may benefit from an attempt to clarify the phylogenic and ontogenic determinants of functional equivalence, the contextual control over its occurrence, and its relation to other variables and processes involved in complex behavior.

References

Augustson, E. & Dougher, M. J. (1992, May). *Transfer of respondent functions and avoidance behavior via stimulus equivalence.* Paper presented at the 18th annual convention of the Association for Behavior Analysis, San Francisco.

Berryman, R., Cumming, W. W., Cohen, L. R., & Johnson, D. F. (1965). Acquisition and transfer of simultaneous oddity. *Psychological Reports, 17,* 767-775.

Bush, K. M., Sidman, M., & De Rose, T. (1989). Contextual control of emergent equivalence relations. *Journal of the Experimental Analysis of Behavior, 51,* 29-45.

Chiasson, C. & Dougher, M. J. (1992, May). *Contextual control of transfer of function through equivalence classes.* Paper presented at the 18th annual convention of the Association for Behavior Analysis, San Francisco.

Cumming, W. W. & Berryman, R. (1965). The complex discriminated operant: Studies of matching-to-sample and related problems. In D. J. Mostofsky (Ed.), *Stimulus generalization* (pp. 284-330). Stanford, CA: Stanford University Press.

Dube, W. V., McDonald, S., & McIlvane, W. J. (1992). A note on the relationship between equivalence classes and functional stimulus classes. *Experimental Analysis of Human Behavior Bulletin, 9,* 5-8.

Gatch, M. B. & Osborne, J. G. (1989). Transfer of contextual stimulus function via equivalence class development. *Journal of the Experimental Analysis of Behavior, 51,* 369-378.

Goldiamond, I. (1962). Perception. In A. J. Bachrach (Ed.), *Experimental foundations of clinical psychology* (pp. 183-224). New York: Wiley.

Goldiamond, I. (1966). Perception, language, and conceptualization rules. In B. Kleinmuntz (Ed.), *Problem solving* (pp. 183-224). New York: Wiley.

Greenway, D. E., Dougher, M. J., & Wulfert, E. (1992, May). *Transfer of consequential functions via stimulus equivalence: The role of generalization.* Paper presented at the 18th annual convention of the Association for Behavior Analysis, San Francisco.

Harzem, P. (1992, May). *Operant reformulation of research on operant analyses of data from "cognitive" literature: Unexplored areas for behavioral research.* Paper presented at the 18th annual convention of the Association for Behavior Analysis, San Francisco.

Hayes, S. C. (1989). Nonhumans have not yet shown stimulus equivalence. *Journal of the Experimental Analysis of Behavior, 51,* 385-392.

Hayes, S. C. (1991) A relational control theory of stimulus equivalence. In L. J. Hayes and P. N. Chase (Eds.), *Dialogues on verbal behavior* (pp. 17-40).

Hayes, S. C., & Hayes, L. J. (1989) The verbal action of the listener as a basis for rule governance. In S. C. Hayes (Ed.), *Rule-governed behavior: Cognition, contingencies and instructional control* (pp. 153-190). New York: Plenum Press.

Hayes, S. C., Kohlenberg, B. S., & Hayes, L. J. (1991). The transfer of specific and general consequential functions through simple and conditional equivalence relations. *Journal of the Experimental Analysis of Behavior, 56,* 119-137.

Kohlenberg, B. S., Hayes, S. C., & Hayes, L. J. (1991). The transfer of contextual control over equivalence classes through equivalence classes: A possible model of social stereotyping. *Journal of the Experimental Analysis of Behavior, 56,* 505-518.

Lazar, R. M., (1977). Extending sequence class membership with matching to sample. *Journal of the Experimental Analysis of Behavior, 27,* 381-392.

Lazar, R. M. & Kotlarchyk, B. J. (1986). Second-order control of sequence-class equivalences in children. *Behavioral Processes, 13,* 205-215.

Lynch, D. C. & Green, G. (1991). Development and crossmodal transfer of contextual control of emergent stimulus relations. *Journal of the Experimental Analysis of Behavior, 56,* 139-154.

Lovaas, O. I., Schreibman, L., Koegel, R. L., & Rehm, R. (1971). Selective responding by autistic children to multiple sensory input. *Journal of Abnormal Psychology, 77,* 211-222.

Lovaas, O. I., Liegel, R. L., & Schreibman, L. (1979). Stimulus overselectivity in autism: A review of research. *Psychological Bulletin, 86,* 1236-1254.

Malatt, R. W. (1991). Equivalence and relational frames: Sniping at the snipe hunters. In L. J. Hayes and P. N. Chace (Eds.), *Dialogues on verbal behavior* (pp. 41-44). Reno, NV: Context Press.

McIlvane, W. J. & Dube, W. V. (1990). Do stimulus equivalence classes exist before they are tested? *The Analysis of Verbal Behavior, 8,* 13-18.

McIlvane, W. J., Dube, W. V., Kledaras, J. B., de Rose, J. C., & Stoddard, L. T. (1992). Stimulus-reinforcer relations and conditional discrimination. In S. C. Hayes and L. J. Hayes (Eds.), *Understanding verbal relations* (pp. 43-67). Reno, NV: Context Press.

McIntire, K. D., Cleary, J., & Thompson, T. (1989). Reply to Saunders and to Hayes. *Journal of the Experimental Analysis of Behavior, 51,* 393-396.

Rhatt, R. S. & Wasserman, E. A. Secondary generalization and categorization in pigeons. *Journal of the Experimental Analysis of Behavior, 52,* 213-224.

Saunders, K. J. (1989). Naming in conditional discrimination and stimulus equivalence. *Journal of the Experimental Analysis of Behavior, 51,* 379-384.

Saunders, R. R. & Green, G. (1992). The nonequivalence of behavioral and mathematical equivalence. *Journal of the Experimental Analysis of Behavior, 57,* 227-241.

Sidman, M., Kirk, B., & Wilson-Morris, M. (1985). Six-member stimulus classes generated by conditional discrimination procedures. *Journal of the Experimental Analysis of Behavior, 43,* 21-42.

Sidman, M. & Tailby, W. O. (1982). Conditional discrimination vs. matching to sample: An expansion of the testing paradigm. *Journal of the Experimental Analysis of Behavior, 37,* 5-22.

Sidman, M., Wynee, C. K., Maguire, R. W., & Barnes, T. Functional classes and equivalence relations. *Journal of the Experimental Analysis of Behavior, 52,* 261-274.

Skinner, B. F. (1935). The generic nature of the concepts of stimulus and response. *Journal of General Psychology, 12,* 40-65.

Spradlin, J. & Saunders, R. R. (1984). Behaving appropriately in new situations: A stimulus class analysis. *American Journal of Mental Deficiency, 88,* 574-579.

Strommer, R., McIlvane, W. J., & Serna, R. W. (1992, June). *Complex stimulus control and equivalence.* Paper presented at Fifteenth Symposium on Quantitative Analysis of Behavior: Stimulus Relations. Cambridge, MA.

Strommer, R. & Strommer, J. B. (1990a). The formation of arbitrary stimulus classes in matching to complex samples. *The Psychological Record, 40,* 51-66.

Strommer, R. & Strommer, J. B. (1990b). Matching to complex samples: Further study of arbitrary stimulus classes. *The Psychological Record, 40,* 505-516.

Thomas, D. R. & Schmidt, E. K. (1989). Does conditional discrimination learning by pigeons necessarily involve hierarchical relationships? *Journal of the Experimental Analysis of Behavior, 52,* 249-260.

Vaughan, W. (1988). Formation of equivalence sets in pigeons. *Journal of Experimental Psychology: Animal Behavior Processes, 14,* 36-42.

Vaughan, W. (1989). Reply to Hayes. *Journal of the Experimental Analysis of Behavior, 51,* 397-398.

Wasserman, E. A. & DeVolder, C. L. (1992, June). *Similarity-based conceptualization.* Paper presented at Fifteenth Symposium on Quantitative Analysis of Behavior: Stimulus Relations. Cambridge, MA.

Wasserman, E. A., DeVolder, C. L., & Coppage, d. J. (in press). Nonsimilarity-based conceptualizations in pigeons via secondary or mediated generalization. *Psychological Science.*

Wulfert, E., Dougher, M. J., & Greenway, D. E. (1991). Protocol analysis of the correspondence of verbal behavior and equivalence class formation. *Journal of the Experimental Analysis of Behavior, 56,* 489-504.

Wulfert, E., & Hayes, S. C. (1989). Transfer of a conditioned ordering response through conditional equivalence classes. *Journal of the Experimental Analysis of Behavior, 50,* 125-144.

Chapter 5

Discrimination of Artificial Polymorphous Categories in Humans and Non-Humans

Masako Jitsumori
Chiba University

In the natural environment, animals frequently display adaptive behavior to novel objects. Categorization of objects play a crucial role in the life of most animals. With controlled laboratory experiments, it has been shown that animals, particularly pigeons, are capable of responding similarly to familiar and novel members of one class of stimuli and differently to familiar and novel members of other classes of stimuli. In most of these experiments, animals are trained to discriminate between two classes of photographic slides of natural objects, usually in a go/no-go successive discrimination procedure. The subjects are then tested with a variety of new instances. Pigeons have demonstrated their capacity to categorize a wide variety of stimuli including people, a particular person, fish, trees, oak leaves, bodies of water, other pigeons, and so forth (Cerella, 1979; Herrnstein & de Villiers, 1980; Herrnstein, Lovland, & Cable, 1976; Poole & Lander, 1971; Siegel & Honig, 1970; Wasserman, Kiedinger, & Bhatt, 1988.) Even pictures of some less natural stimuli were categorized by pigeons, such as alphabetical characters (Morgan, Fitch, Holman, & Lea, 1976), aerial photographs containing and not containing man-made objects (Lubow, 1974), and drawings of cartoon characters (Cerella, 1980.)

Natural categories are defined by a number of relevant features, none of which is necessary nor sufficient for category membership. For example, members of a natural category such as trees contain a wide variety of subsets of features such as leafy, branchiness, woodiness, greenness, verticality, and so forth. Most trees are green and leafy, although a tree that has lost its leaves in winter is not green or leafy. Most trees are larger than bushes, but a *bonsai* tree is very small. Thus, natural categories are polymorphous; no single feature is likely to be a necessary nor sufficient condition for category membership. Herrnstein and others (Herrnstein, 1985; Herrnstein, Loveland, & Cable, 1976; Morgan, Fitch, Holman, & Lea, 1976) have argued that both humans and animals may use similar polymorphous rules to classify natural objects.

It is often difficult to describe photographs of natural objects in terms of physical features. Because of this difficulty, artificial geometric stimuli that were constructed to mimic the supposed feature structure of natural categories have been used to investigate the mechanisms of discrimination of polymorphous categories. An advantage of using artificial categories is that it is possible to analyze the way in which well-defined distinct features control discriminative performance. In a pioneering work by Lea and Harrison (1978), pigeons were trained to discriminate arrays of symbols on colored backgrounds. The positive stimuli contained two positive and one negative feature, and the negative stimuli contained one positive and two negative features (the positive features were black, circle, and a green background; and the negative features were white, triangle, and a red background.) There were three possible combinations of features for the positive stimuli and for the negative stimuli, respectively. Pigeons learned to discriminate the stimuli and showed transfer to stimuli with all three positive or negative features. Instead of artificial geometric stimuli, as used in Lea and Harrison, von Fersen and Lea (1990) used photographs of natural scenes differing along five 2-valued (positive or negative) dimensions, including site, weather, camera distance, camera orientation, andcamera height. Slides containing three or more positive features were positive, and slides containing fewer than three positive features were negative. Seven of 8 pigeons learned to discriminate the 3-out-of-5 polymorphous categories but with substantial difficulties. Lea and his co-workers reported difficulties in training pigeons to use all relevant features to discriminate stylized pictures of pigeons (Lea & Ryan, 1990) and pseudo-seeds (Lea, Lohmann, & Ryan,1993) differing on five dimensions. In contrast, Huber and Lenz (1993) recently reported that pigeons very quickly learned to classify Brunswick faces that differed along four 3-valued (positive, neutral, and negative) dimensions.

With humans, by using similar geometric stimuli like as those used by Lea and Harrison for pigeons, Dennis, Hampton, and Lea (1973) showed that an artificial polymorphous problem is much more difficult than a conjunctive or disjunctive problem. By using a similar training procedure as that used by Lea and Harrison for pigeons, Tanaka and Sato (1983) trained humans to discriminate drawings of human infants wearing a cap. The stimuli differed along three 2-valued dimensions, including gender (a boy or a girl), type of cap (a baseball cap or a hunting cap), and color of cap (green or red). College students and children aged from 6 to 12 years old learned to discriminate among the three positive and three negative stimuli. However, none of them showed transfer to the stimuli containing all three positive or all three negative features.

A Comparative Study o Discrimination of Artificial Polymorphous Categories in Pigeons, Monkeys, and Humans

Jitsumori (1993; 1994, in press) compared category discrimination of artificial polymorphous stimuli by pigeons, monkeys, and people. Subjects were trained to discriminate arrays of symbols on colored backgrounds, like as those used by Lea and Harrison (1978.). The three relevant dimensions of the stimuli were symbol color (black or white), symbol shape (circle or triangle), and background color (green or red). For each subject, one value of each feature was defined as positive and the other as negative. Stimuli containing two of the three positive features were positives, and stimuli containing two of the three negative features were negatives. Stimuli having all three positive or all three negative features were not used for training. A set of three positive stimuli and a set of three negative stimuli were used for training in Lea and Harrison (1978), whereas Jitsumori (1993; 1994) used a total of 60 stimuli (30 positives and 30 negatives) for training. Each type of stimulus was presented in ten different arrays of 3, 4, or 5 identical symbols. Although the number of training stimuli was small enough to allow pigeons (Vaughan & Greene, 1984; von Fersen & Delius, 1989) and monkeys (Jitsumori, Wright, & Cook, 1988; Ringo & Doty, 1985) to learn each individual stimulus, different arrays of symbols were used in order to diminish the possibility that subjects learned to respond just to the individual stimuli. Figure 1 shows representative samples of arrays of symbols.

Discrimination by Pigeons

Five homing pigeons were trained in a go/no-go discrimination task similar to that used by Herrnstein and his co-workers (Herrnstein, 1979; Herrnstein, Lovland, & Cable, 1976; Herrnstein & de Villiers, 1980.) The stimuli were successively presented on a screen positioned in front of a transparent rectangular key. The height and width of the slides as they appeared on the screen were 6.5 and 9.5 cm, respectively.

Each session consisted of 60 trials separated by 5-sec intertrial intervals. The 60 stimuli were randomly ordered each day with the restriction that no more than three positive or negative stimuli could occur in succession. The average duration of each presentation was 30 sec.In the presence of a positive stimulus, pecking was reinforced on a variable interval schedule with an average of 30 sec. The reinforcer consisted of 3-sec access to mixed grain in an aperture positioned below the key. The schedule of reinforcement was independent of the trial duration with the restriction that zero to three reinforcers could be earned during a single positive trial. In the presence of a negative stimulus, pecking was not reinforced. A negative trial terminated after its initial scheduled interval had expired and 5 sec had passed without responding. On positive trials, the number of responses prior to the first reinforcer of the trial was used to calculate response rate. The response rate on negative trials was calculated from the number of responses prior to the time when a reinforcer would have been delivered if the stimulus had been positive instead of negative. The training continued until 90% or more of the total responses occurred in positive trials for three consecutive daily sessions.

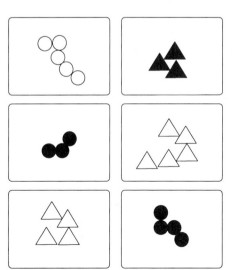

Figure 1. Representative examples of arrays of symbols used as stimuli.

Four of the five pigeons required an average of 90 sessions, with a range from 70 to 105 sessions, to reach the performance criterion. For one bird, symbol shape did not gain control over responding, and this bird was dropped from the experiment after 107 sessions of training.

Discrimination by Monkeys

Five male rhesus monkeys were trained to discriminate the 60 stimuli in the procedure used for pigeons but with minor changes. The front panel of an experimental chamber contained a 35 by 15 cm transparent window. Mounted behind the window was a computer monitor on which the stimuli were presented one by one. A response lever was positioned below the window. Food reinforcers were delivered into a container located to the right of the lever. The reinforcer was accompanied by a single beep.

Three of the 5 monkeys reached the acquisition criterion after an average of 36 sessions, with a range from 23 to 55 sessions. Performance of the other two monkeys was unstable, and they were dropped from the experiment after 45 sessions of training. For the monkeys that reached the acquisition criterion, the schedule of reinforcement on positive trials was changed to a variable interval of 60 sec. Training continued until the monkeys regained the acquisition criterion.

Discrimination by Humans

Ten male and female undergraduate students served as subjects. Each subject sat in front of a computer monitor that displayed stimuli one by one, and classified each stimulus by pressing one of the two keys, "A" or "B." The positive stimuli for pigeons and monkeys were assigned as members of group A and the negative stimuli as members of group B. The stimuli disappeared after each choice. Presses on the correct key added a point on the point counter that was continuously displayed on the computer monitor, and the statement (in Japanese) "Your choice is correct. This pattern belongs to group A (or B)" appeared on the computer monitor. Presses on the incorrect key produced a single beep, and the statement "Your choice is incorrect. This pattern belongs to group A (or B)" appeared. The statement was presented for 3 seconds, and 10 seconds later a new stimulus began the next trial. Subjects were instructed to attempt always to earn points on the point counter.

The subjects required an average of 4.5 sessions, with a range from 2 to 9 sessions, to attain a criterion of 90% correct choices or better in a session of 60 trials.

Transfer to Novel Instances

Subjects who learned the discrimination, 4 pigeons, 3 monkeys, and 10 people, were tested for transfer to novel instances. In the study of Lea and Harrison (1978), pigeons were tested for transfer to only two stimuli; a stimulus containing all three positive features and a stimulus containing all three negative features. In the present experiment, subjects were tested with a variety of new instances in Tests 1 and 2.

The stimuli used in Test 1 included all eight feature-value combinations. With seven new arrays of symbols, there were 56 novel patterns. For pigeons, two test sessions were given in extinction. Each of the 56 stimuli appeared once in a session.

For monkeys, a preliminary test revealed that testing in extinction severely decreased overall rate of responding. Monkeys, therefore, received 7 test sessions each of which consisted of 8 test trials and 60 training trials. Thus, monkeys were tested on each stimulus once in 7 sessions. On test trials, responses had no consequences (no reinforcers and no penalties.) The duration of each test trial was set at 30 s, and response rate was calculated from the number of responses that occurred during the entire trial time. On training trials in which the monkeys were exposed to the training stimuli, the contingencies of reinforcement were in effect.

Human subjects were tested on each stimulus once in a single session of 56 trials. Before the test, the statement "This time you will not get any beeps, points, or feedback statements, but you have to guess whether each stimulus belongs to group A or B as best as you can" appeared on the computer monitor. During the test, the computer monitor darkened for three seconds after each choice.

Subjects who showed transfer even to the stimuli with all three positive or all three negative features in Test 1 received Test 2, with retraining sessions intervening between the tests. The stimuli used in Test 2 had one of the three features replaced with a novel one; the color of the symbols was gray instead of black or white, the shape of the symbols was star instead of circle or triangle, or the background was blue instead of green or red. The remaining two features in a stimulus were both positive, both negative, or one positive and one negative. There was a total of 12 feature-value combinations. With five different arrays of symbols selected from those used in Test 1, a total of 60 novel stimuli was used in Test 2. Testing procedures were basically the same as in Test 1.

Mean response rates (responses per minute) for the novel positive and novel negative stimuli in Test 1 were 79.2 and 6.7 for pigeons, and 51.1 and 1.1 for monkeys, respectively. Response rates to the stimuli with all three positive and with all three negative features were 89.1 and 8.8 for pigeons, and 60.0 and 1.1 for monkeys, respectively. The stimuli with two or more positive features systematically produced higher response rates than those with one or none. All four birds and three monkeys showed high levels of transfer to the stimuli with all three positive or all three negative stimuli. However, discrimination of those stimuli was not significantly better than discrimination of the novel positive and novel negative stimuli. In other words, the "super releaser" effect as suggested by Lea and Harrison (1978) was not obtained. One may argue that the superreleaser effect was not observed because response rates were already at maximum values for the present reinforcement contingencies. In other words, a ceiling effect might have overshadowed the superreleaser effect. However, it should be noted that the superreleaser effect was not obtained with pigeons in Lea and Harrison (1978) in which a simultaneous discrimination task was used in order to eliminate such a effect.

Percentages of correct responses by human subjects to the novel positive and novel negative stimuli were 97.1 and 95.7%, respectively. Response rates to the stimuli with all three positive and with all three negative features were 21.4 and 18.6%, respectively. Eight of the 10 subjects tended to respond A to the stimuli with all three negative features and B to the stimuli with all three positive features (percentages of correct choices were less than 50%). One of the remaining subjects tended to respond A to the stimuli with all three positive or negative features. Only one subject showed perfect discrimination.

Figure 2 shows response rates of pigeons and monkeys for the stimuli containing a novel feature in Test 2. Data from Monkey 2 are not included because this monkey ceased to respond to the stimuli containing any novel feature. Response rates were separately shown for the stimuli in which the remaining two features took both positive, one positive and one negative, and both negative values. All of the birds generally showed high levels of transfer to the stimuli containing a novel feature. However, Bird 5 responded at low rates to the stimuli with a novel background color. Birds 3 and 5 showed relatively higher rates of responding to stimuli containing a novel symbol shape with the other two features, one positive and one negative. The positive shape generalized to the novel shape (star) for these two birds. The positive shape was a triangle for these two birds and a circle for the others.

Monkey 5 generally responded at low rates. Specifically, the novel symbol shape produced very low rates of responding regardless of the remaining two features. Only Monkey 1 showed a high level of transfer to the stimuli with a novel feature. In Monkey 1, high rates of responding were controlled by the combinations of two positive features and the combination of the positive symbol shape and novel symbol color (gray) that might be perceptually similar to the positive symbol color (black for this monkey).

The human subject who showed perfect discrimination in Test 1, received a session in which 30 stimuli containing a novel feature (with the other two features either both positive or both negative) were scrambled with 30 novel positive and novel negative stimuli. He showed perfect discrimination of the novel positive and novel negative stimuli, but his accuracy decreased to 56.6% with the stimuli containing a novel feature.

Verbal Strategies Used by Humans

Human subjects were asked to state the strategies used to classify the stimuli at the end of the experiment. The verbal reports by the eight of the 10 humans, who tended to respond A to the stimuli with all three negative features and B to the stimuli with all three positive features, revealed that they arbitrarily chose a certain feature combination and remembered to respond A (or B) to those stimuli. For example, the stimuli composed of white circles on a green background were remembered as belonging to group A. They learned to change to B with stimuli in which one feature was changed (black circles on a green background, and white circles on a red background), and to respond A to stimuli in which two features were changed (white triangles on a red background, and black triangles on a green background), and to respond B to stimuli in which three features were changed (black triangles on a red background.) According to this rule, stimuli with all three positive features (white triangles on a red background) belonged to group B, because only one feature was changed, and stimuli with all three negative features (black circles on a green background) belonged to group A, because two features were changed. The subject,

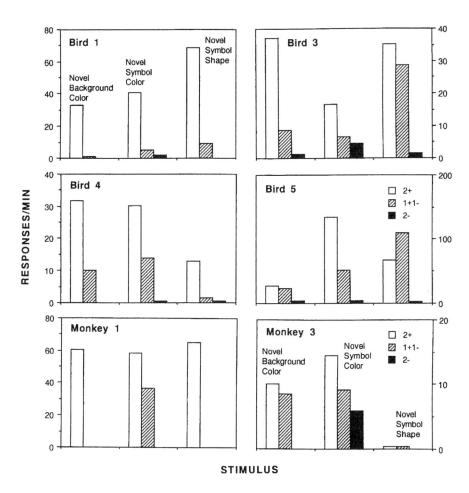

Figure 2. Response rates in responses per minute for pigeons and monkeys in Test 2. (The feature-value combinations are represented by sets of three letters: C=positive symbol color; c=negative symbol color; S=positive symbol shape; s=negative symbol shape; B=positive background color; b=negative background color).

who tended to respond A to the stimuli with all three positive or all three negative features, learned to respond A or B to each of the six feature-value combinations used for the training. This strategy could not be adapted to stimuli that had different feature-value combinations from those of the training stimuli, and this subject arbitrarily responded A to those stimuli. The subject, who showed perfect discrimination in Test 1, gave the rules that "if background is red (taking a positive value for this subject), then if the stimulus is composed of white circles (negative values), then respond B else A", and that "if background is green, then if the stimulus is composed of black triangles, then respond A, else B." Accordingly, the stimuli with all three positive features belong to group A and the stimuli with all negative features belong to group B. This strategy could not be adapted to the stimuli containing a novel feature in Test 2.

The rules reported by the human subjects were all in conditional or "if....., then....." form, and did not describe the category membership at all. None of them found a rule such that an A is composed of black circles, circles on a red background, or black symbols on a red background. A sophisticated version of this rule would be a 2-out-of-3 polymorphous rule; an A is composed of two of three features of black symbol, circular symbol, and a red background. Verbal strategies reported by the humans revealed that they had learned to respond A or B on the basis of conditional discriminations of stimuli rather than to classify the stimuli into two groups. Logical reasoning based on verbal strategies apparently makes it difficult for humans to find polymorphous rules.

Failure to Form Functional Equivalence by Pigeons

Lea (1984) argued that if successful transfer to novel instances of a category is based solely on perceptual similarity but not on functional relations, it is inappropriate to use the term "concept" to describe observed performance. It has been well known that for monkeys and pigeons, members of a conceptual category (verbally defined by humans) resemble one another more than they resemble members of other categories. Vaughan and Greene (1984) and Wasserman, Kiedinger, and Bhatt (1988) showed that pigeons learn to discriminate categories corresponding to those of humans far faster than they learn to discriminate pseudocategories in which the slides to be discriminated are randomly selected from the same categories. With a variety of techniques, Astley and Wasserman (1992), Cerella (1979), Roberts and Mazmanian (1988), and Sands, Lincoln, and Wright (1982) obtained evidence of categorical coherence in monkeys and pigeons. Given these findings, a high level of transfer to new instances might result from simple stimulus generalization due to already-existing categorical coherence, or perceptual similarity.

Vaughan (1988) trained pigeons to discriminate two randomly selected sets of pictures of trees. The reinforcement contingencies for the two sets of stimuli were then reversed. After repeated reversal training, the birds generalized reversal to all of the stimuli after they encountered the reversal contingencies with just a few stimuli. He argued that functions given to one or a few members of a class transferred throughout the class. On the other hand, in an experiment designed to test generalization based on mediating associations among members of a stimulus class (secondary generalization), Bhatt and Wasserman (1989) found no evidence of such interstimulus associations with pigeons.

The question asked by these studies is similar to the issue of stimulus equivalence logically defined by the three behavioral properties of reflexivity, symmetry, and transitivity (cf. Sidman, 1971; Sidman & Tailby, 1982.) Formation of stimulus equivalence in verbally retarded humans has been studied in the paradigm of conditional discrimination (typically, a matching-to-sample task), in the context of verbal relations among members of a conceptual class. So far, clear evidence of stimulus equivalence has not yet been shown in pigeons or monkeys (D'Amato, Salmon, Loukas, & Tomie, 1985; Lipkens, Kop, & Matthijs, 1988; Hayes, 1989).

In Experiment 2 in Jitsumori (1993), a selective reversal design was used to explore whether the birds which showed transfer to novel stimuli in Tests 1 and 2 had formed stimulus classes identified by the common behavioral functions of their members. After Experiment 1, the birds received additional training sessions with 56 stimuli (8 feature combinations x 7 different arrays of symbols) including those with all three positive or all three negative features. The birds were then given reversal training with three stimuli containing the three positive features and three stimuli containing the three negative features, randomly selected from those used during the training sessions, but the contingencies of reinforcement were reversed. The birds that reached the performance criterion were then tested with the 50 remaining stimuli used during the training sessions but not during the reversal sessions. The stimuli were arranged in five sessions of 60 trials. Over the first 12 trials and the last 8 trials in each session, the birds were exposed only to the reversal training stimuli. The remaining 40 trials of a session were made up of 10 blocks of four trials, each containing three reversal training stimuli and one of the 50 test stimuli, chosen at random without replacement. On reversal trials, the reversal training contingencies were in effect. On test trials, responses produced no reinforcers nor penalties. After the 5-day test was completed, the testing procedure was repeated. If concepts of the sort required by Lea (1984) were learned, or class members were functionally connected to one another, then the reversal should generalize to the members not used for the reversal training.

On test trials, all four birds responded at higher rates to the stimuli with three negative features than to the stimuli with three positive features. The mean rates of responding (responses/minute) to those stimuli were 73.8 and 0.8 for Bird 1, 105.9 and 40.8 for Bird 3, 30.0 and 0.3 for Bird 4, and 53.9 and 16.8 for Bird 5, respectively. Thus, reversal training transferred to those stimuli that had the same feature combinations as the reversal stimuli. However, the mean rates of responding were higher to the stimuli with two positive features than to the stimuli with one positive feature for all four birds. The mean rates of responding to those originally positive and originally negative stimuli were 32.6 and 27.1 for Bird 1, 42.1 and 25.1 for Bird 3, 34.6 and 16.8 for Bird 4, and 60.4 and 57.2 for Bird 5, respectively. Thus, reversal training did not transfer to the nonreversed feature combinations. This finding suggests that the birds might have not formed concepts of the sort required by Lea (1984).

Further analyses revealed that only one feature, or two at most, exerted reversal control. None of the birds showed systematic reversals to all three features. The reversal training allowed the birds to rely on either all three features or only one or two features to reverse responding, because reversal training was given on a set of stimuli that contained three positive or three negative features. If a set of positive or negative features had been functionally connected to form a concept, interfeature generalization should have occurred. But it did not. The findings suggested that the pigeons acquired discriminations and successfully classified the novel stimuli in Tests 1 and 2 through feature learning, rather than through concept formation.

Categorization Based on Feature Learning

The findings of the above experiments suggest that transfer to a wide variety of novel instances is a necessary but not a sufficient condition for the formation of concepts of the sort required by Lea (1984). There are at least two possible explanations of category discrimination on the basis of feature learning.

Linear Feature Model

Lea and Ryan (1990) proposed the linear feature model which assumes that response rate is determined by the linear sum of the weighted measures of relevant features that are independent to one another. Simple additivity of feature values predicts the superreleaser effect. However, as noted above, the superreleaser effect was not clearly obtained either with pigeons in Jitsumori (1993), with monkeys in Jitsumori (1994), or with pigeons in the previous study (Lea & Harrison, 1978.) Moreover, at least the findings with monkeys in Test 2 were inconsistent with this model as discussed in Jitsumori (1994).

The linear feature model is simple at a theoretical level, but the underlying mechanism is rather illusive. It is doubtful that pigeons transform various distinctive features into values on a single psychological dimension, such as positiveness or negativeness, and then in some way add up the values to determine responding.

Feature Combination Model

An alternative account on the basis of feature learning is the feature combination model. With 2-out-of-3 polymorphous stimuli, any combination of two positive features is correlated with reinforcement, whereas any of two negative features is correlated with extinction. Combinations of one positive and one negative feature are correlated with reinforcement when they are included in the positive stimuli and with extinction when included in the negative stimuli. If combinations of two features gain control over responding depending on the contingencies of reinforcement, high levels of transfer would occur to stimuli composed of all three positive or all three negative features and even to stimuli containing a novel feature. It should be noted that this model does not necessarily predict the superreleaser effect.

On the basis of the feature combination model, category discrimination learning involves extraction and learning of critical feature combinations that enable the subjects to discriminate the experimenter-determined positive and negative categories. A limited capacity to learn feature combinations would provide difficulties in discriminating sets of stimuli containing a large number of features. On the other hand, when one feature is a good predictor of another, discrimination based on feature combinations may be effective even with stimuli including a large number of feature combinations. In the simplest case, suppose that a subject learns that members of a given category are those including feature combinations ab, bc, or ca. If the subject learns further that stimuli including cd belong to this category, regardless of other features, then stimuli including ad and bd should be readily classified as members of this category through c without direct training. In other words, if there is feature equivalence, transitive relations among the features may eventually make it possible to categorize stimuli including a large number of relevant feature combinations. Artificial stimuli like those used by Jitsumori (1993) do not meet this feature equivalence for pigeons as discussed above. In contrast, features of natural objects are nested in or correlated with one another. For example, greenness of a tree is correlated with leafy, verticality or branchiness is correlated with woodiness, and so on. This model is consistent with the findings with monkeys in Jitsumori (1994) and even with pigeons in Jitsumori (1993). However, a problem in extending this model as an account of excellent discrimination of natural categories by animals is that there has been no evidence that animals can form feature equivalence, or even stimulus equivalence, with photographs of natural objects.

Feature Integration and Learning Theories

Feature Integration by Pigeons

Experiment 3 in Jitsumori (1993) investigated whether and in what way information from several distinct features could be combined to determine pigeons' responses to any given stimulus. In this experiment, only a single feature in each stimulus had a positive or negative value. The remaining two features were uncorrelated with reinforcement contingencies. They are referred to as neutral features. For all birds, the neutral features were gray, star, and a blue background. For example, if black, circle, and a red background were defined as positive, the positive stimuli were black stars on a blue background, gray circles on a blue background, and gray stars on a red background. The negative stimuli were white stars on a blue background, gray triangles on a blue background, and gray stars on a green background. Four experimentally naive pigeons were trained with the 6 feature-value combinations in 10 different arrays of symbols, making a total of 60 stimuli. After training, the birds were tested with all possible combinations of three 3-valued features. With six new arrays of symbols for each of these 27 combinations, a total of 162 novel patterns was tested in extinction.

Mean relative rates of responding averaged among the four birds were shown in the bottom panel of Figure 3. Data for each individual bird (not shown here) revealed systematic differences. The gradients shown by two birds peak at the stimuli containing one positive and two neutral features, POO, the feature-value distribution identical to that of the positive training stimuli. These birds also emitted relatively high rates of responding to stimuli made up of the combination of one positive and one neutral feature, such as PPO and PNO. Thus, the combination of one positive and one neutral feature controlled high rates of responding for these two birds. The gradients shown by the other two birds are bimodal with one peak at the POO and a second peak at the OOO. These birds responded at low rates to stimuli including at least one negative feature. The combination of two neutral features, the OO, as well as the combination of one positive and one neutral feature, the PO, controlled high rates of responding, but only with stimuli that did not include a

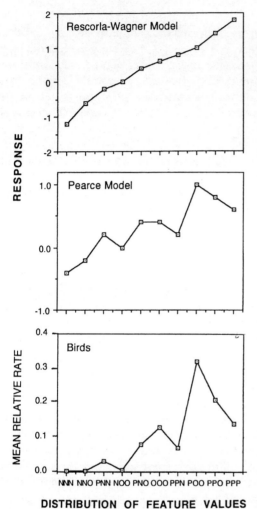

negative feature. Within positive training stimuli (POO), the OO is associated with the PO, which might have resulted control of high rates of responding by the OO and PO. Although the OO was also associated with the NO within negative training stimuli (NOO), the very strong control by a negative feature for these two birds might have overshadowed the association. Overall, the results of this experiment show that responding was not controlled by the simple sum of feature values. Rather, specific combinations of feature values largely determined response rates.

Application of Learning Theories

Investigations of discrimination learning with compound stimuli has long been reported in the literatures of learning theories. Pavlovian conditioning theories have attempted to specify the associations of an element of a compound conditional stimulus that is paired with an unconditioned stimulus. According to an elemental theory, the Rescorla and Wagner (1972) model, the associative strength of a compound stimulus is determined by the algebraic sum of the associative strengths of its elements. This model is in agreement with the linear feature model of category discrimination in such a way that elements of a stimulus are additively integrated to determine responding. Equation 1 shows how this model predicts the change in associative strength on any given trial.

$$\blacktriangle V = \alpha \cdot \beta \cdot (\lambda - V_i). \qquad (1)$$

Figure 3. Gradients derived from the Rescorla-Wagner model (top panel) and the Pearce model (center panel), in comparison to the mean relative rates of responding averaged among the four birds (bottom panel). (The feature values are represented as follows: P=positive; N=negative; O=neutral).

In this equation, $\blacktriangle V$ is the change in the associative strength of a conditioned stimulus; α and β are learning rate parameters with values between 0 and 1; λ is the asymptote of conditioning; and V_t is the combined associative strength of elements on the trial in question.

In an application of this model to the stimuli used in Experiment 3 in Jitsumori (1993), the combined strengths of responding to positive stimuli, V_{POO}, and to negative stimuli, V_{NOO}, are defined in Equation 2 and 3, respectively.

$$V_{POO}=V_P+V_O+V_O \qquad (2)$$
$$V_{NOO}=V_N+V_O+V_O \qquad (3)$$

In Equations 2 and 3, V_P is the strength of responding emitted by a positive feature, V_N by a negative feature, and V_O by a neutral feature. At the end of training, V_{POO} and V_{NOO} are equal to λ: 1 for the positive stimuli and 0 for the negative stimuli. The value of $\alpha \cdot \beta$ in Equation 1 was set at 0.1. The strengths of responding, or feature values, derived from computer simulations based on Equation 1 are 0.6 for positive, 0.2 for neutral, and -0.4 for negative features at the end of training. The magnitude of responding to a test stimulus can be predicted as the sum of feature values of that stimulus.

According to an alternative theory, a configural theory proposed by Pearce (1987), the associative strength of a stimulus is determined by the associative strength of that stimulus as a whole and the associative strength that generalizes to it from other stimuli. Equation 4 shows how the magnitude of generalization is determined:

$$e_Y = \gamma S_X \times E_X \qquad (4)$$

In this equation, e_Y is the magnitude of associative strength generalized from stimulus X to stimulus Y; E_X is the associative strengths of X; and γS_X is the similarity between X and Y. Equation 5 indicates the way in which this model predicts the change in associative strength, $\blacktriangle E$, on any given trial; β is a learning rate parameter with a value between 0 and 1; λ is the asymptote of the conditioning; and e is determined by means of Equation 4.

$$\blacktriangle E = \beta \times [\lambda-(E+e)]. \qquad (5)$$

In an application of Equations 4 and 5 to the stimuli used in this experiment, the changes in the strength of responding to positive stimuli, $\blacktriangle E_{POO}$, and to negative stimuli, $\blacktriangle E_{NOO}$, are defined in Equations 6 and 7, respectively.

$$E_{POO} = \beta \times [\lambda-(E_{POO}+ {}_{NOO}S_{POO} \times e_{NOO})] \qquad (6)$$
$$E_{NOO} = \beta \times [\lambda-(E_{NOO} + {}_{POO}S_{NOO} \times e_{POO})] \qquad (7)$$

The value of S was set at 2/3, because the positive and negative stimuli shared two of the three feature values. The value β was set at 0.1. At the end of the training, λ was 1 for the positive stimuli and 0 for the negative stimuli. The strength of responding to the positive stimuli, E_{POO}, was 9/5 and to the negative stimuli, E_{NOO}, was -6/5 at the end of the training. The magnitude of generalization from the positive and negative stimuli to test stimuli is predicted by Equation 4. The value of S of each test stimulus is determined by the number of feature values shared with the positive or negative stimuli. For example, the magnitude of generalization to stimuli containing two positive and one neutral value, e_{PPO}, is

$$_{POO}S_{PPO} \times E_{POO} + {}_{NOO}S_{PPO} \times E_{NOO} = 2/3 \times E_{POO} + 1/3 \ E_{NOO}$$

Because the Pearce model was applied to sets of stimuli defined by feature-value combinations, this model is in agreement with the feature combination model of category discrimination in a way that feature values are integrated to determine rates of responding.

Figure 3 shows the gradients derived from the Rescorla-Wagner model (top panel) and the Pearce model (center panel), in comparison to the mean relative rates of responding averaged among the four birds (bottom panel.) The mean relative rates of responding are more consistent with the Pearce model than with the Rescorla-Wagner model. Although the birds showed an interesting difference in gradients as discussed above, the applications of the models did not involve assumptions of individual differences among the subjects. The Pearce model might readily describe the differences among the birds if the S parameters could be determined for each bird. It should be also noted here that the application of these models in Experiments 1 and 2 in Jitsumori (1993) revealed that the Pearce model was fairly consistent with the findings.

Logical Reasoning and Feature Learning

The series of experiments presented here demonstrated a fundamental difference in problem solving by humans and animals. Logical reasoning based on verbal strategies with humans made it difficult to find appropriate rules to classify the artificial polymorphous stimuli. By contrast, feature learning, as with the feature combination model, readily explained successful classification of the artificial polymorphous stimuli by animals. Such a difference found between humans and animals might reflect a species-specific difference developed in the course of a cognitive revolution. It should be noted, however, that the tasks and stimuli used in these experiments are highly specific. Some changes in procedure that would promote human subjects to perform on the basis of automatic processing rather than controlled processing might change the outcomes. The distinction between logical reasoning and feature learning may sometimes be analogous to the distinction between rule-governed behavior and contingency-shaped behavior, and sometimes to the distinction between top-down and bottom-up processes. Dreyfus and Dreyfus (1986) argued that learning of complex human skills often begins with rules (rule-governed behavior), and that expertise involves performance that no longer depends on the rules (contingency-shaped behavior.) On the other hand, we can distinguish dogs from other animals, but no one logically learned the concept of dogs by means of rules in his or her early infancy. Comparative studies of cognitive behaviors addressed in other chapters of this book might converge to provide a perspective from which to explore the roles of verbal behavior in the cognitive processes of humans.

References

Astley, S. L., & Wasserman, W. A. (1992). Categorical discrimination and generalization in pigeons: All negative stimuli are not created equal. *Journal of Experimental Psychology: Animal Behavior Processes, 18,* 193-207.

Bhatt, R. S., & Wasserman, E. A. (1989). Secondary generalization in pigeons. *Journal of the Experimental Analysis of Behavior, 52,* 213-224.

Cerella, J. (1979). Visual classes and natural categories in the pigeon. *Journal of Experimental Psychology: Human Perception and Performance, 5,* 68-77.

D'Amato, M. R., Salmon, D. P., Loukas, E., & Tomie, A. (1985). Symmetry and transitivity of conditional relations in monkeys (Cebus apella) and pigeons (Columba livia). *Journal of the Experimental Analysis of Behavior, 44,* 35-47.

Dennis, I., Hampton, J. A., & Lea, S. E. G. (1973). New problem on concept formation. *Nature, 243,* 101-102.

Dreyfus, H. L., & Dreyfus, S. E. (1986). *Mind over machine.* New York: Macmillan.

Hayes, S. C. (1989). Nonhumans have not yet shown stimulus equivalence. *Journal of the Experimental Analysis of Behavior, 51,* 385-392.

Herrnstein, R. J. (1979). Acquisition, generalization, and discrimination reversal of a natural concept. *Journal of Experimental Psychology: Animal Behavior Processes, 5,* 116-129.

Herrnstein, R. J. (1985). Riddles of natural categorization. *Philosophical Transactions of the Royal Society, B, 308,* 129-144.

Herrnstein, R. J., & de Villiers, P. A. (1980). Fish as a natural concept for people and pigeons. In G. H. Bower (Ed.), *The psychology of learning and motivation* (Vol. 14, pp. 59-95). New York: Academic Press.

Herrnstein, R. J., & Loveland, D. H. (1964). Complex visual concept in the pigeon. *Science, 146,* 549-551.

Herrnstein, R. J., Loveland, D. H., & Cable, C. (1976). Natural concepts in pigeons. *Journal of Experimental Psychology: Animal Behavior Processes, 2,* 285-302.

Huber, L., & Lenz, R. (1993). A test of the linear feature model of polymorphous concept discrimination with pigeons. *Quarterly Journal of Experimental Psychology, 46B,* 1-18.

Jitsumori, M. (1993). Category discrimination of artificial polymorphous stimuli based on feature learning. *Journal of Experimental Psychology: Animal Behavior Processes, 19,* 244-254.

Jitsumori, M. (1994, in press). Discrimination of artificial polymorphous categories by rhesus monkeys (Macaca mulatta). *Quarterly Journal of Experimental Psychology.*

Lea, S. E. G. (1984). In what sense do pigeons learn concepts? In H. L. Roitblat, T. G. Bever, & H. S. Terrace (Eds.), *Animal cognition* (pp. 263-276). Hillsdale, NJ: Erlbaum.

Lea, S. E. G., & Harrison, S. N. (1978). Discrimination of polymorphous stimulus sets by pigeons. *Quarterly Journal of Experimental Psychology, 30,* 521-537.

Lea, S. E. G., Lohmann, A., & Ryn, C. M. E. (1993). Discrimination of five-dimensional stimuli by pigeons: Limitations of feature analysis. *Quarterly Journal of Experimental Psychology, 46B,* 19-42.

Lea, S. E. G., & Ryan, C. M. E. (1990). Unnatural concepts and the theory of concept discrimination in birds. In M. L. Commons, R. J. Herrnstein, S. Kosslyn,& D.

Mumford (Eds.), *Quantitative analyses of behavior; Vol. 8. Behavioral approaches to pattern recognition and concept formation* (pp. 165-185). Hillsdale, NJ: Erlbaum.

Lipkens, R., Kop, P. F. M., & Matthijs, W. (1988). A test of symmetry and transitivity in the conditional discrimination performances of pigeons. *Journal of the Experimental Analysis of Behavior, 49,* 279-285.

Lubow, R. E. (1974). Higher order concept formation in the pigeon. *Journal of the Experimental Analysis of Behavior, 21,* 475-483.

Morgan, M. J., Fitch, M. D., Holman, J. G., & Lea, S. E. G. (1976). Pigeons learn concept of an "A." *Perception, 5,* 57-66.

Pearce, J. M. (1987). A model of stimulus generalization for Pavlovian conditioning. *Psychological Review, 94,* 61-73.

Poole, J., & Lander, D. G. (1971). The pigeon's concept of pigeon. *Psychonomic Science, 25,* 157-158.

Rescorla, R. A., & Wagner, A. R. (1972). A theory of Pavlovian conditioning: Variations in the effectiveness of reinforcement and nonreinforcement. In A.H. Black & W. F. Prokasy (Eds.), *Classical conditioning II: Current research and theory* (pp. 64-99). New York: Appleton-Century-Crofts.

Roberts, W. A., & Mazmanian, D. S. (1988). Concept learning at different levels of abstraction by pigeons, monkeys, and people. *Journal of Experimental Psychology: Animal Behavior Processes, 14,* 247-260.

Sands, S. F., Lincoln, C. E., & Wright , A. A. (1982). Pictorial similarity judgments and the organization of visual memory in the rhesus monkey. *Journal of Experimental Psychology: General, 3,* 369-389.

Sidman, M. (1971). Reading and auditory-visual equivalences. *Journal of Speech and Hearing Research, 14,* 5-13.

Sidman, M., & Tailby, W. (1982). Conditional discrimination vs. matching to sample: An experiment of the testing paradigm. *Journal of the Experimental Analysis of Behavior, 37,* 5-22.

Siegel, R. K., & Honig, W. K. (1970). Pigeon concept formation: Successive and simultaneous acquisition. *Journal of the Experimental Analysis of Behavior, 13,* 385-390.

Tanaka, T., & Sato, M. (1983). Formation of polymorphous concepts in humans. *Japanese Journal of Behavior Analysis, 1,* 54.

Vaughan, W. (1988). Formation of equivalence sets in pigeons. *Journal of Experimental Psychology: Animal Behavior Processes, 14,* 36-42.

Vaughan, W., & Greene, S. L. (1984). Pigeon visual memory capacity. *Journal of Experimental Psychology: Animal Behavior Processes, 10,* 256-271.

Von Fersen, L., & Lea, S. E. G. (1990). Category discrimination by pigeons using five polymorphous features. *Journal of the Experimental Analysis of Behavior, 54,* 69-84.

Wasserman, E. A., Kiedinger, R. E., & Bhatt , R. S. (1988). Conceptual behavior in pigeons: Categories, subcategories, and pseudocategories. *Journal of Experimental Psychology: Animal Behavior Processes, 14,* 235-246

Chapter 6

Functional Analysis of Verbal Behavior in Handicapped Children

Jun'ichi Yamamoto
Meisei University

In this chapter, I will discuss on the functional analysis of verbal behavior in handicapped children based on the following points. Verbal behavior is controlled by antecedent and consequent events. Antecedent events largely are organized as equivalent relations in the development of language. Consequent events determine what kind of response emerges. Listener's behavior is critical as a functional consequent events in verbal behavior. Responding in verbal behavior has two kind of repertoires: differential responding and selection-based responding.

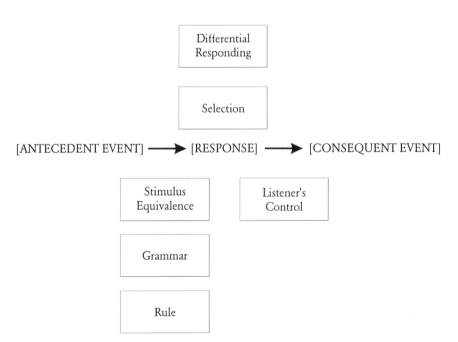

Figure 1. A framework of the analysis of verbal behavior in handicapped children in this chapter.

Figure 1 shows this framemork for analysis of verbal behavior in handicapped children. I will not defend these points now, but instead will refer back to them throughout the chapter.

Stimulus Equivalence and Expansion of the Paradigm

Conditional discrimination tasks have been used to study language functions of handicapped children. In the procedure to develop conditional discriminations, when stimulus A1 appears as the sample, the child is required to select B1 from an array of comparisons which include B2, and when A2 is the sample, the child is required to select B2 from the same array of comparisons. Sidman (1971; 1973; 1974) also demonstrated that conditional discrimination training may generate derived stimulus relations.

Sidman and his colleagues (1982 a,b; 1989) formalized such derived stimulus relations in conditional discrimination as "stimulus equivalence." They argued that stimulus equivalence would consist of the following dimensions: reflexivity, symmetry, transitivity and equivalence. Reflexivity would be demonstrated when generalized identity matching occurs. Symmetry requires the subject to select the related comparison stimulus, even when the role of sample and comparison stimuli was interchanged. That is, symmetry may emerge when the subjects can form the BA derived relation after AB was trained. In transitivity, a new conditional relation AC must emerge after two conditional discriminations, AB and BC, were trained. In equivalence, both symmetry and transitivity were involved. That is, the emergence of CA was required after AB and BC were trained.

Emergence of stimulus equivalence might represent an aspect of relational control across stimuli and responses. Recently, various studies were conducted to expand and to re-formalize Sidman's paradigm on stimulus equivalence. Some authors examined how contextual stimuli may control the emergence of stimulus equivalence (Kohlenberg, Hayes & Hayes, 1991; Lynch & Green, 1991; Steele & Hayes, 1991). The other authors studied whether the stimulus equivalence paradigm could be a model of the acquisition of grammar using sequential responding (Green, Sigurdardottir, & Saunders, 1991; Lazar, 1977; Lazar & Kotlarchyk, 1986; Sigurdardottir, Green & Saunders, 1990; Wulfert & Hayes, 1988).

In almost all of these studies, however, nonhandicapped adults served as participants. These participants already have a language repertoire before the experiment. So, in the experimental situation, they might merely apply the rules which they have already acquired in their language development. In other words, the development of stimulus equivalence by nonhandicapped adults may be a model of the acquisition of a second language, rather than a first language. To model first language learning, the emergence of stimulus equivalence should be analyzed in the persons who have no or few functional language skills (Dixon & Spradlin,1976; Spradlin, Cotter, & Baxley, 1973; Spradlin & Dixon, 1976; Spradlin & Saunders, 1984; VanBierliet, 1977). The purpose of this chapter is to present some experiments on the functional analysis of verbal behavior in handicapped children using stimulus and response equivalence paradigms.

Differential Responding and Selection-Based Responding

Establishment of equivalent relations is required in ordinal language development. When a child says "cup" in the presence of a cup and the child writes c-u-p in the presence of a cup, three stimulus and response relations, that is, a real object, cup, the vocal response "cup" and the writing response c-u-p would be functionally equivalent.

In the above case, topographically differentiated responding such as speaking and writing are involved in the formation of equivalent relations. Alternatively, selection-based responding, such as pointing to symbols, might be involved in language learning for handicapped children. In recent studies, augmentative and alternative communication skills have been trained for language-disabled children (Miller & Allaire, 1987). In these cases, selection-based responding such as pointing to symbols or key pressing is taught as one of verbal responses. For example, when

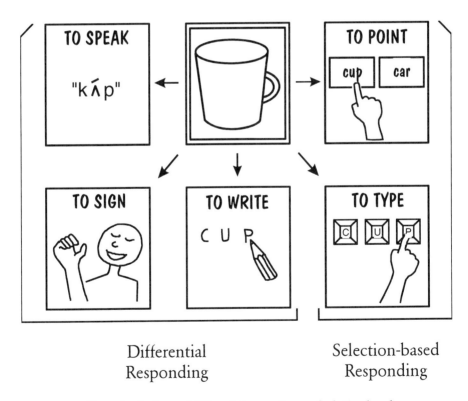

Differential   Selection-based
Responding   Responding

Figure 2. A scheme of differential responding and selection based responding for a real object: cup.

the picture of a cup is presented to the child as sample stimulus, pointing to the written word c-u-p or iconic symbol representing cup on the communication sheet was specified as a verbal response. Figure 2 shows scheme of differential responding and selection-based responding for the real object, cup.

The emergence of stimulus equivalence should be assessed in such selection-based verbal behavior. Devany, Hayes and Nelson (1986) examined whether language skill is associated with the emergence of stimulus equivalence. They demonstrated that completely language-disabled children did not show stimulus equivalence, though both normal children and retarded children with some receptive or expressive language did show it. I examined whether an autistic child with no expressive speech could show stimulus equivalence (Yamamoto, 1990).

Emergence of Stimulus Equivalence in Mute Autistic Child

Method

The participant was a mute autistic child. He was six years and four months old. His mental age was two years and zero months as measured by the Binet Intelligence Scale revised for Japanese children. The subject showed simple motor imitation and could follow simple instruction given by an adult. He did not show any expressive speech. In the reception mode, he could not select a correspondent material or picture in response to the adult's verbal instruction such as "Give me a ball." We used drawings, Japanese Characters, Kana, and Chinese Characters, Kanji, as stimulus sets. Each stimulus set involved two stimuli which represented hand and foot. The child did not name the drawings, Kana and Kanji. He did not chose the corresponding drawing, Kana and Kanji, when the experimenter said the name of it.

The child sat facing the experimenter across the stimulus presentation board. The experimenter first placed two comparison stimuli side by side, 3cm apart in the stimulus presentation board. Then the experimenter placed the sample stimulus in front of the child. The child was required to place the presented sample stimulus adjacent to the corresponding comparison stimulus. In training trials, social reinforcement was offered to the child. In test trials, no feedback was offered.

Figure 3 represents the paradigm of conditional discrimination training, equivalence tests and an exclusion test. In the first conditional discrimination training, Kana was used as the sample and drawings were used as comparisons. In the second training, drawings were used as samples and Kanji was used as comparisons. After the performance met the criterion, tests for stimulus equivalence were conducted. In the first symmetry test, drawings were used as samples and Kana was used as comparisons. In the second symmetry test, Kanji was used as the sample and drawings were used as comparisons. In the transitivity test, Kana was used as sample and Kanji was used as comparisons. In the equivalence test, Kanji was used as sample and Kana was used as comparisons. In the exclusion test (Stromer & Osborn, 1982), a novel Kana stimulus representing head was used as a sample stimulus and a drawing of a head was used as a correct comparison and a drawing of a hand (or foot) was used as an

Equivalence

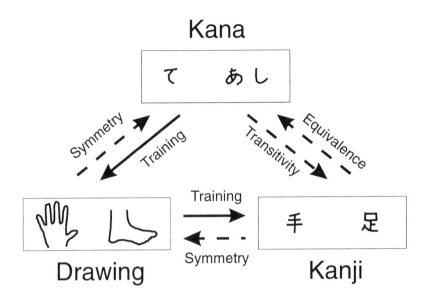

Exclusion

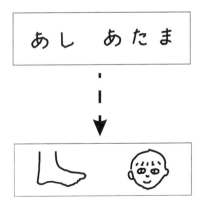

FIgure 3. The stimulus equivalence paradigm in a mute autistic child. The solid line shows conditional discrimination training. The dotted line shows symmetry, transitivity, equivalence and the exclusion test.

incorrect comparison. Each test session consisted of eight reinforced training trials, 16 nonreinforced training trials and eight probe trials.

Results and Discussion

Results showed that the percentage of correct responses in the symmetry, transitivity and equivalence test were 100%, respectively. The percentage of correct responses in the exclusion test was 96% (mean percent correct for three blocks). These results indicated that an autistic child who had no expressive speech showed stimulus equivalence. This suggests that expressive language skills are not a necessary condition for stimulus equivalence. Devany et al (1986) indicated that language disabled children did not show stimulus equivalence. The stimuli used in their work were somewhat different from those of the present study. Devany et al (1986) used nonsense figures. In the present study, on the contrary, drawings representing real objects were used. As such the drawings might be categorized as referents and Kana and Kanji would be categorized as symbols. This may have facilitated the formation of stimulus equivalence in the present subject.

Equivalence of Sequential Responding and Formation of Grammar In an Autistic Child

The formation of grammar could be based on the emergence of stimulus equivalence (Zuriff, 1976). The development of grammar could be described as the formation of specific word orders. In the course of language development, two-word sentences develop in nonhandicapped children by 18 months of age (Slobin, 1971).

From a behavior analytic point of view, the development of two-word sentence involves two components, including a sequence response which would determine word order and a conditional discrimination which would determine the categories of words. Recent studies have demonstrated that sequential responding may be integrated into equivalence relations in nonhandicapped persons (Green, Sigurdardottir, & Saunders, 1991; Lazar, 1977; Lazar & Kotlarchyk, 1986; Sigurdardottir, Green & Saunders, 1990; Wulfert & Hayes, 1988). Few studies have examined the controlling variables in forming word-order in language-disabled children, however. The study described below I examined the emergence of two-word sentences in an autistic child (Yamamoto,1990).

Method

The child was six years and five months old. His mental age was five years and two months (Binet Intelligence Scale). His speech responses were close to echolalia. In naturalistic observations, he often emitted one-word sentences. He could respond appropriately to everyday life instruction by adults.

Six Kanji characters were used, which represent colors, green (A1), black (B1) and red (C1) and objects, clothes (A2), shoes (B2) and car (C2). All stimuli (8.0cm x 6.0cm) were drawn by black ink on white backgrounds. The child did not emit an appropriate verbal response when he was presented with each character as the sample stimulus. The child also did not choose an appropriate character when the

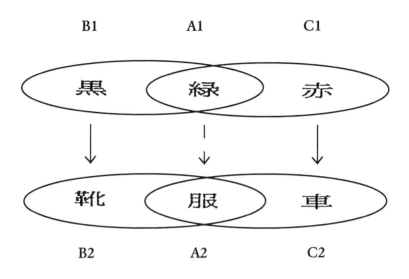

Conditional Discrimination Training

Sample:	A1		A1	
Comparison:	B1	B2	C1	C2
	+		+	

Sample:	A2		A2	
Comparison:	B1	B2	C1	C2
		+		+

Sequence Training

First   Second

B1 —————————————————> B2
C1 —————————————————> C2

Sequence Test

A1 — — — — — — —> A2

Figure 4. The stimuli used in the experiment and the training and testing paradigm. The solid arrow shows sequence training and the dotted arrow shows the sequence test. Ovals show associations established by conditional discrimination.

experimenter spoke the name of the character. Thus, the child did not know the name of each Kanji character neither productively nor receptively. Stimuli used as stimulus set 1 involved B1 (black) and B2 (shoes), and those of stimulus set 2 represented C1 (red) and C2 (car). The experimenter sat facing the subject across the stimulus presentation board. Figure 4 shows stimuli used in the experiment and paradigm of training and testing.

(1) Conditional discrimination: In the conditional discrimination training, the experimenter first placed two comparison stimuli side by side, 3cm apart in the stimulus presentation board which was painted blue. Then the experimenter placed the sample stimulus in front of the child. The child was required to place the presented sample stimulus adjacent to the corresponding comparison stimulus. In training trials, social reinforcement was offered to the child. A1 (green) or A2 (clothes) was presented as a sample stimulus, and B1 (black) and B2 (shoes) (or C1 (red) and C2 (car)) were presented as comparison stimuli. When A1 (green) was presented, selection of B1 (black) (or C1 (red)) was reinforced. When A2 (clothes) was presented, selection of B2 (shoes) (or C2 (car)) was reinforced. Figure 5 (upper panel) shows an example of conditional discrimination training.

(2) Formation of the word sequence: The child also sat facing the experimenter across the stimulus presentation board which was painted orange. The experimenter put stimuli in piles for each stimulus set. For example, C2 (car) was put on C1 (red). Stimulus positions of top and bottom were arranged randomly over trials. The subject was required to place the color character (e.g., C1 (red)) in the left side and then to place the object character (e.g., C2 (car)) in the right side of the stimulus construction board. Correct responses were socially reinforced and a correction procedure was applied for incorrect responses. Figure 5 (lower panel) shows an example of sequence training.

(3) Test for two-word sentences: After conditional discrimination training and sequential responding training had met the criterion, emergence of generalized two-word sentence which had not been trained was tested with the stimulus construction board. A1 (Green) and A2 (clothes) were presented in a pile. The position of stimuli was randomized over trials. The emergence of appropriate sequence responses was examined. That is, the child was expected first to pick up A1 (green) and place it in the left position, and then to pick up A2 (clothes) and place it in the right position. Feedback was not presented in the test trials. One session consisted of 16 trained sequential responding trials, 16 conditional discrimination trials and eight probe sequential responding trials with green and clothes.

Results and Discussion

Results indicated that the percentage of correct responding in the probe trials in successive sessions was 63%, 88%, 100% and 100%, respectively. Figure 6 shows the percentage of correct sequence responding for A1 and A2 in the test trials. These results indicated that generalized sequential responding could occur in a language-disabled autistic child. In other words, sequential response training and conditional discrimination training were sufficient for producing two-word sentences. The child did not name the stimuli used in the experiment neither productively nor receptively. As such, there are no referents in the training and testing. This suggests that referents are not a necessary condition in developing grammar in language-disabled children.

Conditional Discrimination Training

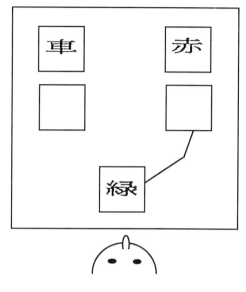

Sequence Training

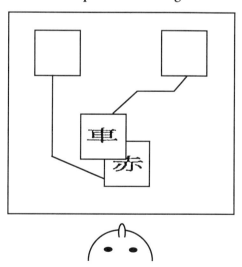

Figure 5. The example of conditional discrimination training (upper panel) and sequence training (lower panel). In conditional discrimination training, the experimenter first placed comparison stimuli, and then placed the sample stimulus in front of the child. The child was required to place the presented sample stimulus adjacent to the corresponding comparison stimulus. In the sequence training, the experimenter put stimuli in piles for each stimulus set. Stimulus position of top and bottom was arranged randomly over trials. The subject was required to place the color character on the left side and then to place the object character on the right side of the stimulus construction board.

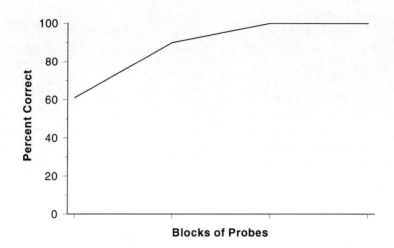

Figure 6. The percentage of correct sequence responding for A1 and A2 in the test trials. One block consisted of eight test trials.

Functional Analysis of the Mand

The Mand and Establishing Operation

The previous studies demonstrated that language-disabled children could acquire equivalence relations of stimuli through conditional discrimination training. In everyday life situations, we select specific symbols from established equivalent stimuli and would use them as functional verbal behavior. Therefore, we have to analyze the situation in which children select a specific symbol from the equivalent repertoire which has been acquired through conditional discrimination training. The "listener" would determine which symbol should be used in the specific situation. The function of the listener will be analyzed in verbal behavior, especially the case of the mand.

Requesting an object or an action is a type of verbal behavior called a "mand," (Skinner, 1957) and is defined as "a verbal operant in which the response is reinforced by a characteristic consequence and is therefore under the functional control of relevant conditions of deprivation and aversive stimulation" (pp.35-36).

Children who have few spontaneous verbal responses would need enough learning opportunities for forming functional manding. To increase learning opportunities for forming manding, one must manipulate an "establishing operation" (Michael, 1982; 1988). An "unconditioned establishing operation" would involve manipulation of deprivation and/or aversive stimulation. A "conditioned establishing operation" would involve a procedure by which reinforcing value of specific stimulus is evoked.

A defining feature of manding is that the response is controlled by the consequent event specific to the establishing operation (Hall & Sundberg, 1987). In other words, a mand "specifies" its reinforcement. So, we have to manipulate an appropriate conditioned establishing operation for forming a mand. To ensure that the acquired mand is controlled by the specified consequence, one would train children to respond differentially to the consequences of their mands.

Listener's Control of Mand

Yamamoto & Mochizuki (1988) established in autistic students a functional verbal response set "Give me _ " and "That's not it" that would specify a consequent event, and determined the degree to which the response was controlled by the specified consequence.

In the verbal behavior chain of manding, the director instructed the autistic students saying "Bring an object (for example, cup) from that teacher (supplier)." The students were trained to request a specific object from the supplier saying "Give me _ " and to deliver the requested object to the director. Subsequently, the degree to which the object offered by the supplier controlled the "Give me _ " response was assessed by delivering to the student an object other than the one requested. There are two types of trials in the experiment. In "matched trials," the supplier offered the object that the student requested. In "unmatched trials," the supplier offered an object other than the one the student requested.

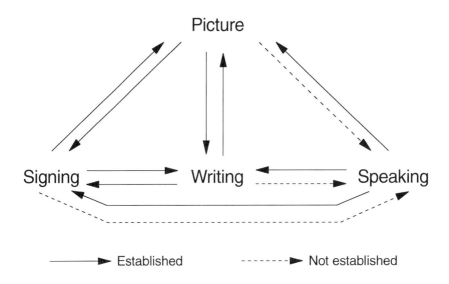

Figure 7. The equivalence relations established through conditional discrimination training in an autistic child. He developed all equivalence relations except for speech responding.

The verbal behavior chain in matched and unmatched trials was as follows. [matched trials]

Director: "Bring _ from that teacher." (Points to the supplier.)

Student : (Comes and stands in front of the supplier.) "Give me _."

Supplier: (Offers the requested object.)

Student : (Receive the requested object from supplier and delivers it to the director.) [Unmatched trials]

Director: "Bring from that teacher." (Points to the supplier.)

Student : (Comes and stands in front of the supplier.) "Give me _.

Supplier: (Offers an object other than the one requested.)

Student : "That's not it. Give me _." Supplier: (Offers the requested object.)

Student : (Receive the requested object from supplier and delivers it to the director.)

With regard to the establishing operation, the analysis of the verbal behavior chain might be as follows. The trial begins with the director's instruction "Bring (a cup) from that teacher." This stimulus probably has multiple effects. That is, it functions as an discriminative stimulus and as a conditioned establishing operation. It is an discriminative stimulus for the behavior chain of getting the object from the supplier and giving it to the director, but the response cannot successfully occur without the object, and the mand "Give me (a cup)." The director's instruction might be a discriminative stimulus for the behavior chain, and it increases the reinforcing value of the object and evokes the mand "Give me _ " by which the student has received that object in the past. The supplier's presentation of the wrong object constitutes a nonverbal stimulus and probably shares control of the "That's not it" response with the establishing operation which controlled the first mand, "Give me (a cup)," which is still at strength. The receipt of the specific object functions as reinforcement.

In our experiment, despite knowing the names of all objects used in the experiment, the students accepted and delivered to the director any object offered by the supplier regardless of its match with the requested object. After training to say "That's not it" when a non--requested object was offered, the students responded differentially to requested and non-requested objects. These results generalized across settings, suppliers and known objects.

The procedure used in this experiment involved the presentation of an incorrect object by the supplier, i.e. the listener. This procedure, thereby, is useful in determining whether the acquired verbal behavior is a mand, under the control of specific consequences mediated by the listener. Verbal behavior is defined by the listener's reaction to it (Silverman, Anderson, Marshall & Baer, 1986; Skinner, 1989). In everyday life situations, listener's responding might not always be consistent. Thus, it is important for speakers to develop flexible communication skills in response to listeners' responding. When the listener emits inappropriate responses, the speaker should reject or re-mand, such as "That's not it" or should change communication modes, such as from signing to writing.

Listener's Control of Equivalent Relations

Listener determining Specific Equivalent Relations of Speaker

Equivalent relations in verbal behavior involve both stimulus-stimulus relations and stimulus-response relations. In the example of word "cup," the object-word relationship would be established not only between the object cup and the symbol cup, but also between the object cup and saying "cup," writing of c-u-p or signing of cup. In the former case, a stimulus-stimulus relationship would be established, in which selection based responding such as pointing would be used. In the latter case, differential responding such as speaking, writing and signing would be used.

In previous studies, equivalence relations have been established through the conditional discrimination procedure. These studies examined how arbitrary stimuli are incorporated into equivalence repertoires. There are, however, few studies which have examined the controlling variables determining which mode of stimulus-response relation (such as speaking, writing, signing or pointing) in an equivalent repertoire would be functional in specific situations. What kind of stimulus-stimulus relation and/or stimulus--response relation would be used under the control of the listener's response in everyday life situations, after the equivalence relations have been established? For example, in the child who has acquired equivalence relations such as speaking, manual signing, writing, and pointing to the word, what kind of response will be used in the everyday life situation? We have examined the controlling variables determining the emergence of communication modes.

Experiments on the Listener's Control over Equivalence Relations

Noro, Yamamoto & Kato (1992) showed that a non-vocal mute autistic child showed communication mode changes in the mand situation in which an establishing operation was involved. The child was 10 years and seven months old. His mental age was four years and eight months (Block Construction Test). He was first trained on equivalence relations across pictures, signing and writing. After the training, the child could form equivalence relations except for vocal responses. He did not emit expressive speech after the training. Figure 7 shows the equivalence relations acquired by the child established through conditional discrimination training.

The communication mode change in equivalence relations was tested in a mand situation. The child sat next to thedirector, and the supplier stood 5m from the director behind a box containing various objects. In this situation, the child was instructed by the director which speech mode he was to use to get the object from the supplier. The child was required to walk to the supplier, to tap the supplier on his shoulder to get his attention, to write (or make the sign of) the name of the instructed object followed by the manual sign of "give me," to take the object from the supplier and to go back to the director. One block consisted of five matched trials and five unmatched trials. In matched trials, the supplier presented a correct object that the child requested. And in unmatched trials, the supplier presented an incorrect object on three occasions regardless of child's responding. This procedure was implemented for two blocks.

The result showed that the child changed the mode (signing to writing and writing to signing) in unmatched trials. The percentage of mode change trials was 100% and 60% in respective blocks. These findings suggest that a mute autistic child could change his communication mode in response to a listener's behavior. He could select one of the stimulus-response relations from the equivalence repertoire in the mand situation which involved the incorrect object presentation procedure.

Mochizuki, Nozaki, Watanabe and Yamamoto (1988) also showed that the controlling variables which determined the selection of response mode had been integrated into equivalent classes in the previous training. Two deaf adults with mental retardation were trained to establish stimulus equivalence among object, word, and sign through word-object and sign-object conditional discrimination training for new vocabularies. Results showed that the subjects could learn untrained sign-word relations and that each subject showed a spontaneous change of expressive mode (e.g., signing to writing, writing to signing), when an incorrect object was offered.

Integrating these two studies, when an incorrect object was offered, the participants changed the communication mode which had been incorporated into equivalence relations through prior conditional discriminations. This indicated that the participants switched the communication mode in response to listener's behavior. Thus, listener's behavior was shown to control the selection of equivalent repertoires. Listener's behavior such as presenting incorrect object, may function as contextual stimuli (or higher-ordered conditional stimulus) to determine which response would emerge in the already integrated equivalence relations.

Conclusion

In developing functional language skills in developmentally delayed or autistic children, a framework of equivalence relation would be effective. However, it should be used to expand the framework of equivalence. With regard to the "structure" of verbal behavior, sequential responding would be involved in equivalent relations to explain the acquisition of grammar. As for the "function" of verbal behavior, a listener's response may determine the speaker's use of specific response repertoire. Studies on equivalence relations have been conducted to explain the process by which relations between stimuli and responses are formed. Additional work is warranted on how the equivalent repertoires were established and how the listener determines what kinds of relations will emerge. Through studies on equivalence, more effective and efficient interventions for establishing functional verbal behavior of handicapped children could be developed.

References

Devany, J. M., Hayes, S. C., & Nelson, R. O. (1986). Equivalence class formation in language-able and disabled children. *Journal of the Experimental Analysis of Behavior, 46*, 234-257.

Dixon, M., & Spradlin, J. (1976). Establishing stimulus equivalences among retarded adolescents. *Journal of Experimental Child Psychology, 21,* 144-164.

Green, G., Sigurdardottir, z. g., & Saunders, R. R., (1991). The role of instructions in the transfer of ordinal functions through equivalence classes. *Journal of the Experimental Analysis of Behavior, 55,* 287--304

Hall, G. & Sundberg, M.L.(1987). Teaching mand by manipulating conditioned establishing operations. *The Analysis of Verbal Behavior, 5,* 41--53.

Kohlenberg, B. S., Hayes, S. C., & Hayes, L. J. (1991). The transfer of contextual control over equivalence classes through equivalence classes: A possible model of social stereotyping. *Journal of the Experimental Analysis of Behavior, 56,* 505-518.

Lazar, R. (1977). Extending sequence--class membership with matching to sample. *Journal of the Experimental Analysis of Behavior, 27,* 381-392.

Lazar, R., & Kotlarchyk B. J. (1986). Second-order control of sequence--class equivalences in children. *Behavior Processes, 13,* 205-215.

Lynch, D. C., & Green, G. (1991). Development and cross model transfer of contextual control of emergent stimulus relations. *Journal of the Experimental Analysis of Behavior, 56,* 139-154.

Michael, J. (1982). Distinguishing between discriminative and motivational functions of stimuli. *Journal of the Experimental Analysis of Behavior, 37,* 149-155.

Michael, J. (1988). Establishing operation and mand. The Analysis of Verbal Behavior. 6, 3-9. Miller, J. & Allaire, J. (1987). Augmentative Communication. In Snell, M. E. (Ed.), *Systematic Instruction of Persons with Severe Handicaps.* (pp. 273-297). Merill.

Mochizuki, A., Nozaki, K., Watanabe, H., & Yamamoto, J. (1988). Acquisition and functional use of signing and writing indeaf adults with mental retardation through conditional discrimination. *Journal of Multihandicapped Person. 1,* 233-249.

Noro, F., Yamamoto, J., & Katoh, T. (1992). Selection of communication modes in a mute autistic child: A training program for the functional use of signing, writing and vocal labelling. *Japanese Journal of Special Education. 30,* 25-35. (In Japanese with English Abstract)

Sidman, M. (1971). Reading and auditory-visual equivalences. *Journal of Speech and Hearing Research, 14,* 5-13.

Sidman, M., & Cresson, O.,Jr. (1973). Reading and crossmodal transfer of stimulus equivalences in severe retardation. *American Journal of Mental Deficiency, 77,* 515-523.

Sidman, M., Cresson, O.,Jr., & Willson-Morris, M. (1974). Acquisition of matching to sample via mediated transfer. *Journal of the Experimental Analysis of Behavior, 22,* 261-273.

Sidman, M., & Tailby, W. (1982 a). Conditional discrimination vs. matching to sample: An expansion of the testing paradigm. *Journal of the Experimental Analysis of Behavior, 37,* 5-22.

Sidman, M., Rauzin, R., Lazar, R., Cunningham, S., Tailby, W., & Carrigan, P. (1982 b). A search for symmetry in the conditional discriminations of rhesus monkeys, baboons, and children. *Journal of the Experimental Analysis of Behavior, 37*, 23-44.

Sidman, M., Wynne, C. K., Maguire, W., & Barnes, T. (1989). Functional classes and equivalence relations. *Journal of the Experimental Analysis of Behavior, 52*, 261-274.

Sigurdardottir, Z. G., Green, G., & Sanders, R. R. (1990). Equivalence classes generated by sequence training. *Journal of the Experimental Analysis of Behavior, 53*, 47-63.

Silverman, K., Anderson, S. R., Marshall, A. M., & Baer, D. M. (1986). Establishing and generalizing audience control of new language repertoires. *Analysis and Intervention in developmental Disabilities, 6*, 21-40.

Skinner, B. F. (1957). *Verbal behavior*. Appleton-Century-Crofts.

Slobin, D. I. (1971). *Psycholinguistics*. Scott, Foresman & Company.

Spradlin, J. E., Cotter, V. W., & Baxley, N. (1973). Establishing a conditional discrimination without direct training: A study of transfer with retarded adolescents. *American Journal of Mental Deficiency, 77*, 556-566.

Spradlin, J. E., & Dixon, M. H. (1976). Establishing conditional discriminations without direct training: Stimulus classes and labels. *American Journal of Mental Deficiency, 80*, 555-561.

Spradlin, J. E., & Saunders, R. R. (1984). Behaving appropriately in new situations: a stimulus class analysis. *American Journal of Mental Deficiency, 88*, 574-579.

Steele, D., & Hayes, S. C. (1991). Stimulus equivalence and arbitrarily applicable relational responding. *Journal of the Experimental Analysis of Behavior. 56*, 519-555.

Stromer, R., & Osborne, J. G. (1982). Control of adolescents' arbitrary matching-to-sample by positive and negative stimulus relations. *Journal of the Experimental Analysis of Behavior, 37*, 329-348.

VanBiervliet, A. (1977). Establishing words and objects as functionally equivalent through manual sign training. *American Journal of Mental deficiency, 82*, 178-186.

Wulfert, E., & Hayes, S. C. (1988). Transfer of a conditional ordering response through conditional equivalence classes. *Journal of the Experimental Analysis of Behavior. 50*, 125-144.

Yamamoto, J., & Mochizuki, A. (1988). Acquisition and functional analysis of manding with autistic students. *Journal of Applied Behavior Analysis. 21*, 57-64.

Yamamoto, J. (1990). On stimulus equivalence. *Annual Bulletin of Personality and Behavior Disorders Research Meeting, 30*, 1522. (In Japanese.)

Zuriff, G. E. (1976). Stimulus equivalence, grammar, and structure. *Behaviorism, 4*, 43-52.

Footnotes

Preparation of this paper was supported in part by a grant-in-aid from the Ministry of Education, Science and Culture, Japan (No.04831009) to Jun'ichi Yamamoto.

Chapter 7

Acquisition of Demand and Reject Behaviors in a Chimpanzee

Takao Fushimi

Primate Research Institute, Kyoto University

In linguistics, one of the main fields of research, called semantics, studies the relation between a signified event and its signifier. For example, the word, "chair" is defined as the signifier which signifies a chair. The central issue in semantics is: which word signifies which event. Behavioral research can approach semantics. From a behavioral perspective, a words are identified as the response which the speaker emits in a given context. For example, the speaker emits the response, "chair", corresponding to what he/she sees. Subsequently, the listener listens to the emission, "chair", guesses the stimulus event the speaker occasioning this response, and responds to the speaker's emission in some manner. The semantic issue in behavioral research is how the speaker and the listener acquire the relation between the stimulus event and the response.

Behavioral Analysis of Pragmatic Repertoires

Another main field of research in linguistics is pragmatics. Pragmatics analyzes how words are used. Skinner's (1957) *Verbal behavior* is a particularly good approach to pragmatics. According to Skinner, the emission of a word can be defined by the preceding event which initiates the emission and the following event which reinforces it. On the basis of Skinner's theory, we can classify the cases in which the speaker emits the response, "chair", as illustrated in Figure 1. For example, in the left panel in the upper row, the speaker is going to eat the food on the table but there is no chair within reach. In this case, the speaker emits "chair" to get the chair from the listener. In the second panel in the upper row, the speaker already sits on the chair and the listener offers another chair. In this case, the speaker emits the response, "(I don't need a) chair", to make the listener withdraw the chair. In each case, the emission is controlled by the chair. Therefore, we can call words like "chair" *object words*. However, the purpose of the emission is different in each case. The purpose of the emission in the first case is to demand the chair which is out of reach, and in the second case the purpose is to reject the offered chair. Therefore, we can discriminate these cases and identify the behavior in each case as a *pragmatic repertoire*, that is, a demand repertoire and reject repertoire. Furthermore, in each repertoire, the emission, "chair", is controlled not only by the chair but also by the *context* in each case. The context which makes the speaker emit "chair" is the necessity of a chair in the demand repertoire and the lack of necessity of a chair in the reject repertoire. Each context also suppresses other possible emissions, such as "table". Furthermore, the speaker can modify his emission to make the purpose of the emission clear to the listener. For example, the speaker can modify the emission, "chair", by "I want" in the demand repertoire and by "I don't need" in the reject repertoire. These emissions for modification are controlled by the contexts: the emission, "I want", is controlled by the occurrence of necessity and the emission, "I don't need", is controlled by the lack of necessity. These emissions can be frames in generating new sequential responses, such as "I want a table", "I don't need a table" and so on (Skinner, 1957). Therefore, we can call words like "I want" and "I don't need" *frame words*.

We can summarize the main points of a behavioral analysis of pragmatic repertoires as follows: 1) What is the purpose of the emission; 2) Which context makes the speaker emit the response; 3) How does the speaker modify the emission to make the purpose clear to the listener? We can apply this scheme to other pragmatic repertoires such as advice, warning, reply, report, and announcement as illustrated in Figure 1.

Recent Research on Language Training in the Chimpanzee

Many experiments have been conducted on the acquisition of artificial language by chimpanzees. It has been demonstrated that the chimpanzee can use object words from human language. We can classify the methods of training used in such research on the basis of pragmatic repertoires. Some methods can be considered as the training of a reply repertoire (Asano, Kojima, Matsuzawa, Kubota, & Murofushi, 1982; Matsuzawa, 1985; Savage-Rumbaugh, Rumbaugh & Boysen, 1978; Savage-Rumbaugh, 1984). In these cases, the experimenter presented an object to the chimpanzee and the chimpanzee was required to press one of several response keys. Each response key displayed a geometric form which could be considered a word. The chimpanzee had to press the correct response key corresponding to the presented object to produce a reinforcer. Another method can be considered as the training of a demand repertoire (Savage-Rumbaugh et al.,1978). In this case, the experimenter placed food at a particular site, for example, an apple was placed in a room with the bolted door, while the chimpanzee watched. First, the chimpanzee was trained to use a tool that corresponded to the food site, for example, to unscrew the bolt by a wrench. Subsequently, the chimpanzee was trained to press a response key corresponding to the tool. If the chimpanzee pressed the correct key, the experimenter provided the tool and the chimpanzee could use the tool to get to the food.

However, we have found no research in which the experimenter trained a chimpanzee to differentiate various pragmatic repertoires. Savage-Rumbaugh et al. (1978) trained chimpanzees to use object words which corresponded to tools, first with a demand repertoire, then with a reply repertoire. In the training of the reply repertoire, the chimpanzees had problems in using the words which they had acquired in the demand repertoire. Though the authors reported that once the

Figure 1. Examples of pragmatic repertoires. The title above each panel indicates the pragmatic repertoire, the purpose of emitting "chair". Each panel illustrates the context which makes the speaker (S) emit "chair". The phrase below each panel illustrates the response which modifies the emission, "chair", to make the purpose of the emission, "chair", clear to the listener.

chimpanzees could use the object words in the reply repertoire (the chimpanzees could use the same object words in both the demand and the reply repertoires), they did not provide any data to document the differentiation between the two repertoires. Furthermore, though they trained the chimpanzee to use the frame word "give" in the demand repertoire, they did not prepare another frame word to be used in the reply repertoire. Therefore, there was no evidence demonstrating that the chimpanzee discriminated the demand context and the reply context when the chimpanzee used the object words.

The Purpose of the Study

The purpose of the present study was to train a chimpanzee to differentiate two pragmatic repertoires, the demand and reject repertoire. First, the chimpanzee was taught to demand and to reject by gestures. Subsequently, we trained or tested the chimpanzee's use of the same object word in two different pragmatic repertoires, the use of frame words like "want" and "don't need", and the use of a 2-word sentence like "want" + "(something)" and "don't need" + "(something)" by combining the frame word and the object word.

Method

Subject and Setting

The subject was a female chimpanzee (Pan *troglodytes)* named Pan. She was laboratory-born and raised by human caretakers from her birth. She was housed in a group cage with cagemates according to the Guide for the care and use of laboratory primates of the Primate Research Institute, Kyoto University. She was 6 years old at the onset of the study. She had been trained on auditory discrimination tasks, conditional discrimination tasks with visual stimuli on a CRT screen, and training of gesticular communication in free play sessions. Throughout the experiments, she was not deprived of food or water.

The experiments were conducted in a small room. The room was divided into three booths. Each booth was separated from the others by a wall which had a slot through which materials could be exchanged. One experimenter was designated as the director, who controlled the start and end of each trial, and the other experimenter was designated as the provider, who provided or withdrew the object that the chimpanzee demanded or rejected.

Materials and Pretraining

Table 1 shows the materials used in the experiments which consisted of 3 sets of wood blocks (Set 1, 2 and 3), 3 pairs (Pair 1, 2 and 3) of 2-part objects. Each wood block was painted with one of six colors. Each set of wood blocks consisted of 4 blocks, 2 painted with one color and the other 2 painted with another color (e.g., red, red, green, green). Each 2-part object consisted of 2 parts, a large part and a small part (e.g., the shaft and head of a hammer).

The chimpanzee was pretrained on a simultaneous matching-to-sample task before the training of the demand and reject behaviors. Only the director conducted this training. First, the chimpanzee was trained with Set 1 of the wood blocks. The director presented one wood block (the sample) in a box to the chimpanzee and 2 wood blocks (the choices) within reach of the chimpanzee; one choice block (called S+) had the same color as the sample and the other had a different color (called the S-). If the chimpanzee picked up the S+ and placed it into the box with the sample, the director presented a reinforcer (a piece of apple, pineapple, or banana) to the chimpanzee. The chimpanzee acquired this identity matching-to-sample behavior and her performance generalized to other sets of the wood blocks. Subsequently, she was trained with the 2-part objects. In training, the director presented the large part of a 2-part object as the sample, the small part of it as the S+ and the small part of another 2-part object as the S-. The chimpanzee acquired this symbolic matching-to-sample behavior with each pair of the 2-part objects.

General Procedure

Figure 2 shows the setting of pretraining and training of the demand, receive and reject behavior. The director and the provider participated in the training of the demand, receive, and reject behaviors. Figure 3 shows the general training procedure. Each trial started with the presentation of the sample and the choices. The director presented the sample in the box and the provider presented the choices in front of him so that they were placed out of reach of the chimpanzee. Then, the provider waited until the chimpanzee demanded the choice objects (demand opportunity). If the chimpanzee demanded incorrectly (e.g. reached for the S-), the sample and the choices were removed and the trial started after a 5-sec timeout (correction procedure). If the chimpanzee demanded correctly (e.g. reached for the S+), the provider offered the S+ with a probability of p (receive opportunity) or offered the

Table 1 - Materials Used in the Experiment

Set or Pair	The sample	The choices
Set 1	Red or green wood block	Red and green wood blocks
Set 2	Purple or pink wood block	Purple and pink wood blocks
Set 3	Blue or Black wood block	Blue and black wood blocks
Pair 1	The can or the shaft of a hammer	The lid of the can and the head of a hammer
Pair 2	The ball with a hole for a stick or the pole of a ringtoss	The stick and the ring of a ringtoss
Pair 3	The box or the bottle	The lid of the box and the cap of the bottle

PRETRAINING

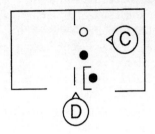

DEMAND

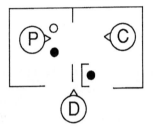

RECEIVE

REJECT

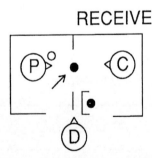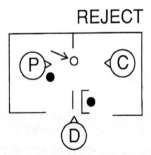

Figure 2. The settings of pretraining and training of the demand, receive, and reject behaviors. C: the chimpanzee. D: the director who controlled the start and end of each trial. P: the provider who provided or withdrew the object that C demanded or rejected. The filled circle between D and C indicates the sample. The filled and open circles other than the sample indicate the choices: the filled circle is the S+ and the open circle is the S- in the example shown. The chimpanzee's matching-to-sample response of placing the S+ in the box with the sample was reinforced in pretraining. Therefore, the chimpanzee was given the demand opportunity when the S+ and the S- were placed out of reach of the chimpanzee, in front of the provider. The chimpanzee was given the receive opportunity when the provider offered the S+; the chimpanzee was given the reject opportunity when the provider offered the S-.

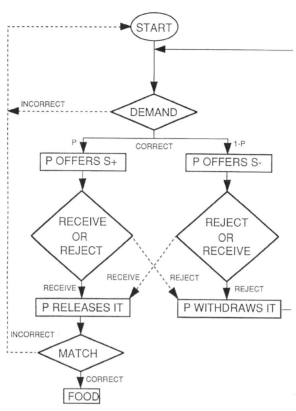

*Figure 3. A flowchart of the general procedure. The diamonds indicate opportunities to respond and the rectangles indicate the outcomes which followed the chimpanzee's response. The solid lines indicate the flow when the chimpanzee responded correctly; the broken lines indicate the flow when which the chimpanzee responded incorrectly. Each trial started with presentation of the sample and the choices. The provider waited to give the demand opportunity to the chimpanzee. The solid lines: if the chimpanzee demanded the object correctly, the provider offered the S+ with a probability of P or offered the S- with a probability of 1-P. When the provider offered the S+, the chimpanzee could receive or reject it. The correct response was to receive it. Receiving it and placing it into the box with the sample produced a reinforcer. In the case that the provider offered the S-, the chimpanzee could reject or receive it. The correct response was to reject it. If the chimpanzee rejected it, the provider withdrew the offered S- and waited for the chimpanzee to demand again. If the chimpanzee demanded again correctly, the provider offered the S+, and the procedure **on the** left side followed. The broken line: if the chimpanzee's demand behavior was incorrect, all materials were removed and the trial was repeated after a timeout (correction procedure). If the chimpanzee rejected the offered S+, the provider withdrew it and waited for the chimpanzee to demand again. If the chimpanzee received the offered S-, the provider released it. In this case, the chimpanzee could not produce a reinforcer even if she placed the S- in the box or placed it outside the box. A correction trial started 5 sec after the chimpanzee released the S-.*

S- with a probability of 1-p (reject opportunity). The value of p was determined dependent on the conditions of the experiment. When the provider offered the S+ or the S-, the chimpanzee was given the opportunity to receive or reject it. The provider waited with the S+ or the S- object in the offered position until the chimpanzee received or rejected it. When the provider offered the S+ and the chimpanzee correctly received it, the chimpanzee was given a reinforcer after she placed the S+ in the box with the sample. When the provider offered the S+ but the chimpanzee incorrectly rejected it, the provider withdrew the offered S+, and the chimpanzee was given the opportunity to demand again (the provider offered the S+ when the chimpanzee demanded correctly). When the provider offered the S- and the chimpanzee correctly rejected it, the provider withdrew the offered S-, and the chimpanzee was given the opportunity to demand again (the provider offered the S+ when the chimpanzee demanded correctly). When the provider offered the S- but the chimpanzee incorrectly received it, all materials were removed after the chimpanzee placed the S- in the box or some other place; the trial was repeated after a timeout. This general procedure was sometimes modified according to the condition of the experiment (see the Procedure section of each experiment).

Demanding and Rejecting by Gestures

Definition of Behaviors

The correct demand behavior was defined as reaching for the S+ in the demand opportunity. The correct receive behavior was to take the offered S+ in the receive opportunity. The correct reject behavior in the reject opportunity was defined as closing the palm near the offered S-. These behaviors were not trained but were the first responses which the chimpanzee made in the demand and reject opportunities.

Procedure

The sessions consisted of training sessions and generalization test sessions. After completion of the pretraining with three sets of wood blocks and Pair 1 of the 2-part objects, training of the demand behavior started with Set 1 of the wood blocks (red and green). First, each session consisted of 48 trials with only the demand and receive opportunities; that is, if the chimpanzee reached for the S+, the provider always offered the S+. Subsequently, 12 trials with both the demand, receive, and reject opportunities were added to each session. In these trials, when the chimpanzee reached for the S+, the provider offered the S+ with a probability of .8 and the S- with a probability of .2. In the reject opportunity, the provider waited for the occurrence of the reject gesture for 2 sec. If the chimpanzee made the reject gesture within 2 sec, the provider withdrew the offered S immediately. If the chimpanzee made no response, the provider withdrew the offered S after 2 sec had elapsed. This procedure was omitted after completion of training of the reject behavior, and the provider did not withdraw the S- until the chimpanzee made the reject gesture.

After completion of training of the demand, receive, and reject behaviors, generalization tests were conducted with other sets of wood blocks and Pair 1 of the 2-part objects. The test trials were reinforcing probes in which the chimpanzee's

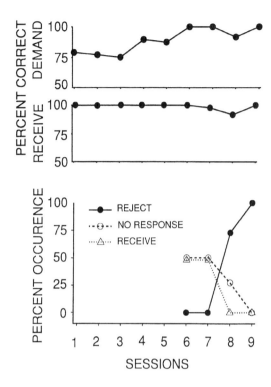

*Figure 4. Acquisition of the demand, receive, and reject behaviors by the use of gesture. The upper and middle panels indicate the accuracy of the demand and receive behaviors, **respectively**. The lower panel indicates the percent occurrence of the reject behavior as well as no response and receive behavior in the reject context.*

correct responses were followed by the same outcome as in the training sessions. The generalization test with each set and pair consisted of 10 trials only to avoid the effect of learning during tests. There were 10 demand opportunities, 8 receive opportunities and 2 reject opportunities in 10 test trials. The test trials were mixed with the trials for Set 1 of the wood blocks.

Results and Discussion

Figure 4 shows the accuracy of the demand behavior and the receive behavior, and the percent occurrence of the reject behavior as well as no-response and receive behavior in the reject opportunity in training. Before training of the demand behavior, the chimpanzee's performance on the matching-to-sample tasks was 100% correct with all sets of wood blocks and with Pair 1 of the 2-part objects. The percent correct for the demand behavior was calculated from 48 (for Session 1 to 5) or 60 (for Session 6 to 9) demand opportunities per session. The accuracy of the chimpanzee's demand behavior was 79% in the first session and it reached near 90% during 5 sessions of training. From Session 6, 12 reject opportunities were added. In Sessions 6 and 7, the chimpanzee either received the offered S- or made no response. From Session 8, the chimpanzee never received the offered S-. In the 4th reject opportunity in Session 8, the chimpanzee made the reject gesture for the first time; the provider withdrew the offered S-, and the chimpanzee was given the same demand opportunity immediately. Once the chimpanzee had made the reject gesture, she never failed to make that gesture in the remaining reject opportunities in that session and in all opportunities of the next session. The percent correct of the receive behavior was calculated from 48 receive opportunities each session. The chimpanzee always received the offered S+ in Session 1 to 5. The receive behavior was also very stable from Session 6 to 9 though the chimpanzee did not receive the offered S+ in one

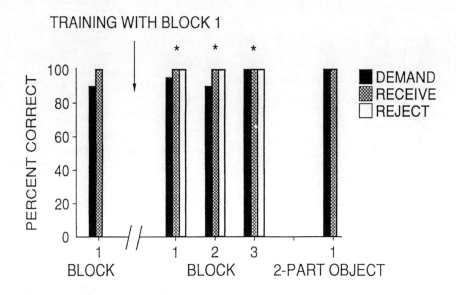

Figure 5. Generalization of the demand, receive, and reject behaviors by the use of gesture. The bars indicate the accuracy of the demand, receive, and reject behaviors in generalization test sessions except for Set 1 of the wood blocks. The data with Set 1 of the wood blocks were derived from the first and the last session of training.

trial in Session 7, and made reject gesture when the provider offered the S+ in two trials in Session 8.

Figure 5 shows the accuracy of the demand, receive, and reject behaviors with each material set. The data were derived from the first 10 demand, 8 receive and 2 reject opportunities with each material set except for the data with Set 1 of the wood blocks after training which was derived from the last 10 demand, 8 receive and 2 reject opportunities. An asterisk above a bar indicates statistical significance in both the occurrence of the correct demand behavior above chance level (binomial test, $p<.5$) and the difference between the occurrence of the receive and reject behaviors across the offered choice (Fischer's exact probability test, $p<.5$). The chimpanzee's performance in the first 10 demand opportunities was 90% correct though it was not stable in the first session in which the total accuracy was 79%. The chimpanzee's demand, receive, and reject behavior generalized to the other sets of the wood blocks. Only the demand and receive behavior generalized to Pair 1 of the 2-part objects; the reject behavior did not occur at all in testing with the 2-part object.

These data illustrate the acquisition of the demand and reject behavior by gestures in the chimpanzee. Both gestures, that is, reaching and palm-closing, appeared spontaneously and were not explicitly trained. The rapidity of acquisition of both gestures indicates that the chimpanzee could easily differentiate these two pragmatic repertoires by her spontaneous gesture when the provider responded according to the chimpanzee's behavior.

Demand and Reject by the Use of "Words"

In the above section, it was demonstrated that the chimpanzee could differentiate the demand and the reject repertoires by spontaneous gestures. Here, the chimpanzee's demand and reject behaviors were analyzed by separating the element which indicated the object of these behaviors and the element which indicated the purpose of these behaviors, by means of object words and frame words.

Features of the "Words"

Six color cards and two frame cards (5.5 cm x 8.0 cm) were prepared. Each color card was assigned as the object word corresponding to the wood block of the same color. Each frame card had a white geometric form on a black background. One frame card was assigned as the demand card meaning "want", and the other as the reject card meaning "don't need". These cards were located on the communication board placed between the chimpanzee and the provider. The communication board had 8 locations for cards, 4 in the upper row and 4 in the lower row from the chimpanzee's view point. The color cards were always located in the upper row, and the frame cards were always located on the lower row. The number of cards located on the board depended on the condition of the experiment.

Demanding by Pointing to the Color Card

Definition of behaviors. Two color cards were located on the upper row of the communication board. The location of each color card was determined randomly for each trial. The correct demand behavior was to point to the color card corresponding to the sample.

Procedure. The sessions in this step consisted of baseline sessions, training sessions, and generalization test sessions. The procedure was similar to the general procedure except that the provider always offered the S+ if the chimpanzee correctly demanded it. Only Set 1 of the wood blocks was used and 2 color cards corresponding to the set were located on the communication board in baseline and training sessions. In baseline sessions, 8 baseline trials in demanding by pointing to the color card were mixed with 24 trials for demanding by reaching. Each baseline trial ended if the chimpanzee did not point to the color card within 5 sec in the demand opportunity. The training sessions consisted of 48 trials of demanding by pointing to the color card. After the completion of training with Set 1 of the wood blocks, the generalization tests to other sets of wood block were conducted. In each generalization test trial, 2 color cards corresponding to the set of wood blocks used in the trial were located on the communication board. Four generalization test trials with each set of wood blocks, 8 trials in total, were mixed with 24 trials using Set 1 of the wood blocks. The generalization tests were conducted as reinforcing probes in which the chimpanzee's correct demand response was followed by the provider offering the

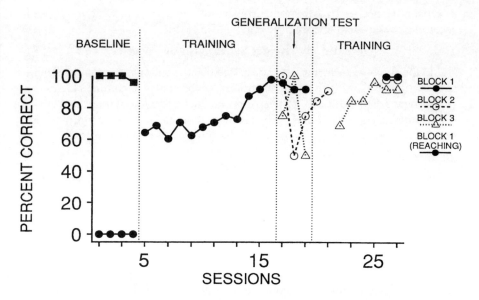

*Figure 6. The accuracy of the demand behavior by the use of color cards in baseline,
training, and generalization test sessions with Set 1, Set 2, and Set 3 of the wood blocks,
respectively. The data for the demand behavior by the use of gesture with Set 1 of the wood
blocks in baseline are also presented.*

S+. After the generalization test, the chimpanzee received intensive training with the
other sets of wood blocks.

    Results and Discussions. Figure 6 shows the accuracy of the chimpanzee's
demand behavior by reaching and by pointing to the color card with 3 sets of wood
blocks during baseline, training, and generalization test sessions. In baseline
sessions, the chimpanzee demanded correctly by reaching (the filled squares in
baseline), but she never pointed to the color card spontaneously (the filled circles in
baseline). Therefore, in the 1st and 2nd training sessions, the director's pointing to
the card was introduced as a prompt in trials where the chimpanzee did not point
to the card. The chimpanzee began to point to the color card in the 1st training
session and the prompting procedure was omitted from the 3rd training session. It
took 11 training sessions for the accuracy of the demand behavior to reach the
criterion of more than 90% correct during two consecutive sessions. The generalization tests were conducted in 12 trials with Set 2 and Set 3 of the wood blocks. The
total accuracy with Set 2 was 75% (non-significant, binomial test) and with Set 3 it
was 83% (p<.5, binomial test). However, 2 and 4 sessions of intensive training with
Set 2 and 3, respectively, increased the accuracy to more than 90%. Finally, the
accuracy with each set reached the 90% criterion.

    The chimpanzee could acquire the demand behavior by pointing to the color
card which had the same color as the sample. Even though the relations between the

sample and the card were not arbitrary, the color card functioned as the object word which signified the object.

Demand and Reject Behavior by Pointing to the Frame Cards

Definition of behaviors. The demand card and reject card were located on the lower row of the communication board with the location of each card determined randomly for each trial. The correct demand behavior was to point to the demand card. The correct receive behavior was to receive the offered S+. The correct reject behavior was to point to the reject card when the provider offered the S-.

Procedure. The sessions in this step consisted of baseline, training, and generalization test sessions. In all conditions each session had 48 trials. In the baseline sessions, all sets of wood blocks were used. Three kinds of trials were prepared in this procedure; demand trials, receive trials, and reject trials. In the demand trial, the provider waited for the chimpanzee's demand behavior. In the receive and reject trials, the provider did not wait for the chimpanzee's demand behavior and offered the S+ or the S- immediately at the onset of the trial. Each baseline trial ended with no reinforcement after 5 sec had elapsed, independent of the chimpanzee's behavior. During 6 baseline sessions, 4 demand trials, 2 receive trials, and 2 reject trials per set of the wood blocks were mixed with other trials for demanding by pointing to the color card on the board.

In the training sessions, only Set 1 of the wood blocks was used and the procedure was identical to the general procedure. When the chimpanzee demanded correctly, the provider offered the S+ with a probability of .75 and the S- with a probability of .25. First, the chimpanzee was required to point to the frame card one

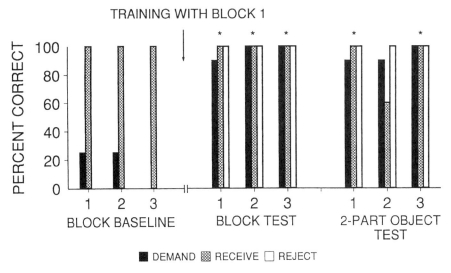

Figure 7. The accuracy of the demand, receive, and reject behaviors by the use of frame cards with each set or pair of materials in baseline and generalization test sessions.

time in each demand and each reject opportunity but subsequently she was required to point to the card 1, 2, or 3 times. If the chimpanzee changed her pointing before the outcome occurred, her response was counted as incorrect.

In the generalization test sessions, all sets of wood blocks and all pairs of the 2-part objects were used. The procedure was identical to that in the training sessions and the chimpanzee's responses were followed by the outcomes. With Set 2 and 3 of the wood blocks and each pair of two 2-part objects, 10 demand, 8 receive, and 2 reject opportunities were mixed with trials with Set 1 of the wood blocks.

Results and Discussion. Figure 7 shows the accuracy of the chimpanzee's demand, receive, and reject behaviors with each set of wood blocks and each pair of the 2-part objects during baseline and generalization test sessions. In baseline sessions, the chimpanzee's total accuracy of the demand, receive, and reject behaviors were 17%, 100%, and 0%, respectively. Subsequently, she was trained to demand, receive and reject according to the context. It took 40 sessions until the chimpanzee's performance reached the criterion of more than 90% during two consecutive sessions with each behavior. In the generalization test sessions, the chimpanzee's performance generalized to the other sets of the wood blocks and to all pairs of the 2-part objects except for a failure of the receive behavior to generalize with Pair 2 of the 2-part objects.

The data demonstrate that the chimpanzee could differentiate the demand and reject behaviors by pointing to cards according to the context across various material sets though the pointing to the demand card also functioned as the starting response. These cards could function as the frames in the combined response such as "want" + "red".

Reject by Pointing to a Color Card and the Appearance of Combined Responses

Up to this point in training and testing, the chimpanzee had acquired the demand behavior by pointing to the color card corresponding to the sample (color-card demand). She had also acquired the demand and the reject behaviors by pointing to the frame cards corresponding to the contexts (frame-card demand and frame-card reject). The next step investigated the acquisition of: 1) reject behavior by pointing to the color card corresponding to the offered S- (color-card reject), and 2) combined responses like "want" + "red" (2-word demand) and "don't need" + "green" (2-word reject).

Definition of behaviors. Two color cards corresponding to the colors of one set of the wood blocks used in the trial were located on the upper row of the communication board and two frame cards were located on the lower row of the board, with the position of the cards determined randomly. The correct 2-word demand behavior was defined as pointing to the demand card and the color card corresponding to the sample. The order of pointing did not matter. If the chimpanzee pointed only to the correct color card or only to the demand card, it was counted as an imperfect response. If the chimpanzee pointed to the other color card or to the reject card, it was counted as an error response. The correct 2-word receive behavior was defined as receiving the offered S+. If the chimpanzee pointed to any card in the receive opportunity, it was counted as an error response. The correct 2-word reject behavior was defined as pointing to the reject card and to the color card corresponding to the offered S-. The order of pointing did not matter. If the chimpanzee pointed to only the correct color card or the reject card, it was counted as an imperfect response. If the chimpanzee pointed to the demand card or the color card corresponding to the sample, it was counted as an error response.

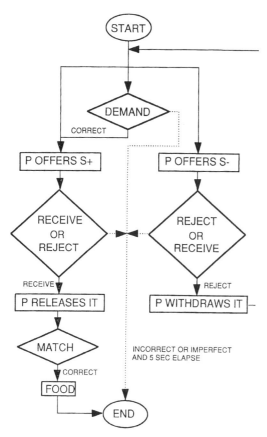

Procedure. The sessions in this step consisted of 4 blocks of test sessions (Test 1, 2, 3, and 4) separated from one another by training sessions. Each session consisted of 48 trials. All sets of the wood blocks were used in test trials. Three kinds of test trials were prepared as shown in Figure 8; in the 2-word demand trials, the provider waited for the chimpanzee's demand response; in the 2-word receive trials, the provider offered the S+ immediately after onset of the trial; in

Figure 8. A flowchart of three kinds of test trials of 2-word demand, 2-word receive, and 2word reject behaviors. The arrow from START, which diverges into three branches, indicates each kind of trial. Each trial started with the presentation of the sample and choices. In the demand trial (center branch), the provider waited for the chimpanzee's demand behavior. In the receive trial (left branch), the provider offered the S+ immediately after the trial started. In the reject trial (right branch), the provider offered the S- immediately after the trial started. The correct 2-word demand behavior was to point to the demand card and the color card corresponding to the sample. The correct 2-word receive behavior was to receive the offered S+. The correct 2-word reject behavior was to point to the reject card and the color card corresponding to the offered S-. The correct responses were followed by the outcome indicated by the solid line from each diamond. If the chimpanzee made an incorrect, an imperfect, or no response, the test trial ended without any reinforcer when 5 sec elapsed from onset of the trial, as indicated by the dotted line.

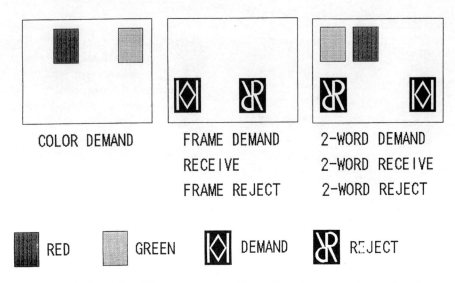

COLOR DEMAND   FRAME DEMAND   2-WORD DEMAND
                    RECEIVE   2-WORD RECEIVE
                    FRAME REJECT   2-WORD REJECT

RED   GREEN   DEMAND   REJECT

Figure 9. Examples of the arrangement of the cards on the communication board.

the 2-word reject trial, the provider offered the S immediately after onset of the trial. The test trials in which the provider offered the S+ or the S- immediately after onset of the trial were adopted to confirm that pointing to the demand card did not function only as a starting response. Each test trial ended when 5 sec elapsed without the chimpanzee making the correct response. If the chimpanzee made the correct response within 5 sec, the outcome followed as shown in Figure 8. In each test, 18 test trials (3 trial types x 6 sample colors) were mixed with the trials for the behavior which the chimpanzee had acquired before each test, that is, color-card demand, frame-card demand, receive, frame-card reject, and 2-word demand behaviors. In the color-card demand trials, only two color cards corresponding to the set of wood blocks were located on the communication board; in the frame-card demand, receive, and frame-card reject trials, only two frame cards were located on the board. Figure 9 shows examples of the arrangement of the cards on the communication board in this step.

After Test 1, the 2-word demand behavior was trained with only Set 1 of the wood blocks by a type of errorless training procedure. The effect of the acquisition of the 2-word demand response was tested in Test 2. After Test 2, the chimpanzee's frame-card reject behavior was trained by the procedure shown in Figure 8, so that the chimpanzee would point to the reject card immediately after the trial started. After this training, the chimpanzee's 2-word reject response was tested in Test 3. The chimpanzee was then trained to point to the reject card with two color cards and two frame cards on the communication board. This training was conducted by an identity pointing procedure in which the chimpanzee was required to point to the same card as the card that the director presented to the chimpanzee as the sample. After this training, the chimpanzee's 2-word reject response was tested in Test 4.

Results and Discussion. Figure 10 shows the accuracy of the behaviors which the chimpanzee had already acquired before each test. These behaviors consisted of color-card demand, frame-card demand, receive, and frame-card reject behaviors. In Test 3 and 4, 2-word demand behaviors were added in place of the color-card demand behavior. The data show that these behaviors were maintained during these test sessions.

Figure 11 shows for each test trial the correct (+) or incorrect (-) responses of the chimpanzee's 2-word demand, 2-word receive, and 2-word reject behavior. Each point in each test was derived from a trial in which one of 6 colored wood blocks was the sample. In the 2-word demand trial and 2-word reject trial, pointing to the correct color card and pointing to the correct frame card were separately plotted. In Test 1, the chimpanzee could point to the correct color card but never pointed to the demand card in the 2-word demand trials; she could receive the offered S+ in half of the 2-word receive trials; she never pointed to any card in the 2-word reject trials. It took 17 sessions of training for the chimpanzee's 2-word demand behavior to reach the criterion of more than 90% correct during two consecutive sessions. In Tests 2,

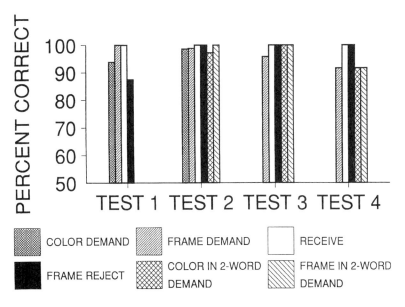

Figure 10. The accuracy of the behaviors which the chimpanzee had already acquired before 2-word demand and 2-word reject tests. These behaviors consisted of color demand, frame demand, receive, frame reject behaviors. The test trails of the 2-word demand, 2-word receive, and 2-word reject behaviors were mixed with trials for these behaviors in each test sessions. In Test 1 and 2, there was no trial for 2-word demand behavior. In Test 3 and 4, there were no trials for color card demand behavior. The accuracy of pointing to the color card and to the frame card was calculated separately for the 2-word demand behavior.

3, and 4, the chimpanzee could point to both the correct color card and the demand card in all demand trials. Furthermore, in the 2-word reject trials, the chimpanzee sometimes pointed to the card corresponding to the offered S though she never pointed to the reject card.

The failure of spontaneous appearance of the 2-word demand response in Test 1 shows the difficulty of combining pointing to the color card and pointing to the demand card. However, the complete performance of the 2-word demand responses in Tests 2, 3, and 4 shows that the chimpanzee could acquire the 2-word demand response through intensive training and it generalized to the other sets of wood blocks.

The absence of spontaneous appearance of the color-card reject, that is, pointing to the color card corresponding to the offered S-, in the reject trial in Test 1 shows the difficulty of changing the object on the basis of which she pointed to the color card. That is, it was difficult for her to change the object of the object word according to the context. In other words, the chimpanzee could not spontaneously use the same object word in a different context or in a different pragmatic repertoire. However, the appearance of pointing to the color card corresponding to the offered S- in Tests 2, 3, and 4 suggests the spontaneous appearance of the color-card reject. The chimpanzee was never trained to point to the color card corresponding to the offered S- and she made almost no errors in pointing to the color card corresponding to the sample in both color-card demand and 2-word demand trials during Tests 2, 3, and 4. Therefore, it is possible that the chimpanzee's pointing to the color card corresponding to the offered S- was controlled by the offered S-, not by the sample. Though this behavior was not stable during Tests 2, 3, and 4, the instability could be attributed to the test procedure because this behavior was counted as an imperfect response and was not followed by an outcome. The spontaneous appearance of this behavior could be attributed to the effect of the acquisition of the 2-word demand behavior. That is, it is possible that the acquisition of the 2-word demand behavior released the pointing response to the color card from the control of the sample to the offered S-, in other words, from the demand context to the reject context. Though other tests are necessary to confirm this possibility, it is possible that the use of the object word in the demand context could spontaneously transfer to the reject context through the acquisition of the 2-word demand behavior. However, the failure of pointing to the reject card was also observed in the 2-word reject trials in Tests 2, 3, and 4. This confirms the difficulty of combining pointing to the color card and pointing to the frame card observed in the 2-word demand trials.

General Discussion

These experiments demonstrate that according to the context the chimpanzee could differentiate the demand and reject repertoires by gestures and by the use of object words and frame words. In the use of the gestures, the chimpanzee could demand the S+ by reaching for it and could reject the offered S- by closing the palm. These gestures appeared spontaneously and were not explicitly trained. Through training of the use of the object word, the chimpanzee could demand the S+ by

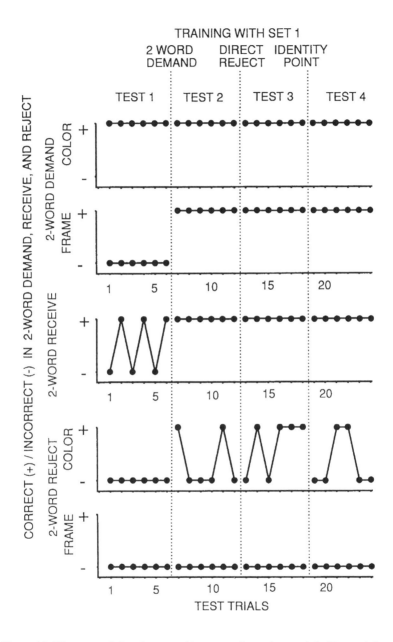

Figure 11. The correct (+) or incorrect (-) response for each test trial of 2-word demand, 2word receive, and 2-word reject behaviors. Each point is derived from a trial in which one of 6 colored blocks was the sample. In 2-word demand and 2-word reject trials, pointing to the correct color card and pointing to the correct frame card were plotted separately.

pointing to the color card corresponding to the sample. Through the training of the use of the frame word, the chimpanzee could demand the object by pointing to the demand card and to reject the offered S- by pointing to the reject card. In the combined use of object words and frame words, the chimpanzee did not spontaneously use 2-word demand or 2-word reject but acquired 2-word demand through intensive training. Furthermore, this training facilitated the use of object words in the reject context, that is, pointing to the color card corresponding to the S- though it was difficult here to identify the function of this behavior.

To confirm that the offered S- controlled the use of the object word in the reject context, we would have to conduct the same test with more than three color cards on the communication board and with the **irrelevant wood blocks within the chimpanzee's visual** field. To confirm the stimulus control of the use of frame words, we would have to conduct other generalization tests with new materials. For example, we can prepare a desirable object such a food or toy item as the S+ and an undesirable object as the S- with no sample presented to the chimpanzee. In such a test, the chimpanzee has to demand the S+ and reject the offered S- on the basis of her preference, not on the basis of the sameness or the combination of the sample and the S+ as in the test using the wood blocks and the 2-part objects. If the use of the frame words generalizes to such new materials, it will be confirmed that the frame words are used based on the contexts of the necessity or lack of necessity.

To confirm the function of the demand and reject behavior, we would have to analyze not only stimulus control but also the reinforcing event of these behaviors: whether the demand behavior is reinforced by the delivery of the S+, and whether the reject behavior is reinforced by the disappearance of the offered S-. Complex test procedures may be needed to identify the reinforcing event for these behaviors. However, we can guess the function of the demand and reject behavior by confirming that the event which controls the use of object words and the frame words depends on the context.

Furthermore, the acquisition of the use of object words and frame words in a combined manner provides us with an approach to analyze the segmentation of the stimulus events which control the demand and reject behaviors. For example, it was demonstrated that the acquisition of the 2-word demand behavior generated the appropriate use of the object word in the reject context, that is, pointing to the color card corresponding to the offered S-. These data illustrate that the stimulus event was segmented through the training of the 2-word demand behavior. It means that the chimpanzee could differentially discriminate the context and the object which was highlighted by the context: she could differentially discriminate the S+ and its necessity in the demand context and the offered S- and the lack of its necessity in the reject context. Such segmentation may generate a response which consists of two components, one of which is controlled by the object which is highlighted by the context and the other is controlled by the context. Such a response may be the most primitive type of subtle and complex responses, the same way that "Give (something)" is the primitive type of "I want (something)", "(something), please", and "I demand (something)".

Skinner (1957) defined a mand as "a verbal operant in which the response is reinforced by a characteristic consequence and is therefore under the functional control of relevant conditions of deprivation and aversive stimulation" (pp.35-36). Michael (1982, 1988) suggests a new term, establishing operation (EO), which alters the reinforcing effectiveness of an event and therefore evokes the response reinforced by the event. Deprivation and aversive stimulation are unconditioned establishing operations (UEOs) because they function as EOs without learning. Michael (1988) also suggested another EO, a conditioned establishing operation (CEO). A CEO momentarily increases the conditioned reinforcing effectiveness of an event and therefore evokes the response reinforced by the conditioned reinforcer. For example, hot soup in a dish without a spoon functions as a CEO which increases the conditioned reinforcing effectiveness of a spoon and evokes the response reinforced by the receipt of a spoon. Therefore, "spoon" may be a mand which is reinforced by the delivery of a spoon and is therefore under control of hot soup in a dish without a spoon.

There has been some research with human subjects in which the experimenter trained the learner to demand objects by manipulating CEOs (Hall & Sundberg, 1987; Reichle, Rogers, & Barrett, 1984; Sigafoos, Reichle, Doss, Hall, & Pettitt, 1990; Sundberg, Juan, Dawby, & Arguelles, 1990; Yamamoto & Mochizuki, 1988). The trained topographies consisted of the object words such as "(tool name)" or the objects word with frame words such as "want" + "(tool name)". There has also been a few experiments in which the learner was trained to reject objects (Reichle, Rogers & Barrett, 1984; Yamamoto & Mochizuki, 1988). The trained topographies consisted of only the frame word such as "no want". However, no research has investigated the use of an object word in the reject context, Sigafoos et al. (1990) suggested the possibility that the acquisition of the frame word facilitated transfer of the use of the object word from the reply context (they called them tact contingencies) to the demand context (they called them mand contingencies). This phenomenon also indicates that the use of object words across contexts may be facilitated by the acquisition of the frame word.

The demand and reject repertoires are considered as subclasses of mands. The CEO of the demand repertoire is the necessity of objects; the CEO of the reject repertoire is the lack of necessity of objects. We can also devise the CEOs of the other subclasses of mands such as question, advice, warning, call, and so on. We can train the use of frame words corresponding to the CEOs and we can test the generalization of the use of frame words within or across the CEOs to investigate the classification of the CEOs. For example, we can test whether the learner uses the reject frame or advice frame when he/she is exposed to a warning context for the first time. We can also investigate the effect of the acquisition of the frame word on the spontaneous use of object words across CEOs and on the combined responses which may be considered as a primitive version of subtle and complex responses such as "You'd better do (something)" or "I advise you to do (something)". Furthermore, we can also devise the context of another verbal operant, a tact, whose subclasses are considered as reply, report, announce, and so on, and we can prepare frame words corresponding to these contexts (see Figure 1). Though the categorization of subclasses of mands and tacts is difficult, we can analyze these repertoires by attending to the use of object and frame words if we can design and control the contexts.

References

Asano, T., Kojima, T., Matsuzawa, T., Kubota, K., & Murofushi, K. (1982). Object and color naming in chimpanzees (*Pan troglodytes*). *Proceedings of Japan Academy, 58*, 118-122.

Hall, G. & Sundberg, M. L. (1987). Teaching mands by manipulating conditioned establishing operations. *The Analysis of Verbal Behavior, 5*, 41-53.

Matsuzawa, T. (1985). Use of numbers by a chimpanzee. *Nature, 315*, 57-59.

Michael, J. L. (1982). Distinguishing discriminative and motivational functions of stimuli. *Journal of the Experimental Analysis of Behavior, 37*, 149-155.

Michael, J. L. (1988). The establishing operation and mands. *The Analysis of Verbal Behavior, 6*, 3-9.

Reichle, J., Rogers, N., & Barret, C. (1984). Establishing pragmatic discriminations among the communicative functions of requesting, rejecting, and commenting in an adolescent. *Journal of the Association for Persons with Severe Handicaps, 14*, 75-80.

Savage-Rumbaugh, E. S. (1984). Verbal behavior at a procedural level in the chimpanzee. *Journal of the Experimental Analysis of Behavior, 41*, 223-250.

Savage-Rumbaugh, E. S., Rumbaugh, D. M., & Boysen, S. (1978). Linguistically-mediated tool use and exchange by chimpanzees (*Pan troglotyes*). *Behavioral and Brain Sciences, 1*, 539-554.

Sigafoos, J., Reichle, J., Scott, D., Hall, K., & Pettitt, L. (1990). "Spontaneous" transfer of stimulus control from tact to mand contingencies. *Research in Developmental Disabilities, 11*, 165-176.

Skinner, B. F. (1957). *Verbal behavior*. New Jersey: Prentice-Hall.

Sundberg, M. L., Juan, B. S., Dawdy, M., & Arguelles, M. (1990). The acquisition of tacts, mands, and intraverbals by individuals with traumatic brain injury. *The Analysis of Verbal Behavior, 8*, 83-99.

Yamamoto, J. & Mochizuki, A. (1988). Acquisition and functional analysis of manding with autistic students. *Journal of Applied Behavior Analysis, 21*, 57-64.

Footnote

All experiments were conducted in collaboration with Masaki Tomonaga at the Department of Psychology, Primate Research Institute, Kyoto University. The author thanks Dr. Iver H. Iversen at University of North Florida for editorial comments on the manuscript.

Chapter 8

Tool Using Behavior and Language in Primates

Toshio Asano

Aichi University

When we discuss the evolution of behavior–the phylogenetic shaping of behavior by contingencies of survival–three classes of change in biological inheritance seem possible. Changes might occur in: 1) the sense organs so as to enhance stimulus control, 2) motor effectors so as to enhance response topography, and 3) releasing mechanisms so as to secure a high probability of occurrence of a given response form (Skinner, 1975).

Conversely, when we discuss the expansion of learned behavior of individual organisms, we tend to focus on the development or modification of behavior under given environmental arrangements, rather than how an organism can learn to modify its environment in order to obtain better contingencies of reinforcement. For example, a hammer is a tool that is made to enhance the effectiveness of a response for hitting or cracking. A hammer represents a kind of artificial expansion of a natural response topography in which what has been changed is the environment rather than in the structural characteristics of organisms. Most anthropologists and primatologists seem to take it for granted that such tools involve merely the expansion of organic effectors, but from a behaviorist's point of view, there are other kinds of tools.

Types of Tools

Tools may be classified into three groups according to their major function in altering particular aspects of contingencies of reinforcement in which they are involved. Table 1 presents examples of this classification (revised from Asano, 1978). Class 1 tools expand discriminative stimuli, thus facilitating the acquisition and maintenance of stimulus control. There seems to be two subsets in this class. Some such tools aid natural sense organs. For example, a telescope produces no permanent change in the environment, but enhances the sensitivity of the eyes and thus greatly expands the range of possible stimulus control. Other tools provide artificial stimuli so as to alter the impact of naturally occurring stimuli. For instance, a map is an artificially produced stimulus that can bring about a change in the impact of discriminative stimuli in the environment.

Class 2 tools expand response topographies. A hammer or chopsticks are direct expansions of the motor effectors (an arm and hands), but the natural feature of the topography, such as hitting or picking, is relatively unchanged. These tools are aids for the natural motor organs. Other Class 2 tools enable us to perform response topographies that do not occur naturally. For example, hang-gliders or boats are artificial products which allow us to perform response topographies that are not provided by inheritance.

Class 3 tools expand the consequential effects of stimuli. Some such tools alter the impact of natural consequences. For example, pain medication reduces the painful consequences of behavior (e.g., vigorous work or exercise is easier having taken aspirin).

Other such tools provide artificial consequences. For instance, money is an artificial consequential stimulus. These three categories are not orthogonal. Some tools may have multiple functions and some tools may change their major function from one class to the other class while they are used.

Table 1
Behavioral Function of Tools

Class 1: Expansion of Discriminative Stimulus
   a) Aids For Sense Organs
      Examples: telescope, candle light
   b) Artificial Products
      Examples: clock, map, characters

Class 2: Expansion of Response Topography
   a) Aids for Motor Effectors
      Examples: hammer, chopsticks
   b) Artificial Products
      Examples: hang-glider, car

Class 3: Expansion of Reinforcing Stimulus
   a) Aids for Sense Organs
      Examples: pain-killer, flavorings
   b) Artificial Products
      Examples: money, Nintendo games

Cultural Contingencies

Having categorized tools in this way, we must still study and specify the environmental features that bring about a given form of tool making or tool usage in a group of organisms. In other words, what kind of shaping environment is provided for a group of organisms to produce or to use a new tool? Often this means a cultural contingency.

Now, let me review some experiments on diffusion of newly acquired behavior in the natural setting done by Japanese primatologists. The first exemplar is a well–known finding on the learning of potato washing behavior by the natural troop of Japanese monkeys on Koshima Islet (Kawai, 1965).

The behaviors of monkeys on Koshima Islet are famous in Japan, since Mrs. Mito wrote a book on how the monkeys (and also the human researchers) have behaved while the research project has been going on (Mito, 1971). She lived near the Islet and helped researchers of Kyoto University from the beginning in 1950 and observed monkeys almost everyday until recently. In the summer of 1953, Mrs. Mito found an one-year old female, named "Imo" later, was playing with a potato rolling in the shallow stream near the beach. The potato was scattered by the feeder, namely Mrs. Mito. There were no naturally grown potatoes in the Koshima Islet. After the play, she ate it. Then Mrs. Mito gave her another potato covered with sand. Imo took it to the stream and played with it for a while then ate. By doing this, Imo caught the attention of Mrs. Mito, and Imo was given a number of tests.

The natural response topography of monkeys to a potato covered with sand is to beat the sand off by their hands, to brush it off with their arm hair, or to rub it on the rocks. However, Imo seemed to show a new repertoire with this potato. After accidentally dropping the sandy potato into the stream several times while she was playing with it, her behavior of carrying the sandy potato near the stream was accidentally reinforced with a cleaned potato. In a year, Imo had developed potato carrying and washing behavior. The water in the stream came from rain water running from the hill to the beach. Hence, once in a while, there was no clear water stream on the beach when the sandy potato was fed by the researcher. Under these conditions, Imo generalized her carrying and washing behavior to the sea water. In the beginning the sea water was used as sand washing liquid like clear water (a class 2-a tool), but soon Imo began to carry clean potatoes to the sea and dip them into the sea water after each bite. This behavior was flavoring (an instance of a Class 3a tool). This behavior spread first among her playmates, then to the mothers, and finally to the adult males by 1970.

Although the diffusion process of those operants of Japanese monkeys in a natural setting has long been explained with "imitation" or "observational learning" by many primatologists (e.g. Kawai, 1965), there seems to be no proof that Japanese monkeys can imitate another monkey's newly acquired operant behavior in a natural setting. Mr. Tokita of Jigokudani natural monkey park (famous for their hot spring bathing in winter) bound horizontally a clear pipe of 102cm long and 12cm diameter on the heavy trunk of a dead tree in December of 1983. He occasionally set an apple in the middle of the pipe, and left a stick near the pipe. By May of 1984, no spontaneous stick use was observed in the troop. He then started to teach monkeys how to use the stick to obtain the apple. Two of the monkeys had succeeded in the learning use of the stick within four months. However, several years later–in July of 1992–Mr. Tokita reported to me that only four monkeys could use the stick by this point, and all of them had learned by direct shaping. No case of observational learning was found, although many others frequently observed the stick using. Asano and Higuchi (1988) had succeeded in shaping token use by only one monkey in a corral of about 30 monkeys from a natural troop of Japanese monkeys. But no diffusion to other members was found despite the fact that the imitator showed this behavior frequently and was reinforced for doing so.

Very large individual differences in acquisition of a tool using behavior in a natural setting seems to be common in the troops of Japanese monkeys. So far, there is no experimental evidence in a natural setting to support the notion that Japanese monkeys can acquire a new repertoire of behavior by observation or imitation of others. Identical behavior patterns might be brought about independently and directly conditioned by reinforcement under the influence of local enhancement (Thorp, 1963; Higuchi, 1992).

Chimpanzees have shown good diffusion of behaviors among the troop without any human intervention, although a detailed analysis of the process is warranted. For example, chimpanzee's termite fishing and sponge usage are well known (e.g. Goodall, 1986) and furthermore they show local traditions and cultural transmission (Nishida, 1987.) Recently, detailed observations of the learning process involved in using stones as a hammer and an anvil to crack oil nuts in chimpanzees in Bossou were reported (Sakura and Matsuzawa, 1991.) Cracking a nut with a stone hammer and an anvil seemed to require highly sophisticated visual-motor coordination and to be very difficult for chimpanzees less than five years of age. They experienced a long unsuccessful imitation period. Also, generalization of a stone anvil to a hard wood trunk was observed. Sakura and Matsuzawa insisted there was evidence for chimpanzees' understanding of relationships between tool and referents.

In summary, comparing Japanese monkeys with chimpanzees, it seems to be clear that a strong human intervention in the contingencies of reinforcement is necessary to shape the Japanese monkey in a natural setting. They do not imitate nor learn response topographies by observation. Local enhancement mostly governs their diffusion process. A high diffusion might be brought about by local enhancement only, if the response topography is simple enough and followed by immediate reinforcement. Educational operants emitted by the successful individual to others have apparently not been reported.

This brings us to the relation between language and tool using behavior. The most versatile tool that can work for all three classes seems to be another organism. In this context, a mand (Skinner, 1957) corresponds to a tool using behavior where another organism is a tool. A tact (Skinner, 1957) is a behavior that works as an information tool for others. Speaking a mand is not a tool but a tool using response, where the tool is a living body of other organism (sometimes different species). So, we can classify our social behaviors into those three classes.

We can see some overlap between the function of cultural contingencies and the verbal community. The most conspicuous difference between the cultural contingency for tool related behavior of non-human primates and tool use and verbal community of humans is that the former have no evidence of Class–1 tools, while the latter utilizes Class–1 tools, particularly Class 1–b, very often. Humans use a lot of the Class–1 tools in our cultural transmission that enable us to communicate with each other beyond the boundaries of time and space. However, there seems to be no evidence that nonhuman primates produce a Class–1 tool by learning. By contrast, humans, even very early man, could draw signs and pictures. Very young children can draw highly sophisticated pictures. What kind of human world can we imagine if humans could speak, but could not draw? It seems to me that it would be very much like a chimpanzee's world.

References

Asano, T. (1978). Behavior of organisms and hominization. (in Japanese). *Kagaku* (Iwanami shoten), *48* (4), 213-220.

Asano, T. and Higuchi, Y. (1988). Shaping a token-use behavior of a Japanese monkey in a corral and lack of its transmission to others. *Abstracts of the XXIV International Congress of Psychology.*

Goodall, J. (1986). *The chimpanzees of Gmbe: Patterns of behavior.* Cambridge, MA: Harvard Univ. Press.

Higuchi, Y. (1992). *Cultural behavior in the Japanese monkev* (in Japanese). Kawashima-shoten, Tokyo.

Kawai, M. (1965). Newly-acquired pre-cultural behavior of the natural troop of Japanese monkeys on Koshima Islet. *Primates, 6,* 1-30.

Mito, S. (1971). *Monkeys in Koshima Islet: Observation for 25 years* (in Japanese). Popura-sha, Tokyo.

Nishida, T. (1987). Local traditions and cultural transmission. In Smuts, B. B. et al. (Eds.), *Primate societies* (pp. 462-474). Chicago: University of Chicago Press.

Sakura, O. and Matsuzawa, T. (1991). Flexibility of wild chimpanzee nut-cracking behavior using stone hammers and anvils: An experimental analysis. *Ethology, 87,* 237–248.

Skinner, B. F. (1957). *Verbal behavior.* New York: Appleton-Century-Crofts.

Skinner, B. F. (1975). The shaping of phylogenic behavior. *Journal of the Experimental Analysis of Behavior, 24,* 117-120.

Thorpe, W. H. (1963). *Learning and instinct in animals.* (2nd ed.). Methuen.

Chapter 9

Thinking

Linda J. Hayes

University of Nevada

No event has suffered interpretation throughout the history of psychology more than the inapparent, complex acts of human beings generally labeled—for lack of a better or more inclusive term—thinking (1). So central to the science of psychology, in fact, is the act of thinking, that the history of the discipline could be told in interpretations of this act alone. It is not my intention to tell that story here, but instead to contribute yet another interpretation to the succession of thinking theories.

Whatever the analysis of thinking articulated, it is founded ultimately on a set of assumptions concerning the nature of psychological events more generally. These assumptions influence the kinds of problems addressed, the methods employed for their solution, and the manner in which findings are interpreted and related to other findings both within and outside a particular scientific domain. When articulated and organized into a postulational system these assumptions serve as criteria against which the internal consistency and cross-disciplinary compatibility of a given scientific enterprise may be evaluated, as well as provide guidelines for the modification of that enterprise so as to achieve these outcomes.

Systemization of assumptions does not always prevail in science, however. This circumstance arises in part because assumptions underlie and strengthen theoretical positions regardless of how well articulated or organized they are. In other words, assumptions influence intellectual work even when scientists are not fully aware of them. Systemization may also be lacking because many scientists, particularly those operating in accordance with inductive procedures and biases, are not fully apprised of the services such systemization affords the scientific enterprise. Unfortunately, when system building efforts of this sort are lacking theoretical inconsistency and categorical incompatibility are the rule. This is because assumptions derived from different intellectual sources are unknowingly intermixed.

Not all aspects of scientific work are influenced equally by incomplete systemic development. Systemic development is of greatest service when understanding a particular phenomenon requires a considerable degree of methodological and theoretical extension, since it is under these conditions that inconsistency and incompatibility are most likely to arise in its absence (Parrott, 1986.) The extremely subtle and transient activities of thinking, imagining, and reminiscing are phenomena of this sort and the history of controversy over their interpretation is a consequence of workers operating on the basis of different, and oftentimes inscrutable, assumptions.

From these analyses of system building, it may be apparent that the most efficient procedure for elucidating any given theoretical position, as well as its points of departure from other positions, is to articulate it in terms of its underlying assumptions. This procedure, while not eliminating the controversy necessarily resulting from the adoption of different assumptions, may at least eliminate that arising from a failure to adequately discern the underlying system. This being the case, I wish to set forth a small number of assumptions upon which the analysis I am about to defend is based so that it may be subjected to a comparison with another analysis bearing some similarity. Interpretations of the phenomenon known nontechnically as thinking, as suggested by B. F. Skinner and J. R. Kantor, will then be presented. Finally, I will provide an evaluation of the relative merits of these two positions.

Postulational Basis for an Interpretation of Thinking

I will begin, then, with the first of five assumptions upon which my subsequent arguments concerning the interpretation of thinking are based. These assumptions have been articulated by Kantor (e.g., Kantor, 1959; Kantor & Smith, 1975) in numerous treatises.

1. Psychological events constitute unique occurrences in the sense of intimacy and fleetingness.

This means that a psychological event—as the interaction of a particular response of a particular individual with a particular stimulus in a particular setting—occurs once and only once. It may appear that events of some sciences are not unique in this sense. To believe it so is to overlook the facts of event measurement, though. For example, some chemical reactions are almost reversible, that is to say, the things transformed or retransformed by way of chemical operations are so similar that it seems possible to describe them as the same event. As Kantor (1922, p. 191) points out, however: "(a)n examination of this case impresses us with the fact that even if the measurements made give us the same results without averaging, which is hardly the case, we could not consider these as repetitions of the same event without abstracting the temporal factor." In short, *all* events are unique events; and the historical character of psychological events makes their uniqueness more than usually important to emphasize.

Intimacy, in this context, may be taken to mean merely that in a given time and place a particular individual with a particular history was involved in some specific event. By fleeting, we mean simply that psychological events are processes of brief duration, not subject to reappearance.

2. Psychological events are ontogenic.

This means that psychological events originate in the lifetimes of particular individuals and evolve during the interbehavior of those individuals with specific stimuli. The particular ways in which individuals and stimuli operate in given situations depend upon the ways they have previously interacted under definite conditions. Psychological acts are, in this sense, historical and cumulative.

3. Psychological events involve the actions of whole organisms not of their parts considered separately from the whole.

This means that from a psychological perspective, parts of the organism, *considered separately from the whole,* do not participate in *psychological* events. Rather, they participate in the events isolated by other sciences, namely biology or physiology. In other words, the spleen and the liver and the stomach and the lungs do not engage in *psychological* acts—and neither does the brain. It is not the eyes that see, the ears that hear, the legs that walk, the brain that thinks—it is rather the whole organism who engages in these acts. And, moreover, the action of a whole organism is always a very complex act.

The whole organism assumption is based on an assumption of broader scope, as implied in the next postulate.

4. The events of one science are not reducible to those of another science.

This statement is true by definition: If the events of one science are defined such that they encompass aspects not included in the definition of events of another science, then reduction changes their nature to an extent that they may no longer be characterized as events of the first science, and the procedure is thereby illegitimate. That is, if psychological events are not mere organismic occurrences but also include stimulating environments, then they cannot be reduced to organismic occurrences—the events of physiology—and still sustain their distinctly psychological character. Hence, one may talk about neural events if one wishes to do so. But what is said about them should not be confused with an understanding of the *psychological* events of thinking, imagining, remembering and so on.

A reductionistic position is rejected by Kantor on utilitarian grounds as well. Kantor was well aware of the value of reductionistic analyses in ordinary science—the value of using the events of one science as explanations for the events of another. He objected to system building on this foundation however because from his standpoint you "couldn't get there from here" and as a consequence the utility of trying was illusory.

Technically, Kantor (1959, P. 139-169) argued that theoretical constructions were developed as abstractions from generalizations made in the handling of events of a particular sort, and pertained thereby to events of that sort, not to events of some other sort. The principle of reinforcement, for example, was developed by way of contacts with whole organism responses to stimulating circumstances and pertains as such to events of this sort, not to the events of photosynthesis, or thermo-regulation, or combustion, or genetic selection. Consequently, even if a causal or explanatory role were possible for events of *some* sort to play, a claim Kantor (1950,

p. 156-158) denied, no such role is possible for the events of one science over those of another. Simply stated, the utilitarian argument for reductionistic explanations in science, in Kantor's view, is false. Moreover, to suggest as much is a *disservice* to scientific system building as it constitutes a distraction from potentially more fruitful avenues of investigation.

The implications of these assumptions for the analysis of private events in particular remain to be articulated. In the first place, privacy may be an apt descriptor of events on the grounds of their inapparence to observers. This inapparence cannot be claimed to follow from the internal location in which such events are held to be taking place, however. That is, private events, like *all* events of the psychological domain, are acts of *whole organisms*. They do not occur within the skin of the organism any more than any other acts of the whole organism.

The only justification for a claim to the contrary—as made by Skinner, among others—is the argument that private events are enacted by parts less that the whole— by parts residing inside the organism's skin. (Bear in mind that the skin is not a boundary that warrants comment if one's intention is to imply an act of the whole organism.) Let me illustrate this point with an example:

If a mother nurses her baby in the dressing room of a department store, the act is private in the sense that it is not accessible to observers. It is *not* private in the sense that Skinner uses this term, however. In Skinner's (1953, p. 257; 1974, pp. 21-25) analysis, private events are private by virtue of the *internal location* of their occurrence—not because of the *circumstantial* inability of others to observe them. For Skinner, the privacy of private events is not a *simple* matter of their inaccessibility to observers; it is a consequence of the fact that such events are enacted by parts other than the whole organism—parts residing inside the whole organism's skin. The inaccessibility of private events to observers, from Skinner's standpoint, is due to the *place* in which they are held to be taking place.

Alternatively, dreaming, imagining, thinking and feeling no more occur within the organism's skin than do walking, talking, scratching and crying. The privacy of events, where such is the case, is a matter of the circumstances of their occurrence, the intricacy of the phenomena, and the reactional biographies of observers—points I will take up momentarily. First, let me articulate a fifth and final assumption upon which my arguments are based.

5. A psychological event is an interdependent relation of responding and stimulating, occurring in a multi-factor field.

This means that a psychological event is, in *every* instance, an interaction with a stimulating environment: It is never a mere organismic occurrence; neither is it ever independent of, nor isolated from, the field or setting of its occurrence.

This assumption bears on the issue of reductionism, as already discussed. In short, it defines a psychological event in such a way that it cannot be reduced to physiological happenings without changing its definition, and the definition is a given. Hence the reduction of psychological events to the events of physiology is rendered illogical.

The concept of interdependence of stimulating and responding articulated in this fifth assumption has other implications for a number of occurrences generally partitioned into the private events class, however, to which we may now turn.

When psychological events are conceptualized as interdependent stimulus-response relations, nothing short of a functional relation has psychological significance. Hence what may be inaccessible to observers, and hence challenging for scientists, are not the responses but rather the functional relations sustained between responding and stimulating and the stimulational phases of such relations may be as inaccessible as their response phases.

Complex Psychological Occurrences

These assumptions lead to a somewhat different organization of complex psychological occurrences, among which are included those of the private events variety. Specifically, responses may be apparent or inapparent to observers, as may be stimulus events, making for four classes of events, only one of which—the case of apparent responses interrelated with apparent stimuli—presents no particular problem for the scientific community. Into the other three classes may be included all other psychological events, and, I should add, all of the problematic cases. Included among them are such events as reminiscing, imagining, dreaming, speaking, planning, feeling, thinking and so on. These cases may be illustrated as follows:

RESPONSE

	Apparent	Inapparent
STIMULUS **Apparent**	talk about a remark	think about a remark
Inapparent	talk about the past	think about the past

With regard to inapparent responses such as thinking, it may not be obvious to an observer that a response has occurred. Likewise, when a person speaks about something that is not present, it is not obvious what stimulates such action. And when a person thinks about something that is not present, it may be very difficult indeed for the observer to know that anything has happened at all.

The classification scheme suggested here is not so important as the intellectual burden it engenders, namely the obligation to account for responding with respect to absent stimuli and to describe the morphological characteristics of inapparent responding. Before attempting to deal with these issues from a Kantorian perspective, it may be illuminating to contrast it with Skinner's treatment of the events making up this matrix.

Skinner's Analysis of Private Events

With regard to events involving inapparent responses with respect to apparent stimuli (as in the case of thinking about a remark), Skinner's general approach has been to point out the difficulties encountered by the verbal community in teaching its members to talk about private events, rather than to discuss the characteristics of the private event itself, either functionally or morphologically. Furthermore, in the case of thinking in particular, Skinner goes to some length in the book *Verbal Behavior* (1957) to interpret thinking as *behavior* plain and simple, not as covert verbal behavior as is more typically held.

There are indications in several sources, however, that private responses, including those of the thinking variety, are regarded as low magnitude or miniature versions of their public counterparts, which we may assume involve muscular activity to some degree (Skinner, 1953, p. 282; 1957, p. 141; 1969, p. 242; 1974, p. 27.) In addition, Skinner suggests that private responses may be of a neurological sort at least in some cases (1957, p. 371.) Functionally, though, private responses are said to operate in the same manner as public events and to be subject to the same laws (1957, p. 437.)

Skinner is much more inclined to talk about private *stimulus* events than private response events however, as in the example of talking about the past in the above matrix. The inaccessibility of the past as a source of stimulation for a current event arises from the fact that the past is by definition not present, hence what is stimulating talk about it is not obvious to an observer.

Skinner does deal with events of this sort, although they are not assumed by him to be complicated by the problem of privacy. For example, stimulus generalization is invoked to explained reminiscence (1974, p. 108), wherein the stimuli involved, both past and present, remain in the public domain. Similarly, recall is explained as a case of intraverbal control, again involving publicly observable stimuli (1974, p. 109.) For Skinner, the problem of privacy, as it concerns stimulus events, prevails only for events inaccessible by virtue of the *place in which they are held to be occurring*, namely, within the organism's skin. It is, thereby not the past time of operation of a stimulus that makes for its privacy, but rather its location. Hence private stimuli tend to include full bladders, dry throats and the like. And much of Skinner's discussion of private stimuli (1957, pp. 130-138; 1945) is again focused on how we learn to *talk* about such events, not what sort of events they are, morphologically or functionally.

Skinner is at times explicit about these issues, and when so, he argues that private stimuli arise from the digestive, respiratory and circulatory systems, from the position and movement of the body, and from conditions associated with behavior but not necessarily produced by it such as inflammation of tissues (1953, p. 258.) In short, private stimuli, morphologically considered, have their sources in bodily conditions. From a functional standpoint private stimuli are regarded as capable of entering into the same kinds of controlling relations with response events as public stimuli, although they are not regarded as having causal status with respect to responding. (For further discussion, see Parrott, 1983.)

In summary, according to Skinner, inaccessibility of events to observers is the criterion upon which they are relegated to the private events class, and inaccessibility—be it with respect to response events or stimulus events—is due to the place in which such events are held to be taking place, namely, inside the organism's skin. I hasten to add that privacy does not imply a *substantive* difference from Skinner's standpoint: Private events are *not* mental events, they are merely natural events obscured from view.

Kantor's Analysis of Subtle Events

Let us proceed now to an alternative interpretation, that derived from the work of J. R. Kantor. To reiterate, given that psychological events involve actions of whole organisms, not their parts considered separately, and given that psychological events are conceptualized as unique occurrences of interdependent stimulating and responding, there exists an obligation first to provide an explanation for the participation of a stimulus in interdependent relation when the stimulus object is not present; and, second, to describe the morphological character of psychological responding of the inapparent sort in such a way that it amounts to something other than sheer biological activity.

Stimulus phase. The stimulational burden is borne by a distinction between stimulus objects and stimulus functions, and an analysis of the means and conditions under which functions transfer from one object to another. The details of this analysis are beyond the scope of the present address. Suffice it to say that when one responds with respect to an object that is not present, the stimulation coordinated with such responding is held to arise from another immediately present object in which a stimulus function of the first object inheres. A stimulus function adhering in an object other than the one with which it was originally coordinated is called a substitute function by Kantor (1924, pp. 295-300; Kantor & Smith, 1975, pp. 198-199.) The transfer of functions from one object to another, implied by this claim, is argued to be a result of a particular set of historical circumstances involving, ultimately, a proximal relation of the two stimulus objects or their functions. In short, the a priori definition of a psychological event is not compromised to accommodate the case of responding with respect to stimuli that do not appear to be participating in the event from the standpoint of the observer. Instead, the definition fosters a distinction between stimulus objects and their functions, a distinction that stands out as one of the most significant contributions of the interbehavioral position to psychology, in my opinion.

Response phase. The intellectual burden posed by the five assumptions discussed previously and the classification of apparent and inapparent interdependent relations as it applies to *responding* is shouldered by the concept of the reaction system in Kantor's (Kantor and Smith, 1975, pp. 33-35) analysis. Let me explain.

Kantor argues that the response phase of a psychological event may be conceptualized apart from the stimulational phase of that same event for analytical purposes. The purpose in this case is to isolate the form of a response from its function. The reaction system is a conceptual component of the response phase of a psychological event analyzed for this purpose. Reaction systems are described by Kantor as activities of the biological organism including acts of a neural, muscular and glandular sort, among others. The organismic or reactional phase of a psychological response, at least with respect to its *form*, is conceptualized upon the occurrence of some configuration of these biological events. As such, different responses may be described as involving different degrees of participation by various reaction systems. For example, one response might be characterized by more glandular or more muscular involvement than another response. (It is important to remember that from an interbehavioral standpoint, a psychological event is not possible of description in purely formal terms. Hence, the discussion to follow concerning reaction systems and response form should not be taken to apply to the psychological event understood in its entirety.)

Psychological events involving inapparent responses may be distinguished, in part, from those involving more apparent responses by the types of reaction systems constituting their response forms. Response forms in which muscular reactions figure prominently constitute readily confrontable stimulus objects for observers; whereas those involving a preponderance of glandular activity may not be as readily confronted. It should be noted that responding on the parts of observers is coordinated with stimulating, not with stimulus objects, as in all other cases of responding. Hence the present argument with respect to the confrontability of stimulus objects is meant to imply only that sources of stimulation having substantive structure may be home to more stimulus functions than insubstantial sources due to the addition of functions based on formal properties in such cases and the opportunities for substitution they afford. That is, when the form of a person's action is such as to generate a thing-like stimulus as a source of stimulation for an observer, the observer is more likely to report observing the action of the first person than when this is not the case.

This is not to say that observation in the latter case is not possible. Inapparent responses are not unobservable in principle, they are just subtle and their observation depends more on the history of interaction between the observed and the observer than is required for apparent events. I will explain this in a moment.

Summary of Skinner's and Kantor's Analyses

Let me summarize up to this point. Skinner argues that private events are those events in which responses or stimuli or both are taking place somewhere inside the organism's skin and as such are inaccessible to observers. Similarly, Kantor argues that when psychological events are inaccessible to observers it may be due to inapparent responses, stimuli or both.

Unlike Skinner, however, a psychological event for Kantor is an interdependent relation of stimulating and whole organism responding, occurring in a multi-factor field. Consequently, when observers are unable to identify the stimuli with which responding is coordinated, it is not because there are no relevant stimuli, neither is it because the relevant stimuli are taking place inside the organism. It is instead because substitute stimuli are involved, and their object sources are therein obscured.

Likewise, when observers are unable detect response occurrences, it is because response forms are constituted of reaction systems of the nonmuscular and nonskeletal sort, not because responding is occurring inside the skin. In short, psychological events may be *subtle* but they are never internal.

Evaluation of the Two Positions

Having thus far identified the events partitioned into the private events class and the analyses made of them by Skinner and derived from Kantor work, we may turn to an evaluation of their analyses of these events. In as much as there is no way of knowing whether or not either of these descriptions of thinking corresponds better to the events described than the other, I will make an evaluation on other grounds, namely, on the criterion of coherence and on the principle of utility.

Coherence

It is difficult to criticize Kantor's position on the grounds of incoherence. The interbehavioral system is built on the principle of coherence. What Kantor has to say about inapparent psychological events is consistent in every detail with what he has to say about apparent events.

Not so of Skinner's position. For example, sometimes psychological events are held to be enacted by the whole organism (e.g., arguments against reductionism, 1938, pp. 418-432); at other times by the organism's parts considered separately (1953, p. 258.) Psychological occurrences are sometimes described as interactions with stimuli (1938, p. 9); sometimes as completely organismic events (1974, p. 215.) Sometimes causality is taken to be synonymous with control (e.g., multiple causation, 1957, p. 227); sometimes not (1953, p. 23.) More specifically, private stimuli, while able to participate in all forms of controlling relations with responses (Skinner, 1953, p. 275), they are not regarded as having causal status with respect to responding (1957, p. 437; 1969, p. 257.) The same is not true of public stimuli.

No doubt there will be those who will argue that I am being selective in my presentation of Skinner's position. I would not disagree. The very fact that it is possible to be selective is indicative of the problem, however. If coherence is a virtue, Skinner's position is in trouble.

Utility

Perhaps the more important criterion, though, is the relative utility of the two positions in achieving such goals as a more thorough understanding, more accurate prediction and better control over events like thinking. It is usually on such grounds that Skinner's position is defended and Kantor's criticized, hence it seems fair to subject both analyses to scrutiny on this criterion as well. Let us consider Skinner's position first.

Skinner's analysis of private events, by locating them inside the organism, suggests that the observational problems posed by private events of psychological significance will eventually be solved by the physiologist of the future (1974, p. 215) using technologies designed to amplify biological occurrences (1953, p. 282.) In other words, *psychologists* have no role to play in the understanding of psychological occurrences of the private sort, at least not in the foreseeable future.

This solution to the problem of private events is valuable if one's goal is to avoid the study of such events. However, it does little to enhance our ability to understand, predict and control them, at least not as *psychological* events and not *now*. In the interests of achieving these goals it seems reasonable to suggest that Skinner's analysis is not particularly useful.

When events of this same sort are conceptualized as subtle interactions occurring in a *field* not an organism, as is the position I am taking, then the opportunities for their study by psychologists are greatly improved. Such events are not unobservable in principle. They are, rather, subtle, requiring special practices of observation and special relations between observers and the events observed.

Observation of Subtle Events

Having argued that events of the sort more typically regarded as private are possible of direct observation, I turn now to an account of observation of subtle events. As previously discussed, the subtleties of events may have to do with their response phases, stimulus phases, or both. I will address each of these cases in turn.

Observation of Events Involving Inapparent Stimulation

In the case of apparent responses with respect to inapparent stimulation (e.g., talking about what happened yesterday), observation of the stimulational phases of such events depends on knowledge concerning the kinds of stimulus objects that might be serving as sources for substitute stimulus functions in the present environment. As previously mentioned, substitution depends, ultimately, on there having been a proximal relation between original and substitute source objects or their functions. To some extent, the source objects involved may be known from cultural or characteristic organizations of stimuli. In other words, for example, since teachers and schools tend to occur together in most people's histories, the functions of one may be actualized by the other in its absence for most people. As such, it might be useful to assume that talk about one's teacher in her absence is coordinated with stimulation arising from a school building. Common cultural circumstances between observers and actors is required for observational practices of this sort to prove useful.

Observation of subtle events of a more idiosyncratic sort depends on an intimacy of the observer with the observed. To the extent that an observer knows how a particular individual is stimulated by immediately *obvious* stimulus objects—a knowledge accumulated over the course of many interactions between the two persons—that is the extent to which the observer may know which objects serve as substitute stimuli for that particular individual. For example, a father might be able to predict that his daughter will fuss when she sees him put on his shoes in the morning—a prediction based on the fact that putting on his shoes immediately precedes his leaving the house and serves as a substitute stimulus for his leaving, with which, in turn, the daughter is interacting when she fusses. A stranger would be unable to predict this action on the part of the daughter, because he would not know which stimuli serve as substitutes for the father's leaving the house due to a lack of intimacy with the girl.

It is for this reason that we know why friends do what they do in what may seem to be ambiguous circumstances to another observer, yet we cannot understand the actions of a stranger. A knowledge of which stimuli serve as substitutes for particular responses by close associates is also the basis of subtle forms of control over their behavior that is not available in the case of unfamiliar persons. For instance, I might instigate a friend's leaving a social situation with the raise of an eyebrow, a stimulus that would not have this effect on a stranger.

Observation of Events Involving Inapparent Responses

Observation of subtle interactions involving inapparent responses is also possible from the present standpoint. In such cases, conventional responding may provide a means of observation: We know what even a stranger is feeling upon witnessing a tragic car accident because shared enculturation enables us to know that a stranger feels much the same as we do ourselves.

Intimacy makes for greater knowledge in this case as well. If I have observed a friend's overt responding with respect to immediately apparent stimulation, I may also observe that friend's response when it is not apparent to a stranger on the basis of the stimulation present. If a couple of friends were on some occasion to make disparaging remarks about some other individual, the arrival of that individual would enable each to know what the other were thinking, despite the fact that a stranger might have no indication that either of them were thinking anything at all. When "I know what you are thinking" it is because I have observed your responding to similar stimulation on previous occasions and I can see that you are responding in the same way on this occasion. I can, as such "read another's mind" and my ability to do so increases with my experience or history with the other person.

Observation of Events Involving Inapparent Stimulation and Responding

In cases where subtleties are present in both the stimulation and response phases of an event, as in the case of thinking about something that happened years ago, observational difficulties are multiplied. Observation is still possible by the same means as made inapparent responses and inapparent stimulation observable, as discussed above. Observation in the present case depends on an even more extensive history of interaction between the observer and the observed, though. The observer must have observed the responses of the observed person with apparent stimulation in its situational contexts so as to know how substitute stimulation might have arisen and be operating in the present situation. The observer must also know how the observed person responds to such stimulation when responding has taken more obvious forms.

With these histories available, the observer may know what a person is thinking when neither the act nor the stimulation for it is observable to an observer without this history of interaction. Couples who have lived together for long periods of time often display this sort of knowing. Often they know so well what the other is thinking that they find the need to express themselves overtly less necessary over time. They finish each others' sentences, or speak in partial sentences that their partners understand fully. They may also find themselves thinking the same thing at the same moment. All of these circumstances are due to extensive histories of intimate interaction between the two persons. Strangers witnessing these interactions may be dumbfounded by them. And occasionally, too, participants in them find them sufficiently noteworthy to attribute them to supernatural forces, as when they refer to their intimate friends as "kindred spirits" or "soul mates."

Summary of Evaluation of Skinner's and Kantor's Views

In summary, what Skinner calls "private events" and deems unobservable by virtue of the internal location of their execution, Kantor calls "subtle events" held to be capable of observation. Observation in the latter case depends minimally on shared histories between observers and the observed as a matter of enculturation, and maximally on the intimacy of the observer and the observed as a matter of shared individual histories. Kantor's analysis suggests, in other words, that what appears to be unobservable is not so in principle, but is instead subtle; and subtlety is not a formal characteristic of the event in question. That is to say, subtlety is not something about a particular event apart from an observer's insufficient history with respect to it. The greater one's history of interaction with subtle events, the more obvious they therein become since, psychologically speaking, observed events are nothing other than loci of response functions for observers.

The two positions may be compared in summary form as follows:

	Skinner's Private Events	Kantor's Subtle Events
Event Type	stimulus or response	stimulus-response interaction
Event Location	inside the skin	in the event field
Problem for Observers	inaccessibility of events to observers	insufficient history of observers with events
Interim Solution	infer events from correlated public accompaniments	develop a history for observers with events and study its unfolding
Ultimate Solution	direct physiological measurement of events	develop a history for observers with events and study its unfolding

Further Comments of the Nature of Observation

No doubt there will be those who will claim that this analysis flies in the face of the obvious fact that some events *are* private, some public, and that private events sometimes have public accompaniments, sometimes not. And that when they are private and do not have public accompaniments they are just plain unobservable. I wish to comment on this issue–again–more directly.

First, the public-private dichotomy is not a statement of fact. It is an interpretation. It is a statement having its source in a particular scientific system, based on a particular set of assumptions that are unlike those to which I am adhering. Hence, to those who would claim that some events of the psychological domain are private, some public, and this argument is based on the *location* in which the events in each case are held to be taking place, I can say only that we operate on different assumptions and, thereby, find different categories useful. As such, we have no legitimate argument.

Secondly, the notion that some so-called private events have public accompaniments, is not relevant, as intended, to my argument. I am not disputing the claim that subtle events may be more readily inferred when correlated public accompaniments are present. I have no argument with this notion. It is not germane to my point though. On the contrary, I am arguing that subtle, or what Skinner calls private events are themselves directly observable with or without observable accompaniments.

With these clarifications behind us, let me address the issue of observation more fully, as this too is a source of disagreement. At issue here is the dichotomy of the observable and the unobservable. While private events may be response events or stimulus events from the standpoint of the person in whom the event is taking place, from the standpoint of an observer, private events on the part of another person are stimulus events. That is, a private event, as it is known in Skinner's treatment, is a stimulus, or *would be* a stimulus were an observer able to respond to it. Events such as these, while sustaining the naturalistic character of other stimulus events, are said to be unobservable; while stimulus events occurring in the public domain are thought observable, at least in principle. These claims suggest that observability is a property of the stimulus events under consideration. To put it another way, it is held that the observability of an event can be determined by an examination of the event independently of the activities of an observer with respect to it.

Alternatively, I would argue that things and events do not have the property of observability or unobservability in and of themselves. Observation of events is an interaction of stimulating—having its source in the events—and perceptual respond-ing—having its source the observing person. In other words, observation is itself a psychological event and is, as such, subject to the same limitations and elaborations as any other type of psychological event. This is not a particularly controversial argument, I should think. The implications of this argument are not immediately obvious, however, and it is these that I wish to explore.

Let me begin by reiterating the view that psychological interactions are historical and cumulative, as postulated earlier. According to this view, the past interactions of a given individual with the environment exist in the *current* interactions of that individual. Current interactions constitute an end point in the evolution of interactions with the environment, which have evolved over the lifetime of the individual. In other words, a psychological event of the present moment is not an isolated, free standing event, but is instead just the most recent elaboration of an historical continuity of action. (See Hayes, 1992, for further discussion of this issue.)

This argument applies to all events of the psychological domain, including the perceptual events of observation. That is, the seeing, hearing, smelling, tasting or feeling in given acts of observing must be understood as historical acts. The implication here is that what one sees or otherwise observes in the present moment can not be accounted for by appeal to the prevailing stimulating circumstances considered *ahistorically*. What one sees in any given moment must be understood as the current end point in an evolution of seeing acts. This is why we appear younger to ourselves than we do to a stranger; why we see a whole object even though only part of it is directly visible; why eye witness testimonies are subject to doubt despite the absence of motivated biases.

One implication of this analysis is that observation is not an instrument of correspondence truth telling. We do not know the world by virtue of our observation of it. We know about our observation of the world; and there is in this knowledge no dichotomy of the known and the unknown; the public and the private, the internal and the external; or the observable and the unobservable. What we know, rather, varies continuously with the intricacy of the phenomena observed and our reactional histories with respect to them. The more intricate the phenomenon the more extensive a history of interaction with it is required to know it.

A more technical analysis of these events and others like them would entail a discussion of implicit fields (Parrott, 1986), stimulus substitution (Hayes, 1991), and the transfer of stimulus functions (Hayes, 1993; Hayes and Hayes, 1992) which is beyond the scope of the present chapter.

Conclusion

In conclusion, I sing praises for Kantor's subtle event construction as an interpretation of such events as thinking, imagining, reminiscing, and so on. Kantor's analysis of subtle events sustains a coherence with his analyses of more obvious events. More importantly, relative to Skinner's formulation, Kantor's position holds greater promise for understanding, prediction, and control of this complex, human phenomenon.

The analysis suggested by Kantor and elaborated in this chapter interprets private events, including the covert verbal events typically entailed in analyses of thinking, as subtle interactions obtaining between the responding of whole organisms and stimulating environments. They are not, as such, actions of parts of the whole occurring inside the whole, as Skinner's interpretation of private events suggests. Thinking is no more private than walking; and thinking no more occurs in the brain than walking occurs in the legs. The virtue of the present analysis is that it eliminates obstacles to the observation of "private" events; and also renders them subject to *psychological* analysis, both formally and functionally.

References

Hayes, L. J. (1991). Substitution and reference. In L. J. Hayes and P. N. Chase (Eds.), *Dialogues on verbal behavior* (pp. 3-14). Reno: Context Press.

Hayes, L. J. (1992). The psychological present. *The Behavior Analyst, 15,* 139-145.

Hayes, L. J. (1993). Equivalence as process. In S. C. Hayes and L. J. Hayes (Eds.), *Understanding verbal relations* (pp. 97-108). Reno: Context Press.

Hayes, S. C. and Hayes, L. J. (1992). Verbal relations and the evolution of behavior analysis. *American Psychologist, 47,* 1383-1395.

Kantor, J. R. (1924). *Principles of psychology* (Vol. I) Chicago: Principia.

Kantor, J. R. (1950). *Logic and psychology.* (Vol. II) Chicago: Principia.

Kantor, J. R. (1959). *Interbehavioral psychology.* Chicago: Principia.

Kantor, J. R. and Smith, N. W. (1975). *The science of psychology: An interbehavioral survey.* Chicago: Principia.

Parrott, L. J. (1983). Systemic foundations for the concept of "private events": A critique. In N. W. Smith, P. T. Mountjoy and D. H. Ruben (Eds.), *Reassessment if psychology: The interbehavioral alternative* (pp. 251-268). Washington: University Press of America.

Parrott, L. J. (1986.) The role of postulation in the analysis of inapparent events. In
    H. W. Reese and L. J. Parrott (Eds.), *Behavior science: Philosophical, methodological
    and empirical advances* (pp. 35-60). Hillsdale, NJ: Erlbaum.
Skinner, B. F. (1938). *The behavior of organisms.* New York: Appleton-Century-Crofts.
Skinner, B. F. (1945). The operational analysis of psychological terms. In A. C.
    Catania and S. Harnad, (Eds.) (1988). *The selection of behavior* (pp. 150-163).
    Cambridge, MA: Cambridge University Press.
Skinner, B. F. (1953). *Science and human behavior.* New York: McMillan.
Skinner, B. F. (1957). *Verbal behavior.* New York: Appleton-
Century-Crofts.
Skinner, B. F. (1969). *Contingencies of reinforcement.* New York: Appleton-Century-
    Crofts.
Skinner, B. F. (1974). *About behaviorism.* New York: Knopf.

Footnote

1 *The term "thinking" is used in this chapter in a generic sense to refer to events commonly
understood as thinking, imagining, reminiscing, and so on. Such events are commonly viewed
as having verbal character to some degree and are held to be hidden from view in some way.
Events of this sort are among those to which Skinner refers with the term "private events."
Skinner's technical analysis of thinking, as it occurs in the book* Verbal Behavior *(Skinner,
1957, pp. 432-452), does not conclude that the term thinking refers to such events, but instead
to behavior, verbal or nonverbal, covert or overt. The present chapter addresses thinking events
when they are among the subclass of behaviors regarded as having the character of being verbal
and covert.*

Chapter 10

"Lying"

Masaya Sato and Naoko Sugiyama
Keio University

Behavior Analysis consists of three parts: the conceptual analysis of behavior, the experimental analysis of behavior, and applied behavior analysis. An important goal of the conceptual analysis of behavior is to redefine behavior analytically the ordinary usage of language terms describing behavioral events. To redefine such terms is to identify the behavioral process of behavioral events which generate discriminative stimuli controlling the usage of the word.

The conceptual analysis of everyday language could contribute to the development of behavior analysis in two respects. First, it may clarify behavioral processes to be studied through experimental analysis. Second, it may help reconstruct cognitive psychology from the view point of behavior analysis. Cognitive psychology has provided very interesting information about behavior but is risks becoming a kind of lay psychology because it takes in everyday language thoughtlessly without redefining lay terms in its own framework. Those ordinary words remain as

---

Table 1 - Dictionary Definitions of "Lie" as a Noun

- an untrue deceptive statement deliberately used to mislead. (Collins Dictionary of the English Language)

- an untrue statement purposely made to deceive. (Longman Dictionary of Contemporary English - New Ed.)

- a statement that the speaker knows to be untrue. (Oxford American English Dictionary.)

- a false statement or piece of information deliberately presented as being true: a falsehood. (The American Heritage Dictionary of the English Language - New College Ed.)

- an intentionally false statement. (The Concise Oxford Dictionary - New Ed.)

- a false statement made with deliberate intent to deceive: a falsehood. (The Random House College Dictionary - Rev. Ed.)

---

mentalistic as ever in cognitive psychology, because cognitive psychology has no firm conceptual framework to construct psychological phenomena within a unified whole.

In this paper, we are trying to analyze conceptually an ordinary word, "lying." Lying is a very interesting theme but it has been seldom discussed, whether by behavior analysts and cognitive psychologists (Parsons, 1989). We will also present some empirical data on the topic.

Definition of "Lie"

What is a lie? Let us begin by examining six dictionary definitions, as shown in Table 1. All of the definitions listed in Table 1 are defined with everyday language. The definitions share much in common, and have as a central theme that a lie is a false statement with intentionality. Thus, to analyze "lie" conceptually we must analyze two more ordinary terms, "a false statement" and "intentionality."

First, let us consider "a false statement." Table 2 shows six statements. Which are the false statements among them ?

If a statement that does not correspond to a state of affairs in the objective world is a false statement, Statements 2, 4, and 6 are false. Conversely, if a statement that does not correspond to subjective knowledge of the world is a false statement, Statements 2 and 3 are false, and we cannot judge whether Statements 5 or 6 are true or false. They are "irresponsible statements."

We can make a false statement when we are talking about our own behavior for the future. Table 3 shows twelve statements. Which are the false statements among them?

If a statement that does not correspond to actual behavior—a state of affairs in the objective world—is a false statement, Statements 2, 3, 6, 7, 10, and 11 are false.

Table 2 - False or True Statement? (1)

When it rains,

1. a person knows it and tells someone "It is raining now."

2. a person knows it but tells someone "It isn't raining now."

3. a person doesn't think so but tells someone "it is raining now."

4. a person doesn't think so and tells someone "It isn't raining now."

5. a person has no knowledge whether it is raining or not and tells someone "it is raining now."

6. a person has no knowledge whether it is raining or not and tells someone "It isn't raining now."

Conversely, if a statement that does not correspond to his own intention–subjective knowledge of the world–is a false statement, Statements 3, 4, 5, and 6 are false, and Statements 9, 10, 11, and 12 are irresponsible.

In this way, when we judge whether a statement is truth or false, we can set two different standards: whether the statement corresponds to a state of affairs in the objective world, or whether the statement correspond to subjective knowledge of the world. We can call a false statement judged by the first standard "an objectively false statement" and a false statement by the second standard "a subjectively false statement."

Table 3 - False or True Statement? (2)

---

1. A person invited to a party was planing to attend it and replied "I will join you." And he attends it.

2. A person invited to a party was planning to attend it and replied "I will join you." But he is absent.

3. A person invited to a party was planning to attend it but he replied "I cannot join you." But he attends it.

4. A person invited to a party was planning to attend it but he replied "I cannot join you." And he is absent.

5. A person invited to a party was planning to decline it, but he replied "I will join you." And he attends it.

6. A person invited to a party was planning to decline it, but he replied "I will join you." And he is absent.

7. A person invited to a party was planning to decline it and he replied "I cannot join you." But he attends it.

8. A person invited to a party was planning to decline it and he replied "I cannot join you." And he is absent.

9. A person invited to a party was in two minds about attending it and he replied "I will join you." And he attends it.

10. A person invited to a party was in two minds about attending it and he replied "I will join you." But he is absent.

11. A person invited to a party was in two minds about attending it and he replied "I cannot join you." But he attends it.

12. A person invited to a party was in two minds about attending it and he replied "I cannot join you."

Behavioral Processes of "Lying"

Objectively False Statement

Now, let us consider the behavioral processes that might bring about an "objectively false statement" in terms of controlling variables. In a verbal community, a verbal response "X" is reinforced in the presence of a physical stimulus X and a verbal response "Y" is reinforced in the presence of a physical stimulus Y. We may call this contingency the "prevailing contingency." However people sometimes tell a lie. They emit verbal response "Y", instead of "X", in the presence of the stimulus X.

Table 4 shows eight behavioral processes that could bring about objectively false statements. In each of the top five processes, a verbal response "Y" is emitted in the presence of a physical stimuli X. In each of the bottom three processes, a verbal response "not X" or "other than X" is emitted in the same condition.

Process 1 brings about the verbal response "Y" emitted as a mand independent of stimulus control. An additional contingency controlling the false statement in this process is that it has been strongly reinforced in the presence of a physical stimulus Y. This additional contingency is a personal contingency experienced by the speaker in the past, even though there is aloso a prevailing contingency in the speaker's verbal community in which true statements are reinforced. A false statement occurs when the statement is controlled by the additional contingency rather than by the prevailing contingency.

Process 2 brings about the verbal response "Y" emitted as an inaccurate tact in the presence of physical stimuli X. The additional contingency controlling the inaccurate tact is that it has been reinforced for some reason in the presence of X and thus $S^D(X)$ generated by the physical stimulus X controls the response "Y."

In Process 3, the verbal response "Y" is emitted as a generalized tact. The additional contingency controlling the response is as follows: a verbal response "Y" has been reinforced and/or a verbal response "X" to a physical stimulus X has been punished or extinguished. As a result, the functional stimulus $S^D(X)$ generated by the physical stimulus X comes to control a verbal response "Y."

In Process 4, a verbal response "Y" is emitted as a mistaken tact. In this case, the physical stimulus X generated not $S^D(X)$ but for some reason generated $S^D(Y)$.

Process 5 is related to conditional discrimination. In the process, a verbal response "Y" is emitted as conditionally discriminated tact. A verbal response "X" to a physical stimulus X has been reinforced without condition L and a response "Y" to the stimulus x has been reinforced with condition L. The additional contingency results in $S^D(X \mid L)$ being generated by the physical stimulus X in combination with the condition L. The S^D comes to control the verbal response "Y."

Process 6 brings about a false statement "not X" or some statement other than "X" as an autoclitic in the presence of stimulus X. The additional contingency is that a verbal response "X" has been punished in the presence of stimulus X. It results in X generating an $S^D(X)$ that controls a covert response "X."

Table 4: Classification of Behavioral Processes that Produce Objectively False Statements

	Additional Contingency	Physical Stimulus	Functional Stimulus	Other Cntrllng Variable	Verbal Respons	Behavioral Process	Sub. False Statmt	Inten- tion- ality
1	Y: "Y" » extra RFT	X	-	EO	"Y"	Mand		
2	X: "Y" » RFT	X	Sd (X)		"Y"	Inaccurate Tact	x	
3	Y: "Y" » RFT &/or X: "X" » EXT or PNSHMNT	X	Sd (X)		"Y"	Generalized Tact	x	
4		X	Sd (Y)		"Y"	Mistaken Tact		
5	X | L: "X" » RFT & X | L: "Y" » RFT	X & L	Sd (X | L)		"Y"	Conditionally Discriminated Tact	x	
6	X: "X" » PNSHMNT	X	Sd [Sd (X) » covert "X"]		"not X"; other than "X"	Autoclitic	x	
7	Situation to tell a lie: lying » RFT	X & S (s.l.)	Sd (X), Sd (s.l.), & Sd [Sd (X) » covert "X"]		"not X"; other than "X"	An instance of lying operant	x	
8	[Situation to tell a lie & rule "lie now will get RFT" or "lie now will avoid PNSHMNT"]: lying » RFT	X & S (s.l.)	Sd (X), Sd (s.l.), & Sd [Sd (X) » covert "X"] & Sd [RULE "lie now will get RFT" or "lie now will avoid PNSHMNT"]	EO	"not X"; other than "X"	An instance of rule-governed operant	x	x

The additional contingency in Process 7 is that lying has been reinforced in a specific situation where lying is always reinforced either positively or negatively. Two functional stimuli, $S^D(X)$ and S^D(situation to tell a lie, or s.l. in the table) control "not X" or some statement other than "X" as a lying operant. It remains to be seen whether lying as a higher-order operant really exists. But if so, autoclitics are related to the lying operant.

In Process 8, the additional contingencies are a situation to tell a lie and a rule "If I tell a lie now, I will get reinforcement and /or avoid punishment." The functional stimuli controlling the false statement are three stimuli; $S^D(X)$, S^D(situation to tell a lie), and S^D(RULE). The response "not X" or some statement other than "X" is a rule-governed response. In this process, autoclitics are related to the response.

We have illustrated eight behavioral processes that bring about "objectively false statements." All of them are defined in terms of the additional contingency that establishes certain functional stimuli. Most of them are discriminated operants.

Sato, Sakagami, & Sugiyama (1988) further divided the discriminated operant into non-transferable and transferable types. The transferable operant can be controlled by a stimulus or compound stimulus under which the operant never has been reinforced. The non-transferable operant can be controlled only by the stimulus under which the operant has been reinforced.

The non-transferable operant can be further divided into simple discriminated operant and conditional discriminated operant. The transferable operant can be also further divided into a conceptual operant and generalized operant. A generalized operant is a higher-order operant such as stimulus equivalence, rule-governed behavior, and the autoclitic. If a "lying operant" exists, it could be a kind of generalized operant.

We find only two experimental studies of lying in operant literature (Lanza, Starr, & Skinner, 1982; Ribeiro, 1989). Both pigeons' lying in the former study and children's lying in the latter are regarded as a simple discriminated operant in our framework.

In the study of Lanza, Starr, and Skinner (1982), two pigeons were taught to use symbols to communicate information about hidden colors to each other. When reporting red was more generously reinforced than reporting yellow or green, both birds passed through a period in which they "lied" by reporting another color as red. In this experiment, the speaker's response was only arbitrary matching to sample in which sample stimuli were the three colors. Arbitrary matching is not considered to be a conditional discrimination but rather a simple discrimination in our framework (Sato, et al., 1988). Arbitrary matching to sample is a what Jack Micael calls a "stimulus-selection based tact." If it corresponds to a topography-based tact in natural language, then it must be a simple discriminated operant, not a conditional discriminated operant, because the topography-based tact (for example emitting a verbal response "red" to red color) is clearly a simple discriminated operant. If choosing a card on which a word "red" is written is reinforced in the presence of red color, the "red card choosing operant" is shaped. The red card choosing operant comes to a discriminated operant controlled by an S^D generated by the red color.

In the experiment of Lanza et al. (1982), when reporting red was more generously reinforced than reporting yellow or green, both birds passed through a period in which they "lied" by reporting another color as red. Which behavioral processes, the first or the third in Table 4, brought about the pigeons' lying? The first is that a previously simple discriminated operant comes to function as a mand–as non-discriminated operant. The third is that tacting "red" to a red stimulus as a simple discriminated operant generalizes to yellow or green color. We cannot conclude which process brought about the pigeons' lying only by the result of this experiment.

In his study of lying in young children, Ribeiro (1989) allowed them to play with as many as three of six different toys and then had another experimenter ask whether they had played with each. When reports were made in the absence of experimenter reinforcement, or were consistently reinforced, they always correct. However, when any report of play was reinforced regardless of actual behavior, some children began to report play with all six toys, even though no more than three had been played with. The children's tacting became inaccurate, because of lack of differential reinforcement in Process 2 in Table 4. Of course, it is possible that lying in humans have something to do with a higher-order process like Process 7 or Process 8 in Table 4. But we can analyze this experiment only in terms of the process of the simple discriminated operant, although many researchers tend to regard lying as more complex higher-order behavior.

When we analyze the discriminated operant in terms of "lying", many problems to be solved even in the simple discriminated operant comes to light. Both Skinner (1957, pp. 149-150) and Keller & Schoenfeld (1950, P. 392) regarded lying as a distorted tact. The distorted tact can be brought about by various behavioral processes, such as Processes 1, 2, 3, and 4 in Table 4. We have to analyze the distorted tact deeply in terms of the additional contingency. The simple discriminated operant has not been analyzed enough, let alone the conditionally discriminated operant and the transferable operant.

Subjectively False Statement

Next, let us consider the "subjectively false statement." From the view point of behavior analysis, it can be defined as a verbal response other than "X" in the presence of a physical stimulus X, although one of the functional discriminative stimuli is $S^D(X)$ generated by the physical stimulus X. Based on this definition, we can exclude Statements 1 and 4 in Table 4 from the subjectively false statement.

Questionnaire Study

We have logically distinguished the objectively false statement from the subjectively subjectively false one. In everyday life, how do we think of these two dimensions? When we judge a statement to be a "lie," is it objectively false or subjectively false ? To analyze this question, we had 64 undergraduate students judge the statements shown in Table 2 using a questionnaire.

Table 5 shows the result. It is clear that the judgments differ from individual to individual, but there are some themes in the data. The statement in Question 3 is

---

Table 5 - False or True Statement? (1)

	Percentages Saying the Statement is a			
	Lie	**Not a Lie**	**Neither**	**No Idea**
When it rains . . .				
1. a person knows it and tells someone "It is raining now."	0	100	0	0
2. a person knows it but tells someone "It isn't raining now."	94	0	6	0
3. a person doesn't think so but tells someone "it is raining now."	66	22	13	0
4. a person doesn't think so and tells someone "It isn't raining now."	17	70	9	3
5. a person has no knowledge whether it is raining or not and tells someone "it is raining now."	27	36	38	0
6. a person has no knowledge whether it is raining or not and tells someone " It isn't raining now."	55	11	33	2

---

* *columns may not sum to 100 due to rounding*

subjectively false while the statement in Question 4 is objectively false. 7.8% of the students (5 of 64) judged that both were lies. Half (32 students) judged only the statement in Question 3, the subjective false statement, to be a lie. 9.4% (6 students) judged only the statement in Question 4 to be a lie. 10.9% of them (7 of 64) judged neither statement to be a lie. In their view, a person tells a lie, when the statement is false *both* objectively and subjectively.

Next, let us consider answers to Questions 5 and 6. Both are irresponsible statements. 26.6% (17 of 64) judged both to be lies. 9.4% (six students) judged neither to be a lie. None of the students judged only the statement in Question 5 (the objectively true but irresponsible statement) to be a lie, while 21.9% of them (14 of 64) judged only the objectively false statement in Question 6 to be a "lie." Thus, in general, irresponsible statements were much more likely to be viewed as "lies" when they were objectively false. 29.7% of the the respondents (19 of 64) could not judge whether the irresponsible statements in Questions 5 and 6 were lies or not.

Judging a statement as a lie or not differed with individuals. On the whole, however, there were three major clusters of response patterns. One group, representing 21.9 % of the students (14 of 64), judged subjectively false statements and irresponsible statements to be "lies." A second group, representing 15.6% of the respondents (10 of 64), judged subjectively false statements to be "lies" but viewed irresponsible statement as ambiguous. A third group, representing 14.1% of the raters (9 of 64) judged all objectively false statements–including irresponsible ones– to be "lies."

A similar pattern was shown in the evaluation of statements about one's own behavior in the future. The statements shown earlier in Table 3about a person responding to an invitation to a party were rated by 65 students in a fashion similar to the judgements just described. Table 6 shows those results. Interestingly, many students felt that a statement such as "I will join you" is a lie, even if the persons *does* attend the party, so long as the person was not planning to attend it. Thus "intention" was an important component of the questions.

Intentionality

Let us now consider the issue of "intentionality." When we judge whether a behavior is done with intention, the judgment might vary according to whose behavior it is, our own behavior or the other's behavior. For example, a pigeon's key pecking reinforced by food might be regarded as a behavior with intention by layman other than most behavior analysts. However, it is impossible to tell whether the pigeon itself regards its own behavior as intentional behavior, because the pigeon has no verbal repertoire. We will give another example. A woman becomes indifferent to a man. It is possible that the man regards it as intentional behavior, while the woman never does so. In this way, "intentionality" is an ambiguous concept without objectivity. But it would be valid to say that a person behaves with intention, when he or she has thought of doing so before doing it. Based on this

Table 6
False or True Statement? (2)

	Lie	Not a Lie	Neither	No Idea
	Percentages Saying the Statement is a			

A person invited to a party was planing to attend it . . .

	Lie	Not a Lie	Neither	No Idea
l. replied "I will join you." And he attends it.	0	100	0	0
2. replied "I will join you." But he is absent.	45	29	25	2
3. replied "I cannot join you." But he attends it.	68	8	23	2
4. replied "I cannot join you." And he is absent.	22	51	25	3

A person invited to a party was planning to decline it . . .

	Lie	Not a Lie	Neither	No Idea
6. replied "I will join you." And he attends it.	25	49	22	5
7. replied "I will join you." But he is absent.	89	0	11	0
8. replied "I cannot join you." But he attends it. *	45	32	18	2
9. replied "I cannot join you." And he is absent.	0	100	0	0

A person invited to a party was in two minds about attending it . . .

	Lie	Not a Lie	Neither	No Idea
l. replied "I will join you." And he attends it.	8	77	14	2
2. replied "I will join you." But he is absent.	74	3	20	3
3. replied "I cannot join you." But he attends it.	58	9	26	6
4. replied "I cannot join you." And he is absent.	9	78	11	2

* two of the respondents did not answer this question. Otherwise, columns may not add to 100 due to rounding.

definition, we can judge our own behavior intentional or not, but we can only infer others' intentionality.

Can this definition of intentionality be translated into behavior-analytic terms? "Thinking of doing something" before doing it actually is a covert verbal behavior. Behavior whose S^D is a stimulus generated by covert verbal behavior is rule-governed behavior in its broad sense. So, rule-governed behavior is behavior with intention. Based on this definition, only Process 8 in Table 4 is behavior with intention.

We sometimes tell a lie with intention, but not always. Sometimes one tells a lie in spite of oneself. Telling a lie in spite of oneself is brought about by any behavioral processes from 1 to 7 in Table 4.

Irony

We make another false statement called *irony* in everyday life. It raises some interesting issues for our analysis. Irony is the use of words to convey the opposite of their literal meaning. We could call it a kind of false statement.

What is an irony? We can start once again by looking up the dictionary definitions, as is shown in Table 7.

Table 7
Definitions of "Irony"

- the humorous or mildly sarcastic use of words to imply the opposite of what they normally mean. (Collins Dictionary of the English Language)

- use of words which are clearly opposite to one's meaning, usu. either in order to be amusing or to show annoyance. (Longman Dictionary of Contemporary English - New Ed.)

- the expression of one's meaning by using words of opposite meaning in order to make one's remarks forceful as that will please him (used of something that will not please him). (Oxford American English Dictionary.)

- the use of words to convey the opposite of their literal meaning. (The American Heritage Dictionary of the English Language - New College Ed.)

- an expression of meaning, often humorous or sarcastic, by the use of language of a different or opposite tendency. (The Concise Oxford Dictionary - New Ed.)

- a figure of speech in which the words express a meaning that is often the direct opposite of the intended meaning. (The Random House College Dictionary - Rev. Ed.)

Table 8: Classification of Behavioral Processes that Produce Irony

	Additional Contingency	Physical Stimulus	Functional Stimulus	Other Cntrllng Variable	Verbal Respons	Behavioral Process
1	X | Ī: "X" » RFT & X | I: "op X" » RFT	X & L	Sd (X | I) & Sd [Sd (X) » covert "X"]		"op X"	Conditionally Discriminated Tact
2	Situation to make an ironic remark: making an ironic remark » RFT	X & S (s.l.)	Sd (X), Sd (s.l.), & Sd [Sd (X) » covert "X"]		"op X"	An instance of making an ironic remark operant
3	[Situation to make an ironic remark & rule "irony now will get RFT"]: making an ironic remark » RFT	X & S (s.l.)	Sd (X), Sd (s.l.), & Sd [Sd (X) » covert "X"] & Sd [RULE "irony now will get RFT"]	EO	"op X"	An instance of rule-governed operant

These definitions share much common. They converge on a definition that irony is the expression of one's meaning by using words of opposite meaning in order to be amusing or show annoyance. As a modification of a primary verbal operant to make a specific effect on the listener is an autoclitic, irony can be regarded as a kind of autoclitic.

Table 8 shows behavioral processes bringing about irony. They correspond to behavioral processes 5, 7, and 8 in Table 4 bringing about "lying" respectively.

Many cognitive psychologists has been interested in implicature as well as irony and have proposed various theories, although they hardly pay attention to "lying." Behavior analysts have a firm conceptual framework–behavioral contingency–to analyze psychological phenomena within a unified whole. In using this framework, we have to make an effort to analyze issues both conceptually empirically.

Experimental Analysis

The following is an experiment we performed (Sugiyama & Sato, in preparation). The purpose of the study is two-fold. One is to examine whether normal adults lie in an experimental condition like the children in Ribeiro(1989). The other is to measure lying responses quantitatively using a free-operant paradigm.

Subjects were one female and three male students. We used two rooms for the experiment—one for the subjects and the other for the experimenter to monitor the subjects' behavior. The rooms wereseparated by around 15m, were two of four rooms in the area, and these other rooms were not used for the experiment. In this way, the subjects had no idea that the experimenter would be able to know what they did.

Experimental session consisted of two parts, a time for solving problem in arithmetic and a report time. The subject was bought to the experimental room and told the following instruction.

> I am carrying out research on the ability to do mental arithmetic. I ask you to solve problems in arithmetic for 10 minutes. Each problem will be presented on the TV monitor one by one. You solve the problems and input the solution through the keyboard in front of you. Press the return key and you will be given another problem. If your answer is incorrect, you will hear a beep and you have to solve the same problem until you can get the correct answer. At the head of each problem you can see a consecutive number. After the calculating time, you will be asked how many problems you solved. So, please remember the numeral at the head of the last problem you would solve. You will be paid 100 yen after 10 minutes calculating time. You are expected to solve problems as many as possible during the 10 minutes. Do you have any questions?

During the calculating time, the experimenter went to another room and watched the monitor on which the same material was presented the subject was given. So, the experimenter knew the exact number of the problems the subject had actually solved.

When 10 minutes passed, the experimenter went into the experimental room and asked the subject how many problems he or she had solved. The answer was recorded as the reported number of problems solved, but the number of problem actually solved was also recorded.

This was an experimental condition for baseline. We introduced two other conditions as intervention according to reinforcement contingencies to reporting behavior; reinforcement of lying condition and reinforcement of honesty (do-say correspondence) condition.

In the reinforcement of lying condition, the subjects were paid some money according to the number of solution they reported. The more the reported number was, the more they could get money, regardless of the number of problems actually solved. The amount of payment was decided based on a particular equation. Just after report time, the experimenter calculated the amount of payment quickly based on the equation and provided him or her with money.

In the reinforcement of correspondence condition, the subjects were paid for accurately reporting the number of solutions. The amount of payment came to maximum when he or she reported the exact number of problems actually solved.

These three conditions were introduced sequentially during the report time using multiple baseline design across subjects. Conditions during the time for calculating remained constant throughout the experiment.

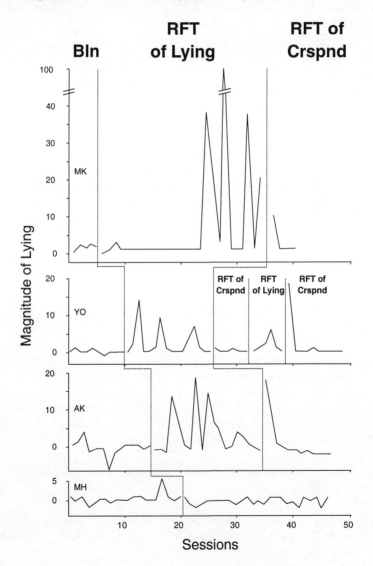

Figure 1. Magnitude of lying (number of problems reported solved minus number actually solved) for each subject in each condition.

Figure 1 shows the magnitude of "lying" in each subject in each session. We defined the magnitude of lying as the difference between the reported number and the number of problems actually solved. In the baseline condition, the magnitude of lying was around zero in all four subjects.

In early sessions in the reinforcement of lying condition, subjects YO, AK started telling lies. YO started lying at the 3rd session and AK at the 4th session. Both

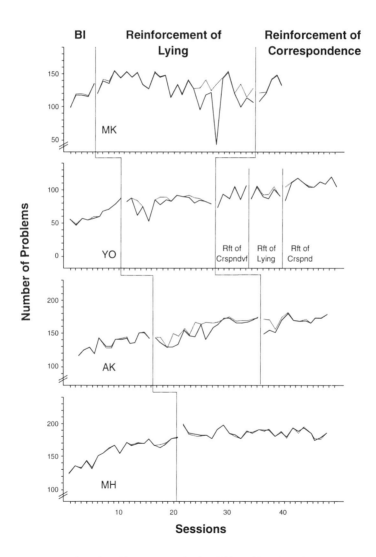

Figure 2. Number of problems reported solved (dotted lines) and number actually solved (solid lines) for each subject in each condition.

of them reported 10 problems more than they actually solved. MK and MH were almost always honest even after many sessions were passed. So, at the 17th session for MK, and at the 36th session for MH, behavior modeling was introduced. A decoy (pretending to be a real subject) solved multiplying problems in front of the subject and reported an inaccurate number and then received a large monetary payoff. Neither subject told a lie under these conditions. At the 22nd session for MK and at the 42nd session for MH, another technique, prompting, was introduced. Another decoy talked to the subject in the absence of the experimenter and told him that he could get more money if he reported completing more problems than the number of problems actually solved.

Two sessions after introducing the prompt, MK started telling lies. The magnitude of lying was significant. At the 27th session, MK reported that he had solved 157 problems, though he had actually solved only 56 problems. He received 1,352 yen (around $13) for the ten minute job.

In the second reinforcement of corespondent condition, honesty returned in the all subjects, although subject MH was always honest throughout the experiment.

In the reinforcement of correspondence condition, all but MH emitted some lying behavior. However, Figure 2 shows they didn't always tell a lie in all sessions during the condition. Each subject reported a relatively constant number during the condition, but they sometimes solved fewer problems than usual and got a bigger payoff than deserved. Figure 2 shows this corner-cutting at Sessions 24 and 27 in MK, sessions 13 and 15 in YO, and session 25 in AK.

Conclusion

Lying is a complex issue and one that has been little analyzed by behavioral psychology, either conceptually or empirically. The present chapter provides one way to begin.

References

Keller, F. S. & Schoenfeld, W. N. (1950). *Principles of psychology*. New York: Appleton-Century-Crofts.

Lanza, R. P., Starr, J., & Skinner, B. F. (1982). "Lying" in the pigeon. *Journal of the Experimental of Behavior, 38*, 201-203.

Parsons, H. M. (1989). Lying. *The Analysis of Verbal Behavior, 7*, 43-47.

Ribeiro, A. (1989). Correspondence in children's' self-report: Tacting and manding aspects. *Journal of the Experimental analysis of Behavior, 51*, 361-367.

Sato, M., Sakagami, T., & Sugiyama, N. (1988). *A behavior analysis of "intelligent" behavior*. Paper presented at the convention of the Association for Behavior Analysis, Philadelphia, PA.

Skinner, B. F. (1957). *Verbal behavior*. New York: Appleton-Century-Crofts.

Chapter 11

Verbal Control of Superstitious Behavior: Superstitions as False Rules

Koichi Ono
Komazawa University

In behavior analysis, the language of superstition sometimes refers to the effects of accidental contingencies on behavior (as in Skinner, 1948). In everyday usage, however, it more often refers to human practices that are reported through verbal behavior. In this chapter we will speak of *superstitions* as rules expressed as verbal behavior, and *superstitious behavior* as nonverbal behavior that may or may not be accompanied by verbal behavior. The relation between superstitions and superstitious behavior can be used to illustrate rules or rule-following in social settings.

A simple example may be helpful for understanding the relation between superstitions and superstitious behavior. Assume a man who likes to eat a lot of spinach whenever his muscles ache. This behavior may be called superstitious behavior. Conversely, if he just says things like, "eating spinach is good for aching muscles," his statement may be called a superstition. Sometimes this type of statement may be spoken by many members of the social community, and sometimes it may be spoken only by one individual. In this example, the behavior of eating spinach may be controlled by one or more of the following possible variables.

A. An accidental contiguity between relief from aching muscles and eating spinach. The muscle ache may once have disappeared some time after the man ate spinach. B. Instructions by a member of community who said that spinach is good for aching muscles. C. His own verbal description (self-instruction), by saying, "I believe that spinach is good for aching muscles."

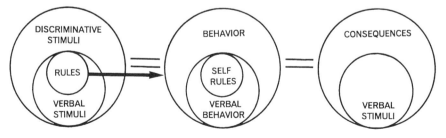

Figure 1. Possible relations between two kinds of behavior and conditions that produce it.

Possible relations between the behavior and the conditions that produce it are shown in Figure 1. Generally speaking, spinach eating is controlled by two main variables. One is three-term contingencies of reinforcement (accidental contingencies in this case); this behavior is contingency-shaped behavior. The other is rules socially presented by others; behavior under the control of rules is called rule-governed behavior. Furthermore, verbal descriptions stated by the individual may control the behavior. In these circumstances, the same individual can be involved in the verbal contingencies for both a listener and a speaker. Thus, superstitions and superstitious behavior involve many issues dealt with by the topic of rule-governed behavior or instructional control in an operant paradigm. The purpose of this chapter is to describe superstitious behavior in relation to such variables as social rules, self-stated rules, and contingencies of reinforcement. Superstitious behavior is a class of operant behavior, so human superstitious behavior can be classified into two types, just like any other variety of operant behavior. These types are contingency-shaped superstitious behavior and rule-governed superstitious behavior.

First, I will discuss studies of contingency-shaped superstitious behavior. Many studies have used nonhuman organisms, and these studies necessarily have not been much concerned with possible verbal components of superstitious behavior. Second, I will describe rule-governed superstitious behavior. In this section, I will begin with the discussion of the characteristics of superstitions as rules and proceed to a review of the major experimental findings on rule-governed behavior or instructional control. Then I will summarize the literature examining the effects of self rules or self-stated rules. Finally, I will describe data from an experiment examining how both social rules and self rules control superstitious behavior in social communication settings such as that illustrated in Figure 1.

Contingency-Shaped Superstitious Behavior

Superstitious behavior has mostly been studied as contingency-shaped behavior. What contingencies can be said to produce superstitious behavior? Since Skinner (1948) defined superstitious behavior in terms of behavior generated by response-independent schedules of reinforcement, subsequent studies have mainly been conducted under these contingencies (e.g., Staddon & Simmelhag, 1971; Fenner, 1980; Timberlake & Lucas, 1985). But some researchers have suggested that superstitious behavior can develop under other contingencies besides response-independent schedules (Brown & Jenkins, 1968; Catania, 1968). For example, Brown and Jenkins (1968) distinguished among three types of superstitious conditioning and then stated:

> Types of superstitious conditioning are classified in terms of procedures, not in terms of behavioral outcomes. ... To say that all three procedures produce superstitious conditioning points only to their common feature; namely, that they entail certain unconditional relations among stimuli, responses, and reinforcements (p. 2).

The rationale of this classification of superstitious behavior seems to be clear and reasonable. Types of superstitious behavior can be distinguished according to where independent relations exist among the three terms of the three-term operant contingency. Figure 2 shows four possible arrangements of such independent contingencies.

The upper two characterize superstitious behavior under the response-independent contingencies, and the lower two under response-dependent contingencies. The first three are the ones suggested by Brown and Jenkins (1968). Three of these kinds of superstitious behavior will be discussed below. Auto-shaping will be excluded because it has been studied in other experimental contexts, even though it is included in superstitious behavior by definition.

《RESPONSE INDEPENDENT》

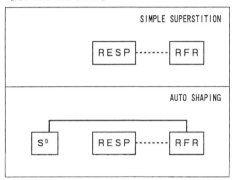

《RESPONSE DEPENDENT》

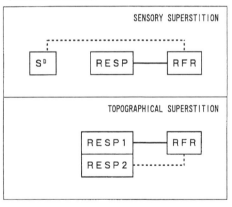

Figure 2. Four types of superstitious behavior. Types of superstitious behavior can be distinguished according to where independent relations exist among three terms of three term contingencies of reinforcement. The upper two characterize superstitious behavior under response independent contingencies, and the lower two under response-dependent contingencies.

Simple Superstitious Behavior

Simple superstitious behavior develops in a contingency in which the delivery of a reinforcer is independent of behavior or of the stimulus that is present. Research on the effects of response-independent food delivery on nonhuman behavior has been controversial with regard to the properties of superstitious behavior. Skinner (1948) demonstrated that pigeons developed idiosyncratic and stereotyped superstitious behavior under fixed time 15 second schedules of reinforcement and explained this behavior in terms of accidental reinforcement.

In contrast to Skinner (1948), Staddon and Simmelhag (1971) found that pigeons rarely showed specific superstitious behavior during intervals of periodic feeding. Instead, they pecked frequently on the magazine wall. Staddon and Simmelhag (1971) argued that the superstitious responses described by Skinner (1948) were members of a class of terminal responses elicited in anticipation of food rather than accidentally reinforced, and they rejected the view that a reinforcer automatically strengthens any operant that precedes it.

Fenner (1980) and Timberlake and Lucas (1985) failed to replicate the

Staddon and Simmelhag (1971) finding that pigeons pecked on the magazine wall at the end of fixed-time intervals. Their data showed consistent wall-directed behavior instead of wall pecking at the end of intervals. Timberlake and Lucas (1985) proposed the alternative explanation that wall-directed behavior under periodic delivery of food is derived from components of species-typical patterns of appetitive behavior related to feeding.

Most research on nonhuman performance under periodic food delivery, including recent studies by Eldridge, Pear, Torgrud, and Evers (1988) and by Justice and Looney (1990), has been concerned with steady state responding. But these studies make limited contributions to our understanding of human superstitious behavior, because human superstitious behavior often seems to be established before long-term exposure to contingencies. It therefore may be important to examine more about the effects of accidental reinforcement from Skinner's original viewpoint. Contrary to the steady state data from nonhumans, studies of human superstitious behavior have shown idiosyncratic and stereotyped superstitious behavior under response-independent contingencies (e.g. Ono, 1987; Wagner & Morris, 1987).

Sensory Superstition

Sensory superstitions develop under contingencies in which the presentation of reinforcers depends on behavior but not on existing antecedent stimuli. Sensory superstitions were first described by Morse and Skinner (1957). When two stimuli were alternated irregularly independently of behavior and reinforcers, the two stimuli often produced different response rates. For example, three pigeons were first exposed to variable interval (VI) 30 minute schedules under orange light. During very long sessions (6-20 hours a day), the key light was changed to blue for 4 minutes per hour. Though the change of the key light had no effect on reinforcement contingencies, response rates increased or decreased during the blue light.

Starr and Staddon (1982) and others (Blue, Sherman, & Pierrel, 1971; Kello, Innis, & Staddon, 1975; Kiefer, 1965; Lander, 1968) have also demonstrated sensory superstitions. Three explanations of this effect have been offered. The first is that different reinforcement rates during the two stimuli in early sessions may cause the different response rates. The second is a history effect in which organisms learn to respond with high rates or low rates during a specific stimulus. The third appeals to an endogenous stimulus effect in which pigeons just tend to respond faster or slower in the presence of some stimuli. Though Starr and Staddon (1982) argue that the endogenous effect is the most important, the possibility that contingencies play a crucial role has not yet been ruled out. In particular, historical effects of discriminative stimuli may be profoundly related to kinds of superstitious behavior.

Topographical Superstition

This type of superstition develops under contingencies in which reinforcers are depend on both antecedents and behavior. In this case, the independent relation exists between such secondary properties of responses as response topography, response sequence, response rate, and response duration and reinforcers.

Catania (1968) called this type of behavior "topographical superstition" and defined it as a superstition in which reinforcement produces and maintains a response topography that varies over a much narrower range than that specified by the limits of the operant class. A specific sequence of behavior developed under concurrent schedules can be also considered as a kind of topographical superstition (Bruner & Revusky, 1961; Catania & Cutts, 1963; Zeiler, 1970).

Herrnstein (1966) stated that the development of such non-instrumental aspects of instrumental behavior in humans correspond to those individual differences discussed as style or preference. Such behavior, however, deserves to be called superstition not only by definition but also on the basis of experimental data. For example, all subjects in the experiment by Bruner and Revusky (1961) who engaged in responding on four concurrent telegraph keys reported being convinced that reinforcers could be obtained only by a pattern of responses on at least one collateral key that "set up" the reinforced key. These statements demonstrate that topographical superstitions should not be limited to those properties called style or preference.

Rule-Governed Superstitious Behavior

Rule-governed superstitious behavior is the behavior that is controlled by the verbal stimulus called a 'superstition'. Superstitions may be regarded as kind of rules because in both form and function they include many properties of rules. To the extent that such superstitions are verbal, they may be distinguished from other rules by whether they are true or false. Before discussing the characteristics of superstition, it may be useful to summarize how rules can be described. In general, rules are specified by the following four criteria.

(1) Rules are defined functionally as antecedent verbal stimuli, rather than by topographic or syntactic forms. Therefore, the most distinguishing attribute of rules pertains to the control they exert upon the first opportunity that an organism has to behave toward a novel problem (Andronis, 1991). Concerning this function of rules, Skinner (1966, 1969) also defined rules as contingency-specifying stimuli (an object in the environment) and stated:

> As a discriminative stimulus, a rule is effective as part of a set of contingencies of reinforcement. A complete specification must include the reinforcement which has shaped the topography of a response and brought it under the control of the stimulus (Skinner, 1966, p. 244).

Rules, however, do not necessarily qualify as discriminative stimuli even though they function as verbal antecedents, because whether rule-following occurs in the presence of a rule is often ambiguous (Catania, 1992; Schlinger & Blakely, 1987). As long as they function as verbal antecedents, verbal stimuli such as instructions, commands, advice, warnings, laws, folklore, maxims, proverbs, and superstitions are assumed to have the same roles as rules (Skinner, 1974, pp. 132-141).

(2) Rules may be distinguished from other verbalizations (for example, simple tacts) by their concentration on relations between two or more events. Therefore, rules can be said to be words that state a relation. Otherwise, a rule is said to describe

or specify a contingency of reinforcement (Skinner, 1969, 1974). In most cases, the relation is between behavior and consequences. But in some cases, the relation is between a number of behaviors (as when the rules of a game specify a sequence of movements). And in other cases, the rule states relations among stimulus events (scientific principles).

(3) Rules can be divided into two categories of verbal operants: tacts and mands. Reese and Fremouw (1984) describe these as descriptive rules and prescriptive rules. A descriptive rule does not specify particular behavior for the listener (for example, principles, laws of nature, etc.). A prescriptive rules, on the other hand, describes a relation that ought to exist in the listener's behavior (for example, laws, commands, advice, guidelines).

(4) Another distinction between kinds of rules is that between social rules (rules states by others) and self rules (self-stated or self-generated rules). This derives from the fact that a person can be both listener and speaker; that is, a person may listen to a rule related to a certain contingency, and at the same time, the person may verbalize his or her own rule about the same contingency. The distinction between social rules and self rules may sometimes be difficult because self rules are originally the verbal behavior of the speaker and sometimes they work in turn as verbal antecedents, whereas social rules are usually just verbal antecedents. But social rules may become especially effective when, because the speaker repeats them to himself or herself, they become self rules.

Characteristics of Superstitions

There seems to be no objection to the idea that superstitions are a kind of rule. Then the critical characteristic of superstitions that distinguish them from other rules may be that superstitions are false rules. Sometimes, folklore, maxims and proverbs are regarded as the same type of rules as superstitions because of their socially maintained style. However, such rules as folklore, maxims, proverbs, are distinguished from superstitions because they are not always false. When they are not false, they may be useful for people.

Furthermore, all false rules cannot be called superstitions; that is, some wrong instructions or inaccurate commands may not be taken as superstitions, though the classification may sometimes be difficult. Being false is a necessary but not a sufficient condition for a superstition. The extent to which a rule is false may depend on the extent to which the rule describes a contingency accurately. In following some cases, a rule may not be called false.

A. A rule can be called a false rule if it describes an independent relation between behavior and consequences as a dependent relation, and vice versa in a few cases. Typical superstitions are this type. B. A rule may be a false rule when it represents a contingency that works in other circumstances but does not work in the present circumstances. For example, the rule was accurate before, but not accurate now. Or the rule is accurate there, but not accurate here. C. A rule may also be called false if it represents only a restricted part of the contingency or if it represents the contingency with extra attributes.

The Effects of Rules on Behavior: Experimental Findings

As a verbal antecedent, how does a rule work on behavior? These issues were initially examined in studies of the effect of instructions on behavior and then in studies on the topic of schedule sensitivity. From the mid-1970s, instructions and instruction following began to be equated with rules and rule-governed behavior, respectively. Is there any difference between the two terms, instructions and rules? In most cases, authors seem to use these two words without any distinction. However, it may be useful to differentiate between the two words as follows; that is, a rule is a description of contingencies while an instruction is a presentation of rules. As there are many reviews of experimental findings about instructional control or rule-governed behavior (e.g., Hayes, 1989), here I will look briefly at experimental findings on how social rules control behavior, and how self rules work.

The Effects of Social Rules

(1) Accurate instructions efficiently control the behavior of verbal organisms (Ayllon & Azrin, 1964; Baron, Kaufman, & Stauber, 1969; Weiner, 1970).

(2) Instructed behavior often interferes with human sensitivity to changing conditions. This research suggests that rules stated by the experimenter can evoke behavior that is neither efficient nor truly sensitive to programmed contingencies, especially when the contingencies change. These studies also show that instructions tend to interfere with responding to changed environments, especially when the changes are ambiguous (Buskist, Bennett, & Miller, 1981; Buskist & Miller, 1986; Galizio, 1979; Hayes, Brownstein, Zettle, Rosenfarb, & Korn, 1986; Kaufman, Baron, & Kopp, 1966; LeFrancois, Chase & Joyce, 1988; Matthews, Shimoff, Catania, & Sagvolden, 1977; Shimoff, Catania, & Matthews, 1981).

(3) The sensitivity of instructed behavior to changing conditions is most likely to occur when responding under previous conditions is punished and changes in behavior are reinforced. Galizio's (1979) results also indicate that once control is established by instructional stimuli, responding is likely to be maintained in that form until notable discrepancies between the rule and the programmed contingencies occur.

(4) Disrupting the social aspects of the contingencies that are part of the instructions is likely to lead to sensitivity to changing conditions (Hayes, Brownstein, Zettle, Rosenfarb, & Korn, 1986).

(5) A history of responding to a variety of instructions is likely to increase the subject's sensitivity to changing conditions (Hayes, Brownstein, Zettle, Rosenfarb, & Korn, 1986; LeFrancois, Chase, & Joyce, 1988).

(6) The variability of behavior when the contingencies change seems to be a critical factor for producing sensitive behavior (Joyce & Chase, 1990).

The Effects of Self Rules

(1) Self rules (self stated rules) are usually consistent with performance on schedules, and these self rules are sometimes correlated with the insensitivity of

human behavior to changes in schedules of reinforcement (Bentall, Lowe, & Beasty, 1985; Harzem, Lowe, & Bagshaw, 1978; Leander, Lippman, & Meyer, 1968; Lippman & Meyer, 1967; Lowe, 1979, 1983; Lowe, Beasty, & Bentall, 1983; Lowe, Harzem, & Bagshaw, 1978). These results imply that if subjects describe their behavior and their behavior is consistent with the description, we can safely assume that their descriptions do not distort what they are doing and we can probably assume that if behavior changes with changes in experimental conditions, so self rules will also change consistently, and vice versa (Catania, Matthews, & Shimoff, 1982).

(2) Stating a self rule can lead to schedule control. Rosenfarb, Newland, Brannon, and Howey (1992) demonstrated that if subjects were asked to verbalize self-generated rules, control by schedule contingencies was likely to develop more quickly than for subjects not asked to verbalize rules.

(3) Shaped self rules may evoke responding that does not change when contingencies change even though the shaped self rules are contrary to the schedule (Catania, Matthews, & Shimoff, 1982).

The material reviewed in this section identified two kinds of rules: one is the ordinary rule given by others, and the other is the rule which an individual states to himself or herself. We have also seen that the effects of each type of rule have been studied separately in previous studies. In contrast, the following experiment treats these two types of rules simultaneously and examines the effects of each type rules on schedule performance during successive interpersonal communication.

Experiment

Two persons were engaged in the experiment at the same time; one was a real subject and the other was a dummy subject (partner). The real subject did not know that. Each person was apparently exposed to a differential reinforcement of high rate (DRH) schedule (actually, the partner was not required to respond). At every change of turn, the subject had to leave a message for the next person about what was the best way to get points, or how the next person should pull the lever.

Messages from the partner are called "social rules," and messages to the partner by the subject are called "self rules." Four different social rules given by the partner in successive phases were all false rules, in that they did not represent the actual contingencies. Therefore this experiment may have some implications for the issue of verbal control of superstitious behavior.

Method

Subjects. Eight pairs consisting of a subject and a partner were assigned to the experimental group, and five subjects are assigned to the control group. They were all university students.

Apparatus. In the experimental room, one large lever was installed on a table. Pulling its pole forward and returning to the right position was regarded as a appropriate response. Three walls were placed on the table around the lever. On the front wall, one orange lamp and a point counter were installed for presenting reinforcers. On the left side wall, one green lamp for a discriminative stimulus and a message board for communication were installed. Scheduling and recording equipment was in an adjacent room.

Procedure. A DRH schedule that required 5 responses per 15 seconds ran continuously throughout the experiment. If the subject responded more than 5 times per 15 seconds, the reinforcement lamp was lit for 5 seconds and the subjects received a point at the end of a trial. Otherwise, the trial ended with five seconds of blackout. Each subject was exposed to this schedule for 9 trials at a time (a total of 3 minutes).

The minimum unit of the experiment was a round. The experiment started with a partner's turn though the partner did not actually engage in the schedule performance. The real subject waited in a waiting room while partner was in an experimental room and wrote a dummy message. Next, after 4 to 5 minutes passed, the experimenter took the partner to the waiting room and brought the subject to the experimental room. Then the subject read the partner's message (social rule) and thereafter engaged in 3 minutes of the schedule performance. After the performance, the subject wrote a message to the partner (self rule) and thereafter took turns with the partner. Both the real subject and the partner were instructed to get as many points as possible by pulling the lever in the right way when the green light was on. They were also asked to write down on the message board what was a good way to get points.

The subjects in the control group were exposed to the DRH schedule alone over a few experimental days. They did not receive any social rules but stated self rules on the message board at the end of each round. Experimental settings:

The effects of social rules in relation to self rules were examined over the four social-rule phases described below.

[Phase 1] Pull more than 20 times [Phase 2] Pull 10 times after 7 seconds
[Phase 3] Pull once after 15 seconds [Phase 4] Pull more than 20 times (same as Phase 1)

The Phase 1 social rule instructed more restricted responding than was required by the contingency (this may be called a rule for topographical superstition). Phase 2 added the irrelevant dimension of latency into the rule that restricted responding. The statement of Phase 3 was inconsistent with the contingency, in the sense that if the subject followed the rule the subject could not get any points. In each phase, the partner wrote the above messages consistently, but in various styles. Sometimes the partner simply wrote the main sentence, and sometimes wrote with some modifiers. For example, "Your way might be a good way to get points, but my way is better. Try it! Pull more than 20 times."

Results and Discussion

The data of the control group are presented first because there were no social rules to interfere with schedule performance for this group. The left column of Figure 3 shows the data from all five control subjects. The mean response rate per trial over four successive rounds is presented for each subject. Mean latencies for each subject are also shown on the top part of Figure 3, which plots the average time to the first response in each trial. The data showed that the subjects were quite sensitive to the DRH schedule and that the appropriate performance was established very quickly. By round 3, mean responding per trial had stabilized from about 5 to 8 responses, and by round 5, all subjects stated the rule exactly. Furthermore, response latencies were very short, within 3 seconds in most cases.

The right column of Figure 3 shows summary data for the experimental group over the four phases. The widely varied performances shown by the experimental group can be attributed to interference by the social rules. In the first half of the experiment (Phase 1 and 2), most subjects were strongly influenced by the social rules, but their performances were not always completely consistent with those rules. In most cases, the subjects established their own performances, while only one subject (TAB) seemed to obey the social rules in three phases. Six subjects in Phase 1 and five subjects in Phase 2 did not satisfy the requirement of the social rules in mean response rate. A finding of special interest was that most subjects did not follow the social rules even after their first trial.

These findings are similar to results of Stoddard, Sidman, and Brady (1988), who found that later subjects who had been informed the best way to perform by earlier subjects did not behave in that way, but behaved in their own way. Thus, the present experiment demonstrates that the effects of social rules are not absolute but relative.

In Phase 3, the social rules contacted the actual contingencies; that is, as long

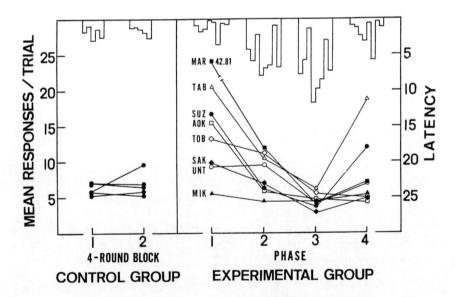

Figure 3. Summary data for the control group and experimental group. The left column of the Figure shows the data from five control subjects, and the right column of the Figure shows the data from experimental group over the four phases.

as the subjects followed the social rules reinforcers were not presented. By Phase 3, seven out of eight subjects showed schedule control similar to that of the control subjects, and they could also state correct descriptions about the contingencies as self rules. These data are consistent with those of Galizio (1979). Response rates, however, tended to shift in the direction of the social rules even after the correct rules had been stated. In Phase 4, six subjects did not follow the social rules even though their content was the same as in Phase 1.

In contrast to the social rules, the self rules produced by the subjects themselves corresponded well with their performances. Figures 4a and 4b show examples of how the self rules and the performances corresponded. The left column in each phase shows the requirement stated in the social rules delivered by the partner. The middle column shows the performances of the subjects. The right column shows the requirement stated in their self rules. The number of plots in each column corresponds to the number of rounds conducted in that phase. These results, however, do not tell us about control of one type of behavior by the other. We cannot say whether self rules caused the schedule performance or the schedule performance caused the self rules. All we can say is that self rules and the performances were correlated, in the sense that they usually changed together. This suggests that if we could control the subjects' self rules, we would also change their performances (Catania, Matthews, & Shimoff, 1982).

Latencies were more strongly influenced by social rules than were response rates. Over a broad range of values, latency was independent of reinforcers, while a dependent relation existed between response rates and reinforcers. Frequently, subjects followed social rules that specified latency even after the correct rules had been stated, as can be seen in Phase 3. Thus, features of behavior that do not contact current contingencies are more likely to be maintained by social rules than those that do contact contingencies.

Conclusion

The present experiment offers some contributions to the study of instructional control or rule-governed behavior. I will make three points here in concluding my chapter.

First, the source of rules must be considered when we refer to rule governance. In other words, to say how effective a rule will be, it is important to know who put the rule. Social rules may control behavior differently depending on speaker variables such as "credibility of the speaker," "prestige of the speaker," and so on. If a person hears that a famous scientist says "Spinach is good for aching muscles," then he may be likely to start eating spinach when his muscles ache. DeGrandpre and Buskist (1991) have also pointed out the effects of accuracy of instructions on human behavior. In the present experiment, most subjects did not show pliance to their partners' advice probably because the low credibility of their partners' rules. On the other hand, rules or instructions given by an experimenter in a popular experimental setting may work more effectively.

Second, we will have to reconsider the difference between social rules given by

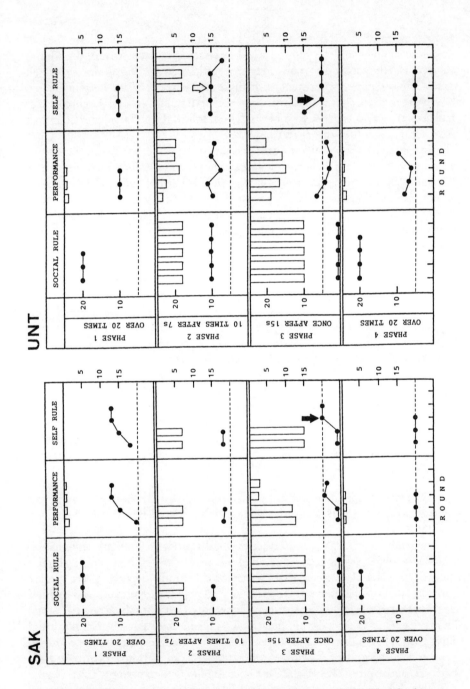

Figure 4a, 4b. Examples of how performances and self rules corresponded. The left column in each phase shows the requirement stated in the social rules, the middle column shows the performances of the subjects, and the right column shows the requirement stated in their self rules.

others and self rules stated by oneself. The present experiment showed that social rules and self rules should not be considered as equivalent events and events having the same function. The difference of these kinds of two rules may derive from their origins; that is, a self rule is initially the verbal behavior of organism itself, so when it functions as verbal antecedent, it may sometimes work as a covert stimulus, whereas social rules are simply verbal antecedents.

Third, response variability is often a good treatment for increasing sensitivity to contingency changes or for reducing superstitious behavior. Generally, the role of rules is to restrict behavior within the area described by the rule (Joyce & Chase, 1990; Andronis, 1991). The restricted behavior is likely to be maintained indefinitely as long as it continues to be correlated with reinforcers. Subjects in the present experiment showed much variability in their responding and consequently acquired appropriate responses because the social rules did not restrict their behavior very much. In the same way, superstitious behavior will not be maintained for a long time if the behavior pattern does not remain stereotyped.

The invention of language surely provided great advantages to humankind. Owing to language, we could acquire tremendous knowledge and a behavior repertoire that we could not have acquired only through nonverbal contingencies. "This plant can be eaten," "It is dangerous to go that way," "You can do it if you do it like this," and so on. In spite of these advantages, however, it can be said ironically that they also make the false functions of language inevitable.

References

Andronis, P. (1991). Rule-governance: Enough to make a term mean. In L. Parrott & P. N. Chase (Eds.), *Dialogues on verbal behavior* (pp. 226-235). Reno, NV: Context Press.

Ayllon, T., & Azrin, N. H (1964). Reinforcement and instructions with mental patients. *Journal of the Experimental Analysis of Behavior, 7,* 327-331.

Baron, A., Kaufman, A., & Stauber, K. A. (1969). Effects of instructions and reinforcement-feedback on human operant behavior maintained by fixed-interval reinforcement. *Journal of the Experimental Analysis of Behavior, 12,* 701-712.

Bentall, R. P., Lowe, C. F., & Beasty, A. (1985). The role of verbal behavior in human learning: II. Developmental differences. *Journal of the Experimental Analysis of Behavior, 43,* 165-181.

Blue, S., Sherman, J. G., & Pierrel, R. (1971). Differential responding as a function of auditory stimulus intensity without differential reinforcement. *Journal of the Experimental Analysis of Behavior, 15,* 371-377.

Brown, P. L., & Jenkins, H. M. (1968). Auto-shaping of the pigeon's key peck. *Journal of the Experimental Analysis of Behavior, 11,* 1-8.

Bruner, A., & Revusky, S. H. (1961). Collateral behavior in humans. *Journal of the Experimental Analysis of Behavior, 4,* 349-350.

Buskist, W. F., Bennett, R. H., & Miller H. L., Jr. (1981). Effects of instructionalconstraints on human fixed-interval performance. *Journal of the Experimental Analysis of Behavior, 35,* 217-225.

Buskist, W. F., & Miller, H. L., Jr. (1986). Interaction between rules and contingencies in the control of human fixed-interval performance. *Psychological Record, 36,* 109-116.

Catania, A. C. (1968). Glossary. In A. C. Catania (Ed.), *Contemporary research in operant behavior* (pp. 327-349). Glenview, IL: Scott, Foresman.

Catania, A. C. (1992). *Learning* (3rd ed.). Englewood Cliffs, NJ: Prentice-Hall.

Catania, A. C., & Cutts, D. (1963). Experimental control of superstitious responding in humans. *Journal of the Experimental Analysis of Behavior, 6,* 203-208.

Catania, A. C., Matthews, B. A., & Shimoff E. (1982). Instructed versus shaped human verbal behavior: Interactions with nonverbal responding. *Journal of the Experimental Analysis of Behavior 38,* 233-248.

Davis, H., & Hubbard, J. (1972). An analysis of superstitious behavior in the rat. *Behaviour, 3,* 1-12.

Davis, H., Hubbard, J., & Reberg, D. (1973). A methodological critique of research on "superstitious" behavior. *Bulletin of the Psychonomic Society, 1,* 447-449.

DeGrandpre, R. J., & Buskist, W. F. (1991). Effects of accuracy of instructions on human behavior: Correspondence with reinforcement contingencies matters. *Psychological Record, 41,* 371-384.

Eldridge, G. D., Pear, J. J., Torgrud, L. J., & Evers, B. H. (1988). Effects of prior response-contingent reinforcement on superstitious behavior. *Animal Learning & Behavior, 16,* 277-284.

Fenner, D. (1980). The role of contingencies and "principles of behavioral variation" in pigeons' pecking. *Journal of the Experimental Analysis of Behavior, 34,* 1-12.

Galizio, M. (1979). Contingency-shaped and rule-governed behavior: Instructional control of human loss avoidance. *Journal of the Experimental Analysis of Behavior, 31,* 53-70.

Harzem, P., Lowe, C. F., & Bagshaw, M. (1978). Verbal control in human operant behavior. *Psychological Record, 28,* 405-423.

Hayes, S. C. (Ed.). (1989). *Rule-governed behavior: Cognition, contingencies, and instructional control.* New York: Plenum.

Hayes, S. C., Brownstein, A. J., Zettle, R. D., Rosenfarb, I., & Korn, Z. (1986). Rule-governed behavior and sensitivity to changing consequences of responding. *Journal of the Experimental Analysis of Behavior, 45,* 237-256.

Herrnstein, R. J. (1966). Superstition: A corollary of the principles of operant conditioning. In W. K. Honig (Ed.), *Operant behavior: Areas of research and application* (pp. 33-51). New York: Appleton-Century-Crofts.

Higgins, S. T., Morris, E. D., & Johnson, L. M. (1989). Social transmission of superstitious behavior in preschool children. *Psychological Record, 9,* 307-323.

Joyce, J. H., & Chase, P. N. (1990). Effects of response variability on the sensitivity of rule-governed behavior. *Journal of the Experimental Analysis of Behavior, 54,* 251-262.

Justice, T. C., & Looney, T. A. (1990). Another look at "superstitions" in pigeons. *Bulletin of the Psychonomic Society, 28,* 64-66.

Kaufman, A., Baron, A., & Kopp, R. E. (1966). Some effects of instructions on human operant behavior. *Psychonomic Monograph Supplements, 1,* 243-250.

Kello, J. E., Innis, N. K., & Staddon, J. E. R. (1975). Eccentric stimuli on multiple fixed-interval schedules. *Journal of the Experimental Analysis of Behavior, 23,* 233-240.

Kieffer, J. D. (1965). Differential response rates correlated with the presence of "neutral" stimuli. *Journal of the Experimental Analysis of Behavior, 8,* 227-229.

Leander, J. D., Lippman, L. G., & Meyer, M. E. (1968). Fixed interval performance as related to subject's verbalization of the reinforcement contingency. *Psychological Record, 18,* 469-474.

LeFrancois, J. R., Chase, P. N., & Joyce, J. H. (1988). The effects of a variety of instructions on human fixed interval performance. *Journal of the Experimental Analysis of Behavior, 49,* 383-393.

Lippman, L. G., & Meyer, M. E. (1967). Fixed-interval performance as related to instructions and to subject's verbalizations of the contingency. *Psychonomic Science, xxx,* 135-136.

Lowe, C. F. (1979). Determinants of human operant behavior. In M. D. Zeiler, & P. Harzem (Eds.), *Advances in xxx analysis of behavior: Vol. 1. Reinforcement and the organization of behavior* (pp. 159-192). Chichester, England: Wiley.

Lowe, C. F. (1983). Radical behaviorism and human psychology. In G. C. L. Davey (Ed.), *Animal models of human behavior: Conceptual, evolutionary, and neurobiological perspectives* (pp. 71-93). Chichester, England: Wiley.

Lowe, C. F., Beasty, R. P., & Bentall, C. F. (1983). The role of verbal behavior in human learning: Infant performance on fixed-interval schedules. *Journal of the Experimental Analysis of Behavior, 39,* 157-164.

Lowe, C. F., Harzem, P., & Bagshaw, M. (1978). Species differences in temporal control of behavior II: Human performance. *Journal of the Experimental Analysis of Behavior, 29,* 351-361.

Matthews, B. A., Shimoff, E., Catania, A. C., & Sagvolden, T. (1977). Uninstructed human responding: Sensitivity to ratio and interval contingencies. *Journal of the Experimental Analysis of Behavior, 27,* 453-467.

Morse, W. H., & Skinner, B. F. (1957). A second type of superstition in the pigeon. *American Journal of Psychology, 70,* 308-311.

Ono, K. (1987). Superstitious behavior in humans. *Journal of the Experimental Analysis of Behavior, 47,* 261-271.

Reese, H. W., & Fremouw, W. J. (1984). Normal and normative ethics in behavioral sciences. *American Psychologist, 39,* 863-876.

Reynolds, G. S. (1968). A primer of operant conditioning. Scott, Foresman.

Rosenfarb, I. S., Newland, M. C., Brannon, S. E., & Howey, D. S. (1992). Effects of self-generated rules on the development of schedule-controlled behavior. *Journal of the Experimental Analysis of Behavior, 58,* 107-121.

Schlinger, H., & Blakely, E. (1987). Function-altering effects of contingency-specifying stimuli. *The Behavior Analyst, 10,* 41- 45.

Shimoff, E., Catania, A. C., & Matthews, B. A. (1981). Uninstructed human responding: Sensitivity of low-rate performance to schedule contingencies. *Journal of the Experimental Analysis of Behavior, 36,* 207-220.

Skinner, B. F. (1948). "Superstition" in the pigeon. *Journal of Experimental Psychology, 38,* 168-172.

Skinner, B. F. (1953). *Science and human behavior.* New York: Macmillan.

Skinner, B. F. (1966). An operant analysis of problem solving. In B. Kleinmuntz (Ed.), *Problem solving: Research, method, teaching* (pp. 225-257). New York: Wiley.

Skinner, B. F. (1969). *Contingencies of reinforcement: A theoretical analysis.* New York: Appleton-Century-Crofts.

Skinner, B. F. (1974). *About behaviorism.* New York: Knopf

Staddon, J. E. R., & Simmelhag, V. L. (1971). The "superstition" experiment: A reexamination of its implications for the principles of adaptive behavior. *Psychological Review, 78,* 3-43.

Starr, B. C., & Staddon, J. E. R. (1982). Sensory superstition on multiple interval schedules. *Journal of the Experimental Analysis of Behavior, 37,* 267-280.

Stoddard, L. T., Sidman, M., & Brady, J. V. (1988). Fixed-interval and fixed-ratio reinforcement schedules with human subjects. *Analysis of Verbal Behavior, 6,* 33-44.

Timberlake, W., & Lucas, G. A. (1985). The basis of superstitious behavior: Chance contingency, stimulus substitution, or appetitive behavior? *Journal of the Experimental Analysis of Behavior, 44,* 279-299.

Wagner, G. A., & Morris, E. K. (1987). "Superstitious" behavior in children. *Psychological Record, 37,* 471-488.

Weiner, H. (1970). Instructional control of human operant responding during extinction following fixed-ratio conditioning. *Journal of the Experimental Analysis of Behavior, 13,* 391-394.

Zeiler, M. D. (1970). Other behavior: Consequences of reinforcing not responding. *Journal of Psychology, 74,* 149- 155.

Chapter 12

Cognitive and Behavioral Approaches to Problem Solving

Hayne W. Reese
West Virginia University

My goals in this paper are to contrast cognitive and behavioral approaches to the analysis of problem solving, to summarize some findings that are especially relevant, and to suggest how each approach can deal with these findings. A preliminary point is that in keeping with the context of an Institute on Verbal Relations, the paper deals for the most part with verbal activities in problem solving. Problem solving fits this context because all modern cognitive theories implicate the use of verbal activities in human problem solving, at least after early childhood. The analogous assumptions in behavior analysis are that human problem solving after early childhood is largely rule-governed behavior and that the rules are verbal. I have argued elsewhere (Reese, 1989, 1992b) that the latter assumption is not only consistent with behavior analysis but also is accepted by most behavior analysts. I will not repeat the argument here other than to note that the genesis of the rules is not at issue: Humans usually solve problems by applying verbal rules, whether the rules came from contingency-shaping or instruction.

Scope of the Paper

The range of topics included in the area of problem solving is indicated by a 125-page bibliography on problem solving and concept identification prepared by Stern (1969). The entire bibliography was alphabetized by authors, and I examined only the first five pages, which turned out to contain 57 references dealing with the following topics: Problem solving, abstract and concrete thinking, achievement motivation, anagrams, classification, cognition, computerized instruction, concept identification (which is traditionally classified as a kind of problem solving), concept learning, conceptual reorganization, creativity, discrimination learning, group problem solving, intellectual development, intelligence testing, learning, learning set, mediation, memory, perception, perception of part-whole relations, probability learning, productive thinking, set, short-term memory, social learning, teaching (in general), teaching (of arithmetic, astronomy, concepts, reading, social studies, and time concepts), thinking, transposition, and verbal learning.

All these topics can involve problems to be solved, but I will cover only a selected sample of studies from the area traditionally called problem solving, rather than the areas traditionally called learning, memory, etc. I will not cover problem solving in the area usually called coping—coping with problems of social relations and with personal problems (relevant references include D'Zurilla, 1986; Folkman & Lazarus, 1980; Heppner, 1978; Krasnor & Rubin, 1981; Nezu, 1987). I will also not cover problem solving by "expert systems," which are computer programs written to solve specific problems such as airline bookings and seat assignments (Hutchison, 1986). Expert systems are often based on task analysis of the way a human solves the problem, but with extensions beyond human capacities of speed and number of rules or variables that can be taken into account (e.g., Davis, 1986; Duda & Shortliffe, 1983; Lemmon, 1986). That is, expert systems are programs for solving problems, not for simulating human problem solving.

Historical Overview

Recognition of the widespread reliance of human problem solving on verbal behavior emerged gradually; but a survey of this history would require a separate paper. In general, problem solving researchers and theorists were different persons and the researchers dealt with the outcomes of problem solving and the theorists dealt with problem solving as a process (Duncan, 1959). The result was little progress in both the description of problem solving and the explanation of problem solving (Duncan, 1959). Gestalt theorists thought that problem solving is based on insight, which they usually viewed as a perceptual rather than verbal phenomenon—that is, insight involved perceptual reorganization of the visual field rather than verbalization. The stimulus-response learning theorist Irving Maltzman (1955) presented a theory of problem solving based on Hullian concepts such as the habit family hierarchy, generalization, response-produced cues, and mediated association; and although he acknowledged that verbal behavior is involved, he did not give verbal behavior a special status. Later, Charles Cofer (1957) emphasized the mediational role of verbal behavior. Still later, in the 1960s, the research and theory of Soviet developmental psychologists, who especially emphasized the role of verbal activities, became influential in developmental psychology in the United States and generated interest in the role of verbal behaviors, such as asking questions as an aid to problem solving (Berlyne, 1970). Thereafter, human problem solving came to be seen as largely a verbal activity (as perhaps implied by the summary of theories in Table 3).

DEFINITION OF PROBLEM SOLVING

In the older literature on problem solving, the definition of *problem* was generally agreed to be a problem; in fact, Berlyne (1970) dismissed problem solving as a separate category of behavior on the argument that *problem* had no widely accepted definition. Thereafter, however, a wide consensus emerged, as shown in the following subsections.

Table 1

Definition of Problem Solving

Original definition[a]	Revised definition	Re-revised definition
Problem solving is "The process involved in the determination of the correct sequence of alternatives leading to a desired goal."	Problem solving is the way to find out how to get to a desired goal.	Problem solving is the way to solve a problem.

Note. See text for explanation. [a]From Wolman, 1989, p. 262.

Two Definitions

The definition of problem solving in Wolman's (1989) *Dictionary of Behavioral Science* is "The process involved in the determination of the correct sequence of alternatives leading to a desired goal" (p. 262). By this definition, maze learning and discrimination learning are kinds of problem solving, which may seem to make the concept overly inclusive; but in any case the definition is problematic for other reasons. Table 1 shows rewordings of each phrase in the definition. As shown, the definition can be reworded as "Problem solving is the way to find out how to get to a desired goal," or better, the last phrase should be simply "a goal," because a goal that is *not* desired is not really a goal.

The actual problem to be solved is how to get to the goal, and actually finding out how to get to the goal is problem solving. Therefore, the revised definition can be reworded by substituting "a problem" for "how to get to a goal" and by substituting "to solve" for "to find out": "Problem solving is the way to solve a problem." Thus, the definition in Wolman's dictionary is circular.

Aside from being circular, however, the definition includes a feature that is not essential and it lacks a feature that is crucial. The nonessential feature is the reference to the *correct* sequence of behaviors. This feature is clearly appropriate for problems that have only one correct solution, such as finding the square root of a specified number. (Actually, a number has two square roots, one positive and the other negative, but this nicety is irrelevant herein because the one correct solution can be expressed as "$\pm N$.") These problems can be solved by the use of an algorithm (Baer, 1982; Reese, 1992a) or by "convergent" thinking (Guilford, 1967, chap. 7 & pp. 214-215), which should yield the one correct solution. However, many problems have no solution that is correct in any absolute sense (examples are given later, in the

Table 2

Self-Reported Strategies and Performance of Old Adults Given Intentional Memory Instructions in the Overcast et al. (1975) Study

Strategy reported	Percentage of group	Correct recall (%)
None	20	53
Miscellaneous	25	69
Categorization	40	82[a]
Cumulative rehearsal	15	83

Notes. (1) Data reported by Brown, Murphy, Overcast, and Smiley (no date); omitted from Overcast et al. (2) Sample size = 20. (3) "Miscellaneous" included naming, scanning, & self-testing.
[a]With one outlying score omitted, the mean correct recall was 90%.

subsection *Divergent Problems*). For these problems, a solution can be correct only in the relative sense that it is successful; "divergent" thinking (Guilford, 1967, chap. 6) should yield such a solution. (But as Davis [1973, p. 22] pointed out, identifying the one *best* solution involves convergent thinking.)

The crucial feature that is omitted from the definition in Wolman's dictionary is included in a definition given by Anderson (1990), which is also simpler than Wolman's definition: Problem solving is *removing obstacles* to a goal (p. 221). If no obstacle hinders progress toward a goal, attaining the goal is not a problem. Like Wolman's definition, Anderson's is very broad; it incorporates maze learning and discrimination learning as kinds of problem solving and also, for example, memory tasks when the number of items to be remembered is greater than the immediate memory span.

The appropriateness of including memory is exemplified by a study in which old adults were given a memory task and were asked to report any memory strategies they used (Overcast, Murphy, Smiley, & Brown, 1975). Table 2 shows the reported strategies in increasing order of theoretical effectiveness (except for Miscellaneous) and the associated percentages correct recall. The finding that the research participants reported using strategies implies that the memory task was a problem to be solved; and although this inference could be wrong–the participants could have been only complying with the instruction to report strategies–the percentage correct recall increased in the theoretically expectable way, providing convergent validation for the inference.

An example implying that a learning task can be a problem to be solved is a study in which verbal-learning performance, memory ability, and intelligence were assessed (Labouvie, Frohring, Baltes, & Goulet, 1973). The results showed that on early trials, the number of items recalled was predicted better by memory ability and on later trials it was predicted better by intelligence. Evidently, the participants initially interpreted the task not as a problem to be solved, but as a test requiring only rote memorization; and on later trials they interpreted it as a problem to be solved and used cognitive activities to solve it. In support of this conclusion, the increasing importance of intelligence was statistically significant only for a group in which the recall tests were made especially difficult by being delayed.

The Role of Obstacles

The role of obstacles in problem solving has often been noted (e.g., Anderson, 1990, p. 221; Garry & Kingsley, 1970, p. 463; Maier, 1940; Meacham & Emont, 1989; Uznadze, 1966, p. 115; Woodworth, 1918, pp. 138-139); and it is certainly implied by research showing the importance of self-generated questions such as "What's in the way?" and "What's gone wrong?" (Berlyne, 1970, p. 971). The role of obstacles is also implied in definitions of *problem* by Duncker and Skinner: "A problem arises when a living creature has a goal and does not know how this goal is to be reached" (Duncker, 1945, p. 1); "A question for which there is at the moment no answer is a problem" (Skinner, 1966, p. 225). Davis (1973) objected that Skinner's definition in terms of questions and answers inappropriately implies a limitation to verbal behavior (p. 13); but from the more modern point of view, this implication would not be objectionable. In any case, however, Skinner clearly did not intend the limitation; many of his examples involved humans giving nonverbal solutions to nonverbal problems.

The Nature of Problem Solving

Anderson's (1990) definition of *problem* is used in the present paper. According to this definition, a problem exists only if two criteria are met: (a) The organism is in a state that is different from a desired or desirable state, called a *goal state*; and (b) coming to be in the goal state is blocked. "State" includes spatial and temporal location, physiological condition or state, and mental condition or state. The blocking may be external or internal. Examples of external blocking are the physical constraints in a maze and the psychological constraint of a rule imposed by a researcher that peeking is not allowed in a discrimination learning task; internal blocking occurs, for example, in moral dilemmas and other conflicts.

This definition is precisely consistent with the root metaphor of pragmatism, and therefore it is entirely compatible with behavior analysis, provided that the goal is not defined teleologically and provided that the behavior is defined appropriately. (For definition and discussion of the root metaphor of pragmatism, or contextualism as Pepper designated this world view, see Hayes, Hayes, & Reese, 1988; Pepper, 1942, chap. 10; Reese, 1991a.)

Problem-solving behavior is goal-directed, or purposeful, but it is not teleological. The purpose of problem-solving behavior is to remove obstacles; that is,
problem solving is behavior emitted in an attempt to remove obstacles to being in
a goal state. Except for being purposeful, the nature of problem-solving behavior is
not constrained in the definition used in the present paper. This minimal constraint
is inconsistent with definitions that require a novel outcome (e.g., Chase &
Bjarnadottir, 1992); but the consensus seems to be that a novel outcome is not
required, that is, fact retrieval can constitute problem solving (e.g., Maier, 1945;
Maltzman, 1955; Mayer, 1983, p. 165). The minimal constraint is also inconsistent
with definitions which specify that problem solving must involve cognitive activities
(e.g., Anderson, 1980, p. 259; Gagné, 1965, pp. 54, 157; Maier, 1929, pp. 2, 92) such
as the use of principles (Gagné, ibid.) or strategies (e.g., Bédard & Chi, 1992) or rules
(e.g., Reese, 1992a) or the occurrence of rule-governed behavior (Chase & Bjarnadottir,
1992; Skinner, 1966). However, the consensus seems to be that although problem
solving can involve cognitive activities, it can be pure trial-and-error behavior (Davis,
1973, pp. 21-22, 40-47; Dewey, 1933, p. 115; Duncan, 1959; Garry & Kingsley, 1970,
pp. 463-464). Davis (1973), in fact, characterized trial-and-error behavior as "the
most basic and pervasive solution-activity of all" (p. 23). Furthermore, trial-and-error
behavior may be systematic rather than random, perhaps in rats (Krechevsky, e.g.,
1932, 1938) and certainly in humans (e.g., Munn, 1954). Also, trial-and-error
behavior is constrained by the task environment (i.e., the problem as objectively
presented—Simon, 1978, p. 275); for example, a person who is ignorant of the
workings of a typewriter and who wants to adjust the line spacing does not try
knocking on the wall as a possible solution (Duncker, 1945, p. 10).

Not all goal-directed behavior is problem-solving behavior. As noted earlier, if
behavior is directed toward being in a goal state and progress toward the goal is being
made, the situation contains no problem to be solved. For example, presenting a
paper orally is goal-directed behavior, but it is not problem solving unless the
presentation is disrupted, for example by a large number of questions from the
audience or by the chairperson's signaling that time has run out; but in the face of
disruption, the speaker's continuing the same presentation behavior would not
remove the obstacle, which constitutes a problem to be solved to allow attainment
of a new goal—presentation of the main points to be made in the paper. In short,
attaining a goal requires behaving in some effective way; but according to Anderson's
(1990) definition, the behaving is not properly called problem solving unless it
includes removing at least one obstacle.

Effective Problem Solving

Effective problem solving is behavior that actually removes obstacles to being in
a goal state; that is, problem solving is effective when the organism comes to be in
a goal state. However, the goal state the organism comes to be in is not necessarily
the initially specified goal state. By this definition, effective problem solving may
involve abandoning the initial goal and substituting a different one. In fact, the

different one that is substituted may be the mere outcome of the attempt at problem solving, selected as a goal after the outcome occurs. An outcome is not necessarily the same as a goal, as Guthrie (1960, p. 140) noted, but it can be accepted as the goal after it occurs, as in the sour grapes and sweet lemon phenomena.

SURVEY OF THEORETICAL APPROACHES

Introduction

For most if not all phenomena, many different theories provide equally adequate explanations. Often, however, as Max Wertheimer pointed out, they do so by fitting a phenomenon to different Procrustean beds, this theorist cutting off this part of the phenomenon, that theorist cutting off that part (Luchins & Luchins, 1970, p. 263). For example, both Davis (1973, p. 58) and Wertheimer said that stimulus-response learning theory explanations of problem solving sacrifice completeness for simplicity. Another example is that the Gestalt theory of discrimination learning and transposition (Köhler, 1918) did not explain how a relation, which is a property of two objects, can result in the choice of one object (Reese, 1968, pp. 230-231), and the alternative theory—that the organism immediately locomotes toward the second of the two objects upon perceiving the correct relation (Lindworsky, 1919; Reese, ibid.) did not explain why the chickens in Köhler's experiment sometimes fell into a stupor when they were confronted with the transposition-test stimuli (Koffka, 1925, note 208, p. 369; Vygotsky, 1929/1981, p. 213).

I will point out the limits of the Procrustean beds in each approach.

Cognitive Approaches

Modern Structuralism

Perhaps the most radical cognitive approach is modern structuralism. This is different from the old structuralisms such as those of Wundt and Titchener, which were mechanistic: The contents of consciousness were revealed by giving tasks that aroused conscious mental activities of reasoning, problem solving, perception, and sensation, for example, and in the mainstream of structuralism these activities were assumed to be merely aggregates of mental elements and to be completely reducible to these mental elements. The mental elements were revealed by the introspective reports of research participants who were thoroughly trained in the method of introspection.

Modern structuralism is exemplified by the work of Piaget, Piagetians, and neo-Piagetians. Like the old structuralists, these researchers are interested in the architecture of the mind, or mental competence, and they use problem-solving tasks as diagnostic instruments. Their primary interest is not in how children or adults solve problems, but in what children's and adults' problem solving reveals about the structure or form of thinking. However, the world view of modern structuralism is organicism, or dialectical idealism, in which the structure of thinking is a whole not reducible to its components and the mind is a construction of reality rather than a reflection of reality.

Interest in competence. During a colloquium at the University of Kansas in the late 1960s, Martin Braine presented a cognitive theory of early language and illustrated it with a flow-chart type of model that he draw on a blackboard as he went along (the theory is described in Braine, 1971–Braine, personal communication, August 9, 1992). During the discussion period, someone in the audience pointed out that his model did not include the child's actually emitting language. Braine's answer was to drew another box, connect the rest of the model to it with an arrow, and label it "Output." Braine's leaving behavior out of the formal theory was correct because he was interested in the structure of language and not its functions, that is, he was interested in language competence and not language performance. For purposes such as his, the only reason to observe performance is to provide evidence that can be used to diagnose or infer competence. In contrast, behavior analysts and others who study language pragmatics are not interested in structure or competence; they are interested in function or performance.

Holism and constructivism. The holism of modern structuralism means that a specific cognitive activity can be understood only by understanding its role in the structure of the mind. The constructive or creative role of thinking is illustrated by words such as "up," "down," and "permanent," which have no actual referents but which are useful for organizing experiences (Hoagwood, 1992). Other illustrations are the concepts of inertia of motion and inertia of rest, which have no empirical referents (Hegel, 1830/1970, p. 52); the concept of *becoming*, which according to Grünbaum (1967) is "mind-dependent," that is, it has no existence in the physical universe independent of mind; and the concepts of classes and probability, which are mental constructions and not physical entities (Furth & Wachs, 1974, pp. 25-26). In other words, what is known and guides thinking is not objective reality, according to modern structuralism, but a subjective construction (Bowers, 1973; Kohlberg, 1968; Lawler, 1975). The effective environment is not external to the individual, but rather it is an abstraction constructed by the individual. Only the part of the environment that is understood (assimilated) can affect behavior (Kohlberg, 1968, p. 1023; Piaget, 1970, p. 707; Wozniak, 1975).

Constructed concepts in behavior analysis. A digression at this point may help to understand the nature of constructed concepts: Such concepts are also used in behavior analysis. Three examples are given in the following paragraphs.

The *operant* is not a behavior that can be observed; rather, according to Skinner's (1969) definition "an operant is a class, of which a response is an instance or member. . . . It is always a response upon which a given reinforcement is contingent, but it is contingent upon properties which define membership in an operant. Thus a set of contingencies defines an operant" (p. 131).

Stimulus functions are not in the objective world outside the organism; they are in the history of an individual organism.

Equivalence relations do not exist as observables; Sidman (1992) said, "We cannot see equivalence relations; we have to infer them from the results of the test [i.e., from the tests of stimulus equivalence]" (p. 17). A behavior analyst who reviewed a stimulus equivalence study that had been submitted to the *Journal of Experimental Child Psychology* criticized the use of the tests, commenting that too many of the results in this area rest on testing rather than training and that if a relation is found to be important, it should be trained rather than merely tested. On the one hand, the reviewer was correct because the point was about educational implications; but on the other hand, as Sidman (1992) showed, stimulus equivalence can be demonstrated only by the tests. An organism trained to exhibit reflexivity, symmetry, and transitivity, which are the defining features of equivalence relations, is exhibiting the effects of training, not stimulus equivalence.

Problem solving in modern structuralism. A person may learn to solve a problem without understanding the nature of the problem (Piaget, 1970); but modern structuralists are interested in the understanding rather than the problem-solving behavior as such. They conceptualize understanding in terms of mental structures that underlie behavior; but the major point here is that they make the distinction by requiring that research participants not only emit solutions to problems but also explain their solutions. The explanation is more important than the solution, not only because a person can solve problems without understanding them but also because the explanation permits an inference about the "logic" (of whatever type) that the person used to find the solution, whether or not the solution was correct.

Piaget's stages of cognitive development end in adolescence with emergence of what he called formal operational thinking. The content of adults' thinking may be different from the content of adolescents' thinking, but the structure of thinking is the same; that is, knowledge changes after adolescence, but the *form* of thinking does not change (e.g., Piaget, 1972). Other theorists, however, have found evidence of a new form of thinking in adulthood (e.g., Commons, Richards, & Armon, 1984). The new form of thinking is often called *the fifth stage* because Piaget's theory included four stages.

Arlin (1975) proposed a fifth stage that is directly relevant here. She renamed the stage of formal operations the *problem-solving* stage because in this stage problems are solved by convergent thinking, and she named the hypothesized fifth stage the *problem-finding* stage because it is characterized by divergent phenomena—creative thinking, formulating generic questions, raising general questions from ill-defined problems, and the like. She obtained supporting evidence (Arlin, 1975, 1977), but it has been challenged (Cropper, Meck, & Ash, 1976; Fakouri, 1976). Another problem with her fifth stage is that other theorists have identified other fifth stages, such as "dialectical operations" (e.g., Labouvie-Vief, 1982; Riegel, 1973). Given these complexities, I will not pursue this line of research and theory any further here except to note that it has led to considerable interest in everyday problem solving (e.g., Puckett & Reese, 1993; Sinnott, 1989a).

The Procrustean bed in modern structuralism. Two major problems with modern structuralism are that it is a teleological system and that it deals with competence rather than performance. Even its advocates evidently feel compelled to explain away the teleology, either by making the system synchronic rather than diachronic (Overton & Newman, 1982) or by making the teleology a "regulative" principle (Murray, 1991; Overton, 1991). A regulative principle is an "as if" principle; it is applied to experience rather than derived from experience (Kant, 1790/1952, Section 66). Murray (1991) said:

> The earlier steps or stages in a developmental sequence of behaviors are made more intelligible by our knowledge of the endpoint toward which they are progressing even though the later periods cannot in any way be the efficient cause of the earlier events because of the unidirectional character of time. Later events cannot cause earlier events, but they can help us make sense of the earlier events by showing what the earlier events lead to. (p. 43)

Regarding performance, the Piagetian Willis Overton argued that the structuralist account is incomplete because it deals only with universals and treats individual differences and environmental effects as epiphenomena, and that the behavioral account is incomplete because it does not explain the universals (Overton, 1976; Overton & Newman, 1982). He argued that neither account will ever be reduced to the other and therefore that the accounts need to be combined. The neo-Piagetian Pascual-Leone and his colleagues have also developed a theory incorporating both competence and performance (e.g., Pascual-Leone & Morra, 1991; Stewart & Pascual-Leone, 1992). However, the performance aspect that both Overton and Pascual-Leone incorporated was cognitive rather than behavioral. This choice is arguably a mistake, in that Piagetian theory is consistent with the organic world view, the cognitive theory used (information-processing theory) is consistent with mechanism, and behavior analysis is consistent with pragmatism (Hayes et al., 1988; Reese, 1986a) and in that organicism and mechanism share fewer conceptual categories than organicism and pragmatism (Pepper, 1942, pp. 146-148).

Information Processing

The information-processing approach is well known and needs only a brief summary here. Briefly characterized, this approach specifies more or less precisely how the components of a presented task are understood or represented by the problem solver, how operations are selected from a repertoire of algorithmic and heuristic operations for dealing with these representations, and how the outcomes of the selected operations are evaluated. The more precise specifications are found in computer simulations of problem solving; the less precise ones are found in flow-chart types of information-processing theories (for discussion, see Klahr, 1973; Reese, 1989; Simon, 1978). Many summaries of the approach and its applications in specific domains are available (e.g., cognitive development, Siegler, 1983; language, Reese, 1991b; rule-governed behavior, Reese, 1989).

Information-processing theories deal with the ways humans operate upon (process) stimulation received (information), usually with some purpose or goal in view, which is usually determined by the task or situation presented. For example, in computer simulations a theoretical account of some phenomenon, such as counting (Siegler & Robinson, 1982) or solving balance problems (Klahr & Siegler, 1978), is tested by programming a computer to run through the hypothesized operations to see if the computer output is the same as the human output. Unfortunately, these theories are also the most limited in scope (Klahr, 1973), dealing with a single phenomenon such as counting or solving balance problems without any attempt to relate the theoretical account to theoretical accounts of other phenomena.

Information-processing theories of another kind resemble flow charts of the type that computer programmers use as a guide or model to help them write the actual computer program. In this kind of theory, however, no program is actually written. Precision is lost without the actual computer runs to "keep the theory honest," but scope is gained. This is the most prevalent kind of information-processing theory, and as Siegler (1983) commented, Newell and Simon's (1972) version has been the most influential information-processing theory of problem solving.

Broadly characterized, information-processing theories of problem solving deal with "problem representation" and problem-solving strategies, that is, the ways persons mentally reconstruct a problem and the ways they attempt to solve the reconstructed problem. Other major issues dealt with include the quality of emitted solutions, the effect of how well a problem is defined, and the role of the knowledge base, that is, how knowledge– especially expertness versus novicehood–influences problem solving (e.g., Bédard & Chi, 1992).

The Procrustean bed of information-processing theories is bounded by limitations of scope and precision. The limitation of scope is that a theory about the way problems of one type are solved is relatively isolated from theories about the ways other problems are solved; the limitation of precision is that although a given theory can be highly precise, a large and perhaps infinite number of alternative theories dealing with the same phenomenon can be equally precise. (The limitation of scope may not be as serious as the limitation of precision, given that relatively little transfer occurs between problems of different types–e.g., Siegler, 1983.)

Behavior Analysis

Behavior analysis is widely misconstrued and misunderstood, especially by many nonbehaviorists (for documentation see, e.g., Catania, 1991). However, the reason seems to be not that behavior analysis is hard to grasp but rather that it is often not examined. I will summarize it briefly here and then further characterize it by contrasting it with the cognitive approach. Elsewhere, colleagues and I have summarized some general features of the behavior analytic approach (Baltes & Reese, 1977; Hayes et al., 1988; Reese, 1986a, 1986b) and examined its application to developmental psychology (Morris, Hursh, Winston, Gelfand, Hartmann, Reese, & Baer, 1982; Reese, 1980, 1982) and rule-governance (Reese, 1989).

A preliminary point is that in behavior analysis, *problem solving* is not an actual behavior, just as *discriminating, generalizing, abstracting,* and *forming concepts* are not actual behaviors (Skinner, 1969, p. 275). A behavior analysis of problem solving should therefore include identifying the actual behaviors that are emitted and the discriminative and contingent stimuli that control them (Catania, 1992, chap. 15). This procedure was in fact used in the reports of problem solving that I found in a casual survey of the 1982-1992 contents of the *Journal of the Experimental Analysis of Behavior* and the *Journal of Applied Behavior Analysis*, but the kinds of problems studied did not require analysis of the behaviors as such—the problems included concept learning, conditional discrimination, discrimination learning, foraging, "hill-climbing" (by pigeons), matching-to-sample and oddity matching, memory, response chaining, rule-governed behavior, stimulus equivalence, and timing-behavior.

Behavior Analysis of Problem Solving

Skinner defined *having a problem* as lacking the behavior needed to occasion reinforcement that is available; he defined problem solution as emitting this behavior; and he defined problem solving as emitting behaviors that change the current situation in such a way that the solution behavior is emitted (1953, p. 247; 1974, p. 111). He also noted (1966) that problem solving is sometimes emitting behaviors that change the situation in such a way that certain other behavior is *not* emitted.

Skinner (and Kantor, 1922) used the adjective "precurrent" to label behaviors that produce such changes (Skinner, 1966; 1968, chap. 6; 1974, p. 104). Thus, problem solving can be said to proceed through a series of at least two steps, the first consisting of precurrent behavior(s) and the second consisting of the solution behavior(s) (Skinner, 1966). If the solution is deemed to be correct, the solution behavior is reinforced; but even then, the precurrent behavior is not specifically reinforced.

Precurrent behaviors can be as direct and simple as feeling, listening, looking, savoring, and sniffing (Skinner, 1968, p. 122; 1974, p. 104) and as complex as putting objects side by side (facilitating comparison), grouping similar things together (facilitating treating them alike), putting things in order if the solution requires a series of behaviors, translating a verbal response from words into symbols (eliminating surplus cues), representing the premises of a syllogism with overlapping circles (clarifying their interrelations), and counting and measuring (clarifying quantities) (Skinner, 1974, p. 111). One type of precurrent behavior that is often highly effective is the use of rules, such as algorithms and plans, which function as discriminative stimuli for other behavior (Skinner, 1966).

Unsuccessful Problem Solving

The foregoing analysis has implications about the causes of ineffective or inefficient problem solving. For example, Parsons (1976) identified five conditions under which precurrent behaviors might fail to occur: (a) The situation (the combination of setting events and discriminative stimuli) does not occasion initiating the behavioral chain. (b) The precurrent behavior is not in the person's behavioral repertoire. (c) The precurrent behavior is not maintained long enough for the solution behavior to occur. (d) The stimuli produced by the precurrent behavior are too weak to have discriminative control over subsequent behavior. They may be especially likely to be too weak if the precurrent behavior is covert, as it often is in problem solving. (e) Inappropriate discriminative stimuli control behavior in the situation; for example, looking for a dictionary as precurrent to checking the spelling of a word might be disrupted by finding instead of the dictionary an appealing novel.

Two further sources of ineffective or inefficient problem solving can be added to Parsons' list: (f) The precurrent behavior occasions insufficiently variable subsequent behaviors (Chase & Bjarnadottir, 1992). In other literatures, insufficient variability is called functional fixedness, set, and rigidity (e.g., Anderson, 1990, pp. 246-251; Chown, 1959; Garry & Kingsley, 1970, pp. 471-472), and variability is called fluency and flexibility (e.g., Jaquish & Ripple, 1981). (g) The rule emitted as precurrent behavior is inappropriate for the problem at hand (e.g., Chase & Danforth, 1991).

A behavior analysis of unsuccessful problem solving could consist of comparing the effects of experimental treatments designed to alleviate each of these conditions. For example: (a) Manipulate the setting events so that the contingent stimulus is a functional reinforcer, or add a new functional reinforcer. Malott (1986) has discussed this possibility. (b) Use shaping or some other procedure to train the required behavior that may be absent. An example is training "say-do" correspondence to make a rule a functional discriminative stimulus (e.g., Baer, Williams, Osnes, & Stokes, 1984; Riegler & Baer, 1989; Ward & Stare, 1990). (c) Make the precurrent behaviors overt and reinforce their occurrences (e.g., Grimm, Bijou, & Parsons, 1973; Parsons, 1976; Parsons & Ferraro, 1977). (d) Make the precurrent behaviors overt, or strengthen the discriminative stimulus by training the use of a precurrent behavior that makes contact with it (in cognitive terms, train the person to attend to internal cues). Examples are training in self-editing (Hyten & Chase, 1991) and self-recording (Young, Birnbrauer, & Sanson-Fisher, 1977). (e) Eliminate irrelevant aspects of the problem, or impose a response cost or punisher on occurrences of behaviors that compete with problem solving. An extreme example may be the use of continuous programmed environments (Bernstein & Brady, 1986); a less extreme example is the traditional advice to work in a quiet room. (f) Introduce behavioral variability by training or instructions (Chase & Bjarnadottir, 1992; Neuringer, 1992). (g) Shape the appropriate rule (e.g., Catania, Matthews, & Shimoff, 1982).

Role of Cognition

An important point, overlooked by most critics, is that behavior analysis is not claimed to be universal in scope. Skinner (1989) said that (a) behavior analysis deals with the relation between antecedent stimulation and behavior and with the relation between consequent stimulation and change in behavior; (b) behavior analysis does not deal with the mediators of these relations; and (c) the mediators are the province of brain science. Skinner did not include cognitive psychology as part of brain science. He often argued against the metaphorical use of "brain" to refer to "mind" and "cognition" (e.g., 1974, p. 77)–as did J. R. Kantor (1977)–but one of his objections seems to have been that many cognitive psychologists treat the mind as an agent even though the person is the actual agent (Skinner, 1989): "Cognitive processes are behavioral processes; they are things people do" (p. 17).

An aside on mind as agent. I think cognitive psychologists agree with the statement quoted at the end of the preceding paragraph, though they might insist that "activities" would be a better term than "behavioral processes." Many of them talk about a ghostly "executive" process or mechanism, but it seems to be only a metaphor for "person." Also, some of them write as though the processes are little persons, but again they generally seem to be using metaphor. For example, Anderson and Schooler (1991) said:

> The memory system tries to make available those memories that are most likely to be useful. The memory system can use the past history of use of a memory to estimate whether the memory is likely to be needed now. This view sees human memory in some sense as making a statistical inference. However, it does not imply that memory is explicitly engaged in statistical computations. Rather, the claim is that whatever memory is doing parallels a correct statistical inference. (p. 400)

I suppose this statement is useful in some sense, but I will no more attempt to specify what sense than Anderson and Schooler did. I believe that treating "the memory system" and other mentalisms as problem solvers without specifying how they solve problems is a misuse of metaphor–it is using a domain (human problem solving) that is not well understood as a metaphor or model of another domain (memory in this case) that is also not well understood. (I must hasten to add, if only parenthetically, that Anderson and Schooler did not actually take their metaphor seriously; they actually used a mathematical model and showed that it fits certain data very well.)

Mind as cause. Skinner (1974, chap. 13) argued that although mind exists (as private events), it and its effects are completely determined by the organism's genetically determined endowments (e.g., the capacity to be operantly conditioned), the organism's history of contingencies, and the current setting. Consequently, although the mind is causal, it is not *uniquely* causal, that is, the mind is not a sui generis cause of behavior. This rejection of the concept of free will is a basic principle in all noncognitive psychologies. The major implication of this principle is that taking the mind into account cannot improve the prediction and control obtainable from knowing the organism's genetic endowments, the organism's history of contingencies, and the current setting. A drawback is that although the organisms genetic endowments and the current setting might often be known well enough, the organism's history of contingencies is very often not known.

An example of unknown origins. A dog can be trained to "whisper" on command (make barking movements without emitting a bark); but although this training and its outcome constitute a behavior analysis of this dog's behavior, it does not tell us why the normal dog annoys its human neighbors–and for all I know, its owners–by barking out loud. The French naturalist Buffon (1791) had a speculative answer:

> The dog seems to have become clamorous and noisy in the society of man, who employs his tongue more than any other being; for the dog, in a state of nature, is almost mute, uttering a kind of howling when pressed with hunger only. He acquired his faculty of barking by commerce with men in polished society. (pp. 403-404; short s substituted for long s)

Buffon accepted a doctrine of inheritance of acquired characteristics; but this doctrine is not available to modern naturalists, who must therefore look elsewhere to explain dogs' barking.

Coppinger and Feinstein (1991) noted that barking is rare in wild dogs and they argued that it is very unlikely to have been deliberately bred during domestication. Their own speculation was that domestication itself was not a result of deliberate selection by humans but rather was an accidental result of natural selection of behaviors useful for scavenging near human settlements. One set of behaviors constituted "juvenilization," including the perpetuation into adulthood of infantile barks. A flaw in this speculation, I would say, is that dogs' infantile barks are actually purposive, that is, they communicate alarm and distress, as Coppinger and Feinstein commented; but in contrast, as they also commented, the barks of adult dogs serve no evident function. Coppinger and Feinstein were left with a circularity: The adult dog barks because it is stuck in adolescence and "Stuck in adolescence, the dog barks so much because barking is what a *juvenile* canid does" (p. 129).

Are these speculations useful? Probably not; but as far as prediction and control are concerned, certain other speculations are also probably not useful–speculations about the origin of operant conditioning, food preferences, and social behaviors in natural selection and, more to the point, speculations about an unknown history of present behavior.

Prediction and control when history is unknown. When the history of present behavior is unknown, speculations about the history may be useful as guides to further research, but they are are not useful for present prediction and control because they are necessarily post hoc. Such speculations cannot add anything to the prediction and control of behavior beyond the prediction and control obtainable from knowing the present behavior. In fact, as Baer and Sherman (1970) pointed out with respect to behavior modification, the history is generally not relevant to remediation efforts because the issue is not how the behavior originated but how it is being maintained. A study by Repp, Felce, and Barton (1988) supports this contention: They observed problem behaviors and concomitant stimuli in the natural environment, and showed that experimentally manipulating the occur- rences of the stimuli changed the frequencies of the behaviors. (The title of their report referred to "causes" of the behaviors, which perhaps implies–incorrectly–that they studied the history of the behaviors.)

Similarly with respect to problem solving, one issue is how the behaviors originate; however, given that they did originate–given that they are now in an organism's behavioral repertoire–the issue is to predict and control when the behaviors will occur. This "given" is generally all we can know about an individual human, even in the newborn period; we know that the behaviors occur now and that they must have originated somehow, but very often we do not know how they originated. Therefore, the relevant issue is generally the latter one–to predict and control the occurrences of the behaviors. I suggest that the first gap identified by Skinner, that is, the gap between antecedent stimulation and behavior, needs to be filled in order to make such prediction and control possible. In short, when the relevant history of the organism is unknown, it cannot be used as a basis for prediction and control of behavior; in this case, knowing the current status of the organism's mind may provide a basis for prediction and control of behavior.

Another role of cognitive research. Developmental behavior analysts have an additional reason for needing to know the current status of the organism's mind. (I use the phrase "developmental behavior analysis" as an analogue of "developmental psychology.") Developmentalists are interested in *what* changes with development and *how* the changes come about. Baer (1973) outlined a three-stage research program that could be used to find out how the changes come about. The first stage involves experimental analysis: A behavior is selected for study and is taken into the laboratory and shown to be operant behavior (it is brought under stimulus control). The second stage involves naturalistic observations: The behavior is observed in the natural environment to see whether any stimulus changes are correlated with occurrences of the behavior. The third stage involves intervention: The stimulus changes that are identified in the second stage are manipulated in the third stage to see whether they have effective stimulus functions. The point I want to make here is that behavior analysis as such does not indicate what behaviors might be fruitfully selected for study; it deals with *how* the changes come about, not with *what* changes normally occur. Research on the mind–preferably experimental research rather than naturalistic–can identify what the normal changes are–the behaviors that seem to be worth studying.

The study by Repp et al. (1988) cited earlier involved the second two stages (although they did not identify them as such and did not cite Baer's article). First, they observed correlations of problem behaviors with occurrences and terminations of stimuli and, depending on which of these correlations was predominant, they hypothesized that positive or negative reinforcement was maintaining the behaviors. Second, they manipulated the contingencies experimentally. The method was successful.

Private Events

Butterfield, Siladi, and Belmont (1980) demonstrated the usefulness of task analysis in terms of cognitive activities, including not only the cognitive activities of research participants but also the cognitive activities of researchers in conducting the

Table 3 - Examples of Analyses of Problem Solving into Steps

Composite	Bransford & Stein (1984)	Skinner & Chapman (1984)[a]	Polya (1948)	Luria (1973)	Butterfield et al. (1980)	Kingsley & Garry[b]	D'Zurilla (1986)	Osborn[c]
0. Difficulty is felt	Identify the problem					Feeling of difficulty	Problem orientation	
1. Define the problem	Define the problem		Understand the problem			Clarify & define the problem	Define the problem	Define the problem
2. Gather information	Select a goal	Set a goal			Set a goal	Gather information		Gather & analyze information
3. Identify possible solutions	Explore possible strategies	Generate plans and	Devise a plan	State a plan		Try possible solutions	Generate solutions	Generate, Refine, & Evaluate possible solutions
4. Select a plan	select a plan			Concretize the plan	Select a strategy[d]		Make a decision	Select a solution
5. Carry out the plan	Act on the strategies	Operate the plan	Carry out the plan		Implement the strategy	Adopt a solution[e]	Implement solution	
6. Test the outcome	Look back and evaluate	Evaluate the outcome	Look back	See if problem is solved	Assess the outcome	Test the solution	Verify the solution	
7. Change the plan		Adjust the plan		React to preceding[f]				

Note. Adapted in part from Reese, 1992a, Table 6, p. 175. [a]Frese & Stewart (1984) identified the same steps. [b]Kingsley & Garry, 1957; different in Garry & Kingsley, 1970, pp. 464-466: (1) Search, gather information, and define the problem, (2) find possible solutions, (3) develop an actual solution and test it. [c]Osborn (1962). Elsewhere, he (1963) included more preparatory steps: Identify all phases of the problem; Select problem(s) to be attacked; Identify needed information; Identify relevant sources of information; Generate possible solutions; Select possible solutions; Generate possible tests of solutions; Select best tests; Generate possible obstacles; Select best solution (pp. 207-208). [d]Includes Estimate outcomes, Compare estimates of goals, and Select strategy with smallest goal/estimate discrepancy. [e]Includes as an alternative, abandon the problem. [f]If problem has been solved, stop problem-solving activity; if not solved, start over.

research and analyzing the data. In behavior analysis, cognitive activities are in the class called private events.

Assumptions about private events. Private events are assumed to be behaviors that are covert, that is, unobserved because they occur "inside the skin" (Skinner, 1974, p. 207); but they are assumed to operate in accordance with all the laws of overt behaviors except those involving direct, verifiable observation (e.g., Morris, Higgins, & Bickel, 1982). These two assumptions are necessary because without them, the only alternatives open to behavior analysts would presumably be to assume that (a) private events do not exist, (b) private events exist but they are not behaviors, or (c) private events are behaviors but they operate in accordance with laws other than the laws of overt behaviors.

(a) Behavior analysts (e.g., Baer, 1982) reject the first alternative, which asserts that private events do not exist. They argue that acceptance of the reality of private events is one of the major differences between behavior analysis and what they call methodological behaviorism, which is what White called the learning theory tradition (White, 1970) or theoretical behaviorism (White, 1976) rather than what Bergmann (1956) called methodological behaviorism. Their argument is that methodological behaviorists denied the existence of private events, which is not true (Bergmann, 1956; Reese, 1971), and that behavior analysts not only accept the existence of private events but also study them, which is true although in practice most behavior analysts neither acknowledge nor study private events. In any case, behavior analysts clearly accept the reality of private events.

(b) Behavior analysts also reject the second alternative, which asserts that private events are not behaviors. I believe they must reject this assumption in order to retain their mechanistic model of the organism. Many of them deny that their model of the organism is mechanistic, apparently in an attempt to distinguish between behavior analysis and methodological behaviorism; but colleagues and I (Hayes et al., 1988; Reese, 1986a) showed that the organism is conceptualized as mechanical in behavior analysis even though the method of studying it is pragmatic. As Skinner (1969) said, "Man *is* a machine, but he is a very complex one" (p. 294); the alternative to this view, he said, is that human behavior can be explained only by taking account of consciousness and free will (p. 295), that is, by assuming that mind is uniquely causal. The components of a machine are a structure and its functions, or hardware and operations of the hardware, and the analogues in the organism are physical parts (bones, muscles, nerves, brain matter) and behavior. Private events are not usefully represented as physical parts; they are usefully represented only as behaviors.

(c) Behavior analysts also reject the third alternative assumption, which asserts that the laws of private events are different from the laws of other behaviors. This assumption is inconsistent with the mechanistic model of the organism because the machine operates in accordance with a universal set of laws whether or not the operations are visible. Thus, given that private events are assumed to be behaviors, the universal laws of behavior must operate. However, because private events are inaccessible to direct, verifiable observation, the assumption that the relevant laws are the same as for overt behavior and the alternative assumption that the laws are different are equally untestable and whichever assumption is accepted, it is accepted as an unverifiable presupposition. One consequence is that when behavior analysts talk about rule-governed behavior, they generally conceptualize the rule as covert behavior, and although Skinner (1957, p. 449) explicitly said that such covert behavior constitutes thinking and can be nonverbal as well as verbal (and can be overt as well as covert), in practice behavior analysts conceptualize rules as verbal behavior, that is, overt or covert speaking (e.g., Skinner, 1966; Sulzer-Azaroff & Mayer, 1991; Vaughan, 1989). I have argued elsewhere (Reese, 1992b) that this conceptualization is the only reasonable way to interpret rules that can control behavior, as contrasted with rules that describe behavior or that are instantiated by behavior.

The necessity of inference. Occurrences of covert rules and other private events are directly available only to first-person observation, if indeed they are available even to that. Any science based on such first-person reports would be solipsistic because although the reports would be directly available for verification by others, the occurrences purported to be reported would not be verifiable. Consequently, statements about occurrences of private events in a nonsolipsistic science must reflect inference and not direct observation and they must be excluded from any science that excludes statements about events that occur at levels other than the level of observation. Behavior analysis has been said to exclude statements about events and processes occurring at other levels (e.g., Morris, Higgins, & Bickel, 1982); therefore, either the concept of private events is rejected after all or the "other levels" assertion is nonfunctional. Private events are not denied; therefore, the "other levels" assertion is nonfunctional. Given that it is nonfunctional, inferences about cognitive activities can be entirely consistent with behavior analysis. That is, the observations that are examined are reports of private events, and the private events occur at a different level from these observations; but nevertheless, behavior analysts use the observations—legitimately—as a basis for inferring occurrences of the private events at their "other level."

In short, Butterfield et al. (1980) analyzed tasks into cognitive activities and behavior analysts analyze tasks into behaviors, which include speaking and private events. The next step in both approaches is to check the task analysis experimentally; but this insistence on successful working, or successful practice, does not mean that the approaches are compatible. They fit the data into different Procrustean beds by the nature of their inferences about cognitive activities—mental processes versus covert behaviors.

One final point is that in both approaches, the inferred cognitive activities are correctly identified as hypothetical constructs, not as intervening variables (as these phrases were defined by MacCorquodale and Meehl, 1948). Hypothetical constructs designate entities that are presumed to be ontologically real but that are unobserved (if they were observed, the terms designating them would not be called "hypothetical"). Examples in Hull-Spence theory are the fractional anticipatory goal response and unobserved emotional responses (e.g., Spence, 1956, pp. 49-51). Intervening variables, in contrast, are defined as mathematical functions of empirical variables and they have no other empirical reference. The constructs of habit ($_sH_R$) and drive (D) in Hull-Spence theory are examples of intervening variables; they were defined not as the names of ontologically real entities but as mathematical functions of, respectively, the frequency of rewarded occurrences of a response and time of deprivation or strength of noxious stimulation (e.g., Spence, 1956, chap. 4). Intervening variables are useful only for simplifying descriptions of empirical relationships and for facilitating the deduction of as yet unknown empirical relationships. Improvements in measuring instruments might someday make the referents of hypothetical constructs directly observable; the ontologically real aspects of intervening variables are already observable.

Summary of the Behavior Analytic Approach

As Skinner (1989) said, behavior analysts want to understand the origins of behavior—"why people behave as they do" (p. 18). Thus, for example, Baer's (1982) answer to the question of how a person extracts square roots with paper and pencil was that the person learned to emit that behavior in those situations. Cognitive psychologists want to understand the mediation of behavior—how people behave as they do. For example, what is the mental algorithm that leads a person to make particular marks on a piece of paper such that the final marks represent the square root of the number represented by the initial marks?

Skinner (1974) argued that mental activities need not be taken into account in the prediction and control of behavior because these activities are actually behaviors and as such their occurrences and outcomes are completely determined by the genetic endowments and reinforcement history of the organism and the current setting. Thus, knowing the genetic endowments, the history, and the current setting yields all the accuracy of prediction and efficacy of control that can be obtained. Taking mind into account is unnecessary. However, even if one grants the premise that mind and its effects are completely determined, which is a rejection of the concept of mind as uniquely causal, one could still point out that except in highly circumscribed laboratory settings, behavior analysts seldom if ever actually know enough about the history of an individual organism and its current setting to yield accurate prediction or effective control. Thus, one can argue that knowing (diagnosing; inferring) the organism's mental activities may often yield better prediction and control of the organism's behavior.

The situation is entirely the same with respect to genetic endowments and mental activities. On the one hand, if one knows the phylogenetic history of the organism, the genetic endowments are known; and if one knows the reinforcement history of the organism, the mental activities are known. On the other hand, when these histories are unknown, as is usually the case, knowing the products of the histories—the genetic endowments and the mental activities—can be as useful for prediction and control as knowing the histories.

Practical Approach

Specialized guidelines have been developed for dealing with personal problems, for example for use by counselors, parents, and teachers (e.g., Carkhuff, 1973) and for dealing with problems in business and industry (e.g., Nadler & Hibino, 1990). All of them divide problem solving into several steps, some of which may occur simultaneously or may occur in various sequences. A set of steps and principles about how the steps are interrelated reflect a task analysis of problem solving and constitute a heuristic system. Most of the specialized heuristic systems that have been developed overlap considerably with heuristic systems developed for dealing with laboratory problems or with practical problems, as will be seen later. One exception is Nadler and Hibino's (1990) system, which they called Breakthrough Thinking™ and which includes seven rules none of which is in the standard systems. It is not summarized herein because of space limitations.

Table 3 summarizes several heuristic systems developed to represent problem solving, reflecting information-processing theory (Bransford & Stein, 1984), European "action theory" (Skinner & Chapman, 1984), mathematical and practical problem solving (Polya, 1948), theories of intelligence (Soviet psychology: Luria, 1973; information processing: Butterfield et al., 1980), learning theory (Kingsley & Garry, 1957), clinical intervention (D'Zurilla, 1986), and problem solving in business and industry (Osborn, 1962). Davis (1973, p. 16) suggested that all systems such as these could be reduced to two steps identified by John Dewey: Recognizing a perplexity and searching for information that resolves the perplexity (Dewey, 1933, p. 12). However, this is the kind of reduction that is possible only if all the other steps are already known and are implicitly included, much like the parental admonition to a child, "Use your head." Actually, Dewey also identified five steps between these two; they are the "phases" of "reflective thinking" (pp. 106-115). Dewey's complete set of seven steps is: (a) Recognizing a perplexity (Step 0 in Table 3); (b) inhibiting direct action to permit thinking about the problem (related to Step 2 in Table 3); (c) defining the problem—"a question well put is half answered" (p. 108) (Step 1 in Table 3); (d) generating hypotheses, or possible solutions (Step 3); (e) using relevant knowledge as a basis for reasoning about the possible solutions (related to Steps 2 and 4); (f) enacting a selected solution, testing it, and if desirable, modifying it (Steps 5, 6, and 7); and (g) reacting (emotionally) to success (not in Table 3).

According to the definition of problem solving used in the present paper, Step 1 in the table needs to be divided into two steps. Step 1a is to define the goal state and Step 1b is to identify obstacles to being in the goal state. Additional steps have been described in systems not included in the table. For example, Luria (1929/1978) identified three steps that do not fit well with the others: Work out a plan, check it against the situation, and if it fits the situation, implement it. Another example is Wallas (1926, chap. 4), who thought that problem solving is a matter of incubation and illumination, or insight, which involve a predominantly unconscious train of associations. Wallas said that introspective reports often reveal an Intimation that the insight is about to emerge, and he said that conscious effort at that point can disrupt the train of associations and thus prevent emergence of the insight. However, Osborn (1963, chap. 22), who also discussed the virtues of incubation and illumination, noted that incubation can be promoted in several ways, including deliberately beginning a project early enough to allow time for incubation to occur. The validity of the insight is tested in a stage of "verification," which includes stating the insight precisely. In the older literature, insight was often considered to be nonverbal and the problem was said to be not actually solved until the insight had been precisely stated.

Another step not included in Table 3 is found in several systems for problem solving in business and industry: *Get the plan accepted*. This step would come between Steps 4 and 5 in the table; it is needed when the plan must be approved by someone other than the problem solver before it can be implemented, for example by a higher-level manager or by the persons who will implement the plan (Parnes, Noller, & Biondi, 1977, pp. 348-351).

These systems are theoretical task analyses, or idealizations, not descriptions of empirically observed problem solving. That is, these are theoretical prescriptions, not empirical descriptions. Nevertheless, research has demonstrated that the use of steps works, and although the criterion of success has often been scores on tests (e.g., Reese & Parnes, 1970; Reese, Parnes, Treffinger, & Kaltsounis, 1976), the criterion has sometimes been success in solving real problems (Soll, 1982) or simulations of real problems (Dillon, 1982; Sappington & Farrar, 1982).

RESEARCH METHODOLOGY
Variables Affecting Problem Solving

The variables assumed or known to influence problem solving include personal characteristics such as motivation, personality traits, rigidity, and set, (e.g., Duncan, 1959; Garry & Kingsley, 1970, pp. 469-471), intelligence, knowledge, and personal involvement (Garry & Kingsley, ibid.), culture and socioeconomic status (Sinha, 1982), other individual difference variables (Kagan & Kogan, 1970), and training in problem-solving skills (Reese & Parnes, 1970; Reese et al., 1976; Rubin, Fein, & Vandenberg, 1983; Weinert & Treiber, 1982). The relevant variables also include task characteristics such as complexity (Garry & Kingsley, ibid.) and virtually unknown variables that presumably account for the pervasive finding of little transfer between different problem-solving tasks (e.g., Laboratory of Comparative Human Cognition, 1983; Siegler, 1983). The effects of these variables are not reviewed herein, even though the effects of training are especially relevant in light of Skinner's (1968) remarks about the need to train precurrent behaviors in school (pp. 118-119)—a topic included in Weinert and Treiber's (1982) review.

Methods for Studying Problem Solving
Erroneous Use of Group Means

Cognitive psychologists are often interested in the cognitive activities of the individual person; and they design studies that allow them to infer these individual activities. When designs like these are used, the researcher receives the punt in good field position; but many cognitive psychologists then fumble the ball on the next play by using group means to infer the cognitive activities of the group-as-a-whole, which of course is a fiction.

The point is obvious, yet I have found—as editor of the *Journal of Experimental Child Psychology*, as a reviewer for several other journals, and as a general reader—that an amazingly large number of cognitive psychologists make this mistake, including some who are well known and highly regarded in the field. They seem not to understand their own research methodology, and they probably would not see the point of Skinner's (1956, p. 228) remark that nobody goes to the circus to see the average dog jump through the hoop.

Erroneous Use of Mean Performance

One of the standard tasks in Piagetian research involves the conservation of mass. The examiner shows the research participant two equal balls of plasticine and after the participant agrees that they are the same in amount, the examiner molds one of them into a different shape and asks the participant whether the lumps are still equal or whether one of them now has more plasticine. In the best research, the examiner also asks the participant to explain his or her judgment (the characterization of this procedure as the best is controversial; e.g., Chapman & Lindenberger, 1992).

Many North American Piagetian researchers give multiple trials on a task such as this one, with different shapes or other differences, and assign one point for each correct judgment and, if explanations are asked for, one point for each correct explanation. Thus, if 6 trials are given and explanations are asked for, the scores can range from 0 to 12. In a typical study of this sort, the test is given before and after a training period and then the scores are assessed with a condition (experimental versus control) by test (pretest versus posttest) analysis of variance. This approach is wrong because only qualitative scores are meaningful on a task such as conservation; quantitative scores on such a task are uninterpretable. Unless the performance is completely ambiguous, it indicates that a child understands the logical basis of conservation, does not understand this basis, or is "transitional," that is, about to learn the basis. A child cannot two-thirds or three-fourths understand that conservation has a logical basis, because this understanding is all-or-none. A "transitional" child is not a child with a particular score; he or she is a child with a particular pattern of performance.

Some of the research reviewed by Marc Branch (this volume) also illustrates the erroneous use of mean performance; for example, mean performance curves that appear to reflect continuous gradations of response times may reflect variations in the proportionate rates of a fast and a slow response.

The Analysis of Performance Patterns

Understanding any domain requires organizing the information in it. Organizing the information starts with identifying a unit of analysis; and in many domains, the unit of analysis is not the individual element but the pattern of elements. In the domain of research on problem solving, patterns of performance are often the units that are used as bases for inferring the problem-solving rules that were used.

Hypothetical example. Table 4 shows the performance of two hypothetical children, both with a score of 6 on a 6-trial conservation task. Child A gives 3 correct judgments and 3 correct explanations, not all on the same trials, and Child B gives 6 correct judgments and no correct explanations. A correct judgment is saying "same" and the gist of a correct explanation is saying "because you didn't add anything and you didn't take anything away." The number of "same" judgments expected to result from guessing is hard to estimate, but a reasonable expectation is that guessing might yield 3 correct judgments and is very unlikely to yield 6 correct judgments. Therefore, Child B seems to know something that Child A does not know.

Table 4

Performance of Two Hypothetical Children on a 6-Trial Conservation Task

	Child A		Child B	
Trial	Judgment	Explanation	Judgment	Explanation
1	-	-	+	-
2	+	+	+	-
3	+	-	+	-
4	-	+	+	-
5	+	+	+	-
6	-	-	+	-

Guessing seems to have virtually no likelihood of yielding a correct explanation, although a child who gives only one correct explanation might be repeating something heard but not understood. Child B in the hypothetical example may not understand the question being asked about explanation or may not know how to express the explanation verbally (cognitivists believe that nonverbal knowing is not only possible but also prevalent in childhood—for brief discussion see Chapman and Lindenberger, 1992). Despite these possibilities, the best inference from this hypothetical child's pattern of performance is that he or she does not understand the logical basis of conservation. If the incorrect explanations seem to be based on empirical evidence, then this child might be classified as "transitional." That is, the child who believes that the conservation of mass is an empirical truth—a law of nature—is well on the way to realizing that it is actually a logical truth.

If a child gives some correct judgments and they are always accompanied by a correct explanation, then either the child learned these responses by rote, without understanding, or the child understands the logic of conservation but does not always apply it to specific problems. The latter interpretation is generally the more plausible one. Child A's pattern of performance does not fit this model because Trials 3 and 4 show mismatches of judgments and explanations. Therefore, the best inference is that the pattern of performance is ambiguous and that Child A is unclassifiable. Some Piagetian researchers would classify this child as "transitional" because the score is in the middle range, but "unclassifiable" is more appropriate because the pattern of performance provides no evidence that the child is about to realize that conservation has a logical basis.

A research example. Figure 1 shows schematic drawings of six kinds of balance-scale problems used by Klahr and Siegler (1978). The apparatus consists of a beam with a fulcrum at the midpoint and with four equally spaced pegs on each side of the midpoint. Metal washers, all the same weight, can be placed on the pegs. On a given trial, blocks are placed under the two ends of the beam so that it does not move when the weights are placed on the pegs. After the blocks and weights are placed, the research participant is asked to predict whether the scale will remain balanced when the blocks are removed, will go down on the left, or will go down on the right. The only two variables that are manipulated are the number of weights on each side of the fulcrum and the distances of the weights from the fulcrum. In an actual experiment, several problems of each type are given and the correct prediction as to side is counterbalanced across the problems. However, for ease of describing the results, the specific problems shown in Figure 1 are referred to in the following discussion.

Klahr and Siegler tested children and adolescents, but only the data for the youngest group--5- and 6-year-olds—are described here. (a) In the problem labeled Balance, the number of weights at each distance is the same on both sides. The children correctly predicted that the scale would balance. (b) In the Weight problem, the distances are the same but the left side has more weights at one of the distances. Almost all of the children's predictions were again correct—left side down. (c) In the Distance problem, the number of weights is the same on both sides but the distance is greater on the left side. Almost all of the predictions were "balance," which is incorrect. The results for these three problems imply that the children were basing their predictions on a "Weight rule": Balance and imbalance depend only on whether or not the number of weights is the same on both sides.

(d) In the Conflict-Weight problem, weight and distance are potentially conflicting cues in that the left side has more weights but these weights have less "distance"–they are closer to the fulcrum than the weights on the right side. Most

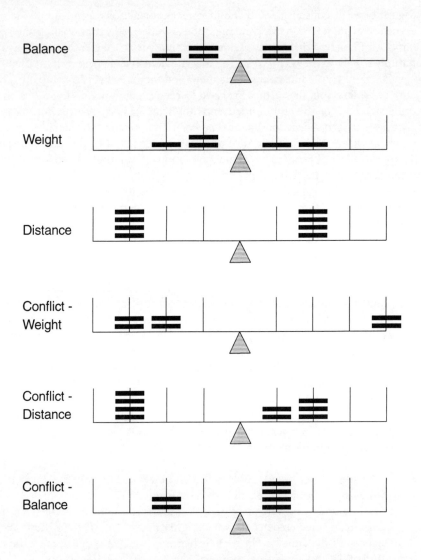

*Figure 1. Symbolic representation of the balance-scale problems
used by Klahr and Siegler (1978).*

of the children's predictions were left side down, which is correct. Thus, most of the
children evidently used the Weight rule and ignored the conflict with distance. (e)
Use of the Weight rule yields incorrect responses on the Conflict-Distance and
Conflict-Balance problems. Most of the children's predictions were wrong on these
problems.

The middle column in Table 5 shows the group results just described and the last column shows the percentages correct that are expected if the Weight rule is used correctly and consistently across all problems of a given type. (A person who correctly uses the fully correct rule—"compute torque"—will make correct predictions on all the problems, including left down on the Conflict-Distance problem and balance on the Conflict-Balance problem.)

The group results in Table 5 are means of means: The mean across children of the mean correct for a child across the problems of each type. These group means are not informative because the obtained percentages did not correspond precisely to the expected percentages. Therefore, Klahr and Siegler also compared each participant's pattern of predictions with patterns that would be expected if various rules were used. They found that 77% of the 5- and 6-year-olds exhibited patterns consistent with the Weight rule and the other 23% exhibited patterns that were unclassifiable, that is, not consistent with any rule that could be inferred from performance on the selected set of problems. Thus, about three-quarters of the children can be inferred to have used the Weight rule.

The finding that almost a fourth of the group was not classifiable is disturbing, but Klahr and Siegler used a very strict criterion of fit and young children are notoriously variable in applying their knowledge, partly perhaps because they are

Table 5

Performance of 5- and 6-Year-Olds in Klahr and Siegler's (1978) Study

Problem type	Percentage obtained	Percentage expected
Balance	94	100
Weight	88	100
Distance	9	0
Conflict-Weight	86	100
Conflict-Distance	11	0
Conflict-Balance	7	0

Note. "Percentage obtained" is the mean percentage correct responses across multiple problems of each type. "Percentage expected" is the percentage correct expected if the Weight rule (see text) is used correctly and consistently. (Means from Klahr & Siegler, 1978, Table II, p. 70.)

often impulsive and often inattentive. This variability was taken into account by most of the non-Skinnerian experimental child psychologists by the use of learning criteria that allowed a small number of errors (a popular criterion in studies of young children's two-stimulus discrimination learning was 9 correct out of 10 consecutive correct responses, which has a chance probability of .01).

Another research example. Another example is a study of moral reasoning by Leon (1984). He was interested in the relation between mothers' and sons' moral reasoning, and like Klahr and Siegler (1978), he used the pattern of performance across conditions as the basis for inferring the rules being used. Briefly, Leon presented scenarios varying in the amount of damage resulting from a child's behavior (none, moderate, severe) and in the child's intent to do damage (accident, displaced anger, malice), with repetitions of the scenarios to permit analysis of variance of each research participant's scores. The scores were the amounts of punishment said by the participant to be deserved. Leon defined several rules that would yield different patterns of significant and nonsignificant effects in an analysis of variance of an individual's performance. The results showed that three rules were sufficient to classify all the mothers tested. The rules were: (a) A *linear rule* weights damage and intent equally and additively, yielding significant positive main effects of damage and intent and no significant interaction. (b) A *configural rule* is the same as the linear rule except that no punishment is assigned for accidents, yielding significant positive main effects of damage and intent and a significant interaction reflecting increased punishment with increasing damage only when the damage was intended. (c) A *damage-only rule* assigns punishment on the basis only of amount of damage, yielding a significant positive main effect of damage, a nonsignificant effect of intent, and a nonsignificant interaction.

Figure 2 shows the mean ratings for the three groups of mothers Leon identified. The curves had to turn out about as they did because they reflect the patterns of significant and nonsignificant effects that Leon used to form the groups.

This study illustrates two important methodological points (aside from its relevance to the development of moral reasoning). One point is that a group method of statistical analysis can be used for evaluation of an individual's performance. The issue is how to get a precise specification of an individual's pattern of performance. One way, endorsed by behavior analysts, is visual examination of the measures; another way, disfavored by behavior analysts, is statistical analysis. However, Leon's use of statistical analysis is not the use that behavior analysts should disfavor; he used inferential statistics for description, which is a legitimate kind of data reduction, rather than for hypothesis testing, which is the use behavior analysts properly disfavor.

The second point is illustrated in Figure 3, which shows the means of the ratings over all the mothers, disregarding inferred rule groupings. As can be seen, if these group means were used to infer the punishment rule the mothers endorsed, the group would be inferred to have endorsed the linear rule: main effects of intent and of damage, no interaction. Thus, the overall group means are accurately descriptive

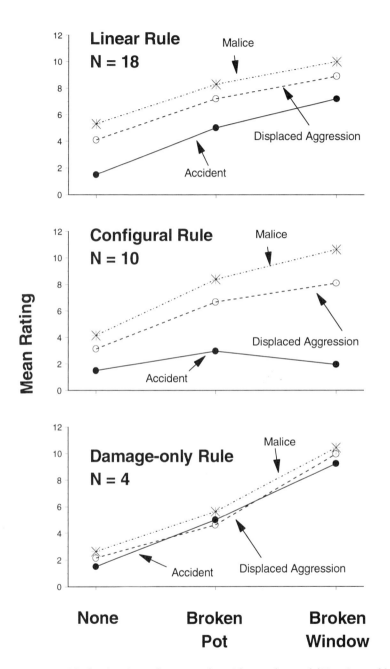

Figure 2. Mothers' ratings of amount of punishment deserved (12-point scale) by hypothetical children varying in intent and amount of damage done. The mothers were grouped using the rules described in the text. (Adapted from Leon, 1984, Fig. 1, p. 2109. Used by permission.)

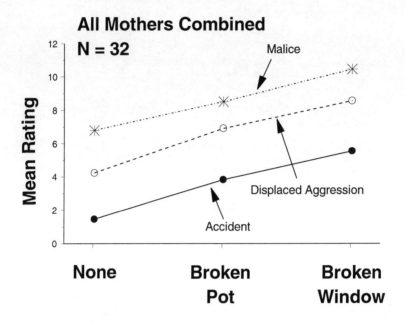

Figure 3. Group means of ratings over all the mothers in Leon's (1984) study, disregarding the groupings shown in Figure 2.

only for the 18 mothers in the linear rule group, that is, only 56% of the mothers in the study.

Examples in behavior analysis. The pattern of performance is often the appropriate unit of analysis in behavioral research. One example is research on schedule effects, in which the focus is usually on the shape of the cumulative response curve rather than on individual key pecks or other individual responses. Hyten and Madden (1990) argued on the basis of such patterns that fixed interval schedules do not lead to scalloping, contrary to the standard interpretation (e.g., Catania, 1992, p. 168), but rather lead to break-and-run responding, which is usually associated with large-ratio variable ratio schedules and fixed ratio schedules (Catania, pp. 161, 169).

Another example is stimulus equivalence research, in which the inference of stimulus equivalence depends on the pattern of responding across tests of reflexivity, symmetry, and transitivity (e.g., Sidman, 1992).

A final example is Place's (1991) method of conversation analysis, which is based on behavior analytic principles and in which the unit of analysis is the actually spoken sentence or sentence fragment rather than the word as such. The unit consists of a particular semantic content, or set of words, emitted by a speaker or received by a listener in a particular syntactic frame. The Marxist psychologist A. R. Luria (1969) also used the sentence, or "connected utterance," as the basic unit of speech (but the word as the basic unit of language). Luria mentioned that for toddlers the connected utterance is a unit and the words in it are inseparable; for example, the toddler who understands "Come here" and "Where is Daddy?" might not understand the recombination of the words into the connected utterance, "Come to Daddy" (p. 139).

Guidelines for Inferring Cognitive Activities

Even the most radical cognitivists–the Piagetians–do not freely invent cognitive activities, but rather they constrain their inventions on the basis of objective evidence. As indicated in the preceding subsection, the objective evidence is often a certain pattern of performance. Other kinds of objective evidence include verbal reports by the research participants. Whatever kind of objective evidence is used, it is used in accordance with guidelines about criteria. I have discussed such guidelines elsewhere (Reese, 1989) in some detail and will only summarize them here: The occurrence of a cognitive activity is implied by (a) regularity of behavior; (b) behavioral discontinuity or the "insight curve"; (c) reported awareness of cognitive activity; (d) consistency of behavior with a rule; (e) certain concomitant behavior, such as moving the lips (an "adjunctive" behavior in young children) and scratching the head (a "collateral" behavior in adults); and (f) generalization. No one criterion is compelling by itself, and as I pointed out elsewhere (Reese, 1971, 1989), the inference that a cognitive activity occurred is always theory-based. The inference is essentially a syllogism of the following form:

Major premise: If a person performs A (a specified cognitive activity), then the person will exhibit B (e.g., a specified regularity in behavior, or a specified concomitant behavior).

Minor premise: The person exhibits B.

Conclusion: The person performed A.

The major premise is a more or less well articulated "theory"; the minor premise is the evidence observed; and the conclusion is the inference about the cognitive activity. This is the standard method of scientific inference; it involves the logical fallacy of affirming the consequent, but this logical flaw is understood not as an invalidation of the method but as a warning against overconfidence in the conclusion.

Classification of Tasks

In cognitive research, problem solving is often described as moving through a "problem space," which consists of an initial state, a desired or desirable goal state that is different from the initial state, perhaps intermediate states, operations for moving from state to state (e.g., Anderson, 1990, p. 223; Mayer, 1983, p. 169), and "the total knowledge available to the problem solver" (Newell & Simon, 1972, p. 810). Except for the part about total knowledge, which is seldom mentioned in the relevant literature, this description is consistent with the definition of problem solving adopted in the present paper–in fact it is the basis for this definition.

Many different systems for classifying problems have been developed (e.g., Arlin, 1989), usually (e.g., Wood, 1983) but not always (e.g., Simon, 1978) because of anticipated differences in how different classes of problems are solved. Many dimensions of difference have been proposed, but most of the current systems include the dimension of problem definition or structure.

Definition and Structure

Problems differ in the ease of identifying the relevant problem space (Anzai, 1987; Reitman, 1965, p. 151). A problem is said to be well-defined or well-structured if the relevant problem space is easy to identify and ill-defined or ill-structured if it is hard to identify. Some writers seem to distinguish between definition and structure, but the distinction is not clear (e.g., in Arlin, 1989); other writers seem to use definition and structure as synonyms (e.g., Simon, 1978); and still others refer only to definition (e.g., Galotti, 1989). I will use the last two conventions and refer only to "definition."

The relevant problem space may be hard to identify because of uncertainty about (a) the initial state, (b) the goal state, (c) the operations that will be effective, or (d) the criteria for effectiveness, that is, for correct or optimal solutions. In some systems, the last feature is the only essential one: A well-defined problem has a single correct solution and an ill-defined problem has multiple acceptable solutions, though perhaps only one optimal solution (e.g., Lee, 1989; Sinnott, 1989b; Wood, 1983). However, a problem may be well- or ill-defined with respect to the initial state as well as the goal state (Reitman, 1965, p. 151).

Divergent and Convergent Problems

Whether or not the definition of correct or optimal solutions is central, problems vary in the extent to which the criteria defining solution accuracy or effectiveness are explicitly and clearly specified (Reitman, 1965, p. 148). Problems also vary in the number of solutions that can satisfy these criteria. Problems that do not have a single objectively correct solution are best approached by means of divergent thinking; consequently, they are herein designated as "divergent" problems. Divergent problems are generally ill-defined at least in the sense that the path to the goal is initially unclear and often in the sense that the goal is also initially unclear. Problems that have one objectively correct solution are best approached by means of convergent thinking; therefore, they are designated herein as "convergent" problems. Convergent problems can be well- or ill-defined. Well-defined convergent problems have strong task demands and therefore these problems give research participants little leeway for defining the problem to suit their problem-solving capabilities. Convergent problems can be solved by trial and error, and if they are, then behavioral variability can have an important influence (Maier, 1940; see also herein the discussion of principle f in the subsection *Unsuccessful Problem Solving*).

Contrived and Practical Problems

Another important dimension on which problems differ seems to be universally accepted even though it is hard to define. The distinction is between artificial laboratory problems, or "contrived" problems (Arlin, 1989), and real-life, everyday, or practical problems; the difficulty of defining the distinction can be seen in Sinnott's (1989a) edited book, *Everyday Problem Solving*. One difficulty in making the distinction is that it may be confounded with familiarity (Arlin, 1989). Examples that are considered later in the present paper are the Refrigerator problem, which is a familiar practical problem of dealing with broken appliances, and the Poisoned Meals problem, which involves familiar materials but is a contrived concept-identification problem. Sinnott and Cook (1989) suggested that the distinction can be made by asking, "Is this ever likely to happen to anyone, and if it did, would they care?" (p. 40). This criterion is problematic, but it will serve.

Both contrived and practical problems can be well- or ill-defined, although practical problems are believed to be usually ill-defined (e.g., Luszcz, 1989; Meacham & Emont, 1989). In research on creativity, the usual problems have been ill-defined, divergent, and contrived. In most of the other research on problem solving, the problems used have been well-defined and convergent, but still contrived. Practical problems or, more often, laboratory simulations of practical problems have also been used, especially in research on cognitive aging (Reese & Rodeheaver, 1985; see also the chapters in Sinnott, 1989a, and selected chapters in Puckett & Reese, 1993). The practical problems and simulations used have included both well- and ill-defined problems and both divergent and convergent problems. Some of this research is reviewed in the next section.

SURVEY OF SELECTED RESEARCH FINDINGS

Divergent Problems

The problem used by Leon (1984), summarized earlier (in the subsection **Another research example**), is an example of problems that are intended to be ill-defined and divergent. Other examples are problems used by Max Wertheimer in his seminars on problem solving and thinking, Maier's two-string problem, and the Refrigerator problem, which are discussed in this order in the following subsections.

Examples of Wertheimer's Problems

Wertheimer's seminars on problem solving and thinking were reconstructed by Luchins and Luchins (1970). According to the reconstruction, Wertheimer gave the seminar many problems to solve in order to illustrate points about these topics. The following three problems are examples. All three are ill-defined, divergent, and, for most persons, contrived. (a) "How would you reverse a locomotive in a railroad station?" (b) "A table has a drawer that can be pulled open from two sides. How is it constructed?" (c) "A door in a certain room can be opened from both sides. It is not a swinging door. How is this brought about?" (Luchins & Luchins, 1970, p. 257). These are divergent problems because they do not have single objectively correct solutions. The obstacle in each case is that no solution is immediately apparent.

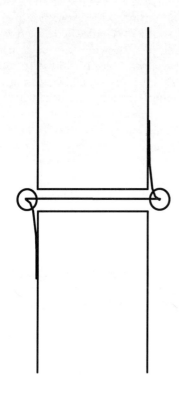

Figure 4. Duncker's solution to the Door problem: A two-way hinge. (Redrawn from Duncker, 1945, Fig. 10, p. 27. Used by permission.)

In the reconstruction by Luchins and Luchins, only the solution for the Locomotive problem was described in detail. The students in the seminar suggested some workable solutions: Build a loop in the track; install a crane that can lift the locomotive and turn it around. Wertheimer disallowed these solutions by introducing a boundary condition: The station is too small to hold the loop and the crane. A student eventually said build a turntable. This solution satisfied Wertheimer's aim, which was to illustrate the principle of reorganization in problem solving; in this problem, the reorganization was to interchange the functions of the track and the locomotive—the one that is ordinarily stationary moves and the one that ordinarily moves is stationary (p. 258). When I read the problem, I attempted to solve it before reading the discussion, and I turned out to have had a simpler solution: Put the locomotive in reverse gear. (My colleague Joseph Laipple had the same solution—personal communication, June 9, 1992.)

Wertheimer's solution for the Drawer problem involved running the drawer on two sets of tracks, one forward and backward and the other left and right (p. 259). I do not see how this solution could work; but again I had a simpler solution before reading the discussion. In my solution, the "two sides" of the table were the front and back, requiring only one set of tracks. My drawer had no stop to prevent its being pulled completely out of the table; I later thought that a pivoting stop might work, but I did not work out the details.

For the Door problem, Wertheimer's solution was to have "a hinge that has a double function; one part of the hinge serves as a hinge for the door to swing on when it turns in one direction, but this part becomes a part of the door when it swings in the other direction" (p. 258). Again, I had a simpler solution before reading the discussion: Push the door outward from one side and pull it inward from the other side. After reading the discussion, I worked out a drawing of Wertheimer's hinge, and I later found that Duncker (1945) had earlier drawn essentially the same hinge—it is shown Figure 4.

Figure 5. The two-string problem as illustrated by Maier. (From Maier, 1945, Figure 1, p. 351. Used by permission.)

These considerations illustrate a basic principle of problem solving: Even a divergent problem can be solved in an objectively satisfactory way, but not unless the problem solver and the solution evaluator interpret the problem in the same way. My solutions would not have been satisfactory to Wertheimer because he and I turned out to be implicitly using different interpretations of "reverse" in the Locomotive problem, "two sides" in the Drawer problem, and "opened" in the Door problem. In other words, his and my interpretations of the problems differed because of different interpretations of the goal states. (Incidentally, Duncker stated the Door problem in an unambiguous way: "A door is to be constructed so as to open *toward* both sides" [p. 26; emphasis added].)

Maier's Two-String Problem

In Maier's (1931, 1945) two-string problem, two strings are suspended from the ceiling of a room and the goal is to tie the ends of the two strings together. The obstacle is that the research participant cannot reach one string while holding the other one. Figure 5 illustrates Maier's version of the problem; the task environment seems to have been an ordinarily furnished room, containing an easy chair, a lamp on a table, a picture on a wall, and drapes on a window. In later versions, the task environment included pliers or other heavy objects (e.g., Anderson, 1990, pp. 246-247; Mayer, 1983, pp. 57-59). The desired solution is to convert one string into a pendulum by tying a weight to it, set it swinging, and catch it while holding the other string.

Meacham and Emont (1989) pointed out an easier and quicker solution: Ask a friend for help. They commented that such solutions are rarely permitted in research on problem solving even though problem solving in real life is very often an interpersonal enterprise. An exception to this comment is a fairly large amount of research that has been done specifically on group problem solving and group learning (for reports of primary research and reviews, see Amigues, 1988; Anderson, 1961; Duncan, 1959; Garry & Kingsley, 1970, pp. 472-473; Hartup, 1983; Lorge, Fox, Davitz, & Brenner, 1958; Parnes, 1962; Thorndike, 1938; Yager, Johnson, & Johnson, 1985). Although the findings of this research are of course complex, the general trend is that groups are often more effective than individuals, especially when the group includes one very able individual, though perhaps not one seen as *too* able. The effectiveness of the group also depends on group size and, at least for young children, whether rewards are shared by the members of the group—as in almost all of the research—or one winner in the group takes all.

Refrigerator Problem

The Refrigerator problem is an ill-defined, divergent, simulated practical problem. A typical version is, "Let's say that one evening you go to the refrigerator and notice that it is not cold inside, but rather it's warm. What would you do?" One obstacle is that the problem is ill-defined. It is ill-defined because at least two different goals could be set—fix the refrigerator or save the food—and because several paths to each goal are possible, such as check the fuse, repair the refrigerator yourself, or call a family member, neighbor, or repair shop to repair it. This is a divergent problem because no one solution is objectively correct.

In Denney and Palmer's (1981) scoring system, the best solution was effective self-reliance. However, this kind of solution is not necessarily the best for the problem *as defined by the participant*, and in any case, Meacham and Emont's (1989) comment about problem solving as an interpersonal enterprise is relevant.

Laipple (1990) used the Refrigerator problem and found that more young than old adults solved the problem consistently with the researcher's intentions, all participants who interpreted the problem differently from the researcher solved the problem they defined, and more old than young adults referred to personal experience in solving the problem. The implications of these findings are discussed later.

Convergent Problems

Water-Jars Problem

Laipple (1990) used the Luchins (1942) water-jars problem as a representative of well-defined convergent problems. In this problem, the participant is given word problems in which three jars with specified volumes are available for obtaining a specified volume of water. For example, in one problem the volumes were Jar A 14 units, Jar B 163 units, and Jar C 25 units, and the goal was to obtain 99 units; and in another problem the volumes were Jar A 18 units, Jar B 43 units, and Jar C 10 units, and the goal was to obtain 5 units. Luchins used these problems to study the development of *Einstellung*, or set, which is why he made the same algorithm relevant (goal volume $= B - A - 2C$).

Laipple found that many of the participants failed to solve the problem because they made arithmetic errors, but his interest was in how the participants interpreted

Figure 6. Drawings used in the House Plants problem. (After Kuhn & Brannock, 1977, Fig. 1, p. 10. Used by permission.)

the task rather than whether they solved it. He found that almost all the participants interpreted it in the way intended by the researcher.

House Plants Problem

The problem. Kuhn and Brannock's (1977) House Plants problem was designed to assess Piagetian formal operational thinking. The participant is shown the top four drawings in Figure 6, representing four potted plants varying orthogonally on four dimensions: healthy versus drooping plant, large versus small glass of water, dark versus light plant food, and leaf lotion versus no leaf lotion. The drawings are presented one at a time, and the qualities on the four dimensions are described as each drawing is presented. The participant is then shown the bottom drawing in the figure, representing a pot with no plant, a small glass of water, light plant food, and no leaf lotion. The examiner describes this drawing, asks how a plant would turn out in this situation, and then asks the participant to explain his or her answer. Plant food is the effective dimension in this example; the expected answer is that the new plant will do well either because light plant food made the plants healthy, or because dark plant food made them unhealthy, and because the other variables are irrelevant. The obstacle is that this solution is not immediately apparent.

The problem seems to be well-defined: Logically analyze the empirical evidence to isolate the effective element. The participants' answers are classified according to relevance to this solution, using the categories shown in Table 6.

Table 6

Types of Performance Exhibited on the House Plants Problem

Type	Definition
0	Exhibits no concept of experimentally isolating an operative variable
1	Exhibits attempt at isolating operative variables, but does not isolate the operative variable
2	Isolates the operative variable but does not logically exclude alternative variables
3	Does not isolate the operative variable, but logically excludes an inoperative variable
4	Isolates the operative variable and logically excludes the inoperative variables

---

Note. Adapted from Kuhn and Brannock, 1977, Table 1, pp. 12-13. Copyright 1977 by the American Psychological Association. Adapted by permission.

Representative findings. Kuhn and Brannock (1977) gave the House Plants problem to children 10, 11, and 12 years old and to college students, and obtained the distribution of solutions shown in Table 7. Kuhn and Brannock interpreted Level 0 solutions as reflecting operational thinking, as defined in Piaget's system, Level 1 as reflecting emergent formal operational thinking, Levels 2 and 3 as transitional, and Level 4 as formal operational thinking. Thus, Table 7 shows that most of the children in the two youngest groups were either concrete operational (Level 0) or transitional (Levels 2 and 3), most of the oldest children were either transitional or formal operational (Level 4), and most of the college students were formal operational.

Table 7

Number of Participants Exhibiting Each Performance Type on the House Plants Problem in the Kuhn and Brannock Study

	Age group			
Type	10	11	12	College
0	7	8	3	1
1	3	2	2	1
2 & 3	7	6	7	5
4	3	4	8	13

Note. Adapted from Kuhn & Brannock, 1977, Table 2, p. 13. Copyright 1977 by the American Psychological Association. Adapted by permission.

Kuhn and Brannock gave the same participants another traditional Piagetian task, the Pendulum problem, in which the goal is to discover by experimentation what determines a pendulum's speed. The scoring system was the same as for the House Plants problem, but as Table 8 shows, the levels of the solutions were different on the two problems. Only 30% of the participants were at the same level on both problems, and 71% of these participants were in one cell (the formal-formal cell). Neimark (1975) reviewed similar research and concluded that the relations across tasks are not strong. One possible interpretation of the intertask discrepancies is that the levels and types of thinking they are assumed to reflect are too far removed from the actual observations to be meaningful. Another possible interpretation is that the tasks are not equivalent in validity. Behaviorists might prefer the first interpretation

Table 8

Cross-Classification of Participants on the House Plants and Pendulum Problems in the Kuhn and Brannock Study

	Pendulum			
House Plants	0	1	2 & 3	4
0	1	4	9	5
1	3	0	0	5
2 & 3	3	6	6	10
4	0	2	9	17

Note. Adapted from Kuhn & Brannock, 1977, Table 3, p. 14. Copyright 1977 by the American Psychological Association. Adapted by permission.

and cognitivists the second one, but the second one is also plausible from a behavioral viewpoint: Different tasks involve different stimulus materials and even if the abstracted levels or types of thinking are the same, the actual behaviors are different.

Puckett, Cohen, and I (Reese, Puckett, & Cohen, 1990) used the House Plants problem in a study of cognitive aging, but our interest was in how the participants dealt with the problem rather than in trying to identify Piagetian stages of thinking. As shown in Table 9, we found that young and middle-aged adults were more likely to use logic than old and old-old adults, who were more likely to use personal experience. In other words, the young and middle-aged adults apparently interpreted the problem as convergent, requiring logical evaluation of empirical evidence, and the old and old-old adults apparently interpreted it as divergent—a test of personal knowledge about house plant lore.

As indicated in Table 3, one of the early steps in problem solving is said to be interpreting the problem. Laipple (1990, 1991) showed that old adults are more likely than young adults to interpret a laboratory problem differently from the researcher—who by the way is likely to be closer in age to young adults. Furthermore, Laipple found that old adults' interpretations are likely to be based on personal experience. On the House Plants problem, the use of personal experience is seen in such solutions as "Over-watering is bad for plants and leaf lotion doesn't do anything, so the plant will do OK." Laipple (1991) found that the way this task and an analogous

Table 9

Percentages of Performance Types Exhibited on the House Plants Problem in the Reese, Puckett, and Cohen Study

	Age group (and age range)			
Type	Young (17-22)	Middle-aged (40-50)	Old (60-70)	Old-old (75-99)
Personal experience	20	32	42	62
Partial logic	29	25	36	28
Full logic	51	43	22	10

Note. "Personal experience" is Types 0 and 1 in Table 6 because all of the participants' solutions of these types turned out to be based on personal experience; "Partial logic" is Types 2 and 3 in Table 6; "Full logic" is Type 4.

one involving automobiles were interpreted accounted for 73% of the variance in performance and age accounted for only 3% of the variance. Thus, taking account of the task interpretation yielded remarkably good predictions of performance and when the effect of task interpretation was removed from the effect of age, age yielded remarkably poor predictions.

Laipple did not use the circular technique of inferring the participant's interpretation of a problem from the solution given. Rather, in the 1990 study, he asked the participants to think aloud throughout the task, and he inferred the problem interpretation from the transcribed protocols. The thinking-aloud procedure is not an introspective technique; as Duncker (1945) said, in introspection the participant's attention is directed to the self-as-thinking and in the thinking-aloud procedure the participant's attention is directed to the problem being solved. Thinking-aloud protocols vary in length and richness of detail: Laipple's protocols were relatively brief; but Anzai and Simon (1979) obtained a 1 1/2 hour protocol from one person, and it was rich enough in details that Anzai and Simon were able to use it to develop a computer simulation of "learning by doing" during problem solving. Laipple also used the thinking-aloud procedure in his 1991 study and in addition, after the participant had finished working on a problem, he asked the participant to administer the task to him. He borrowed the latter method from cross-cultural research (Scribner, 1976).

Theoretical analysis. Variations in how a problem is interpreted are expected from the cognitive view because although the problem as objectively presented–the "task environment" (Simon, 1978, p. 275)–is a determinant of problem-solving activities, the major determinant is the internalized representation of the task environment. In information-processing theory, this is the "problem space." ("Problem space" is defined at the beginning of the section, *Classification of Tasks*. An issue that is debated in the cognitive literature but that is not relevant here is how the problem space is represented in memory. The representation might be encoded in some modality–enactive, iconic, lexical, or whatever [e.g., Kail & Siegel, 1977]–and it might be an abstract of the information presented or a more or less faithful copy, as in gist versus verbatim representation of the sentences in a word problem [e.g., Brainerd & Kingma, 1985; Brainerd & Reyna, 1988].)

The use of personal experience indicates that a problem is being solved by retrieval of facts from memory. This cognitively worded statement can be reworded to be consistent with behavior analysis: The person emits behavior that is not reinforced in the current setting but that has been reinforced in the person's history of similar settings. The two formulations can be expressed as follows:

Cognitive formulation: House plants –>[serve as a retrieval cue for]–> certain experiences stored in memory –>[which are verbally output as]–> problem solution.

Behavioral formulation: House plants –>[occasion]–> covert form of certain behaviors that in overt form were reinforced in the presence of house plants –>[occasion]–> certain overt verbal behavior.

The cognitive formulation is unsatisfactory (even for a cognitivist) because of another finding in Laipple's (1990, 1991) research: Whether a person's interpretation of a problem is the same as or different from the researcher's interpretation, the person is very likely to emit a solution that is satisfactory from his/her own point of view. That is, persons who interpret the House Plants problem as a problem of formal logic are likely to use formal logic and to arrive at the logically correct solution; and persons who interpret it as a problem of experience are likely to use experience and to arrive at an experientially relevant and plausible solution. In short, persons tend to interpret a problem in such a way that they can solve it.

Expanded theoretical analysis. The cognitive formulation given above can be expanded to account for this finding and to account for another finding in Laipple's (1990) research. He gave further instructions to participants who did not use the highest level of reasoning shown in Table 6: "Pretend for the moment that you know nothing about gardening, and use your reasoning to determine why two of the four plants turned out fine, and two of the plants turned out poorly" (p. 16). Of 14 young adults and 18 old adults given these instructions, 11 (79%) young adults and only 6 (33%) old adults shifted to the highest level of reasoning.

A question that arises is why so many old adults failed to shift to the highest level of reasoning. A cognitive psychologist might hypothesize that many of the old adults did not know how to use this kind of reasoning–they were incompetent. A behaviorist might say that this explanation is circular because knowing means the same thing as behaving, and might therefore ask why many of the old adults did not behave consistently with the highest level of reasoning. Taking a cue from the behaviorist, the cognitive psychologist might tentatively reject the hypothesis that the old adults who did not shift to the highest level of reasoning were incompetent ("did not know") and might suggest as a working hypothesis that they simply did not change their initial interpretation of the problem. The tentative rejection of the incompetence hypothesis is supported by research showing that even minimal training has a strong effect on learning (e.g., Treat & Reese, 1976) and problem solving (e.g., Laipple, 1990) by old adults, implying that ineffective performance does not necessarily reflect a deficiency in problem-solving competence (Reese & Rodeheaver, 1985).

The proposed alternative to the incompetence hypothesis is that many old adults did not shift to the highest level of reasoning because their interpretation of the problem did not call for reasoning. The same principle has been used to explain a finding from other research: Children and adults given conditional reasoning problems often commit the logical fallacy of "affirming the consequent." For example, given the premises "If it is raining, then the ground is wet" and "The ground is wet," the conclusion "It is raining" is consistent with this fallacy. However, Chapman (1993) pointed out that this conclusion is not a fallacy if the participant interprets the task as a problem of understanding conversation rather than as a conditional reasoning problem. One of the "rules" of conversation is that the speaker states all the information needed for comprehension of the message. The listener (the participant) assumes that the speaker (the researcher) abides by this rule and would have mentioned alternative causes of wet ground if any existed in the context of the message. On this assumption, the only possible cause of wet ground is rain, that is, the conditional rule is interpreted as a biconditional rule ("If and only if it is raining, the ground is wet"). For a biconditional rule, affirming the consequent is a valid argument rather than a fallacy; therefore, if the task is interpreted as conversation rather than reasoning, the conclusion "It is raining" is true and not a fallacy.

With respect to the House Plants problem, the hypothesis is that a participant who interpreted the task as a test of knowledge about house plants would set as the goal emitting this knowledge, and attaining this goal would be blocked only by trouble in remembering. Even if the participant has trouble remembering, however, the way to overcome this obstacle is not by logical reasoning but by trying various memory-retrieval strategies. This hypothesis could be testing by asking each participant for a self-report of memory troubles in the task and if memory troubles are reported, asking how the participant dealt with them.

This kind of analysis would lead the cognitivist to the next question, why did many of the old adults not change their initial interpretation of the problem? Some cognitive psychologists have explained this rigidity by proposing that old adults have greater "functional fixedness" or are more "rigid" than young adults; but of course,

A. Young Adults   B. Old Adults

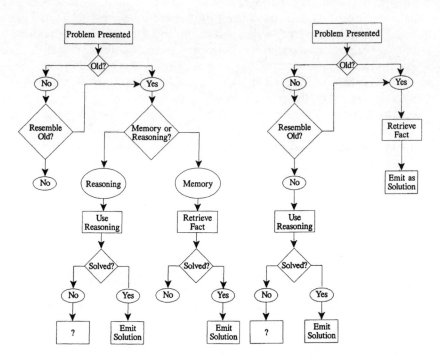

Figure 7. Flow charts representing problem solving by young and old adults. Rectangles represent instructions or situations, diamonds represent decisions to be made, and ovals represent outcomes of decisions. "Old?" means "Have I experienced this problem before?" "Solved?" means "Does the outcome (of reasoning or fact retrieval) solve the problem?"

this explanation is circular unless these constructs are assessed independently of the performance to be explained. In fact, it is still pretty circular if the independent assessment is on a similar kind of problem, because the data would be exhibiting only a correlation of performance across tasks, or as behaviorists might say, transsituational generalization. Attributing a finding to rigidity is unsatisfactory also because it instantly raises another question: Why do old adults exhibit rigidity?

Of course, behavioral rigidity is often observed in old adults. A remarkable example is in a study by Levinson and Reese (1967) on discrimination learning set: Three of the old adults in the study required from 35 to 37 days of training, at a rate of ten 4-trial problems per day, to attain a learning-set criterion of about 93% correct responses on five consecutive problems, which is only a moderately strict criterion. Throughout the precriterion period, all three exhibited a very strong position-alternation tendency, which is entirely insensitive to the reinforcement contingency but which requires keeping track of performance to stay on the alternation. In the same study, five old adults failed to reach criterion in 35 to 45 days; and all five exhibited strong position habits: Two exhibited position alternation, one position preference, one win-stay-position/lose-shift-position, and one position preference and then win-stay-position/lose-shift-position. The last two are particularly noteworthy because they exhibited sensitivity to the reinforcement contingency but not to the discriminative stimuli. However, behavioral rigidity is not an explanation, it is a phenomenon needing explanation. Further speculation would be idle, so I will not pursue the point herein.

Revised theoretical analysis. The cognitive formulation given earlier can be revised as shown in Figure 7. The flow charts represent young and old adults as exhibiting different problem-solving behavior. The flow charts can be construed as hypotheses to be tested or, to say the same thing differently, as hypothesized task analyses. According to the flow charts, both the young adult and the old adult initially classify a task environment or, more accurately, a problem space as having been experienced before (right-hand path) or as new (left-hand path), and if new, they classify it as resembling or not resembling any problem experienced before. If they classify it as entirely new, then both the young adult and the old adult use reasoning and evaluate whether or not they have solved the problem and if not, then they muddle through somehow (research would be needed to determine how). They are hypothesized to differ in what they do when they classify the problem as old or as resembling an old problem: (a) The young adult proceeds to classify the problem as solvable by retrieval of a fact or by reasoning and then acts on the basis of that classification and evaluates the outcome. (b) The old adult proceeds as though the problem is solvable entirely by retrieval of a fact and takes the retrieved fact as the correct solution.

The behavioral formulation does not require revision: The participant emits certain verbal behavior and the researcher infers from it the participant's interpretation of the problem. The behavior constitutes a solution of the problem inferred to have been interpreted because in the participant's history this was in fact the problem in the presence of which the emitted behavior was reinforced. A slight revision of the formulation might make this analysis clearer:

Revised behavioral formulation: House plants as a stimulus class–>[occasion]–> covert form of certain behaviors that in overt form were reinforced in the presence of this stimulus class –>[occasion]–> certain overt verbal behavior.

The revision is intended to show that "interpretation" is attributable to stimulus generalization; no cognitive activity needs to be invoked because stimulus generalization is itself a matter of the organism's history of contingencies (Stokes & Baer, 1977).

Two final points about the behavioral formulation are: (a) The reference to the history of contingencies is almost always post hoc speculation and does not add to the prediction and control of the problem-solving behavior. (b) Therefore, the functional part of the formulation is the inferred interpretation of the task.

Figure 8. One of the menus in the Poisoned Meals problem.

Poisoned Meals Problem

Puckett, Cohen, and I (Reese et al., 1990) used an adaptation of a Poisoned Meals problem developed by Arenberg (1968). It is intended to be a convergent contrived concept-identification problem with familiar materials; it is well-defined in the specification of the initial and goal states; but it is ill-defined with respect to the way to solve it. The adaptation involves a "20-questions" format that permits only 3 questions. The participant is told that one item in the daily special at the Ace Cafe has been poisoned and that he or she is allowed three Yes-No questions to identify it. Three trials are given, each with a different menu, and protocols are scored for the strategy used most often and second most often ("primary" and "secondary" strategies) and for the highest-level strategy used. The results were the same for all three scores.

Figure 8 shows the content of the first of three menus used by Puckett, Cohen, and I; Table 10 shows the scoring system; and Table 11 shows some of the results that were obtained. Two salient findings were: (a) Use of an item-checking strategy (each question is about one specific item) was most frequent in old-old age (significantly greater than in young adults and middle-aged adults, but not significantly greater than in old adults). (b) Use of a constraint-seeking strategy (each question eliminates half or nearly half of the previously untested possibilities) declined significantly across the age groups. Again, Laipple's (1991) follow-up research explained this pattern of findings: Using the modified Poisoned Meals problem and an analogous problem—the Accountant problem illustrated in Figure 9—he found that old adults tended to use personal experience more than young adults (e.g., "Select the food that would cover up the poison"; "Select the person who looks like an accountant"). The way the participants interpreted the tasks accounted for 67% of the variance in performance on these problems and age accounted for none—a remarkable finding because the age range was extremely large (age 18 to age 75 years).

CONCLUSIONS

Given that even minimal training has a strong effect on learning and problem solving by old adults, ineffective performance does not necessarily reflect a deficiency in problem-solving competence. One reason old adults tend not to use their maximal competence is suggested by Laipple's (1990, 1991) research showing that when given ill-defined problems (the Refrigerator, House Plants, and Poisoned Meals problems, plus analogues of the last two problems), young adults are more likely than old adults to define the problems in the ways intended by the researcher (self-reliance for the Refrigerator problem, logic for the House Plants type of

Table 10

Performance Types on the Poisoned Meals Task

Code	Type	Definition	Examples
1	Unscorable	Unclear what items are referred to	"Is it served hot?"
2	Pseudo-constraint seeking	Tests 1 item without directly referring to it	"Does it come from a pig?"
3	Item checking	Tests 1 item with a direct question about it	"Is it the cocoa?"
4	Pair checking	Tests 1 item from each of 2 courses	"Is it the ham or the peas?"
5	Course checking	Tests 2 items from 1 course	"Is it a main dish?" "Is it the ham or chicken?"
6	Incomplete con-straint seeking	Tests about half of the items, but fewer/more than exactly half	"Is it the ham, the peas, or the cocoa?" "Is it a main dish, a vegetable, or a dessert?"
7	Focusing	Tests exactly half of the remaining items	"Is it a main dish or a vegetable?"

Note. The examples are for the first question asked.

problem, and concept identification for the Poisoned Meals type of problem). Furthermore, adults who define the problems differently are likely to define them as problems they can solve on the basis of personal experience. Thus, adults who interpret a problem differently from the researcher, or who initially interpret it in the same way but do not or cannot solve it, effectively maximize the probability of self-perceived success by interpreting the problem in such a way that they can solve it.

The messages are, first, that treating the research participant's different interpretation as a *mis*interpretation is a mistake, as proved by the participant's self-perceived success—and as suggested by Skinner's principle that the subject is always right (1953, p. 13; 1976, p. 271). Progress in understanding age changes in problem solving is likely to be faster and better if researchers focus on all the problem-solving steps, such as interpretation, and not only on outcomes that have been predetermined on theoretical grounds to be successful or unsuccessful. The second message is that

Table 11

Percentages of Strategies Exhibited on Poisoned Meals Problem

| | Age group (and age range) | | | |
Strategy	Young (17-22)	Middle-aged (40-50)	Old (60-70)	Old-old (75-99)
	Best strategy exhibited			
Item checking	12	19	30	42
Pair checking	45	55	59	55
Large constraint	43	26	11	3
	Predominant strategy exhibited			
Item checking	23	27	38	49
Pair checking	41	50	54	50
Largeconstraint	36	23	8	1

Note. "Item checking" means asking about one item at a time; "pair checking" means asking about two items at a time (including "course checking"); "large constraint" means asking about exactly half of the previously unchecked items or nearly half.

cognitivists should look more at performance and behaviorists should look more at normal development, which should be interpreted to include the inferred development of inferred competence and mind because a person's individual history of reinforcements is so often virtually unknown.

In problem-solving tasks, persons generally exhibit behavior that is consistent with use of a step or rule in a problem-solving routine. However, behavior can be consistent with a rule without being rule-governed. Contingency-shaped behavior is consistent with a rule but is not rule-governed, just as the acceleration of a falling body is consistent with the law of gravity, which is a stated rule, but is not governed by that rule. Because relevant parts of persons' histories are generally not known, a researcher cannot know whether the behavior is consistent because it was contingency-shaped or because it is rule-governed. Researchers should not care whether the consistency reflects contingency-shaping or rule-governance unless knowing makes a difference in practice. However, it evidently makes a difference with respect to theories of stimulus equivalence (e.g., Dugdale & Lowe, 1990; Hayes, 1991; Sidman, 1990, 1992) and perhaps with respect to the opposition between contingencies of reinforcement and rules (e.g., Bentall & Lowe, 1987; Bentall, Lowe, & Beasty, 1985), and it certainly makes a difference with respect to behavior modification.

Therefore, when knowing whether behavior was contingency-shaped or rule-

Figure 9. The stimuli in Laipple's Accountant problem. The problem requires using a maximum of three Yes/No questions to identify the one who is an accountant. (From Laipple, 1991, p. 75. Used by permission.)

governed makes a difference—as is often the case—and when the available history is uninformative, the only way to know is to make an inference from current performance. Such inferences are often useful; and in general they can be plausible, as I believe the work of cognitive psychologists has shown.

References

Amigues, R. (1988). Peer interaction in solving physics problems: Sociocognitive confrontation and metacognitive aspects. *Journal of Experimental Child Psychology, 45,* 141-158.

Anderson, J. R. (1980). *Cognitive psychology and its implications.* New York: Freeman.

Anderson, J. R. (1990). *Cognitive psychology and its implications* (3rd ed.). New York: Freeman.

Anderson, J. R., & Schooler, L. J. (1991). Reflections of the environment in memory. *Psychological Science, 2,* 396-408.

Anderson, N. H. (1961). Group performance in an anagram task. *Journal of Social Psychology, 55,* 67-75.

Anzai, Y. (1987). Doing, understanding, and learning in problem solving. In D. Klahr, P. Langley, & R. Neches (Eds.), *Production system models of learning and development* (pp. 55-97). Cambridge, MA: MIT Press.

Anzai, Y., & Simon, H. A. (1979). The theory of learning by doing. *Psychological Review, 86,* 124-140.

Arenberg, D. (1968). Concept problem solving in young and old adults. *Journal of Gerontology, 23,* 279-282.

Arlin, P. K. (1975). Cognitive development in adulthood: A fifth stage? *Developmental Psychology, 11,* 602-606.

Arlin, P. K. (1977). Piagetian operations in problem finding. *Developmental Psychology, 13,* 297-298.

Arlin, P. K. (1989). The problem of the problem. In J. D. Sinnott (Ed.), *Everyday problem solving: Theory and applications* (pp. 229-237). New York: Praeger.

Baer, D. M. (1973). The control of developmental process: Why wait? In J. R. Nesselroade & H. W. Reese (Eds.), *Life-span developmental psychology: Methodological issues* (pp. 185-193). New York: Academic Press.

Baer, D. M. (1982). Applied behavior analysis. In G. T. Wilson & C. M. Franks (Eds.), *Contemporary behavior therapy* (pp. 277-309). New York: Guilford.

Baer, D. M., & Sherman, J. A. (1970). Behavior modification: Clinical and educational applications. In H. W. Reese & L. P. Lipsitt (Eds.), *Experimental child psychology* (pp. 643-672). New York: Academic Press.

Baer, R. A., Williams, J. A., Osnes, P. G., & Stokes, T. F. (1984). Delayed reinforcement as an indiscriminable contingency in verbal/nonverbal correspondence. *Journal of Applied Behavior Analysis, 17,* 429-440.

Baltes, M. M., & Reese, H. W. (1977). Operant research in violation of the operant paradigm? In B. C. Etzel, J. M. LeBlanc, & D. M. Baer (Eds.), *New developments in behavior research: Theory, method, and application In honor of Sidney W. Bijou* (pp. 11-30). Hillsdale, NJ: Erlbaum.

Bédard, J., & Chi, M. T. H. (1992). Expertise. *Current Directions in Psychological Science, 1*, 135-139.

Bentall, R. P., & Lowe, C. F. (1987). The role of verbal behavior in human learning: III. Instructional effects in children. *Journal of the Experimental Analysis of Behavior, 47*, 177-190.

Bentall, R. P., Lowe, C. F., & Beasty, A. (1985). The role of verbal behavior in human learning: II. Developmental differences. *Journal of the Experimental Analysis of Behavior, 43*, 165-181.

Bergmann, G. (1956). The contribution of John B. Watson. *Psychological Review, 63*, 265-276.

Berlyne, D. E. (1970). Children's reasoning and thinking. In P. H. Mussen (Ed.), *Carmichael's Manual of child psychology* (3rd ed., Vol. 1, pp. 939-981). New York: Wiley.

Bernstein, D. J., & Brady, J. V. (1986). The utility of continuous programmed environments in the experimental analysis of human behavior. In H. W. Reese & L. J. Parrott (Eds.), *Behavior science: Philosophical, methodological, and empirical advances* (pp. 229-245). Hillsdale, NJ: Erlbaum.

Bowers, K. S. (1973). Situationism in psychology: An analysis and a critique. *Psychological Review, 80*, 307-336.

Braine, M. D. S. (1971). On two types of models of the internalization of grammars. In D. I. Slobin (Ed.), *The ontogenesis of grammar: A theoretical symposium* (pp. 153-186). New York: Academic Press.

Brainerd, C. J., & Kingma, J. (1985). On the independence of short-term memory and working memory in cognitive development. *Cognitive Psychology, 17*, 210-247.

Brainerd, C. J., & Reyna, V. F. (1988). Generic resources, reconstructive processing, and children's mental arithmetic. *Developmental Psychology, 24*, 324-334.

Bransford, J. D., & Stein, B. S. (1984). *The IDEAL problem solver: A guide for improved thinking, learning, and creativity*. New York: Freeman.

Brown, A. L., Murphy, M. D., Overcast, T., & Smiley, S. S. (no date). *The effects of instructions on recall & recognition of categorized lists in the elderly*. Unpublished manuscript, Children's Research Center, University of Illinois.

Buffon, Count de. (1791). *Natural history, general and particular* (W. Smellie, trans.; 3rd ed.; Vol. 7). London: Strahan & Cadell.

Butterfield, E. C., Siladi, D., & Belmont, J. M. (1980). Validating theories of intelligence. In H. W. Reese & L. P. Lipsitt (Eds.), *Advances in child development and behavior* (Vol. 15, pp. 95-162). New York: Academic Press.

Carkhuff, R. R. (1973). *The art of problem-solving: A guide for developing problem-solving skills for parents, teachers, counselors and administrators*. Amherst, MA: Human Resource Development Press.

Catania, A. C. (1991). The gifts of culture and of eloquence: An open letter to Michael J. Mahoney in reply to his article, "Scientific psychology and radical behaviorism." *The Behavior Analyst, 14* 61-72.

Catania, A. C. (1992). *Learning* (3rd ed.). Englewood Cliffs, NJ: Prentice-Hall.

Catania, A. C., Matthews, B. A., & Shimoff, E. (1982). Instructed versus shaped human behavior: Interactions with nonverbal responding. *Journal of the Experimental Analysis of Behavior, 38,* 233-248.

Chapman, M. (1993). Everyday reasoning and the revision of belief. In J. M. Puckett & H. W. Reese (Eds.), *Life-span developmental psychology: Mechanisms of everyday cognition.* Hillsdale, NJ: Erlbaum.

Chapman, M., & Lindenberger, U. (1992). Transitivity judgments, memory for premises, and models of children's reasoning. *Developmental Review, 12,* 124-163.

Chase, P. N., & Bjarnadottir, G. S. (1992). Instructing variability: Some features of a problem-solving repertoire. In S. C. Hayes & L. J. Hayes (Eds.), *Understanding verbal relations: The second and third International Institute on Verbal Relations* (pp. 181-193). Reno, NV: Context Press.

Chase, P. N., & Danforth, J. S. (1991). The role of rules in concept learning. In L. J. Hayes & P. N. Chase (Eds.), *Dialogues on verbal behavior: The first International Institute on Verbal Relations* (pp. 205-225). Reno, NV: Context Press.

Chown, S. M. (1959). Rigidity—A flexible concept. *Psychological Bulletin, 56,* 195-223.

Cofer, C. C. (1957). Reasoning as an associative process: III. The role of verbal responses in problem solving. *Journal of General Psychology, 57,* 55-68.

Commons, M. L., Richards, F. A., & Armon, C. (Eds.). (1984). *Beyond formal operations: Late adolescent and adult cognitive development.* New York: Praeger.

Coppinger, R., & Feinstein, M. (1991). 'Hark! Hark! The dogs do bark...' and bark and bark. *Smithsonian, 21*(10), 119-129.

Cropper, D. A., Meck, D. S., & Ash, M. J. (1976). The relation between formal operations and a possible fifth stage of cognitive development. *Developmental Psychology, 13,* 517-518.

Davis, G. A. (1973). *Psychology of problem solving: Theory and practice.* New York: Basic Books.

Davis, R. (1986). Knowledge-based systems. *Science, 231,* 957-967.

Denney, N. W., & Palmer, A. M. (1981). Adult age differences on traditional and practical problem-solving measures. *Journal of Gerontology, 36,* 323-328.

Dewey, J. (1933). *How we think: A restatement of the relation of reflective thinking to the educative process.* Boston: Heath.

Dillon, J. T. (1982). Problem finding and solving. *Journal of Creative Behavior, 16,* 97-111.

Duda, R. O., & Shortliffe, E. H. (1983). Expert systems research. *Science, 220,* 261-268.

Dugdale, N., & Lowe, C. F. (1990). Naming and stimulus equivalence. In D. E. Blackman & H. Lejeune (Eds.), *Behavior analysis in theory and practice: Contributions and controversies* (pp. 115-138). Hove, UK: Erlbaum.

Duncan, C. P. (1959). Recent research on human problem solving. *Psychological Bulletin, 56*, 397-429.

Duncker, K. (1945). On problem-solving (L. S. Lees, trans.). *Psychological Monographs, 58*(5, Whole No. 270).

D'Zurilla, T. J. (1986). *Problem-solving therapy: A social competence approach to clinical intervention*. New York: Springer.

Fakouri, M. E. (1976). "Cognitive development in adulthood: A fifth stage?": A critique. *Developmental Psychology, 12*, 472.

Folkman, S., & Lazarus, R. S. (1980). An analysis of coping in a middle-aged community sample. *Journal of Health and Social Behavior, 21*, 219-239.

Frese, M., & Stewart, J. (1984). Skill learning as a concept in life-span developmental psychology: An action theoretic analysis. *Human Development, 27*, 145-162.

Furth, H. G., & Wachs, H. (1974). *Thinking goes to school: Piaget's theory in practice*. New York: Oxford University Press.

Gagné, R. M. (1965). *The conditions of learning*. New York: Holt, Rinehart & Winston.

Galotti, K. M. (1989). Approaches to studying formal and everyday reasoning. *Psychological Bulletin, 105*, 331-351.

Garry, R., & Kingsley, H. L. (1970). *The nature and conditions of learning* (3rd ed.). Englewood Cliffs, NJ: Prentice-Hall.

Grimm, J. A., Bijou, S. W., & Parsons, J. A. (1973). A problem-solving model for teaching remedial arithmetic to handicapped young children. *Journal of Abnormal Child Psychology, 1*, 26-39.

Grünbaum, A. (1967). *Modern science and Zeno's paradoxes*. Middletown, CT: Wesleyan University Press.

Guilford, J. P. (1967). *The nature of human intelligence*. New York: McGraw-Hill.

Guthrie, E. R. (1960). *The psychology of learning* (rev. ed.). Gloucester, MA: Peter Smith.

Hartup, W. W. (1983). Peer relations. In P. H. Mussen (Ed.), *Handbook of child psychology: Volume IV. Socialization, personality, and social development* (E. M. Hetherington, Ed.; pp. 103-196). New York: Wiley.

Hayes, S. C. (1991). A relational control theory of stimulus equivalence. In L. J. Hayes & P. N. Chase (Eds.), *Dialogues on verbal behavior: The First International Institute on Verbal Relations* (pp. 19-40). Reno, NV: Context Press.

Hayes, S. C., Hayes, L. J., & Reese, H. W. (1988). Finding the philosophical core: A review of Stephen C. Pepper's *World hypotheses: A study in evidence*. *Journal of the Experimental Analysis of Behavior, 50*, 97-111.

Hegel, G. W. F. (1970). *Hegel's Philosophy of nature* (A. V. Miller, trans.). Oxford: Clarendon Press. (Trans. from 1959 Nicolin & Poggeler ed. of Hegel's *The encyclopaedia of the philosophical sciences*, 3rd ed., originally published 1830, and from editorial supplements [Zusätze] in Michelet's text originally published 1847)

Heppner, P. P. (1978). A review of the problem-solving literature and its relationship to the counseling process. *Journal of Counseling Psychology, 25*, 366-375.

Hoagwood, T. (1992). Fictions and freedom: Wordsworth and the ideology of Romanticism. In J. N. Cox & L. Reynolds (Eds.), *Power's presents* (pp. ??). Princeton, NJ: Princeton University Press.

Hutchison, W. (1986, May). *Artificial intelligence: Demonstration of an operant approach.* Paper presented at the meeting of the Association for Behavior Analysis, Milwaukee, WI.

Hyten, C., & Chase, P. N. (1991). An analysis of self-editing: Method and preliminary findings. In L. J. Hayes & P. N. Chase (Eds.), *Dialogues on verbal behavior: The first International Institute on Verbal Relations* (pp. 67-81). Reno, NV: Context Press.

Hyten, C., & Madden, G. J. (1990, May). *Can you spot the scallop? Problems in human fixed-interval research since the beginning.* Paper presented at the meeting of the Association for Behavior Analysis, Nashville, TN.

Jaquish, G. A., & Ripple, R. E. (1981). Cognitive creative abilities and self-esteem across the adult life-span. *Human Development, 24*, 110-119.

Kagan, J., & Kogan, N. (1970). Individual variation in cognitive processes. In P. H. Mussen (Ed.), *Carmichael's Manual of child psychology* (3rd ed., Vol. 1, pp. 1273-1365). New York: Wiley.

Kail, R. V., Jr., & Siegel, A. W. (1977). The development of mnemonic encoding in children: From perception to abstraction. In R. V. Kail, Jr., & J. W. Hagen (Eds.), *Perspectives on the development of memory and cognition* (pp. 61-88). Hillsdale, NJ: Erlbaum.

Kant, I. (1952). *Critique of judgement: Part II. Critique of teleological judgement* (pp. 1-180 following p. 246). Oxford: Oxford University Press. (Original work published 1790)

Kantor, J. R. (1922). The nervous system, psychological fact or fiction? *Journal of Philosophy, 19*, 38-49.

Kantor, J. R. (1977). Evolution and revolution in the philosophy of science. *Revista Mexicana de Análisis de la Conducta, 3*(1), 7-16.

Kingsley, H. L., & Garry, R. (1957). *The nature and conditions of learning* (2nd ed.). Englewood Cliffs, NJ: Prentice-Hall. (Cited from Davis, 1973, p. 16)

Klahr, D. (1973). An information-processing approach to the study of cognitive development. In A. D. Pick (Ed.), *Minnesota symposia on child psychology* (Vol. 7, pp. 141-177). Minneapolis: University of Minnesota Press.

Klahr, D., & Siegler, R. S. (1978). The development of children's knowledge. In H. W. Reese & L. P. Lipsitt (Eds.), *Advances in child development and behavior* (Vol. 12, pp. 61-116). New York: Academic Press.

Koffka, K. (1925). *The growth of the mind: An introduction to child psychology* (R. M. Ogden, trans.). New York: Harcourt.

Kohlberg, L. (1968). Early education: A cognitive-developmental view. *Child Development, 39*, 1013-1062.

Köhler, W. (1918). Simple structural functions in the chimpanzee and in the chicken. In W. D. Ellis (Ed.), *A source book of Gestalt psychology* (pp. 217-227). London: Routledge & Kegan Paul.

Krasnor, L. R., & Rubin, K. H. (1981). The assessment of social problem-solving skills in young children. In T. V. Merluzzi, C. R. Glass, & M. Genest (Eds.), *Cognitive assessment* (pp. 452-476). New York: Guilford.

Krechevsky, I. (1932). 'Hypotheses' in rats. *Psychological Review, 39*, 516-532.

Krechevsky, I. (1938). A study of the continuity of the problem-solving process. *Psychological Review, 45*, 107-133.

Kuhn, D., & Brannock, J. (1977). Development of the isolation of variables scheme in experimental and "natural experiment" contexts. *Developmental Psychology, 13*, 9-14.

Laboratory of Comparative Human Cognition. (1983). Culture and cognitive development. In P. H. Mussen (Ed.), *Handbook of child psychology: Volume I. History, theory, and methods* (W. Kessen, Ed.; pp. 295-356). New York: Wiley.

Labouvie, G. V., Frohring, W., Baltes, P. B., & Goulet, L. R. (1973). Changing relationship between recall performance and abilities as a function of stage of learning and timing of recall. *Journal of Educational Psychology, 64*, 191-198.

Labouvie-Vief, G. (1982). Dynamic development and mature autonomy: A theoretical prologue. *Human Development, 25*, 161-191.

Laipple, J. S. (1990). *Solving everyday problems in young and old adulthood.* Unpublished master's thesis, West Virginia University, Morgantown.

Laipple, J. S. (1991). Problem solving in young and old adulthood: The role of task interpretation (Doctoral dissertation, West Virginia University, 1991). *Dissertation Abstracts International*, (University Microfilms No. ???)

Lawler, J. (1975). Dialectical philosophy and developmental psychology: Hegel and Piaget on contradiction. *Human Development, 18*, 1-17.

Lee, D. (1989). Everyday problem solving: Implications for education. In J. D. Sinnott (Ed.), *Everyday problem solving: Theory and applications* (pp. 251-265). New York: Praeger.

Lemmon, H. (1986). Comax: An expert system for cotton crop management. *Science, 233*, 29-33.

Leon, M. (1984). Rules mothers and sons use to integrate intent and damage information in their moral judgments. *Child Development, 55*, 2106-2113.

Levinson, B., & Reese, H. W. (1967). Patterns of discrimination learning set in preschool children, fifth-graders, college freshmen, and the aged. *Monographs of the Society for Research in Child Development, 32*(7, Serial No. 115).

Lindworsky, J. (1919). [Review of Köhler's *Nachweis einfacher Strukturfunktionen . . .* (1918).] *Stimmen der Zeit, 97*, 62ff. (Cited from Koffka, 1925, op. cit.)

Lorge, I., Fox, D., Davitz, J., & Brenner, M. (1958). A survey of studies contrasting the quality of group performance and individual performance, 1920-1957. *Psychological Bulletin, 55*, 337-372.

Luchins, A. S. (1942). Mechanization in problem solving: The effect of *Einstellung*. *Psychological Monographs, 54*(6, Whole No. 248).

Luchins, A. S., & Luchins, E. H. (1970). *Wertheimer's seminars revisited: Problem solving and thinking* (Vol. 3). Albany, NY: Faculty-Student Association, State University of New york at Albany.

Luria, A. R. (1969). Speech development and the formation of mental processes (R. Glickman, D. G. Nichols, E. Schuman, & L. Solotaroff, trans.). In M. Cole & I. Maltzman (Eds.), *A handbook of contemporary Soviet psychology* (pp. 121-162). New York: Basic Books.

Luria, A. R. (1973). *The working brain: An introduction to neuropsychology* (B. Haigh, trans.). New York: Basic Books.

Luria, A. R. (1978). Paths of development of thought in the child. In *The selected writings of A. R. Luria* (M. Cole, Ed.; pp. 97-144; M. Vale, trans.). White Plains, NY: Sharpe. (Original work published 1929)

Luszcz, M. A. (1989). Theoretical models of everyday problem solving in adulthood. In J. D. Sinnott (Ed.), *Everyday problem solving: Theory and applications* (pp. 24-39). New York: Praeger.

MacCorquodale, K., & Meehl, P. E. (1948). On a distinction between hypothetical constructs and intervening variables. *Psychological Review, 55*, 95-107.

Maier, N. R. F. (1929). Reasoning in white rats. *Comparative Psychology Monographs, 6*(3, Serial No. 29).

Maier, N. R. F. (1931). Reasoning in humans: II. The solution of a problem and its appearance in consciousness. *Journal of Comparative Psychology, 12*, 181-194.

Maier, N. R. F. (1940). The behavior mechanisms concerned with problem solving. *Psychological Review, 47*, 43-58.

Maier, N. R. F. (1945). Reasoning in Humans: III. The mechanisms of equivalent stimuli and of reasoning. *Journal of Experimental Psychology, 35*, 349-360.

Malott, R. W. (1986). Self-management, rule-governed behavior, and everyday life. In H. W. Reese & L. J. Parrott (Eds.), *Behavior science: Philosophical, methodological, and empirical advances* (pp. 207-228). Hillsdale, NJ: Erlbaum.

Maltzman, I. (1955). Thinking: From a behavioristic point of view. *Psychological Review, 62*, 275-286.

Mayer, R. E. (1983). *Thinking, problem solving, cognition*. New York: Freeman.

Meacham, J. A., & Emont, N. C. (1989). The interpersonal basis of everyday problem solving. In J. D. Sinnott (Ed.), *Everyday problem solving: Theory and applications* (pp. 7-23). New York: Praeger.

Morris, E. K., Higgins, S. T., & Bickel, W. K. (1982). Comments on cognitive science in the experimental analysis of behavior. *The Behavior Analyst, 5*, 109-125.

Morris, E. K., Hursh, D. E., Winston, A. S., Gelfand, D. M., Hartmann, D. P., Reese, H. W., & Baer, D. M. (1982). Behavior analysis and developmental psychology. *Human Development, 25*, 340-364.

Munn, N. L. (1954). Learning in children. In L. Carmichael (Ed.), *Manual of child psychology* (2nd ed., pp. 374-458). New York: Wiley.

Murray, F. B. (1991). Questions a satisfying developmental theory would answer: The scope of a complete explanation of developmental phenomena. In H. W. Reese (Ed.), *Advances in child development and behavior* (Vol. 23, pp. 39-47). San Diego, CA: Academic Press.

Nadler, G., & Hibino, S. (1990). *Breakthrough Thinking: Why we must change the way we solve problems, and the seven principles to achieve this.* Rocklin, CA: Prima Publishing & Communications.

Neimark, E. D. (1975). Intellectual development during adolescence. In F. D. Horowitz (Ed.), *Review of child development research* (Vol. 4, pp. 541-594). Chicago, IL: University of Chicago Press.

Neuringer, A. (1992). Choosing to vary and repeat. *Psychological Science, 3*, 246-250.

Newell, A., & Simon, H. A. (1972). *Human problem solving.* Englewood Cliffs, NJ: Prentice-Hall.

Nezu, A. M. (1987). A problem-solving formulation of depression: A literature review and proposal of a pluralistic model. *Clinical Psychology Review, 7*, 121-144.

Osborn, A. F. (1962). Developments in creative education. In S. J. Parnes & H. F. Harding (Eds.), *A source book for creative thinking* (pp. 19-29). New York: Scribner's.

Osborn, A. F. (1963). *Applied imagination: Principles and procedures of creative problem-solving* (3rd rev. ed.). New York: Scribner's.

Overcast, T. D., Murphy, M. D., Smiley, S. S., & Brown, A. L. (1975). The effects of instructions on recall and recognition of categorized lists by the elderly. *Bulletin of the Psychonomic Society, 5*, 339-341.

Overton, W. [F.] (1976). Environmental ontogeny: A cognitive view. In K. F. Riegel & J. A. Meacham (Eds.), *The developing individual in a changing world: Vol. II. Social and environmental issues* (pp. 413-420). Chicago, IL: Aldine.

Overton, W. F. (1991). The structure of developmental theory. In H. W. Reese (Ed.), *Advances in child development and behavior* (Vol. 23, pp. 1-37). San Diego, CA: Academic Press.

Overton, W. F., & Newman, J. L. (1982). Cognitive development: A competence-activation/utilization approach. In T. M. Field, A. Huston, H. C. Quay, L. Troll, & G. E. Finley (Eds.), *Review of human development* (pp. 217-241). New York: Wiley.

Parnes, S. J. (1962). Do you really understand brainstorming? In S. J. Parnes & H. F. Harding (Eds.), *A source book for creative thinking* (pp. 283-290). New York: Scribner's.

Parnes, S. J., Noller, R. B., & Biondi, A. M. (1977). *Guide to creative action: Revised edition of Creative behavior guidebook.* New York: Scribner's.

Parsons, A. J. (1976). Conditioning precurrent (problem solving) behavior of children. *Revista Mexicana de Análisis de la Conducta, 2*, 190-206.

Parsons, A. J., & Ferraro, D. P. (1977). Complex interactions: A functional approach. In B. C. Etzel, J. M. LeBlanc, & D. M. Baer (Eds.), *New developments in behavioral research: Theory, method, and application. In honor of Sidney W. Bijou* (pp. 237-245). Hillsdale, NJ: Erlbaum.

Pascual-Leone, J., & Morra, S. (1991). Horizontality of water level: A new-Piagetian developmental review. In H. W. Reese (Ed.), *Advances in child development and behavior* (Vol. 23, pp. 231-276). San Diego: Academic Press.

Pepper, S. C. (1942). *World hypotheses: A study in evidence.* Berkeley: University of California Press.

Piaget, J. (1970). Piaget's theory. In P. H. Mussen (Ed.), *Carmichael's manual of child psychology* (3rd ed., Vol. 1, pp. 703-732). New York: Wiley. (Reprinted in P. H. Mussen, Ed., *Handbook of child psychology: Volume I. History, theory, and methods,* W. Kessen, Ed., pp. 103-126; New York: Wiley)

Piaget, J. (1972). Intellectual evolution from adolescence to adulthood. *Human Development, 15*, 1-12.

Place, U. T. (1991). Conversation analysis and the analysis of verbal behavior. In L. J. Hayes & P. N. Chase (Eds.), *Dialogues on verbal behavior: The first International Institute on Verbal Relations* (pp. 85-109). Reno, NV: Context Press.

Polya, G. (1948). *How to solve it: A new aspect of mathematical method* (5th printing: text slightly changed & appendix added). Princeton, NJ: Princeton University Press.

Puckett, J. M., & Reese, H. W. (Eds.). (1993). *Life-span developmental psychology: Mechanisms of everyday cognition.* Hillsdale, NJ: Erlbaum

Reese, H. W. (1968). *The perception of stimulus relations: Discrimination learning and transposition.* New York: Academic Press.

Reese, H. W. (1971). The study of covert verbal and nonverbal mediation. In A. Jacobs & L. B. Sachs (Eds,), *The psychology of private events: Perspectives on covert response systems* (pp. 17-38). New York: Academic Press.

Reese, H. W. (1980). A learning-theory critique of the operant approach to life-span development. In W. J. Hoyer (Chair), Conceptions of learning and the study of life-span development: A symposium. *Human Development, 23*, 368-376.

Reese, H. W. (1982). Behavior analysis and life-span developmental psychology. *Developmental Review, 2*, 150-161.

Reese, H. W. (1986a). Behavioral and dialectical psychologies. In L. P. Lipsitt & J. H. Cantor (Eds.), *Experimental child psychologist: Essays and experiments in honor of Charles C. Spiker* (pp. 157-195). Hillsdale, NJ: Erlbaum.

Reese, H. W. (1986b). On the theory and practice of behavior analysis. In H. W. Reese & L. J. Parrott (Eds.), *Behavior science: Philosophical, methodological, and empirical advances* (pp. 1-33). Hillsdale, NJ: Erlbaum.

Reese, H. W. (1989). Rules and rule-governance: Cognitive and behavioristic views. In S. C. Hayes (Ed.), *Rule-governed behavior: Cognition, contingencies, and instructional control* (pp. 3-84). New York: Plenum.

Reese, H. W. (1991a). Contextualism and developmental psychology. In H. W. Reese (Ed.), *Advances in child development and behavior* (Vol. 23, pp. 187-230). San Diego, CA: Academic Press.

Reese, H. W. (1991b). Mentalistic approaches to verbal behavior. In L. J. Hayes & P. N. Chase (Eds.), *Dialogues on verbal behavior: The first International Institute on Verbal Relations* (pp. 151-177). Reno, NV: Context Press.

Reese, H. W. (1992a). Problem solving by algorithms and heuristics. In S. C. Hayes & L. J. Hayes (Eds.), *Understanding verbal relations: The Second and Third International Institute on Verbal Relations* (pp. 153-179). Reno, NV: Context Press.

Reese, H. W. (1992b). Rules as nonverbal entities. In S. C. Hayes & L. J. Hayes (Eds.), *Understanding verbal relations: The Second and Third International Institute on Verbal Relations* (pp. 121-134). Reno, NV: Context Press.

Reese, H. W., & Parnes, S. J. (1970). Programming creative behavior. *Child Development, 41*, 413-423.

Reese, H. W., Parnes, S. J., Treffinger, D. J., & Kaltsounis, G. (1976). Effects of a creative studies program on Structure-of-Intellect factors. *Journal of Educational Psychology, 68*, 401-410.

Reese, H. W., Puckett, J. M., & Cohen, S. H. (1990). *Mechanisms underlying cognitive aging processes.* Final report, National Institute on Aging Grant No. R01 AG06069, West Virginia University, Morgantown, WV.

Reese, H. W., & Rodeheaver, D. (1985). Problem solving and complex decision making. In J. E. Birren & K. W. Schaie (Eds.), *Handbook of the psychology of aging* (2nd ed.; pp. 474-499). New York: Van Nostrand Reinhold.

Reitman, W. A. (1965). *Cognition and thought: An information-processing approach.* New York: Wiley.

Repp, A. C., Felce, D., & Barton, L. E. (1988). Basing the treatment of stereotypic and self-injurious behaviors on hypotheses of their causes. *Journal of Applied Behavior Analysis, 21*, 281-289.

Riegel, K. F. (1973). Dialectic operations: The final period of cognitive development. *Human Development, 16*, 346-370. (Reprinted 1979 as "Dialectical operations: The first and final period of cognitive development" In K. F. Riegel, *Foundations of dialectical psychology*, pp. 35-55. New York: Academic Press)

Riegler, H. C., & Baer, D. M. (1989). A developmental analysis of rule-following. In H. W. Reese (Ed.), *Advances in child development and behavior* (Vol. 21, pp. 191-219). San Diego: Academic Press.

Rubin, K. H., Fein, G. G., & Vandenberg, B. (1983). Play. In P. H. Mussen (Ed.), *Handbook of child psychology: Volume IV. Socialization, personality, and social development* (E. M. Hetherington, Ed.; pp. 693-774). New York: Wiley.

Sappington, A. A., & Farrar, W. E. (1982). Brainstorming vs. critical judgment in the generation of solutions which conform to certain reality constraints. *Journal of Creative Behavior, 16*, 68-73.

Scribner, S. (1976). Situating the experiment in cross-cultural research. In K. F. Riegel & J. A. Meacham (Eds.), *The developing individual in a changing world: Volume 1. Historical and cultural issues* (pp. 310-321). Chicago, IL: Aldine.

Sidman, M. (1990). Equivalence relations: Where do they come from? In D. E. Blackman & H. Lejeune (Eds.), *Behavior analysis in theory and practice: Contributions and controversies* (pp. 93-114). Hove, UK: Erlbaum.

Sidman, M. (1992). Equivalence relations: Some basic considerations. In S. C. Hayes & L. J. Hayes (Eds.), *Understanding verbal relations: The Second and Third International Institute on Verbal Relations* (pp. 15-27). Reno, NV: Context Press.

Siegler, R. S. (1983). Information processing approaches to development. In P. H. Mussen (Ed.), *Handbook of child psychology: Volume I. History, theory, and methods* (W. Kessen, Ed.; pp. 129-211). New York: Wiley.

Siegler, R. S., & Robinson, M. (1982). The development of numerical understandings. In H. W. Reese & L. P. Lipsitt (Eds.), *Advances in child development and behavior* (Vol. 16, pp. 241-312). New York: Academic Press.

Simon, H. A. (1978). Information-processing theory of human problem solving. In W. K. Estes (Ed.), *Handbook of learning and cognitive processes: Vol. 5. Human information processing* (pp. 271-295). Hillsdale, NJ: Erlbaum.

Sinha, D. (1982). Sociocultural factors and the development of perceptual and cognitive skills. In W. W. Hartup (Ed.), *Review of child development research* (Vol. 6, pp. 441-472). Chicago: University of Chicago Press.

Sinnott, J. D. (Ed.). (1989a). *Everyday problem solving: Theory and applications.* New York: Praeger.

Sinnott, J. D. (1989b). A model for solution of ill-structured problems; Implications for everyday and abstract problem solving. In J. D. Sinnott (Ed.), *Everyday problem solving: Theory and applications* (pp. 72-99). New York: Praeger.

Sinnott, J. D., & Cook, J. (1989). An overview–if not a taxonomy–of "everyday problems" used in research. In J. D. Sinnott (Ed.), *Everyday problem solving: Theory and applications* (pp. 0-54). New York: Praeger.

Skinner, B. F. (1953). *Science and human behavior.* New York: Free Press.

Skinner, B. F. (1956). A case history in scientific method. *American Psychologist, 11*, 221-233.

Skinner, B. F. (1957). *Verbal behavior.* New York: Appleton-Century-Crofts.

Skinner, B. F. (1966). An operant analysis of problem solving. In B. Kleinmuntz (Ed.), *Problem solving: Research, method, theory* (pp. 225-257). New York: Wiley. (Reprinted in Skinner, 1969, op. cit.)

Skinner, B. F. (1968). *The technology of teaching.* New York: Appleton-Century-Crofts.

Skinner, B. F. (1969). *Contingencies of reinforcement: A theoretical analysis.* Englewood Cliffs, NJ: Prentice-Hall.

Skinner, B. F. (1974). *About behaviorism.* New York: Knopf.

Skinner, B. F. (1976). *Walden two.* New York: Macmillan.

Skinner, B. F. (1989). The origins of cognitive thought. *American Psychologist, 44*, 13-18.

Skinner, E. A., & Chapman, M. (1984). Control beliefs in an action perspective. *Human Development, 27*, 129-133.

Soll, H. P. (1982). Creativity in the marketplace. *Journal of Creative Behavior, 16*, 212-222.

Spence, K. W. (1956). *Behavior theory and conditioning.* New Haven, CT: Yale University Press.

Stern, C. [1969]. *Problem solving and concept formation: A comprehensive bibliography.* [Inglewood, CA: Southwest Regional Laboratory for Educational Research and Development.]

Stewart, L., & Pascual-Leone, J. (1992). Mental capacity constraints and the development of moral reasoning. *Journal of Experimental Child Psychology, 54*,

Stokes, T. F., & Baer, D. M. (1977). An implicit technology of generalization. *Journal of Applied Behavior Analysis, 10*, 349-367.

Sulzer-Azaroff, B., & Mayer, G. R. (1991). *Behavior analysis for lasting change.* Fort Worth, TX: Holt, Rinehart and Winston.

Thorndike, R. L. (1938). On what type of task will a group do well? *Journal of Abnormal and Social Psychology, 33*, 409-413.

Treat, N. J., & Reese, H. W. (1976). Age, pacing, and imagery in paired-associate learning. *Developmental Psychology, 12*, 119-124.

Uznadze, D. N. (1966). *The psychology of set* (B. Haigh, trans.). New York: Consultants Bureau.

Vaughan, M. E. (1989). Rule-governed behavior in behavior analysis: A theoretical and experimental history. In S. C. Hayes (Ed.), *Rule-governed behavior: Cognition, contingencies, and instructional control* (pp. 97-118). New York: Plenum.

Vygotsky, L. S. (1981). The development of higher forms of attention in childhood. In J. V. Wertsch (Ed. & trans.), *The concept of activity in Soviet psychology* (pp. 189-240). Armonk, NY: Sharpe. (Original work published 1929)

Wallas, G. (1926). *The art of thought.* New York: Harcourt, Brace.

Ward, W. D., & Stare, S. W. (1990). The role of subject verbalization in generalized correspondence. *Journal of Applied Behavior Analysis, 23*, 129-136.

Weinert, F. E., & Treiber, B. (1982). School socialization and cognitive development. In W. W. Hartup (Ed.), *Review of child development research* (Vol. 6, pp. 704-758). Chicago: University of Chicago Press.

White, S. H. (1970). The learning theory tradition in child psychology. In P. H. Mussen (Ed.), *Carmichael's Manual of child psychology* (3rd ed., Vol. 1, pp. 657-701). New York: Wiley.

White, S. H. (1976). The active organism in theoretical behaviorism. In H. W. Reese (Ed.), Conceptions of the 'active organism.' *Human Development, 19*, 69-119. Pp. 99-107.

Wolman, B. B. (1989). *Dictionary of behavioral science* (2nd ed.). San Diego: Academic Press.

Wood, P. K. (1983). Inquiring systems and problem structure: Implications for cognitive development. *Human Development, 26*, 249-265.

Woodworth, R. S. (1918). *Dynamic psychology*. New York: Columbia University Press.

Wozniak, R. H. (1975). Dialecticism and structuralism: The philosophical foundation of Soviet psychology and Piagetian cognitive developmental theory. In K. F. Riegel & G. C. Rosenwald (Eds.), *Structure and transformation: Developmental and historical aspects* (pp. 25-45). New York: Wiley.

Yager, S., Johnson, D. W., & Johnson, R. T. (1985). Oral discussion, group-to-individual transfer, and achievement in cooperative learning groups. *Journal of Educational Psychology*, 77, 60-66.

Young, P., Birnbrauer, J. S., & Sanson-Fisher, R. W. (1977). The effects of self-recording on the study behavior of female juvenile delinquents. In B. C. Etzel, J. M. LeBlanc, & D. M. Baer (Eds.), *New developments in behavioral research: Theory, method, and application. In honor of Sidney W. Bijou* (pp. 559-577). Hillsdale, NJ: Erlbaum.

Chapter 13

Models and Problem Solving: Effects of Use of the "Views of Probability"

Yuji Itoh
Keio University

In this paper, I will present a cognitive model of knowledge representation on a mathematical concept, that is, the concept of probability, and some data that would support the model. As a cognitive psychologist, I believe that constructing cognitive models is a useful way of conducting psychological research that can not only provide good explanations but also enable prediction and control of human behavior. Of course, we cannot observe the structure of knowledge directly. Many cognitive psychologists analyze verbal reports to construct cognitive models of knowledge representation and other cognitive structures. My hope is that cognitive modeling and the use of verbal reports as data will interest all the readers of this book, and that this chapter will provide materials for consideration of these things.

Multiple Interpretation of Probability

Mathematical concepts are powerful and have wide applicability because of their abstractness. However, it is often very difficult for nonmathematicians to understand abstract mathematical concepts. Therefore, it may be hypothesized that (1) an individual often has several interpretations or views that mediate an abstract mathematical concept as well as concrete situations in which to apply the concept; and (2), that learners sometimes lack some of the components of the possible knowledge structure or abstract concept, among them several concrete views or their interconnections.

I have examined the above hypothesis with the concept of probability and the experiment reported here is one of a series of experiments on this problem. I have shown that at least two views of probability are held by people, and both of them are often seen in the same individual (Itoh, in preparation). I call these views the case view and the frequency view.

In the case view, which roughly corresponds to theoretical or mathematical probability, people think of probability as the reciprocal of the number of the cases (in this chapter I will refer to kinds of outcomes as "cases" and to individual outcomes as "instances."). For example, they may think the probability of tossing a die and getting one is 1/6 because there are six possible outcome cases. Or, in a slightly more sophisticated version of the case view, people think of probability as the ratio of the number of desired cases to the number of all possible cases. In the frequency view, which corresponds to empirical or statistic probability, people think of probability as the relative frequency of an event. For example, knowing that the probability of getting one in a single toss of a die is 1/6, they conclude that, in many tosses of the die, the result will be one in 1/6 of the tosses. Alternatively, they may think the initial value of 1/6 was determined by an experiment.

For novices in this domain, the frequency view seems useful for solving probability problems. Two advantages of using the frequency view of probability may be hypothesized. First, taking this view, people may be able to avoid the error of thinking that the probabilities of unequally probable events are equal. For example, let us suppose that some people think the probability of a success in a surgical operation is 1/2 because there are two cases, a success or a failure. We can say that they have an incorrect version of the case view. They may notice their misconception when they think of the probability as the relative frequency of successful operations, which may be much higher or lower than 1/2.

Second, with the frequency view, people may be more likely to imagine concrete instances when considering frequencies. This may lead them to pay attention to aspects of the instances that are relevant to the solution and should be considered, and/or to grasp set relations correctly (Johnson-Laird, 1983; Tversky, & Kahneman, 1983). For example, consider a person who is asked to determine the probability of tossing two dice and getting a sum of seven. If she reasons abstractly and simply applies the case view considering the 11 cases from two (1+1) to 12 (6+6), she will answer 1/11. Conversely, assume that she applies the frequency view and imagines what will happen when she tosses two dice many times. She may notice that there are many combinations of the two faces and that there is more than one combination that adds to seven. This may lead her to think of the 36 possible outcomes and to get the correct answer. Analyzing the event into 36 possibilities does not involve the frequency view of probability itself. In this example, the analysis is consistent with the case view and theoretical probability. The point I am trying to make here is that trying to apply the frequency view may lead people to analyze the possible cases appropriately.

The Three Prisoner Problem

Using a notoriously difficult problem, the three prisoner problem, I have quantitatively demonstrated the first advantage of adopting the frequency view. The following is a version of the problem used in Shimojo and Ichikawa (1989, Problem 5), Itoh (1991, the 1/5-prisoner problem), and in this research.

There were three prisoners named A, B and C, and they knew that two of them were to be executed and one was to be released. Probabilities of being released were 1/4, 1/4 and 1/2 for A, B and C, respectively, and they knew the probabilities, too. A said to the jailer, who knew who was to be released, "It is certain that either B or C is executed, at least. You will give me no information about my own chances if you tell me the name of one man, B or C, who will be executed. Will you tell me the name?" The jailer accepted this argument and said "B will be executed." After hearing this answer, what is the probability for A to be released. Assume that the jailer never tells a lie, and if B and C are executed, he answers either name with probability of 1/2.

One can solve the three prisoner problem using Bayes' theorem. The probability can be expressed:

$$P(A|Sb) = \frac{P(Sb|A)P(A)}{P(Sb|A)P(A) + P(Sb|B)P(B) + P(Sb|C)P(C)}$$

where P(A) is the probability that Prisoner A is to be released, P(Sb|A) is the probability that the jailer answers "B will be executed" when Prisoner A is to be released, and so on. All the probabilities on the right side of the equation are given in the problem and we can calculate the probability required as:

$$P(A|Sb) = \frac{1/2 \times 1/4}{(1/2 \times 1/4) + (0 \times 1/4) + (1 \times 1/2)} = 1/5$$

Researchers revealed that very few college students, including those who were majoring in technical subjects, could solve this problem (Itoh, 1991; Sayeki, 1987; Shimojo, et al., 1989). Researchers have been studying the causes of the difficulty that students find with this problem (e. g. Ichikawa, 1989; Ihara, 1988a; 1988b; Itoh, 1991; Mori, 1988a; 1988b; Shimojo, et al., 1989).

I hypothesized that one cause of the difficulty with the three prisoner problem is the difficulty of applying the frequency view to the problem (Itoh, 1991). The events in the three prisoner problem happen only once, and it is difficult to imagine the repetition of the events. I compared the three prisoner problem to another problem (the jewel problem, see Figure 6) in which the repetition of the events was easier to imagine. I also examined the effects of experience in solving the jewel problem on the solution of the three prisoner problem and the effects of some hints that were expected to introduce the frequency view into the solution of the three prisoner problem. The percentage of correct answers to the jewel problem was much higher than for the three prisoner problem. However, neither experience with jewel problem nor the hints improved subjects' performance on the three prisoner problem. There was, however, a difference in the error pattern that was consistent with the first advantage argued for above.

My previous study was unable to demonstrate an increase in the percentage of correct solutions to the three prisoner problem by the introduction of the frequency view. It only implied one of the two hypothesized advantages of the frequency view. One possible explanation of this result is that the subjects in my study did not actually apply the frequency view to the problem. In this study, many subjects correctly answered hint questions intended to introduce the frequency view. However, this does not necessarily imply that they adopted the frequency view. Another possible reason for the lack of hint and experience effects is that, although introduction of the frequency view might facilitate some appropriate reasoning in the problem solving processes, there are other obstacles to be overcome, which overshadow the benefits of this reasoning. So the purpose of this study was to show which view of probability subjects take and the effects of hint questions that could not be detected in the subjects' final answers. In this study, I asked subjects to report out loud what occurred to them and videotaped their problem solving sessions in order to capture the effects that might not be evident in the final answer. Though there have been many discussions on the problem solving processes of the three prisoner problem, there were very few studies that focused on protocol analyses of subjects solving this problem. Presenting this kind of detailed analysis therefore should contribute to the discussion around the three prisoner problem.

Overview of Experiment

Method

Materials. The three prisoner problem (discussed above) and three hint questions were the same as those used in Itoh (1991, the 1/5-prisoner problem). The hint questions were:

Question 1: Assume there are 1000 "parallel worlds" in which three prisoners and a jailer are in the same situation. (A has not asked the jailer a question.) In how many worlds is it expected that A will be released? Probabilities for prisoners to be released in each world are same as the ones in the problem. (Correct answer: 250 worlds)

Question 2: Among the worlds in which A is to be released, in how many worlds is it expected that the jailer answers "B will be executed?" (Correct answer: 125 worlds)

Question 3: In worlds other than in question 2, in how many worlds is it expected that the jailer answers "B will be executed?" (Correct answer: 500 worlds)

The hint questions were expected to introduce the frequency view and make it possible to apply this view to the problem. Question 2 also suggested that there were two different cases where Prisoner A was to be released. The ratio of the answer to Question 2 to the sum of the answers to Questions 2 and 3 (125/(125+500)) is the correct answer to the original problem.

Procedure. First, subjects were told that they would be asked to solve a probability problem and to say aloud whatever occurred to them as they solved it. They were also told that they could use paper and pen, and that there was no time limit. They were then given the problem statement. When subjects said that they were stuck, or when the experimenter judged that they were, a hint question was given to them with the experimenter's comment that it might or might not serve as a hint. They were asked to answer the question and to reconsider the original problem. Three hint questions were given one by one in the same manner. After the third question was given, subjects were allowed to continue until they were stuck or finished, or until the experimenter judged so, and the session was over. Subjects were interviewed about their perception of the problem and their background in statistics and probability.

The experimenter tried not to intervene, but he helped subjects understand the meaning of the problem and the hint questions if they showed confusion or misunderstanding. He also answered some of the subjects' questions.

Subjects. Seven graduate students and post doctoral fellows of University of California at Berkeley participated in the experiment. They were studying problem solving and learning in mathematics and were familiar with the think aloud method. Though they were not unbiased samples in this sense, none of them had a specific interest in problem solving involving probability. All of them had studied probability in a statistics course but none had taken a course in probability theory.

Summary of Results

All the sessions took about one hour, though there was no time limit. Table 1 shows each subject's answers to the problem before answering any hint questions and after answering each hint question, with the subject's answers to the hint questions. Only one subject arrived at the correct answer to the problem after Question 3. The most frequent answer was 1/3. Four out of seven subjects answered

Table 1. Answers to the Original Problem and the Hint Questions

		Subjects				
S1	**S2**	**S3**	**S4**	**S5**	**S6**	**S7**

Answer to the original problem

Before Qs	1/3 (2/3)*	3/8 (5/8)	1/3 (2/3)	1/4	1/3 (2/3)	4/9	1/2 (1/2)
	2/5 (3/5)	1/3 (2/3)					
After Q1	n.c.**	n.c.	n.c.	n.c.	n.c.	3/16	n.c.
After Q2	1/8 (3/4)	n.c.	1/8 (1/2)	n.c.	n.c.	n.c.	1/4
After Q3	n.c.	1/5	n.c.	stuck	n.c.	1/3	n.c.

Answer to the hint questions

Q1	250	250	250	250	250	1/4	250
Q2	125	125	125	125	125	n.a.***	125
Q3	375	500	500	750	500	n.a.	500

* Explicitly answered probability of C to be released.
** Not changed from previous answer to the problem.
*** No answer to the question.

Table 2. Summary of Problem Solving Processes of each Subject

Phases	Representation, domain knowledge

Subject: S1

0	Accepted unequal prior probabilities without any difficulty.
1	P(A)+P(C)=1, P(A)/P(C) is constant.
2	P(A)+P(C)=1, P(A)/P(C) is constant.
3	Focus on A & Sb, qualitative judgment of P(A)'s change.
4	Focus on A & Sb, qualitative judgment of P(A)'s change.
V	Partial use of the frequency view after hint questions.

Subject: S27

0	Accepted unequal prior probabilities without any difficulty.
1	P(A)+P(C)=1, P(A)/P(C) is constant.
2	World model, ratio of world numbers, sample space.
3	World model, ratio of world numbers, sample space.
4	World model, ratio of world numbers, sample space, focusing on A & Sb.
V	Extensive use of the frequency view.

Subject: S3

0	Accepted unequal prior probabilities without any difficulty.
1	P(A)+P(C)=1, P(A)/P(C) is constant.
2	World model, ratio of world numbers.
3	Focus on A & Sb, qualitative judgment of P(A)'s change.
4	Focus on A & Sb, qualitative judgment of P(A)'s change.
V	Use of the frequency view after hint questions.

Subject: S4

0	Accepted unequal prior probabilities without any difficulty.
1	P(A)=1/4 in the problem statement.
2	P(A)=1/4 in the problem statement.
3	P(A)=1/4 in the problem statement.
4	Fragmented application of mathematical knowledge and skills.
V	No use of the case view.

Subject: S5

0	Uncomfortable with unequal prior probabilities.
1	Marble model.
2	Marble model.
3	Marble model.
4	World model, ratio of world numbers.
V	Use of the case view before Question 2 and partial use of he frequency view after Question 2.

Subject: S6

0	Uncomfortable with unequal prior probabilities.
1	Formulas of conditioned probability.
2	Formulas of conditioned probability.
3	Formulas of conditioned probability.
4	Formulas of conditioned probability.
V	Extensive use of the case view.

Subject: S7

0	Uncomfortable with unequal prior probabilities.
1	Incorrect application of the case view.
2	Incorrect application of the case view.
3	$P(A)=1/4$ in the problem statement.
4	$P(A)=1/4$ in the problem statement.
V	Use of the case view at least before hint questions.

Key for Phases:

0:	Acceptance of unequal prior probabilities
1:	Before questions
2:	After Question 1
3:	After Question 2
4:	After Question 3
V:	The use of the views of probability.

1/3, at least once, before Question 1 was presented, and another subject answered 1/3 after answering Question 3. Six subjects answered Questions 1 and 2 correctly, and four subjects gave the correct answer to Question 3. Five subjects changed their answers after answering hint questions.

I used subjects' utterances, notes, and drawings on scratch paper as data. The video recordings were used to locate when subjects made the notes and drawings. I analyzed these data in terms of three questions. First, what view of probability was the subject taking? Second, what kinds of external representations (e. g. diagrams and algebraic expressions) did the subject use? Third, what domain knowledge did the subject access and use? Table 2 shows the summary of this analysis. It shows subjects' acceptance of the unequal prior probabilities (0), representations and domain knowledge that they used, and things that they focused on before any hint questions had been given (1) and after each hint question had been given (2, 3, and 4). It also shows the views that subjects took during the session. In the rest of this section, I will describe the results of the analysis further, presenting some excerpts from subjects' utterances and drawings that support the analysis. First, I will present data that shows what view a subject was taking and how hint questions affected the kind of view taken by a subject. Second, I will present data that show how a subject's taking a specific view affected the course of problem solving.

Detailed Analyses of Problem Solving Behavior

Acceptance of unequal probabilities

First, we can see that there are two kinds of reactions that subjects had just after reading and understanding the problem statement. Four out of seven subjects (S1, S2, S3, and S4) easily accepted the assumption of unequal prior probabilities for the release of the three prisoners, whereas the other three subjects (S5, S6, and S7) did not. S5 and S6 wondered where the prior probabilities came from. They started their solution attempts based on the idea that the answer would be 1/2 if no prior probabilities had been given. They understood that this was not the case, but they were uncomfortable with the unequal prior probabilities.

> S5: ...Ok, so, initially, yeah, ok, how does this work? Probability of being released for these three prisoners are 1/4, 1/4, and 1/2. Why is that? No reason, I guess. Ok, two of the three are going to be executed. All right, now. The jailer tells prisoner A that prisoner B will be executed. Well then, if it's true, jailer accepted this argument. Ok, so if it's true, prisoner B is executed. Then, that leaves only prisoners A and C. Now, without knowing these probabilities, without knowing 1/4 and 1/2, you think that each of these prisoners A and C had about 1/2, fifty percent chances of being released or executed. Now I'm gonna try to figure out whether, I guess it can't be true, given that there is only 25% chance that A would be released to start with. So, I don't think these numbers are right.

S7 arrived at the answer 1/2 soon after reading the problem statement. However, he seemed uncomfortable with his answer because of the unequal prior probabilities. He also wondered where this came from. On the other hand, S1, S2, S3, and S4 did not express any discomfort or difficulty in accepting the unequal prior probabilities.

> S4: Because you said that, uh, probabilities of being released were 1/4, 1/4, and 1/2, for A, B, and C. And, uh, assume A said, asked the jailer, I mean, under every circumstance, 1/4 of the chance for A to be released. No no, the probability for A to be released is 1/4 under every circumstance.

This difference seems to be attributed to whether the case view was dominant when the subject understood the problem statement. For those for whom the case view was dominant (S5, S6, and S7), the unequal prior probabilities were unacceptable. They might have tried to understand the unequal prior probabilities with the case view and have failed. On the other hand, other subjects (S1, S2, S3, and S4) could accept the unequal prior probabilities because they did not interpret them with the case view.

Adoption of the case view

Other observations also suggest the dominance of the case view by the subjects who could not accept the unequal prior probabilities. S5 found it difficult to understand the differences in prior probabilities of the prisoners' release, and stated that the answer would be 1/2 if no prior probabilities were given. She then devised a different situation with the same probabilities, 1/4, 1/4, and 1/2, where four marbles of three colors were in a jar and someone was drawing one of them out (Figure 1). Instead of three unequally probable cases, she thought of four equally probable cases two of which could be seen as the same outcome. This implies that the case view of probability was dominant for her in solving this problem. She thought that knowing B's execution corresponded to removing one (black) marble, and got 1/3 for the probability of A's release and 2/3 for C's.

S5: So, instead of talking about prisoners whatever, we could imagine there are, that there are,
four different like marble in a jar or something
like that, and that two of them are, let's see, how
they work, two of them are white, one of them
is black, one of them is some other color, it
doesn't matter, but so that, so to make a mapping here, it's like there's 1/4 chance that pulling out this, 1/4 chance pulling out this, and this
1/2 chance that pulling out white ones. Uhm, so
this information is equivalent to pulling this, to
knowing that, that this is gone. So that means
the probability of pulling out this one is now 2/
3 and this is 1/3 (Figure 1).

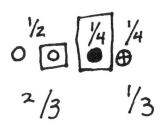

Figure 1. S5's marble model.

S6 remembered some formulas of conditioned probability and tried to use them to solve the problem. She devised a representation of the problem situation in terms of the combination of each prisoner's release and execution (see Figure 2) to figure out the probability where A is released and B is executed. She assigned 1/3 probability to each of the three possibilities without referring the unequal prior probability. Of course, the correct probabilities for three possible combinations are 1/4, 1/4, and 1/2, the unequal prior probabilities of the prisoners' release. S5 also made the same mistake. These observations also suggest the dominance of the case view for these subjects.

Adoption of the frequency view

S1, S2, S3, and S4 accepted the assumption of unequal prior probabilities
for the release of the three prisoners. This
means, at least initially, that they were not
looking at the problem in terms of the
case view. It is not clear from the data
whether they took the frequency view at
this point, although, when S2 was given
Question 1, he mentioned that the idea of
imagined worlds had occurred to him
earlier.

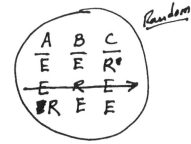

Figure 2. S6's diagram of the three possible combinations of the events. Each row represents a combination. E and R stand for execution and release.

When the Question 1 was given, S2 and S3 among others used the numbers of the worlds to confirm their previous answers (1/3, the wrong answer). They mentioned the three possible combinations of one's release and execution for the first time.

> S2: Ok, we're gonna have A, B, and C. We are gonna have some trials. So the question isexecuted, or released. I wanna do, I wanna some trials ... So. (Drawing Figure 3) A can be executed and B executed and C released, or A can be executed B released and C executed, or A can be released B can be executed C can be executed ... Or A can be released, oh, they are only the possibilities of that. If A is executed then either one of those is released, there really are three possible outcomes. One is released, and each one. This one, this one, or this one is released. A, B, or C. So, there are three possible outcomes of this thing, of each experiment..

S2 and S3 tried to represent the imaginary worlds and what happened in them on paper. They successfully represented three kinds of worlds, indicating who would be released, and who would be executed in each world. However they did not indicate the name the jailer specified (either "B" or "C") in each world. They did not ask whose name the jailer would answer in a given world. Instead, they asked in which worlds the jailer would answer Prisoner B's name (i. e. the worlds where Prisoner B would be executed).

> S2: So the question is in the case where B is executed, what are the possible outcomes?

Both S2 and S3 then decided how many worlds fell into each category (they indicated these values in their figures) and found two sets of worlds where Prisoner B was to be executed. They confirmed their previous answers using the ratio of the numbers of the different types of worlds.

> S2: The case where B is executed, which is either here or here (drawing two arrows in Figure 3). So these are the ones proposed by the jailer. Either A is released or, no, either A is executed or A is released. Jesus. Thing is, in 1000 trials, I'm getting that, 250 of these. I know that. Two fifty with A released.

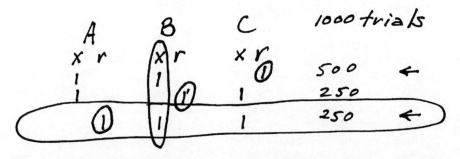

Figure 3. S2's diagram for the three possible combinations of events. Each row represents a possible combination of the prisoners' execution and release. Marks in the x and r columns mean the prisoners' execution and release, respectively.

How many with B released, 250. How many, 500 of these. Ok. How interesting! So the thing that I have done, I've said either this one or this one. So the things I need are in this 500 and in this 250. What am I sampling out of? I'm sampling out of 750. So probability of A being released is 250/750. Just getting my original answer... Ok, my third answer is 1/3.

Answering Question 1 seemed to make S2 and S3 adopt the representation of imaginary worlds. They seemed to imagine individual worlds (trials, in S2's word) and calculated the probability using the numbers of the different types of worlds. Thinking about what would happen in each possible world seems to have made S2 and S3 notice a way to combine the events to make the three possible cases. Or, at least, it gave them a chance to externalize explicitly their thoughts about the cases. This gave them another way of looking at the problem and another solution strategy, which happened to give the same answer of 1/3.

In other words, they adopted the world model of the problem situation that is based on the frequency view of probability. However, taking the frequency view was not enough to make them notice that there were two cases where Prisoner A would be released, one where the jailer specified Prisoner B's name and another where he specified Prisoner C's name. Although S1 and S4 gave the correct number of worlds in response to Question 1, they seemed not to adopt the world model or the frequency view.

After that S2 and S3 continued to use the world numbers to calculate the probabilities. For example, after answering Question 2 correctly (125 worlds), S3 asked herself in how many worlds the jailer was expected to answer B's name without explicitly recognizing its relation to the solution. She got 625 (125+500) and then calculated its ratio to 1000 (.625). She wondered what this probability (.625) was andconcluded that it was not the answer.

S3: So I expect that answer ("B will be executed.") in 500 of these worlds and in 125 of these worlds. So going back to the original question, I expect that answer in 125 plus 500 worlds. So that would be 625. So that would be .625. And, gee it doesn't work at all like 1/3, isn't that 2/3 or something? Hum. It's not even 2/3. 'Cause it's .625. Well, what is the probability of. I want to make sure I'm talking about release. Oh, no not, no not, no not, no not. Ok, maybe those don't matter, I believe that. Because A is killed here, so, this is just the chance, ok, so .625 is just, oh, I don't know what this is. It is something to do with when the jailer answers B will be executed, but this is not the answer, because A is executed in this world.

S3 later got another possible answer to the original problem, .125 (125 worlds out of 1000), and converted it to the fraction 1/8. She mentioned that she had thought that the probabilities of A's and C's release should add up to one and focused on the probability of C's release. She got 1/2 from the number of the worlds (500) where Prisoner C would be released and felt it strange that the probability did not change.

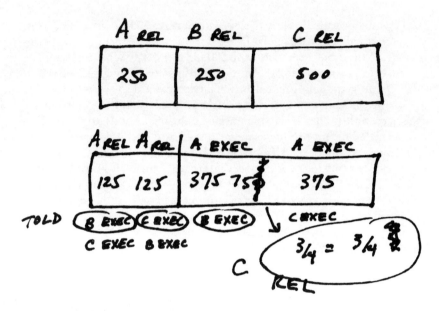

Figure 4. S1's diagram of the division of the worlds.

When Question 3 was given, S2 did not answer Question 3 directly and stated that the jailer's answer "B will be executed" was expected in 125 worlds when Prisoner A would be released, and in 500 worlds when Prisoner A would be executed. S2 calculated the probability of the jailer's answering B's name as 625/750. This made him focus on the 625 worlds as a "new sample size." He then calculated the ratio of the number of worlds from Question 2 to the "new sample size," and got 1/5. He seemed unable to believe his new answer.

> S2: So, it's been said, B is executed. In 625 situations. So 625 could be the new sample size. Question is, out of how many of those A is released. And the answer is 125. So that's 5, 1/5. Ooh, god, probability of A, no, this can't be. This can't be. The probability of A released is 1/5? Oh, I hate this ... So we definitely find the way of getting new sample size here. No, I wouldn't go with this. No.

S2 tried to retrace his solution path but he was not able to. However, he accepted 1/5 as his final answer.

From these episodes, we can say that S2 and S3 were taking the frequency view in their problem solving attempts at least after Question 1 was given. As for S1, there are no direct observations that imply the adoption of the frequency view. Answering Question 2 correctly (125 worlds), he got a new answer to the original problem, 1/8, but it is not clear whether it came from 125/1000 or 1/4 ¥ 1/2. Then S1 tried to make sense of his answer using a diagram of the division of the possible worlds (see Figure 4). In this diagram, he indicated the combinations of the prisoners' release and execution. In contrast to S2 and S3, he labeled each set of worlds with prisoners' fates (and made some errors doing this).

S1: Oh, make that make sense, let's see, if these 250 cases where A is gonna be released, these are 750 cases where A is gonna be executed. Sine we know that, we know later on that B is possibly executed, in all of these 750 cases C gets released. So these all come down as C release. And. It's A release. B is executed, A is released, C is executed, so that's the only. So, not appear. Maybe, this isn't the right way togo, I thought I could, I thought I could break down, I thought I could include all possibilities for everybody in one set of 1000 situations.

In this attempt, S1 focused on the numbers of the worlds. He might have used the frequency view, at least partly. However, it is not clear that he used a world model similar to that used by S2 and S3. For example, he never calculated ratios of the world numbers.

There are no evidences that S4 took any view of probability. She answered Question 1 easily and Question 2 with some help from the experimenter. However, she did not change her original answer, 1/4, after answering them, saying neither of them helped her with the original problem. S4 seemed not to understand Question 3 completely and she came up with 750 worlds using a diagram of the division of the possible worlds like S1's (see Figure 4). After all she never tried to relate the world numbers to any probabilities though she answered the world numbers to the hint question.

Effects of hint questions on switching view

Now we will examine the effects of hint questions on switching of the view of probability. The hint questions were intended to introduce the frequency view into the problem solving activity. Among three subjects who could not accept the unequal prior probabilities, one subject (S5) took the frequency view and used the world model after Question 3 was given. One (S6) never answered the numbers of the worlds to the hint questions and stuck to the case view and the abstract procedures (i. e. application of some equations). Another (S7) seems not to have adopted the frequency view, but abandoned the case view he initially took. Let us look at the case of S7 first and then S5.

S7 first answered 1/2 to the problem. This could be attributed to his application of the case view to the situation. However he seemed uncomfortable with his answer because the prior probabilities of the prisoners to be released were different. He was wondering where this difference came from.

S7: My first, my first, first comes to mind in this problem is that since B will be executed and we're gonna have a new, a new, say, probably a new problem, new set of conditions, that include the fact that one person is going to be released and the other one is going to be, uh, executed. My first thing is that the each one's gonna have half of chance to be the one released? ... I'm beginning to question what, what does it mean. Of course half, yeah. It's not 2/3? Why these guys have different probabilities?

When Question 1 was given, S7 expressed his discomfort with the unequal prior probabilities again. S7 considered the case where the prior probabilities were equal, and then considered the case of unequal probabilities and answered Question 1 with 250. However, he did not change his answer to the original problem. For Question 2, S7 thought a while about the situation where the jailer answered Prisoner B's name, and got the answer 125.

After answering Question 2, S7 thought that the probabilities would not change after hearing the jailer's answer and the answer to the original question was 1/4.

S7: Uh, B will be executed. What is the probability of A to be released? You know, it's 1/4. I mean the probability of A to be released, it's 1/4. It can't change. I mean, the probability of the jailer say, to say, that A is going to be executed or released. Oh, but he never lies. Oh oh, but it doesn't matter. I mean A can still be executed, so the probability that the jailer is gonna say, either A or C is the possible answer to which one is going to, the second one to be killed is 1/2. Probability of A to be executed remains the same. 1/4.

When Question 3 was given, S7 forgot that the jailer would never answer Prisoner A's name. The experimenter pointed it out and S7 answered 500 world to Question 3. Then S7 thought that the probability of A's release should stay or go up, and he concluded that it would not change because it should not be related to whether Prisoner A knew or did not know that B will be executed.

S7: Say, it was A and B. It was more probable. It is more probable because the probability of being executed are higher than C. All right. So, suppose that A and B are going to be executed, and A now knows that B is going to be executed. But he asks the jailer to give no information about his or her own chances. Uhm, so the chances that he has to be released improve or stay the same. That's the question. And I think, think about C. C can either equally be released or. I don't think it changes the answer. My reason is that, uh, what matters is not whether he knows or not that C is going to be released or B is going to be released. But the probability to that, the original probability is my answer.

It is possible that the hint questions stressed the unequal prior probabilities and this made S7 give up the application of the case view. However, he did not mention the world numbers as evidence for his second answer. He did not take the ratio of the world numbers, either. So the hint questions might or might not have introduced the frequency view into his problem solving attempts.

S5 was the only subject who switched from the case view to the frequency view. As discussed earlier, the case view was dominant in the initial part of the session. She devised a marble model of the problem situation, which is consistent with the case view, and used it to calculate the probabilities for a while. After she answered Question 3, she at last adopted the world model and used the ratio of world numbers to calculate the probabilities. What was needed for this change to happen?

Before the hint questions were given, S5 obtained the incorrect answer 1/3 based on her marble model. However she could not relate her marble model and the answer

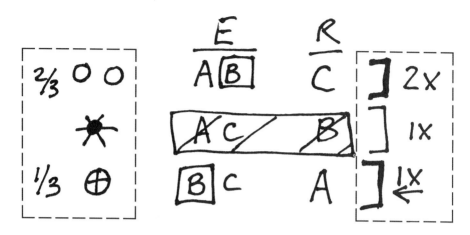

Figure 5. S5's diagram of the three possible combinations of events. The correspondence to the marble model and weights were added later. (Dotted lines added by the author.)

1/3 to the problem situation with three prisoners and a jailer. With the help of Questions 1 and 2, she noticed that the jailer's statement ruled out one of the three possible cases, and that this would change the probabilities. S5 could not map the three possibilities onto the initial probabilities at first, and then thought to give them weights and found the mapping. S5 also mapped them onto her marble model, and got 1/3 for the probability of A's release. However she did not assign numbers of worlds to the three possibilities this time, either.

> S5: If the jailer never tells a lie and he said that B will be executed, then I already ruled this out of the possibility, correct, ok. Well this doesn't change the probabilities? It must ... But, according to these three, each prisoner is equally likely to be executed and equally likely to be released. It's 2/3, 2/3 of the time A will be executed, 2/3 of the time B will be executed, 2/3 of the time C will be executed. But, that's, or changed, for all being released is 1/3, 1/3, 1/3, but that doesn't go along with this at all. So I don't understand, I don't understand. It's kind of like, somehow, it's kind of like saying this situation is two times likely to happen than either these situations (see Figure 5, areas in dotted lines added).

S5 had trouble interpreting Question 3 at first, but then she got 500 worlds as an answer after reinterpreting the question. She confirmed that the jailer would answer B's name in 125 worlds where Prisoner A would be released and in 500 where Prisoner A would be executed. Although she added them atone point and got 625, she did not hit upon taking the ratio 125/625. Instead, S5 focused on the proportions of worlds where the jailer would answer B's name to the worlds where Prisoner A would be released and where he would be executed (1/2 and 2/3, respectively). S5 tried to combine these results but was unable to.

S5 got 1/3 again dividing 250, where Prisoner A was to be released, by 750, where Prisoner B was to be executed. Thus at this time, she took the ratio of the world numbers, which might mean that she took the frequency view for the first time. A possible explanation for this is as follows. S5 had mapped the world numbers onto both of her marble model and the case view. This might have made it possible for her to apply the frequency view to the situation.

Some Differences in Problem Solving Activities

Whether one takes the case view or the frequency view affects the process of problem solving in various ways. Here I will argue the advantage of taking the frequency view. That is, how the problem solver makes the representation of the problem situation in terms of prisoners' release and execution.

As mentioned before, some of the subjects explicitly represented the problem situation with combinations of prisoners' releases and executions. In fact, five out of seven subjects made such representations. The reasons, or the triggers of their devising such representations were diverse.

S2 and S3, who took the frequency view at least after Question 1, devised the possible combination representation after answering Question 1. Answering Question 1 and taking the frequency view seemed to trigger the possible combination representation. They might have imagined some hypothetical worlds and tried to categorize those worlds. They assigned the numbers of worlds to each possible combination.

For S1, the situation was somewhat different. As mentioned before, he devised the possible combination representation when he tried to make sense of the fact that his new answer, 1/8, was smaller than the prior probability of A's release. He drew a diagram with world numbers and assigned prisoners' fates to the groups of the worlds. As for S1's case, we could say that taking the frequency view triggered the possible combination representation, too.

For the cases of S5 and S6, who did not take the frequency view at least at first, there were some other triggers of the possible combination representation. When Question 2 was given, S5 first asked herself how the jailer could never tell a lie and answer the name of Prisoner B or C half the time. Then she went back to the end of the problem statement and noticed that she had ignored the information about the jailer's choice. This might have made her focus on the relationship among A's release, B's execution, and C's execution. S5 considered the case where the jailer said "C will be executed" in terms of four marbles and came to the conclusion that in this case the probability of A's release was 1/2. She then mentioned the three possible combinations of release and execution for the first time.

S5: Yeah, I don't wanna think about the world representation, I wanna think about this some more. All right. There are three possibilities here. There are, there is that A and B get executed, C gets released. A and C get executed, B gets released, or B and C get executed and A gets released (Figure 5, center part)..

In contrast to S2 and S3, S5's representation of the problem situation came from considering what would happen if Prisoner A was released, instead of from considering individual worlds using the frequency view. Unlike S2 and S3, S5 did not count how many worlds fell into each of the three possible cases. She also made a mistake in interpreting these three possibilities, that is, she thought that they were equally likely.

S6, who tried to apply a formula of conditional probability, devised the possible combination representation to figure out the probability that A is released and B is to be executed. She seemed to come to this representation in her consideration of the dependency between A's release and B's execution. She assigned 1/3 probability to each of the three possibilities, as mentioned earlier.

S6: If they (A's release and B's execution) were independent events, I don't know if this is gonna lead down the right track, but, but, if these were independent, I could think of it by this. How about think of it? ... Ok, now what's the chance that A will be released and B executed ... Ok, I could be having, I could have A executed, B executed, and C released. Or this way. Or I could have, released, executed, executed. So the chance that A is released, and B is executed is 1/3.

These observations, though the sample size is too small, might indicate that taking the frequency view facilitates the possible combination representation that is important for the solution of the problem, and without the frequency view some other trigger is required to devise the representation.

Another important difference that may have been caused by the difference in the view taken is the event for which the probability was calculated. It is necessary to divide the case where Prisoner A will be executed into two cases, one where the jailer says "B will be executed" and one where he says "C will be executed." No subjects mentioned this separation directly. However, S1, S2, and S3, who might have taken the frequency view, actually used it in their solution. That is, they tried to calculate the probability of the conjunction of A's release and the jailer's answering B's name. It is noteworthy that two of them (S2 and S3) did this in terms of the number of worlds where A is released and the jailer answers B's name.

On the contrary, the other subjects who did not apply the frequency view to the situation when Question 2 was given did not mention the conjunction of A's release and the jailer's answering B's name. S5 did mention the cases where the jailer answered either B's or C's name when Prisoner A was to be released. But this did not lead her to realize that what was needed was the probability of A's release and the jailer's answering B's name. In other words, S1, S2, and S3 were able to relate the problem assumption of the jailer's answer to the solution by taking the frequency view and imagining the individual worlds.

We can say that the application of the frequency view leads people to categorize the individual instances and to list the possible cases appropriately. However this alone seems insufficient to reach the correct solution to the three prisoner problem.

Only one subject who asked himself what the sample space was ("sample size" in his words) achieved the correct answer to the problem.

The Views of Probability and Mental Models

Detailed analyses of subjects' problem solving activity, using subjects' verbal reports as data, revealed what cannot be accessed by quantitative analyses of ratios of the correct answer and errors. For some subjects, the case view of probability was so dominant that they could not accept the unequal prior probability in the problem situation. They tended to adhere to the case view and only one of them adopted the frequency view after getting three hint questions. Other subjects easily accepted the unequal probability and some of them adopted the world model that was based on the frequency view after getting a hint question. Taking the frequency view triggered subjects to devise the possible combination representation of the problem situation, which was essential to the solution of the problem. For subjects using the case view, some other triggers were necessary to devise the representation.

Though only one subject got the correct answer to the three prisoner problem, the results indicate that the frequency view has some advantage in probability problem solving. This does not mean that the frequency view is better than the case view. Both views might not only have their own advantages but also are accompanied by their particular misconceptions. Both views might be necessary as precursors of the mathematical concept of probability (Hawkins & Kapadia, 1984). However, we could say that the results here identified some of the advantages of the frequency view.

The Jewel Problem

An artificial jewel produced by a factory may have a blur or a crack, or may not have a blur nor a crack. One never has both a blur and a crack. The probability of having a blur is 1/4, the one of having a crack is 1/4, and the one of having neither a blur nor a crack is 1/2. In order to take inferior jewels away, all jewels produced are fed into an automatic checker. Put through this machine, all the jewels with a crack and no jewel without a blur nor a crack are taken away, but only 1/2 of the jewels with a blur are taken away. Now, what is the probability that a jewel that passed the machine check has a blur?

---

j	=	good	=	passed
j	=	good	=	passed
j	=	with crack	=	removed
j	=	with crack	=	removed
j	=	with blur	=	passed
j	=	with blur	=	removed

Figure 6. A mental model for the jewel problem.

What then accounts for the advantage of taking the frequency view in the solving of probability problems? Johnson-Laird's theory of mental models provides a good explanation. Johnson-Laird (1983, 1989) argued that people use mental representations called mental models in reasoning. Mental models are representations of which components correspond to perceivable objects. When problem solvers read the problem statement, they try to construct a mental model of the problem situation. Many problem solvers might be able to construct a mental model like Figure 6 for the jewel problem, which is much easier than the three prisoner problem, though it has the same mathematical structure as the three prisoner problem (at least in the form of tree diagram or Bayes' formula). In this model, there are several nodes for individual jewels and attributes like "with crack", "passed" are attached. The structure of the mental model represents the important partition of the probability space that is essential to the solution of the problem.

The structure of mental models for the three prisoner problem might be influenced by the view that a problem solver is taking. If problem solvers construct a mental model for the problem without the frequency view, components of the natural model might be the prisoners and the jailer. So the mental model may look like Figure 7 (a) or (b). The structures of these models never reflect the structure of the probability space and therefore the problem solvers can not use the model for solution. In such cases, the problem solvers cannot solve the problem unless they have abstract procedures like use of three diagrams or Bayes' formula.

(a)

$A = ex$
$A = rel$
$B = ex$
$B = rel$
$C = ex$
$C = rel$

$J = $ "B is released."
$J = $ "C is released."

(b)

$A = ex$ or rel
$B = ex$ or rel
$C = ex$ or rel

$J = $ "B is released." or "C is released."

Figure 7. A mental model for the three prisoner problem (1).

On the other hand, if problem solvers could apply the frequency model to the problem situation using the possible world representation, they would make mental models like one in Figure 8. Attention to the individual instances leads problem solvers to construct models of which components are the individual instances. The model consists of nodes representing "worlds." This model, like the model shown in Figure 8, reflects the essential structure of the probability space for the solution. However it is much more complex than the model for the jewel problem and this may make the three prison.

$$W = \begin{bmatrix} A = \text{rel} \\ B = \text{ex} \\ C = \text{ex} \\ J = \text{``B is released.''} \end{bmatrix} \qquad W = \begin{bmatrix} A = \text{ex} \\ B = \text{rel} \\ C = \text{ex} \\ J = \text{``C is released.''} \end{bmatrix}$$

$$W = \begin{bmatrix} A = \text{rel} \\ B = \text{ex} \\ C = \text{ex} \\ J = \text{``C is released.''} \end{bmatrix} \qquad W = \begin{bmatrix} A = \text{ex} \\ B = \text{ex} \\ C = \text{rel} \\ J = \text{``B is released.''} \end{bmatrix}$$

Figure 8. A mental model for the three prisoner problem (2). The structure reflects the necessary division of the probability space for the solution.

In this series of experiments, I used several probability problems, some of which were easy and others were difficult. Structures of mental models that seem natural and easy for problem solvers to construct for the problems were a good predictor of the performances. If the mental model reflects the division of the probability space that is necessary for the solution, subjects tend to get the correct answer to the problem. It seems natural and easy to construct such mental models for a problem when it is easy to apply the frequency view to the problem. This may be because it is easy for problem solvers to think of the repetition of an event in these problems and each trial (like a jewel in the jewel problem) can be a component of the mental model. On the other hand, if it is difficult to apply the frequency view to a problem, a trial does not tend to be perceivable for problem solvers and they tend to construct a mental model with other perceivable objects (like the prisoners in the three prisoner problem) as components. In such cases, mental models do not represent the necessary division of the probability space for the problem solution and this seems to make the problems difficult.

Results of the present experiment indicate that dominance of a certain view of probability in a problem solver is a good predictor of the problem solving process and the performance. If the frequency view is dominant in a problem solver, he or she might tend to construct mental models of which components are trials and of which structures reflect the essential structure of the probability space for the solution. On the other hand, if the case view is dominant, and the problem solver cannot analyze the probability space in an abstract way, he or she might tend to construct mental models with components other than trials and not to be able to construct useful problem representations.

References

Hawkins, A. S., & Kapadia, R. (1984). Children's conceptions of probability - A psychological and pedagogical reviews. *Educational Studies in Mathematics, 15,* 349-377.

Ichikawa, S. (1989). The difficulty of the problem of three prisoners: Analysis by the abstract description. *SIGR & I (Japanese Cognitive Science Society), 88-2,* 1-12. Tokyo.

Ihara, J. (1988a). A schematic representation of solution to the three- prisoner problem and its incomplete information theoretic consideration. *The 5th Conference of Japanese Cognitive Science Society,* 86-87.

Ihara, J. (1988b). A theoretical inquiry into Lindley's three-prisoner problem. In Japanese Cognitive Science Society (Ed.), *Advances in Japanese Cognitive Science* (pp. 33-71). Tokyo: Kodansha.

Itoh, Y. (1991). The role of the frequency view of probability in solving the "problem of three prisoners." Technical Report, No. 19. Japanese Cognitive Science Society.

Johnson-Laird, P. N. (1983). *Mental models.* Cambridge, MA: Harvard University Press.

Johnson-Laird, P. N. (1989). Mental models. In M. I. Posner (Ed.), *Foundations of cognitive science* (pp. 469-499). Cambridge, M. A.: MIT Press.

Mori, K. (1988a). What makes the "problem of three prisoners" difficult? *Journal of the Faculty of Education, Shinshu University, 62,* 45-50.

Mori, K. (1988b). Mathematical problems of probability estimation: Why are they so difficult? *Journal of the Faculty of Education, Shinshu University, 63,* 21-30.

Sayeki, Y. (1987). Analysis of the "problem of three prisoners" from the viewpoint theory. *Proceedings of the 4th Conference of the Japanese Cognitive Science Society,* 26-27. Chiba.

Shimojo, S., & Ichikawa, S. (1989). Intuitive reasoning about probability: Theoretical and experimental analyses of the "problem of three prisoners." *Cognition, 32,* 1-24.

Tversky, A., & Kahneman, D. (1983). Extensional versus intuitive reasoning: The conjunction fallacy in probability judgment. *Psychological Review, 90,* 293-315.

Chapter 14

On Introspections and Verbal Reports

Jay Moore
University of Wisconsin–Milwaukee

Introspection has been a controversial topic throughout the history of psychology. The "behavioral revolution" precipitated by John B. Watson in 1913 is often credited with the overthrow of introspection, but the matter is extremely complex. Consider the following famous passage from Watson's (1913) "behaviorist manifesto":

> Psychology as the behaviorist views it is a purely objective experimental branch of natural science. Its theoretical goal is the prediction and control of behavior. Introspection forms no essential part of its methods, nor is the scientific value of its data dependent upon the readiness with which they lend themselves to interpretation in terms of consciousness. (p. 158)

On the basis of this passage, one might conclude behaviorists generally thought introspection was irrelevant to psychology.

In contrast, consider the following passage from the work of the behaviorist B. F. Skinner (1974):

> [Radical behaviorism] restores introspection.... Radical behaviorism restores some kind of balance. It does not insist upon truth by agreement and can therefore consider events taking place in the private world within the skin. It does not call these events unobservable, and it does not dismiss them as subjective. (p. 14)

Admittedly, this passage is taken from a larger set of material on introspection, but the point remains that the nature of introspection and verbal reports, as well as their place in a science of behavior, may not be fully appreciated. The purpose of the present paper is to examine the nature of introspection and verbal reports, in an attempt to clarify their roles in psychological science.

Historical Background

Classical Introspection

In the late 1800s, much of science consisted of simply observing and then describing what were presumed to be nature's mechanisms (Suppe, 1977, p. 8 ff.). As psychology began to be regarded as a science in Western culture, the conscious mind was regarded as the subject matter of psychology. Observation of mental life and the workings of the conscious mind was quite naturally regarded as the way to gather scientific knowledge about that subject matter. Introspection was a special technique of observation, and therefore a special source of data about mental life.

 Accordingly, psychologists of the time made much of "observing" or introspecting the sensations, images, or feelings they experienced when they were engaged in some act of perception, cognition, discrimination, choice, or judgment. To be sure, psychologists of the time debated how well trained a subject needed to be (at least 10,000 training trials were thought necessary), whether the "stimulus error" had been committed (subjects should describe the conscious experience of the stimulus, rather than report its meaning), and whether "imageless thought" was possible (yes according to Kulpe, no according to Wundt). In addition, Titchener, a structuralist, and Baldwin, a functionalist, got into a nasty little quarrel about whether reaction times were faster when subjects concentrated on the stimulus or on the response. Structuralists who performed such experiments found that reaction times were faster when subjects concentrated on the response. In contrast, functionalists who performed the same experiments found that reaction times were faster when subjects concentrated on the stimulus. The matter was somewhat resolved when J. R. Angell and A. W. Moore proposed that there were two different types of people, and that different amounts of training would affect the types differently, thereby allowing each side to be correct. In any case, both structuralists and functionalists regarded conscious experience as the appropriate subject matter for psychology, and regarded introspection as the appropriate methodology to investigate that subject matter (Boring, 1953).

 Few psychologists of the time were concerned with behavior as the subject matter of psychology. At best, behavior was regarded as the subject matter of biology or physiology, rather than psychology. If one was concerned about so pedestrian a phenomenon as behavior, the assumption was that an understanding of behavior would quite naturally fall into place, once introspection had revealed the workings of the conscious mind.

 However, even though introspection was the dominant methodology of its time, it was not universally well-received. For example, Maudsley (1867, as cited in Turner, 1965, p. 11) offered this set of trenchant criticisms:

1. By focusing upon itself, by its rendering the introspective state static, introspection falsifies its own subject matter. As explicitly stated by Kant and Comte, one cannot introspect the act of introspection.
2. There is little agreement among introspectionists.
3. Where agreement does occur, it can be attributed to the fact that introspectionists must be meticulously trained, and thereby have a bias built into their observations.
4. A body of knowledge based on introspection cannot be inductive. No discovery is possible from those who are trained specifically on what to observe.
5. Due to the extent of the pathology of mind, self-report is hardly to be trusted.

6. Introspective knowledge cannot have the generality we expect of science. It must be restricted to the class of sophisticated, trained adult subjects.
7. Much of behavior occurs without conscious correlates.
8. Mind and consciousness are not coextensive.
9. Introspection and consciousness cannot give an adequate explanation of memory.
10. The arousal of a conscious image is not itself introspectible.
11. The brain records unconsciously. Its response is a function of organic states which themselves are not introspectible.
12. Emphasis on introspection minimizes attention given to physiological processes without which there would be no mental states.

Noteworthy is that Maudsley's criticisms anticipate many of those made by the behaviorists some fifty years later. Representative of the behaviorists' criticisms of introspection are the writings of John B. Watson and Max Meyer, to which we now turn.

Watson's Classical S-R Behaviorism

The classical S-R behaviorism of John B. Watson is probably the most widely-recognized criticism of introspection. As most readers know, Watson's program represented a dramatic break with both structural and functional psychology. His heroic effort to guarantee the "objectivity" of psychological science was fundamentally opposed to the inclusion of centrally-initiated processes. As an alternative, he attempted to interpret many of the topics of traditional psychology in terms of peripheral events. Hence, he regarded thinking as subvocal speech habits occurring in the larynx, emotion as peripheral responses (e.g., lust was a "fluttering in the foreskin"), and the verbal report as a legitimate research method. He also relied heavily on the notion of "implicit responses," which were unobservable responses that sometimes occurred between stimulus and the resulting explicit, publicly observable behavior.

However, the specifics of his program were not always well-formulated. For example, his early writings conceded that his program of conceiving of psychology "as [a science of] behavior will have to neglect but few of the really essential problems" with which introspective psychology concerned itself (Watson, 1913, p. 177). His early concession proved damaging because it implied that there might be something valuable about introspection and traditional psychology after all. His later writings, in which he railed bitterly against the metaphysics of consciousness, were less congenial to the possibility that traditional psychology was of much value, but he still had little to offer as a constructive substitute except chains of reflexes linked by peripheral intradermal stimuli. As a result, behaviorism has traditionally been regarded as an approach that subordinated subject matter in psychology to method, in order to be "objective," and by so doing overlooked significant aspects of human conduct. Boring (1953) makes the following point:

Watson's reaction in 1913, away from the pedantry and unreliability of
introspection, as he saw it, toward the more positive psychology of stimulus
and response, was an attempt, not so much to create behaviorism as a new
psychology with consciousness left out, as it was to reformulate the old
psychology in new terms.... The important thing is to see that Watson, in
attacking introspection, was objecting not to the use of words by the
subject, but to trusting the subject to use the words only with those
meanings that the experimenter wishes the words to have. (pp. 184, 185)

In retrospect, perhaps Watson's greatest contribution consists in his emphasis
of behavior as a subject matter in its own right. This emphasis made possible the
causal analysis of behavior as an event that occurred in context. Thus, Watson (1913)
was able to say quite clearly that:

In a system of psychology completely worked out, given the response the
stimuli can be predicted [sic]; given the stimuli the response can be
predicted. (p. 167)

His celebrated rejection of introspection is significant, of course, but needs to be
considered in light of his pioneering concern with behavior as an acceptable subject
matter of psychology.

Meyer and the "Other-one"

Max Meyer's often-cited book, *The Psychology of the Other-one* (Meyer, 1922), also
contains material relevant to the early behaviorist position on introspection. Here
Meyer attempted to present the case in an introductory level book for psychology
as an objective, positivistic science of behavior, concerned with measurable properties. A representative passage from early in the book provides the flavor of Meyer's
(1922) approach:

In times past one used to turn to psychology books when he wanted to learn
something about his Self–his soul.... Modern science owes its triumphs to
the fact that it has learned to restrict itself to describing what one can
measure. The psychology of the Other-one follows the same road. Why
should Robinson Crusoe, wanting information [on Friday], use the anti-
quated, the sterile method?.... Crusoe's desire to know as much more as
possible about his man Friday cannot be satisfied by psychology of selves.
He needs the psychology of the Other-one. He needs the psychology which
applies sense organs to the object of study, compares what the sense organs
perceive, counts and–leaves the question whether Friday has a Self, a Soul,
a Mind, a Consciousness to the single being whom it might concern, to
Friday. (pp. 3, 4)

As had Watson before him, Meyer attempted to call attention to the pragmatic
issue that science was primarily concerned with phenomena that could be touched
and measured. Conscious experience could not be measured as such. Consequently,
psychology had to deal with what it could touch and measure: behavior. The
dominant position was therefore to rule consciousness and mind out of bounds, not

so much because consciousness and mind didn't exist, but rather because they could not be reached by methodology. Introspection was largely irrelevant to psychology as a science.

Zuriff's Summary

Zuriff (1979a, 1979b, 1980, 1985) has recently discussed implications of the general behaviorist position regarding introspections. For example, in his book *Behaviorism: A conceptual reconstruction* (Zuriff, 1985, chap. 2), he summarizes five themes of the behaviorist argument against introspection:

1. Introspection does not work. It is flawed. It doesn't achieve what it claims. Its reports are distorted, inconsistent, and vague.
2. Its contents are not objective, where by objective is mean unbiased and unprejudiced by personal taste.
3. Introspection is private. The hallmark of science is its public nature. There is therefore no way to check or verify the accuracy of introspective statements, either simultaneously or successively.
4. Introspection does not achieve intersubjective agreement, which is necessary to establish a data base.
5. Introspection is unreliable.

These points recapitulate many of those made by Maudsley (1867) over a century earlier, as well as those of Watson and Meyer, and give evidence of continued behaviorist concerns about the status of introspection. With the possible exception of the first point--that it does not work and is flawed in principle, the concerns are again more methodological than ontological or epistemological. In any case, the discipline of psychology clearly began to drift away from the introspective study of the workings of the conscious mind, and toward the study of behavior, with the influence of classical S-R behaviorism and such figures as Watson and Meyer. The question was, and to some extent still is, what form is that study to take.

Introspection and Methodological Behaviorism

Methodological Behaviorism Defined

Methodological behaviorism is usually defined as the attempt to explain behavior solely in terms of publicly observable variables. Watson and Meyer, reviewed above, are often cited as early examples of methodological behaviorism. Perhaps the most familiar statement of methodological behaviorism is from Bergmann (1956; see also Addis, 1982; Natsoulas, 1984):

It must in principle be possible to predict future behavior, including verbal behavior, from a sufficiency of information about [publicly observable] present (and past) behavioral, physiological, and environmental variables. (p. 270)

In this article Bergmann suggests that behavior and the publicly observable environment are ultimately all anyone has with which to work. Thus, psychology as a science should recognize this state of affairs, and work within its boundaries.

Bergmann (1956, p. 269) concludes that Watson's most important contribution was his methodological behaviorism.

Actually, contemporary usage suggests a somewhat expanded definition of methodological behaviorism may actually be more appropriate than Bergmann's (1956) treatment. According to this expanded definition, methodological behaviorism is the attempt to explain behavior in terms of (a) publicly observable variables, (b) intervening variables operationally defined in terms of publicly observable variables, and (c) hypothetical constructs operationally defined in terms of publicly observable variables (see also Moore, 1981, 1990). Following MacCorquodale and Meehl's (1948) convention, intervening variables are considered as logical or theoretical constructs that are exhaustively defined in terms of observations. In contrast, hypothetical constructs are considered as logical or theoretical constructs that are only partially defined in terms of observations. Thus, intervening variables do not admit surplus meaning, whereas hypothetical constructs do. Worth noting is that by these criteria, most of contemporary psychology qualifies as one variety or another of methodological behaviorism, by virtue of the appeal to "mediating" variables.

The Contribution of Kenneth W. Spence

The distinguished learning theorist Kenneth W. Spence was the prototypical methodological behaviorist. According to Spence (1948),

The philosophers of science, particularly the logical positivists ..., philosophically minded scientists such as Bridgman ..., and within psychology, such writers as Boring ..., Pratt ..., and Stevens ..., have succeeded, I believe, in making the point that the data of all sciences have the same origin—namely, the immediate experience of an observing person, the scientist himself. That is to say, immediate experience, the initial matrix out of which all sciences develop, is no longer considered a matter of concern for the scientist qua scientist. He simply takes it for granted and then proceeds to talk of describing the events in it and discovering and formulating the nature of the relationships holding among them. (p. 68)

Spence (1948) continues on the specific topic of introspection:

The introspectionist, it should be recalled, assumed a strict one-to-one relationship between the verbal responses of his subjects and the inner mental processes. Accordingly, he accepted these introspective reports as facts or data about the inner mental events which they represented. The behavior scientist takes a very different position. He accepts verbal response as just one more form of behavior and he proposes to use this type of data in exactly the same manner as he does other types of behavior variables. Thus he attempts to discover laws relating verbal responses to environmental events of the past or present, and he seeks to find what relations they have to other types of response variables. He also makes use of them as a basis for making inferences as to certain hypothetical or theoretical constructs which he employs. In contrast, then, to the introspectionist's conception of these verbal reports as mirroring directly inner mental events, i.e., facts, the behaviorist uses them either as data in their own right to be related to other data, or as a base from which to infer theoretical constructs which presumably represent internal or covert activities of their subjects. (pp. 69-70)

Thus, Spence argued here for the same point that Boring (1953) made about Watson. The issue is that introspections or verbal reports cannot to be taken as veridical reports of events in immediate experience. The assumption was that even though a dimension of immediate experience exists, events in that dimension cannot constitute a subject matter for the science of psychology because they are private and ineffable. Psychology must remain silent on them because like other sciences, psychology can only deal with publicly observable phenomena (see also discussion in Zuriff, 1980, p. 341). Rather, introspections or verbal reports were to be regarded as data in their own right. They were public and could be related to surrounding circumstances. As Boring (1953) notes, methodological behaviorism "shifts the locus of scientific responsibility from an observing subject to the experimenter who becomes the observer of the subject" (p. 184). Thus, methodological behaviorists, at least as they later evolved, could use the introspections or verbal reports as behavioral variables to support inferences about covert events, where those covert events had the status for science of hypothetical constructs. The commitment was to a coherence theory of truth, where at issue was how well all the available data, including verbal reports, supported a common theme.

Methodological behaviorism, of course, follows from a set of assumptions about how humans become knowledgeable, and how inner phenomena contribute to that knowledge (for extended discussion of the epistemological validity of these points, see Alston, 1972). Radical behaviorism represents a contrasting approach that follows from a different set of assumptions. Let us now turn to a discussion of radical behaviorism.

Introspection and Radical Behaviorism

Skinner's radical or thoroughgoing behaviorism (Schneider & Morris, 1987; Skinner, 1945) is markedly different from the methodological behaviorism reviewed above. Radical behaviorism may be defined in terms of four metatheoretical themes.

Radical Behaviorism Defined

Ontology. The first theme concerns ontology. In Skinner's behaviorism, nothing even remotely associated with any aspect of a dualistic ontology is countenanced. The world is regarded as homogeneously physical and material. Organisms interact with respect to features of that world in the process called behavior. All aspects of these processes are physical and material.

In particular, there is no "epistemological dualism" of known and knower that has been common in other forms of psychology, especially methodological behaviorism, since Tolman (see discussion in Boring, 1950, p. 667; Smith, 1986, pp. 116

ff., particularly p. 130). Dichotomies between subjective and objective, knower and known, or observer and agent may imply unique access to a part of the world, but not dichotomous ontologies.

Radical behaviorism views a broad range of locutions as having troublesome ontological implications. Academic pedantry is not the issue. Rather, our language is our calculus. An effective way of talking about phenomena is seen as an important first step in dealing effectively with those phenomena (e.g., Hineline, 1980, p. 72). In particular, radical behaviorism regards the appeal to the mediating phenomena of methodological behaviorism—where the phenomena take the form of intervening variables or hypothetical constructs, as simply a legacy of the Platonic dualistic commitment to explanations that appeal to inner attributes. Radical behaviorism insists that dualistic ontological issues associated with S-O-R mediational neobehaviorism and methodological behaviorism be addressed, rather than swept under the rug. As Skinner (1945) stated,

> It is agreed that the data of psychology must be behavioral rather than mental if psychology is to be a member of the Unified Sciences, but the position taken is merely that of "methodological" behaviorism.... [Methodological behaviorism] is least objectionable to the subjectivist because it permits him to retain "experience" for the purpose of "nonphysicalistic" self-knowledge. The position is not genuinely operational because it shows an unwillingness to abandon fictions. (pp. 292-293)

The "fictions" in question are precisely the elements of immediate experience that methodological behaviorism legitimates as dualistic entities. Mediational neobehaviorism attempts to circumvent ontological problems by using such logical devices as intervening variables and hypothetical constructs, but as discussed elsewhere (Moore, 1981, 1984, 1990), this approach is itself dualistic as well.

Behavior as a subject matter in its own right. The second theme is that the interaction between organism and environment (i.e., behavior) is regarded as a subject matter in its own right. In particular, behavior is not regarded as important because it provides logical grounds for speaking about causal entities that dwell elsewhere, at some other level of observation, and that are measured if at all in different terms (cf. Skinner, 1950).

Most of the variables with respect to which the human organism behaves, and no doubt other organisms as well, are publicly observable. However, not all the relevant variables need to be intersubjectively verifiable. Private phenomena may be important in the control of behavior, but they need not be approached in the traditional way as theoretical inferences about causal phenomena from another dimension. The private phenomena may be incorporated as either stimuli or responses, in the same way as public stimuli and responses are incorporated, but accessible only to one person.

Some private phenomena are felt conditions of the body, such as aches, pains, and other interoceptive states. Others are covert forms of behavior that exercise stimulus control over subsequent behavior. For example, covert verbal behavior might serve as a discriminative stimulus for controlling subsequent behavior. The subsequent behavior may be either verbal or nonverbal, and may be at either the overt or the covert level. Other private phenomena might involve covert perceptual behavior, as in "seeing in the absence of the thing seen," or covert manipulative behavior, as in privately examining the consequences of various moves when playing chess or privately performing "mental" arithmetic (see Moore, 1980; Zuriff, 1979a). Nevertheless, the private phenomena are homogeneous with respect to the behavioral dimension. These private stimuli do not cause behavior in the sense that the inferred entities of the methodological behaviorist cause behavior. For the radical behaviorist, the private stimuli are functionally related to the environmental context in which they are located (Hayes & Brownstein, 1986). Importantly, consideration of private events means that radical behaviorists can say quite legitimately that they "do not believe there is a world of mentation or subjective experience that is being, or must be ignored" (Skinner, 1978, p. 124). The difference is that the facts are regarded as behavioral, rather than mental. (For additional discussion of the origin of mental and cognitive terms, see Skinner, 1989, 1990).

Verbal behavior and explanation. A third theme concerns verbal behavior. Verbal behavior is defined as behavior reinforced through the mediation of other persons. Verbal behavior is therefore behavior that affects the social, rather than the mechanical environment (Skinner, 1957, pp. 1-2). Importantly, verbal behavior is regarded as a behavioral, rather than a logical phenomenon (Skinner, 1945). As such, it is to be accommodated at the same level as other behavior, and does not require a special analysis, with principles fundamentally different from those that apply to the analysis of other operant behavior (Skinner, 1957, chap. 2).

From the perspective of radical behaviorism, the theories and explanations that are so honored in science are to be analyzed as verbal behavior (Skinner, 1957, chap. 18). Theories and explanations function as forms of discriminative stimulation that guide future action, whether through (a) direct manipulation or (b) collateral action when direct manipulation is not feasible (Moore, 1990, p. 25). Radical behaviorism is not opposed to theories in principle. As Skinner (1969) has said, "experimental psychology is properly and inevitably committed to the construction of a theory of behavior. A theory is essential to the scientific understanding of behavior as a subject matter" (p. viii). Rather, radical behaviorism rejects the traditional view of theories as formal statements that appeal to events and entities in other dimensions. The kind of theory that radical behaviorism does endorse is based on an economical collection of facts, noting uniformities of functional relations.

The term "disposition" is often taken as central to a behaviorist position. Interestingly, however, the term "disposition" rarely occurs in Skinner's own writings. When it does, the context is altogether different from traditional approaches. In traditional approaches, mental terms are given the status of dispositions. The dispositions then are treated as hypothetical constructs. In contrast, for radical behaviorism the term typically means that certain motivating operations have been carried out, or that certain antecedent events have established stimulus control, such that the probability of a given response is increased. When physiological techniques are more advanced, perhaps we will know how an organism's microstructure differs as a function of these operations and events. The intriguing relation is that if anything, dispositions are descriptors on the dependent variable side of the ledger. They are not mediators, nor are they on the independent variable side. If dispositions are used in predictions, the prediction is from effect to effect, rather than from cause to effect.

Pragmatic orientation. A fourth theme concerns the pragmatic orientation of radical behaviorism. Absent from radical behaviorism is any rigid claim that "Truth" is derived by conducting hypothesis-testing experiments that involve random assignment of subjects and tests of statistical inference. These methodological concerns are more properly related to methodological behaviorism and mentalism, with the attendant commitment to the supremacy of logic, than to radical behaviorism. Radical behaviorism adopts a pragmatic theory of truth, where truth is a matter of successful working in everyday life (Hayes & Brownstein, 1986). Indeed, radical behaviorism is extraordinarily libertarian when it comes to alternative verbal practices (cf. Mahoney, 1989). As Skinner said,

We may quarrel with any analysis which appeals to ... an inner determiner of action, but the facts which have been represented with such devices cannot be ignored. (1953, p. 284)

No entity or process which has any useful explanatory force is to be rejected on the ground that it is subjective or mental. The data which have made it important must, however, be studied and formulated in effective ways. (1964, p. 96)

The issue of interpretation is especially important in connection with a pragmatic orientation. From the radical behaviorist perspective, interpretation is the making sense out of events when those events cannot be further investigated. A representative statement is found in Skinner (1974):

Obviously we cannot predict or control human behavior in daily life with the precision obtained in the laboratory, but we can nevertheless use results from the laboratory to interpret behavior elsewhere.... [A]ll sciences resort to something much like it.... [T]he principles of genetics are used to interpret the facts of evolution, as the behavior of substances under high pressures and temperatures are used to interpret geological events in the history of the earth. (pp. 228-229)

Interpretation plays a focal role in radical behaviorism. Skinner felt his most important book was *Verbal Behavior*, even though it was "an exercise in interpretation rather than a quantitative extrapolation of rigorous experimental results" (Skinner, 1957, p. 11). Most everyday functioning, of course, involves a considerable degree of interpretation because the knowledge claims of everyday life simply do not come as a result of conducting experiments under carefully controlled conditions. Rather, they come as a result of applying what has been learned elsewhere to beneficial effect, that is, of interpretation.

Radical Behaviorist Stance Regarding Introspection

Given the above outline of radical behaviorism, what then is the radical behaviorist stance regarding introspection? We may start in a general way examining Skinner (1953) on the matter of public observability:

> Modern science has attempted to put forth an ordered and integrated conception of nature. Some of its most distinguished men have concerned themselves with the broad implications of science with respect to the structure of the universe. The picture which emerges is almost always dualistic. The scientist humbly admits that he is describing only half the universe, and he defers to another world—a world of mind or consciousness—for which another mode of inquiry is assumed to be required. Such a point of view is by no means inevitable, but it is a part of the cultural heritage from which science has emerged. It obviously stands in the way of a unified account of nature. (p. 258)

Skinner (1964) continues on this same theme:

> Behaviorists have, from time to time, examined the problem of privacy, and some of them have excluded so-called sensations, images, thought processes, and so on from their deliberations. When they have done so not because such things do not exist but because they are out of reach of their methods, the charge is justified that they have neglected the facts of consciousness. The strategy is, however, quite unwise. It is particularly important that a science of behavior face the problem of privacy. It may do so without abandoning the basic position of behaviorism. Science often talks about things it cannot see or measure.... An adequate science of behavior must consider events taking place within the skin of the organism, not as physiological mediators of behavior, but as part of behavior itself. It can deal with these events without assuming that they have any special nature or must be known in any special way. (p. 84)

With particular regard to introspection, Skinner has said:

> [Radical behaviorism] restores introspection but not what philosophers and introspective psychologists believed they were "specting."... Radical behaviorism restores some kind of balance. It does not insist upon truth by agreement and can therefore consider events taking place in the private world within the skin. It does not call these events unobservable, and it does not dismiss them as subjective. It simply questions the nature of the object observed and the reliability of the observations. The position can be stated as follows: what is felt or introspectively observed is not some nonphysical world of consciousness, mind, or mental life but the observer's own body. This does not mean ... that introspection is a kind of physiological research, nor does it mean (and this is the heart of the argument) that what are felt

or introspectively observed are the causes of behavior.... What are introspectively observed are certain collateral products of [a person's genetic and
environmental] histories. (Skinner, 1974, pp. 14-15)
Feelings are ... collateral products of the conditions responsible for the
behavior (Skinner, 1974, p. 47)
What is felt or seen through introspection is only a small and relatively
unimportant part of what the physiologist will eventually discover. In
particular it is not the system which mediates the relation between behavior
and environment revealed by an experimental analysis. (Skinner, 1974, p.
256)
We do not, through introspection, observe the physiological processes
through which behavior is shaped and maintained by contingencies of
reinforcement. (Skinner, 1978, p. 111)
Here Skinner is very clearly speaking in favor of the contingencies as the factors
responsible for behavior. As noted earlier, the analysis of contingencies is important
for the causal explanation of behavior, not the analysis of the inner phenomena
generated by the contingencies.

Nevertheless, Skinner does admit phenomena that are not publicly observable
into his accounts. Skinner's notion of private events is important in a discussion of
introspection because private phenomena are typically what is introspected. Given
that there are clearly private phenomena that can be introspected, what then is the
causal status of those phenomena?

[T]he private event is at best no more than a link in a causal chain, and it
is usually not even that. We may think before we act in the sense that we
may behave covertly before we behave overtly, but our action is not an
"expression" of the covert response or the consequence of it. The two are
simply attributable to the same variables. (Skinner, 1953, p. 279)
Thus, private phenomena are not initiating causes. Typically, they are located in a
matrix of circumstances. Some of these circumstances are accessible to all. Others,
such as private phenomena, are not. In any case, the private phenomena do not
explain behavior. Rather, they are more behavioral phenomena to be explained. Two
issues are important: (a) How do introspections develop? and (b) How do the private
stimuli that are the object of introspections come to guide subsequent behavior?

How do introspections develop? Introspections are verbal phenomena.
Verbal behavior develops through differential reinforcement arising from the verbal
community. However, in the case of verbal behavior concerned with private events,
such as introspections and verbal reports, the verbal community operates with a
handicap. The verbal community cannot administer differential reinforcement if
important aspects of the contingency are private. Skinner (1945, pp. 273-274) points
out at least four ways in which a verbal response may nevertheless develop to a private
stimulus, despite such a handicap:

1. The verbal community may administer differential reinforcement based on
a public accompaniment to a presumed private stimulus.

2. The verbal community may administer differential reinforcement based on a collateral public response to a presumed private stimulus.
3. The private stimulus may come to exert control in virtue of the stimulus control shared between public and private stimuli.
4. The private stimulus may come to exert control by virtue of stimulus generalization from public to private stimuli.

In these four ways the verbal community overcomes the problem of privacy, and speakers gain the ability to describe events with which they alone are in contact.

How do the private stimuli that are the object of introspections come to guide subsequent behavior? Most forms of covert behavior were acquired in their overt form. The behavior then receded to the private form, where as private stimulation it then joins with other stimuli to form a complex. The private stimuli gain control in the same way that other stimuli gain control. Such control is by no means inevitable, any more than control by a given public stimulus is inevitable. Control might even be enhanced if verbal behavior, however incipient, is occasioned by the private stimuli. The verbal behavior might then exert supplemental control over subsequent behavior. Again, the control exerted by this verbal behavior does not differ from that which would develop if the same verbal behavior arose as a public event.

A common case occurs when the public form of the verbal behavior recedes to the covert level, in a process something akin to the familiar fading out of a public stimulus. There are several situations where such a process might take place. For example, the public form might be punished. Someone speaking out loud might encounter mild verbal punishment for being bothersome from others who are nearby. The resulting verbal behavior might then become "quieter." Another reason why the verbal behavior might be made at a reduced level relates to a lack of environmental support for the overt form. Thus, in the absence of the full set of stimuli necessary to occasion the overt form, the response is made at the covert level, instead of at the overt level. Once the covert form works just as well as the overt, the possibility that others may punish the overt form keeps the behavior at a covert level. The verbal behavior might also be more expedient in a covert form, particularly in its incipient stages, and result in faster, less troublesome execution. Of course, the verbal behavior might re-emerge in an overt form when persons are alone, and begin to "talk to themselves out loud" as they attempt to solve a difficult problem.

An interesting point is how central any of these processes will prove to be. For classical S-R behaviorism, all such behavioral processes were regarded as peripheral. Taken literally, however, the thesis of classical S-R behaviorism implies that persons who were paralyzed cannot think. This thesis strains credulity. In many ways, the radical behaviorist thesis sets the agenda for the neurophysiologist who is interested in studying the behavioral relevance of complex internal events. The neurophysiological evidence will aid in the confirmation of the radical behaviorist interpretation.

A Comparison of Classical Introspectionism, Methodological
Behaviorism, and Radical Behaviorism on the Nature and Role of
Introspective Verbal Reports

Table 1 below provides an overview of the relation between classical introspection, methodological behaviorism, and radical behaviorism on the nature and role
of introspective verbal reports. Three rhetorical questions are posed, and then either
a "yes" or "no" response is given to indicate how each position answers each
questions. The rationale for each answer is then given.

Question	Introspection	Methodological Behaviorism	Radical Behaviorism
Are introspective verbal reports a source of data about phenomena that are immediately legitimate aspects of psychological science?	Yes	No	Yes
Are introspective verbal reports a source of data about inner/mental causes of a subject's behavior?	Yes	No	No
Do introspective verbal reports provide data about unobservables, which must in turn be accommodated as inferred, hypothetical constructs?	No	Yes	No

Table 1. An overview of the relation between classical introspection, methodological behaviorism, and radical behaviorism on the nature and role of introspective verbal reports.

Question 1. Let us begin by analyzing responses to the first question. Classical
introspection answers yes because of the fundamental assumption that the subject
matter for psychology is the contents of consciousness.

In contrast, methodological behaviorism answers no because there the contents
of consciousness cannot be agreed upon. As noted earlier, methodological behaviorism insists that a phenomenon must be capable of being agreed upon, at least in
principle, for it to be considered part of science.

Radical behaviorism answers yes, but for a different reason than does classical
introspectionism. Radical behaviorism rejects the dualistic conception of the
contents of consciousness held by classical introspectionism. However, radical
behaviorism does feel that introspective verbal reports are legitimate phenomena

that must themselves be explainable in an adequate science of behavior, even if only for one person.

Radical behaviorism and methodological behaviorism hold contrary positions on this question because they subscribe to different theories of truth. Radical behaviorism subscribes to a pragmatic theory of truth, whereas methodological behaviorism subscribes sometimes to a correspondence theory, and other times to a coherence theory of truth. Moreover, radical behaviorism notes that methodological behaviorism does not attempt to explain how introspective verbal reports come to be made. Methodological behaviorism simply accepts them as a given, and that uncritical acceptance creates its own set of problems. Of course, a radical behaviorist must infer whether private events are genuinely occurring for another person, given introspective-like statements. Nevertheless, the fact remains that something controls the verbal behavior of the speaker. How is it possible for private phenomena to control that verbal behavior? Whether they do or not in any given instance is a subsidiary question.

Question 2. Let us now analyze responses to the second question. Classical introspection answers yes. According to classical introspection, insofar as it is appropriate to speak of causal analyses, introspective verbal reports may be regarded as providing valid information about those inner or mental causes.

Methodological behaviorism answers no. The concern is not that the introspected phenomena might not be causally relevant in the same way they are to introspectionist. Rather, methodological behaviorists answer no because there can be no agreement about the inner or mental causes.

Radical behaviorism also answers no, but for a different reason than does methodological behaviorism. As noted earlier in the quotes from Skinner, the objects of introspective verbal reports are not regarded as inner causes of behavior (in the sense of initiating causes), mental or otherwise, because there are no initiating inner causes of behavior, mental or otherwise. Information about the causes of behavior is provided through an analysis of contingencies of reinforcement, not introspection.

Of course, from the radical behaviorist perspective introspection may give some information about the physiological states of the body or covert responses that accompany certain aspects of behavior, but even that information is limited. First, we do not have nerves going to the right places in our bodies to allow us to come into contact with much of the important physiology at work. Second, because of the problem of privacy, the verbal community can't sharpen our verbal-descriptive skills sufficiently to allow us to make fine-grain statements about the physiology that is active. Third, the verbal statements may be under the control of variables other than the physiology that is active (Skinner, 1945, pp. 274-275), as in self-deception.

Question 3. Let us now analyze responses to the third question. Classical introspection answers no. It disagrees that introspective verbal reports provide data about unobservables, which must then be accommodated as inferred, hypothetical constructs. As noted in the analyses of responses to the first question, classical introspection accepts the phenomena as immediately given in the contents of consciousness. They may then enter directly into the science.

In contrast, methodological behaviorism answers yes, saying that the phenomena must be regarded as theoretical entities to ensure the enterprise is scientific. As noted earlier, the phenomena are private, and methodological behaviorism argues that the subject matter must be public in order to be objective and part of science. The phenomena in question can therefore enter the science only through the theoretical language, as hypothetical constructs (e.g., Zuriff, 1985, pp. 85-90).

Radical behaviorism answers no for at least two reasons. First, as noted earlier, talk of intervening variables or hypothetical constructs as theoretical entities instead of as verbal behavior concedes the mentalistic premises of reference and coherence theories of language. Second, radical behaviorism feels that an account must be provided of how introspective verbal reports come to be given. This account will never be achieved if the phenomena under study are isolated from analysis by being classified as "logical" or "theoretical" entities.

Thus, radical behaviorism does represent a unique position, particularly with respect to introspective verbal reports (cf. Zuriff, 1980, p. 340). The particular pattern of yes and no answers to the questions above serves to define each position. The pattern also differentiates methodological from radical behaviorism.

Summary and Conclusions

Introspection has historically been regarded as a means of observing and describing the contents and workings of the mind so that conscious mental experience could be properly understood. Classical S-R behaviorism argued against this general orientation. It argued that the aim of psychology was to predict and control behavior, rather than to understand conscious mental experience.

However, classical behaviorism had its own problems. The result was that mental phenomena soon returned as organismic variables, for example, as operationally defined hypothetical constructs, under various S-O-R models of methodological behaviorism (Skinner, 1945). The rationale was that the appeal to hypothetical constructs would yield a theoretical but appropriately scientific understanding of how the mind works, which would lead in turn to a theoretical but appropriately scientific understanding of behavior. Introspective verbal reports came into play as data that could be used to operationally define the hypothetical constructs.

Radical behaviorists, of course, are interested in causal analyses of behavior. However, they regard the traditional conception of the "mind" as causally responsible for behavior as mischievous and deceptive. Neither introspection nor the appeal to hypothetical constructs sheds light on the workings of the mind, because the very conception of a causal mind on which such positions are based is in error.

But if the traditional conception of introspection is in error, are introspections and verbal reports of no psychological significance? For radical behaviorists, the answer is "Not necessarily."

Let us now consider a series of questions that attempt to place introspections and verbal reports in perspective.

1. *What is introspection?* Introspections are instances of verbal behavior under the control of private events.

2. *How do introspections develop?* They develop in four ways. Accepting them as data supporting hypothetical constructs contributes nothing to an understanding of how they develop, and indeed perpetuates mentalistic reference theories of verbal behavior.

3. *What is introspected?* The dimensional issue is at stake here. What is introspected are private physical events and states of body, not mental states that are irreducibly distinct from physiological states. Feelings reported in introspective episodes are not fundamentally different from other behavioral phenomena. What one "feels" during introspection is a state of the body.

4. *What is relation between the objects of introspection and the causes of behavior?* Private events are sometimes links in a behavioral chain, or concomitants that enter into multiple control over subsequent behavior. They are not initiating causes. Classical introspection is mistaken in its tacit assumption that the mind or mental phenomena are responsible for behavior. Contingencies are responsible for behavior.

5. *What problems are created by the methodological behaviorist's approach to introspections and verbal reports?* The answer is mentalism. Mentalism may be defined as an orientation to the study of behavior which holds that a unique, a necessary, and the primary contribution to the causal explanation of behavior consists in proposing various internal acts, states, mechanisms, or processes, presumed to be operating in neural, conceptual, or psychic dimensions (Moore, 1990).

6. *What problems are created by mentalism?* If the way that persons learn to speak of their internal states cannot be effectively explained, we end up with a mentalistic version whereby such phenomena as sensations and feelings are presumed to be mental and to cause such overt behavior as introspections and verbal reports. If there are mental phenomena that cause this kind of behavior, why are there not other mental phenomena that cause other forms of behavior? Thus, as argued elsewhere (Moore, 1990), mentalism is objectionable because it (a) is misleading and vague, (b) obscures important details, (c) impedes the search for relevant variables, (d) misrepresents the facts to be accounted for, and (e) gives false assurances about the state of our knowledge by inducing us to accept fanciful statements about fictitious way stations as explanations.

In short, mentalism fundamentally interferes with an effective explanation of behavioral events. Introspection is a behavioral phenomenon that must be analyzed meaningfully, in order to prevent methodological behaviorism and mentalism from making further inroads into a naturalistic science of behavior.

References

Addis, L. (1982). Behaviorism and the philosophy of the act. *Nous, 16*, 399-420.

Alston, W. F. (1972). Can psychology do without private data? *Behaviorism, 1*, 71-102.

Bergmann, G. (1956). The contribution of John B. Watson. *Psychological Review, 63*, 265-276.

Boring, E. G. (1950). *A history of experimental psychology* (2nd ed.). New York: Appleton-Century-Crofts.

Boring, E. G. (1953). A history of introspection. *Psychological Bulletin, 50*, 169-189.

Hayes, S. C., & Brownstein, A. J. (1986). Mentalism, behavior-behavior relations, and a behavior-analytic view of the purposes of science. *The Behavior Analyst, 9*, 175-190.

Hineline, P. N. (1980). The language of behavior analysis: Its community, its functions, and its limitations. *Behaviorism, 8*, 67-86.

MacCorquodale, K., & Meehl, P. (1948). On a distinction between hypothetical constructs and intervening variables. *Psychological Review, 55*, 95-107.

Mahoney, M. (1989). Scientific psychology and radical behaviorism. Important distinctions between scientism and objectivism. *American Psychologist, 44*, 1372-1377.

Maudsley, H. (1867). *The physiology and pathology of the mind.* London: Macmillan.

Meyer, M. F. (1922). *The psychology of the other-one* (2nd ed., revised). Columbia, MO: Missouri Book Company.

Moore, J. (1980). On behaviorism and private events. *Psychological Record, 30*, 459-475.

Moore, J. (1981). On mentalism, methodological behaviorism, and radical behaviorism. *Behaviorism, 3*, 55-77.

Moore, J. (1984). On behaviorism, knowledge, and causal explanation. *Psychological Record, 34*, 73-97.

Moore, J. (1990). On mentalism, privacy, and behaviorism. *Journal of Mind and Behavior, 11*, 19-36.

Natsoulas, T. (1984). Gustav Bergmann's psychophysiological parallelism. *Behaviorism, 12*, 41-69.

Schneider, S. M., & Morris, E. K. (1987). A history of the term *radical behaviorism*: From Watson to Skinner. *The Behavior Analyst, 10*, 27-39.

Skinner, B. F. (1945). The operational analysis of psychological terms. *Psychological Review, 52*, 270-277, 291-294.

Skinner, B. F. (1950). Are theories of learning necessary? *Psychological Review, 57*, 193-216.

Skinner, B. F. (1953). *Science and human behavior.* New York: Macmillan.

Skinner, B. F. (1957). *Verbal behavior.* New York: Appleton-Century-Crofts.

Skinner, B. F. (1964). Behaviorism at fifty. In T.W. Wann (Ed.), *Behaviorism and phenomenology* (pp. 79-97). Chicago, IL: University of Chicago Press.

Skinner, B. F. (1969). *Contingencies of reinforcement*. New York: Appleton-Century-Crofts.

Skinner, B. F. (1971). *Beyond freedom and dignity*. New York: Knopf.

Skinner, B. F. (1974). *About behaviorism*. New York: Knopf.

Skinner, B. F. (1978). *Reflections on behaviorism and society*. Englewood Cliffs, NJ: Prentice Hall.

Skinner, B. F. (1989). The origins of cognitive thought. *American Psychologist, 44*, 13-18.

Skinner, B. F. (1990). Can psychology be a science of mind? *American Psychologist, 45*, 1206-1210.

Smith, L. D. (1986). *Behaviorism and logical positivism*. Stanford, CA: Stanford University Press.

Spence, K. W. (1948). The postulates and methods of "behaviorism." *Psychological Review, 55*, 67-78.

Suppe, F. (1977). *The structure of scientific theories* (2nd ed.). Urbana, IL: University of Illinois Press.

Turner, M. B. (1965). *Philosophy and the science of behavior*. New York: Appleton-Century-Crofts.

Watson, J. B. (1913). Psychology as the behaviorist views it. *Psychological Review, 20*, 158-177.

Zuriff, G. E. (1979a). Covert events: The logical status of first person reports. *Psychological Record, 29*, 125-133.

Zuriff, G. E. (1979b). Ten inner causes. *Behaviorism, 7*, 1-8.

Zuriff, G. E. (1980). Radical behaviorist epistemology. *Psychological Bulletin, 87*, 337-350.

Zuriff, G. E. (1985). *Behaviorism: A conceptual reconstruction*. New York: Columbia University Press.

A portion of this paper was presented at the convention of the Association for Behavior Analysis held in Nashville, Tennessee in May, 1990.

Chapter 15

The Context of Pigeon And Human Choice

Howard Rachlin
State University of New York at Stony Brook

Suppose you are watching a very brief film clip of a man swinging a hammer. You have not seen the parts of the film that come before and after the clip; the thing the hammer is hitting is out of the frame. These events and objects, the ones you do not see, constitute the context of the man's act. What the man is *really* doing depends on this context. In principle context is infinite in temporal and spatial extent. For you to understand what this man is really doing the film might have to go back to the man's birth or forward to his death. He might be swinging the hammer at his mother's head and he might eventually be put to death for this act. Even better understanding might be attained by going further forward to the lives of his descendants, further back to the lives of his ancestors, and further outward to the lives of his relatives, friends, acquaintances–to larger and larger social spheres.

But the man might not be doing something so grizzly as hammering his mother's head. He might be hammering at a piece of glass, a piece of metal, or most likely at a nail in a piece of wood. In the latter case he might be building a floor, building a wall, or hanging a picture hook. If he were building a floor, he might be building a house, building a deck, or building a barn. If a house, he might be a contractor building the house on speculation, or he might be an accountant building his own house in his spare time. In the latter case he might be getting exercise, engaging in his hobby, preparing for his retirement, providing shelter for his family, or some mixture of all of these. Ultimately, you might see the man's act as part of his attempt to live a good life or obey God or both concurrently. The *meaning* of this man's hammer swing, like the meaning of any act, obviously depends on its context.

But there is another possible interpretation of the context of the man's hammer swing–one framed in terms of his mental life–his pleasures, pains, hopes, dreams, wishes, and fears while swinging the hammer. Let us call the film-clip context, the overt context, "Context OB" (OB stands for overt behavior–the sort that might be captured in a film), and the mental context, "Context M." Still another kind of context might be the set of physiological, muscular and skeletal events causing the man's arm to swing–including his muscle movements, his peripheral nervous impulses and the states of the various cognitive/physiological centers in his brain.

Let us call this context, "Context CP" (CP stands for cognitive/physiological). Of course, Contexts OB, M, and CP all must correspond in some way. We would expect the relevant physiological context of a hammer swing to be found in the man's arm muscles rather than his foot muscles.

The first point of this article is that you may achieve better and better understanding of a given act wholly on the level of overt behavior (more and more of Context OB) and that there is *infinite* room for the development of that understanding without going "deeper" into any other sort of context.

The second point is that the *mental* context of the act, Context M, is embraced wholly by Context OB plus Context CP. Context OB constitutes the *mental life* of the hammer-swinging man and Context CP constitutes the man's internal *mental mechanisms*. If contrary to fact there were some way you could understand the man's act completely in both Context OB and Context CP, there would be no further gain in understanding from Context M. You would already know all there is to know about Context M. (Rachlin, in press a, b, develops this argument and relates Context OB and Context CP to Aristotle's sciences of final and efficient causes.)

The third point is that the first two points apply not only to *your* understanding of the man's act but also to *his own* understanding of that act. If the man understands his own mental life better than you do, it is because he has seen more of the film than you have—not because he has some power of introspection unavailable to you. He cannot directly observe his own physiology (we do not see our retinas—we see the world); and his ability to observe his own overt behavior may in any instance be no better than yours—may in fact be a good deal worse.[1]

Perhaps this third point may be better illustrated with another example. Suppose a film-clip shows a grocer giving a free loaf of bread to a poor customer. His motives are so far ambiguous. He might be giving the customer the bread out of a true spirit of generosity or as part of a publicity campaign or both. What his true motives are depends on what he does "off-stage." Relevant questions are: Has he been generous in the past? Will he be generous in the future? How is his business doing? Is there a publicity campaign going on? You could obtain relevant information by sending poverty-stricken customers into the store at various times (similar to the technique of princes and princesses in fairy tales when testing the character of potential brides and grooms). Both his past and future behavior are relevant, and he can test his own behavior in the same way. The information thus obtained, the data, is not just an indication of what might have been going on in one of his brain centers or what he might have been saying to himself at the moment he gave the customer the bread. If there is an apparent contradiction between the mental state revealed in his behavior, widely observed, and his contemporaneous brain state or internal verbalizations, then it is the brain state and internal verbalizations rather than his behavior that fail to correspond to his true motives. A true motive, a true mental state of any kind, *is* an abstraction of overt behavior; each individual act is a projection of this abstract conception.[2]

A specific act may be a mere sign of a mental event in the sense that it signals a wider pattern of acts (as a specific melody may be a sign that we are hearing a

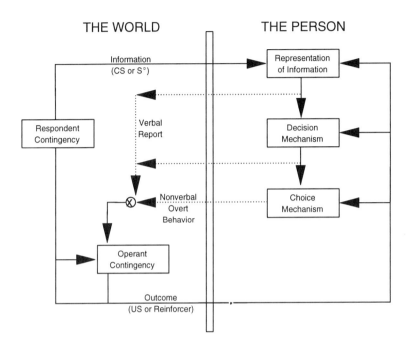

Figure 1. Cognitive and behavioral views (from right and left) of person-world interaction.

symphony by Brahms). The grocer's act as it relates to his mental state is a sign of other corresponding acts (other projections). But the grocer's overt act is not a mere sign of some other more meaningful specific event taking place inside him and accessible only to him. One of the few correspondences between Freudianism and behaviorism is their mutual insistence that people are not the best judges of their own motives.

Thus, Context M is superfluous. Now let us turn to a comparison of Contexts OB and CP using, as a relatively simple example, a pigeon's concept of probability. Then we will return to discuss language and human conceptions of probability. The great advantage of doing psychology experiments with pigeons as opposed to human subjects is that the most relevant context of the pigeon's immediate behavior—its history of reinforcement—can be, at least to some extent, controlled.

The Pigeon's Conception of Probability

Figure 1 (from Rachlin, in press, b) diagrams cognitive and behavioral views of psychological investigation and theory. From the cognitive viewpoint (from the right) incoming stimuli make contact with a representational system; the representations thus created are combined with previous information to generate decisions, choices and judgments, the consequences of which may in turn affect the representational and decision mechanisms. Cognitive decision experiments with human subjects typically use verbal inputs such as, "The probability of gaining $10,000 is 1/2." The probability itself is held to be fundamentally the internal "degree of certainty" elicited by the verbal stimulus. This subjective conception of probability strongly depends on the verbal stimulus and thus is not possible to maintain for pigeons.

If you want to study pigeons' choices among probabilistic events (Mazur, 1989) you have to (at least initially) expose the pigeons to the probabilistic events themselves, not verbal expressions. Probability of gain for pigeons must be varied in terms of objective relative frequencies: reinforcers per trial; reinforcers per response; reinforcers per unit of time. Since trial durations and response rates may be manipulated and evaluated, all probabilistic reinforcement may be expressed in terms of reinforcers per unit time. But this variable is the familiar one of reinforcement *rate*, the most common independent variable in experiments on animal choice (Williams, 1988).

There is a degree of dispute currently in choice research whether reinforcement rate is an unanalyzable molar variable in itself or is analyzable into a series of delays from the moment of choice. In either case, however, probability discounting is held to be a form of *temporal* discounting: if reinforcement rate is fundamental then animals discount value by means of a variable but limited "time window." If delay is fundamental then probability acts like delay: each probability is reducible to a (binomial) distribution of strings of losses followed by a win; the lower the probability the longer the average string's duration (Rachlin, 1990). The value of a probabilistic reinforcer would then be the sum of the values of all possible strings leading to reinforcement (non-reinforcement equivalent to a loss, reinforcement, to a win). The value of each string would be discounted by its own delay and its own probability according to the following formula (Raineri & Rachlin, in press):

$$v = \frac{V}{(1 + kD)(1 + h)} \qquad (1)$$

where V is the undiscounted value of the reward, v is the discounted value, D is the delay imposed by the duration of the string and is equal to $(1-p)/p$ where p is the probability of the string (not the probability of the reward). The constants, k and h represent degree of discounting due to delay and probability.

Equation 1 may or may not be the last word in discount functions of delayed or probabilistic reward. The point here is that Equation 1 predicts and explains choice among probabilistic rewards in terms of delays and probabilities as objective *contingencies in the environment* (from the left in Figure 1) rather than as *internal representations* (from the right in Figure 1). It would be gratuitous after deriving Equation 1 to assume that pigeons internalized this function and then chose among internal representations of the equation's various outputs rather than among the rewards themselves. The equation describes overt choices in the pigeon's past and predicts those in its future (Context OB). The equation is not a description of an engram within the pigeon's nervous system (Context CP). Equation 1 describes a contingency, a relationship between a whole organism and its environment, a relationship that does not (necessarily) correspond to a relationship within the organism between or among its parts.

The distinction between cognitive/physiological and behavioral approaches to probability is important because probability is a paradigm case, a prime example, of an abstract, mentalistic concept. Implications may be drawn from this distinction to (a) other mentalistic concepts, (b) to the relationship between language and behavior–to the function of language, and (c) to the relationship between an individual and society.

Probability And Other Mentalistic Concepts

Experiments with delayed rewards, probabilistic rewards and delayed-probabilistic rewards with human subjects with both hypothetical and real rewards (Rachlin, Castrogiovanni & Cross, 1987; Rachlin & Raineri, in press; Rachlin, Raineri & Cross, 1991; Raineri & Rachlin, in press) indicates that the vast difference between human and pigeon choice lies mainly in the value of the constants h and k for the two species. Whereas pigeons drastically discount valuable rewards over delays of seconds, equal degrees of human discounting are obtained only for delays of many years. (Fry & Green, 1992, found childrens' degree of delay discounting to lie somewhere between that of pigeons and adult humans but reassuringly much closer to that of adults than that of pigeons. Older adults had the flattest discount functions.) A more molar analysis would say that the temporal duration of the patterns of events to which pigeons' behavior is sensitive (their "time window") is far narrower than that of humans.

However, pigeons have minds. The fact that pigeons are sensitive to probabilistic reinforcement indicates that their behavior cannot be described in terms of instantaneous events. A probability (conceived as a relative frequency) cannot exist in an instant. In an instant an event either occurs or does not occur. A probability (like a grocer's motives) requires context. A pigeon's peck may be reinforced on *this* trial but, given that fact, the probability of its being reinforced may range from unity to zero (as an asymptote) depending on what happens on other trials–depending on its context.

Furthermore, like humans, pigeons may learn to enlarge the span of time over which their behavior is affected by reinforcement (their discount functions may flatten or their time windows expand). Let us consider the ways in which such learning has been accomplished.

Commitment

One implication of Equation 1 is that preferences may reverse over time. For instance a pigeon may prefer a larger to a smaller reward when they are both temporally distant, say 4 pellets of grain 10 seconds from now preferred to to 2 pellets of grain 8 seconds from now. But after 7 seconds pass the pigeon's preference may reverse; the smaller 2-pellet reward, 1 second away, is now preferred to the larger 4-pellet reward, 3 seconds away. If, at the earlier point (with the 8 and 10 second delays in effect), the pigeon has the opportunity to prevent its own subsequent choice (its choice when the delays would have diminished to 1 and 3 seconds) it will do so (Ainslie, 1974; Rachlin & Green, 1972). Thus, when commitment contingencies are available pigeons will learn to commit themselves to the larger, more delayed reward. However, pigeons will sometimes learn to choose a larger more delayed reward even with no explicit commitment. Mazur and Logue (1978), by gradually increasing the delay to the larger reward, trained pigeons to choose that reward in preference to the smaller, more immediate reward they otherwise prefer, without any explicit commitment strategy. The *mechanism* by which the pigeons do this is a subject for cognitive/physiological psychology. Ainslie (1992) believes that all self control is a form of commitment–if not explicit and external then implicit and internal. According to Ainslie, an internal commitment (an entire internal bargaining process) mediates (as does the cognitive/physiological mechanism on the right side of Figure 1) between presentation of reward alternatives and choice.[3]

Response Patterning

In experiments now being conducted in my laboratory hungry pigeons chose between small-immediate and large-delayed reinforcers under two conditions. The first is a simple choice condition. A single peck on one key produces the small-immediate reinforcer. A single peck on the other key produces the larger, more delayed reinforcer. After reinforcement there is a brief wait and the choice opportunity is repeated. During each session the pigeon is exposed to many such choices. The result in this simple condition is that pigeons choose the small-immediate reinforcer 90% of the time. The other condition requires 30 pecks (distributed in any way on the two keys) to produce reinforcement. Whichever key receives the 30th peck determines the reinforcer, small-immediate or large-delayed, obtained. In other words, after the pigeon has made 29 pecks the contingencies are the same as they were in the simpler condition: a single peck (the 30th) on either key produces either the small-immediate or large-delayed reinforcer. Nevertheless *all* of the pigeons drastically alter their former preference, most of them reversing and now obtaining the large-delayed reinforcer more frequently than the small-immediate reinforcer.

Several control conditions remain to be run but let us suppose they do not alter the picture painted above. At the moment of its 30th peck each pigeon faces the same choice as it did when it had only one peck to make. What did those 29 pecks do to the pigeon to cause its preference to reverse? In some sense the 29 pecks are a "sunk cost." Logically they are over and done with and should not affect the pigeon's choices. How then do the first 29 pecks direct the 30th? (When the pigeon was about to make the first peck, both reinforcers would be delayed by the time to make the 30 pecks and, according to Equation 1, at that point the pigeon really preferred the larger more delayed reinforcer.) The answer I believe is that the 30 pecks constitute a response unit. The 30 peck contingency organizes the pigeon's behavior into a pattern that extends over a relatively long period. Choice of the larger delayed reinforcer is the consequence of the pattern once it has begun. A switch to the small-immediate reinforcer interrupts the pattern. In the simpler condition the decisive peck is isolated; in the 30 peck condition the decisive peck is embedded in a contextual pattern. So in a sense the pigeon uses its own behavior to obtain the larger reinforcer. There is no external commitment here, any more than you are committed to watch the ninth inning of a baseball game or read the last chapter of a mystery book or hear the last 10 bars of a symphony. Why is it that interruption of these activities diminishes their value out of proportion to the fraction of time missed? If the orchestra failed to play the very last note of a symphony comprised of perhaps 5,000 notes your enjoyment of the symphony would not be reduced by just 1/5,000. You would more likely complain that the whole thing was ruined. Why? Because listening to the symphony as a whole is a single behavioral unit. Your enjoyment (the symphony's value) does not even exist until the music is over. But still it exists simultaneously with the symphony (listening to the symphony is thus a true Aristotelian final cause of listening to each bar of music). Listening to the symphony as a whole cannot precede listening to its parts (as efficient causes would) but neither does the symphony as a whole strictly follow its parts (movements, bars, notes) as a food pellet follows a pigeon's peck. It is a characteristic of modern reinforcement theory (Premack, 1965; Timberlake & Allison, 1974; Rachlin, Green, Kagel & Battalio, 1976) that the value of an activity consists of the activity itself plus its consequences as they occur in a pattern. Behavior and reinforcement are not separate activities but a single patterned activity that itself has a value perhaps higher than that of any of its individual components.

The difference between the cognitive capacity of people and pigeons then lies in the complexity of these patterns. Pigeons are capable of forming simple brief patterns—like 30 pecks followed by a large delayed reinforcer. It is meaningful therefore to say that pigeons can think. But people can form much more complex patterns than pigeons can—the meaningful context of a person's actions are much wider than those of a pigeon. Thus, it is wrong to say (as I have said) that a college degree or the job that the degree gets you is the reinforcer for studying in school or that the worker's pay is the reinforcer for the worker's work. Rather, the patterns of study-degree-job and work-pay-leisure as *wholes* are valuable in themselves and may be more valuable than the reinforcer alone—as the symphony is more valuable than the last few notes or, perhaps more aptly, as the meal is more valuable than the dessert. The student might well not study without the grades, the degree, the job, the status, and so forth. But studying is not simply a neutral response reinforced by correlation with its consequences. Rather, studying is like the first three movements of a symphony or the first three courses of a meal—just as necessary as the rest for the behavioral pattern to attain its full value. You might prefer a cheap meal with dessert to an expensive meal without dessert or a complete popular song to a symphony without its last note but this is not because the value of the meal or the symphony is wholly contained in its ending. The value of complex events is not in their ending but in their *pattern* which may be destroyed when the ending is removed.

What then is the (principal) function of language in human behavior? The answer is that language expands the context of behavior—its variety, its temporal extent, its special extent, its complexity. Language thereby enhances the value of life.

Human Conceptions of Probability

Equation 1 not only describes the behavior of hungry pigeons choosing among food rewards, it also describes the verbal behavior of quite satiated human subjects choosing among hypothetical (i.e., verbally presented) rewards consisting of money and other commodities with various delays, various probabilities and various delays and probabilities (Rachlin & Raineri, in press; Raineri & Rachlin, in press). Although other experiments used "real" rewards with human subjects (for instance, Rachlin, Castrogiovanni & Cross, 1987) their results' conformance to Equation 1 was no better than that of the hypothetical experiments, consisting of nothing but a verbal interchange between experimenter and subject. The experimenter would ask a question such as: "Which do you prefer: $100 now and for certain or $1,000 next week with a probability of 1/2?" Or, "Which do you prefer, $100 now or 1-week's use of an economy car one year from today?" Using the psychophysical up-down staircase method indifference points were obtained and tested for conformance to Equation 1. With some slight modifications, Equation 1 described the results well. In (unpublished) tests with 400 Stony Brook undergraduates answering a paper-and-pencil questionnaire, individual probability and delay discount functions were obtained; the constants h and k were significantly correlated. In other words, subjects who tended to sharply discount delayed rewards also tended to sharply discount probabilistic rewards and vice-versa.

Let us now consider how language operated in these experiments and then try to generalize to the function of language in everyday life.

From the cognitive/physiological viewpoint the function of language is obvious. The experimenter's words enter the subject's nervous system (like the typist's strokes enter the word processor) and create an internal representation for further processing. The representation created is assumed to be the same as that created by an actual probabilistic situation in everyday life. The experimenter's words are tied to the real-life situation by virtue of the common internal representation they both create. The internal representation is the relevant context and the *meaning* of the words as it is of the probabilistic choice situation itself.

From the behavioral point of view the words are tied to the situation by virtue of the common overt choice behavior (rather than the common representation) they evoke. The function of the words is to place the subject's individual act into a specific pattern of actual environmental events. When the experimenter says, "The probability of $100 is 1/2," the subject behaves as if a coin were being flipped and $100 were riding on heads or tails. The words are already a representation of the situation. No further representational mechanism is assumed to exist. Unless the subject has had some experience in the represented situation (with coins, wheels of fortune, dice, dredles, and so forth) the experimenter's words would be as meaningless to him or her as they would be to a pigeon.

There is no such thing as a one-shot probability. The odds of an atomic war breaking out have no meaning unless they refer to either (a) the spatial and temporal coincidence of a series of component acts all of which have themselves repeatedly occurred or (b) the frequency of other events similar to the one-shot event in some respect deemed to be crucial.

What language does is to take the "booming buzzing confusion" of events as they occur, occurred, and will occur and pick out some pattern of those events as the context relevant to present behavior. In behavioral jargon, the experimenter's instruction is a "discriminative stimulus" for a complex behavioral pattern.

The sentences "Hot fudge sundaes taste good," and "Hot fudge sundaes make you fat," may both be true but each is a discriminative stimulus for a different act of choice. The former sentence sets the choice into a narrow context—the context of the *present state* of the eater's body. In the presence of a hot fudge sundae the truth value of the former sentence is equivalent to: "This hot fudge sundae will taste good now." The latter sentence is a general rule. It puts the present act of choice into a relatively wide context. But the sentence "Hot fudge sundaes make you fat," is *not* equivalent to its specific version: "This hot fudge sundae will make you fat now." The more general statement is true but the specific version is false. You will not become fat now if you eat this particular hot fudge sundae.

Of course, the wider statement may not succeed in its function. You might recite the general rule, write it 100 times on the blackboard, or have it drummed into your head, and still eat the hot fudge sundae. In this case, the choices signalled by the more particular and the more general discriminative stimuli conflict with each other. You cannot eat this particular hot fudge sundae now and also not eat it now. However, a still more general discriminative stimulus, "It is good to indulge yourself once in a while," makes it possible that a person eating a hot fudge sundae on this particular occasion might be behaving consistently with all three verbal statements:

1. Hot fudge sundaes taste good.
2. Hot fudge sundaes make you fat.
3. It is good to indulge once in a while.

This could be the one time all this week when the person ate something that, if he ate it frequently, would make him fat.

The more abstract the verbal rule, the wider the temporal slice of behavior one would need to observe in order to classify any given act as controlled by the verbal rule. But you, or the person in question himself, could never be 100% sure whether his behavior was or was not controlled by any verbal rule no matter how narrowly defined—just as you could never be 100% sure whether a coin were unbiased even after a million or even a million million tosses. But, you may say, if the coin were two-headed you could look at it and thus be sure it would always fall heads up. Then, the behaviorist says, you would not be observing the coin's *behavior* but the *mechanism* by which the behavior was brought about. In the case of human beings, as opposed to coins, we are far from being able to directly observe the workings of decision mechanisms. Cognitive psychologists at present must infer the nature of those mechanisms from behavioral observations–as the behaviorist infers the relevant contingencies. Even 100 heads in a row might conceivably be part of a much longer entirely random series of tosses. (In fact if the probability of heads were indeed 1/2, it would have a non-zero, probability of falling heads 100 times in a row; therefore, in a huge number of tosses, a googolplex, say, you might suspect the coin was biased if you did *not* find any instances of 100 heads in a row.)

The power of language to shift the context of particular acts is perhaps nowhere more vividly demonstrated than in the experiments described by Mischel, Shoda & Rodriguez (1989). In the standard version of these experiments, a 4-5 year old child plays the following game with the experimenter: the experimenter places a less-valued reward (a pretzel in this case) in front of the child and leaves the room. If the child summons the experimenter back to the room (by ringing the bell) the child may have the less valued reward right then. However if the child waits for the experimenter to come back herself the child may have a more valued reward (a marshmallow in this case). The experimenter comes back after 15 minutes but few children wait that long. The dependent variable is how long under various conditions children wait before ringing the bell. Mischel et. al.'s first critical observation was that the children waited significantly longer with the pretzel exposed to view than with the pretzel covered. But these results could be reversed depending on what the experimenter told the children before she left the room. Children told to think of how crunchy, salty, and tasty the pretzel was, waited less time, even with the pretzel covered, than children told to think of the pretzel as a log that might be used to build a toy house, even with the pretzel exposed.

The cognitive interpretation of these experiments (Mischel's own interpretation) relies on the influence of the child's thoughts ("hot" thoughts versus "cold" thoughts), caused by the experimenter's verbal statements, on the child's decision mechanism (as on the right of Figure 1). George Ainslie's (1992) cognitive interpretation assigns hot and cold thoughts not to the child but to internal "interests," within the child, who bargain with each other in an internal marketplace. The usefulness of such interpretations will depend on the procedures they suggest for manipulating choice and developing the child's ability to cope with real world problems. Neither of them are necessarily inconsistent with a potential behavioral explanation framed in terms of narrower versus wider temporal contingencies. From a behavioral viewpoint, the instructions to think of the pretzel's sensory qualities (like judgments of the lengths of luminous rods in a dark room) frame the present choice narrowly both spatially and temporally–within the child's body and now; the instructions "think of the pretzel as a log" frame the present choice widely–in the environment and in the future (when the toy house might be played with).

Gustave Flaubert (1856-7/1950, p. 49) describes Madame (Emma) Bovary's character as follows. As an adolescent, "...she rejected as useless whatever did not minister to her heart's immediate fulfillment–being of a sentimental rather than an artistic temperament, in search of emotions, not of scenery." Flaubert is here holding up the narrow (emotional) context of Emma's choices as the key flaw in her character–the trait that is going to get her into trouble later in life.

Theories of behavior concentrating wholly on cognitive control of emotions miss the point that the wider aspects of the environment (the toy log cabin of Mischel's subjects or the "scenery", in Flaubert's terms) are valuable not just because they give rise to pleasant emotions or not just because they help us control and regulate unpleasant emotions but *in themselves*. "Subtility" of behavior (like subtility of a painting) lies not behind the behavior, not inside the organism, but in the patterns on the behavior's surface. The 19th century critic and lyricist Hoffmenstahl, as quoted by Italo Calvino, (in *Six Messages For The Next Millenium*) said, "Depth is hidden. Where? On the surface." A Mozart symphony is not better than a popular song because the emotions to which it gives rise are somehow better or "deeper," but because the pattern of the Mozart symphony is more complex and of longer duration; its context is wider, it is more abstract. And, as Plato pointed out long ago, goodness lies in abstraction.

The most important function of language, therefore, is to expand the context of current behavior. Human happiness (perhaps the reader will agree) lies ultimately in molding one's life into an interesting pattern, one that is neither lost in its environment, nor one that clashes with it. Language, ranging from "pass the salt," to the contents of *Anna Karenin,* is primarily a tool to achieve that end. Since our relations with other people constitute the most influential parts of our environments (Society is the main component of the framework of an individual's life story.) let us now go on to discuss the above considerations in the context of people's interactions in the social sphere.

Social Context

Ainslie (1992, p. 156) quotes the economist J. G. March (1978) as follows:
The problem of intertemporal comparisons...is technically indistinguishable from the problem of interpersonal comparison of utilities. When we compare the changing preference of a single person over time to make [trade offs] across time, we are in the identical position as when we attempt to make comparisons across different individuals at a point in time. The fact that the problems are identical has the advantage of immediately bringing to bear on the problems of intertemporal comparisons the apparatus developed to deal with interpersonal comparisons [1978, p. 600]

The central idea has been around at least since Plato; temporal and spatial domains of human relations are analogous. Ainslie's development of this analogy is the most precise, the best, we have in modern times. This section will follow Ainslie's development but alter it slightly to conform to the present behavioral analysis of context.

According to Ainslie the essence of social conflict is captured by the prisoner's dilemma game. In the standard version of the game, two players, A and B, each choose between two alternatives: C (cooperate) or D (defect). If both players choose C, both gain a moderately high amount (say, +10 points). If both choose D, both lose a moderately high amount (-10 points). However, if one chooses D while the other chooses C, the one choosing D gains a larger amount (+15 points) while the one choosing C loses a larger amount (-15 points). The "rational" strategy for an individual player (A) playing the game one with a person (B) he does not know is to choose D (defect): If, on the one hand, player B chooses D, player A should choose D because A will then lose only 10 instead of 15 points. If, on the other hand, player B chooses C, player A should still choose D because then he will gain 15 instead of only 10 points. If both players follow the "rational" strategy both will lose 10 points. Most people, faced with this sort of game do in fact choose D. However, if both had behaved "irrationally," choosing C, both would have gained 10 points. Hence, the dilemma.

When the players know each other well, however, or when they play the game repeatedly, they more frequently choose C (cooperate). But if a person who initially tends to cooperate is playing the game repeatedly with a persistent defector the cooperator will eventually come to defect.

Social dilemmas like the "tragedy of the commons" (an individual gains when he overgrazes his cattle on the commons as long as other people do not overgraze. But the individual loses if everyone overgrazes their cattle because then the commons will be depleted) and the "free-rider problem" (an individual gains by not contributing to a public good, public television for instance, but loses if no one contributes because then the public good is lost to everyone) are similar in structure to the two-player prisoner's dilemma problem.

Consider the problem of littering and dirty streets. Say the advantage of living in a neighborhood with clean streets is worth +10 points to you while the disadvantage of living in a neighborhood with dirty streets is worth -10 points. Say the advantage of being able to throw your litter anywhere you want is worth +2 points while the disadvantage of looking for a litter can is worth -2 points. Then your "rational" choice is to litter. On the one hand, if everyone else litters (assuming your own actions will not significantly affect the appearance of the streets) and you do not litter you will lose 12 points whereas if you litter too you will lose only 8 points. If on the other hand everyone else does not litter you will gain 10 points for clean streets but if you do not litter either you will gain only 8 points due to the disadvantage of looking for litter cans all the time. However if everyone else does not litter and you do litter you gain the most, 10 points for clean streets plus 2 points for throwing your litter anywhere you want, making +12 points. You would be a "free rider." Of course if everyone followed this same "logic" the streets would be dirty and everyone would lose 8 points.

Ainslie believes that the way societies overcome such "social traps" is by mutual agreement (sometimes in the form of laws) not to litter. I believe that the issue is one of the context of choice (where the mechanism underlying the context might well be a series of mutual agreements and laws). Consider a simpler problem (from 3rd-grade arithmetic): Which would you rather have, $1 for yourself or $2 shared equally between you and three other people? The "correct" answer is $1. Otherwise you would get only 50 cents. However, if the three other people sharing the money were family members (who might spend the money on a mutual good) you might well prefer the $2. The deciding factor it seems is not so much a particular agreement or law but how you perceive yourself in relation to the group. Sharing is really a form of discounting, expressible by the following modification of Equation 1:

$$v = \frac{V}{(1 + kD)\,(1 + h)\,(1 + sN)} \qquad (2)$$

where the old symbols mean what they did before, the new symbol, N stands for number of other people sharing the good and s (ranging from 0 to 1) stands for "selfishness." Assume for the moment that probability of reward is unity ($=0$) and there is no delay ($D=0$). Then according to Equation 2, $v=V/(1+sN)$. If you were completely unselfish ($s=0$) then the value of a good to you (v) would be equal to its absolute value (V) regardless of how many other people were sharing the good. If on the other hand you were completely selfish ($s=1$) then the value of a good would be only what you yourself got ($v=V/(1+N)$).

In any particular instance, the constant, s, would depend on your degree of common interest with the others in the group. In the 3rd-grade arithmetic problem, the choice is between $1 with $N=0$ ($v=$ 1) and $2 with $N=3$ ($v=$ $2/(1+3s)$). If your constant, $s=1/3$, you would be indifferent between the alternatives.

If the reader will bear with me, I would like to describe a very informal experiment that failed. I posed the following question to a group of 10 American psychologists and 10 Japanese psychologists:

Imagine I were to present you with the following choice. I give you $100 [translated into Yen for the Japanese] which you may keep or put in a box. If you choose to keep the $100 it is yours. If however you put it in the box I will add another $100 to the box making $200 in the box from you. After presenting this same choice individually to each member of this group [of 20 psychologists] I will open the box and divide its contents equally among all of you *regardless of whether you put your money in the box or kept it.* No other member of the group will know what you chose.

I then did some sample calculations on the board to show them that they need not worry about what anyone else would chose because, whatever any of the rest of the group chose, any one of them would have $90 more if he or she kept their $100 than if they put it in the box. I asked each of them to indicate on an index card what they would actually do in such a situation—whether they would put the money in the box or keep it—and also to indicate by a J or an A whether they were Japanese or American.

I had previously given this problem to groups of Americans (Stony Brook undergraduates and New York University psychologists) and found that about half of the subjects said they would put their money in the box and half said they would keep it. In this case, I expected more Americans would chose to keep the money and more of our Japanese hosts, members of a tightly-knit society known for its unity of purpose, would put the money in the box. But no. The Americans, as I thought, mostly chose to keep the money but the Japanese also mostly chose to keep it! My hypothesis then was that the Japanese figured the Americans would keep their money so the common cause was already lost. But later I asked a female Japanese participant (sample of one) why the Japanese kept their money. Her instant answer was, "It would have cost *you* [i.e., me] $100 more." So perhaps like other Americans before me I had simply underestimated Japanese social consciousness. Given that my sample of one was typical, the Japanese had low s-values as I suspected but the social context imposed by my verbal instructions (other people in the group) ranged over a further extent than I had imagined.

The analogy between the social (spatial) and delay (temporal) terms of Equation 2 is clear. The constants s and k correspond to the degree of discounting with extent of spatial and temporal groupings; the variables D (delay) and N (number of other people) correspond to spatial and temporal distance (where N specifies the relevant context—the width of a "social window" corresponding to the "time window").

In the unpublished experiments previously discussed, where a significant positive correlation was found between the individual constants h and k (of Equation 1) of 400 Stony Brook undergraduates, subjects were also given a social dilemma similar to the one I presented to the Japanese-American group. The results from these subjects were more predictable. About half of the subjects said they would keep their money and those who did had significantly steeper temporal discount functions (higher k) than the other half, who said they would put their money in the box.

Given the analogy between temporal and social discounting, we may take a social dilemma and (as March suggests) translate it directly into a strictly personal dilemma. Recall for instance the littering problem discussed above. Table 1a reiterates the hypothetical gains and losses involved. Table 1b transposes those values to the personal one of smoking addiction. In Table 1b let us assign +10 points for being healthy, not coughing, not having to buy cigarettes, and other general advantages of not smoking; let us assign -10 points for being unhealthy, coughing, buying cigarettes, and other general disadvantages of smoking; for the immediate pleasure of *this* cigarette, let us assign +2 points and the immediate deprivation of a cigarette, -2 points. Then if you do not smoke generally and do not smoke now you get +10 points for being healthy but -2 points for loss of pleasure of a cigarette right now, totalling +8 points. If you do not smoke generally but have just this one cigarette you get +10 points for being healthy and +2 points for the immediate pleasure of a cigarette totalling +12 points—which is the best of all possible smoking worlds; you have your cake and eat it too.[4] If you generally smoke but deprive yourself of a cigarette now you lose 10 points for being unhealthy and lose another 2 points for your current deprivation, a total of -12 points; you neither have your cake *nor* eat it. Finally, if you generally smoke and you smoke now you are unhealthy (-10 points) but at least you get the pleasure of a smoke (+2 points) for a total of -8 points.

Table 1

a)   Social Dilemma:

Point Assignments
clean streets: +10
dirty streets: - 10
littering: + 2
not littering: - 2

		Person A	
		doesn't litter	litters
Other	don't litter	+ 8	+ 12
people	litter	- 12	- 8

b) Intrapersonal Dilemma:

Point Assignments
being healthy: +10
being unhealthy: - 10
smoke now: + 2
don't smoke now: - 2

		Person A Now	
		doesn't smoke	smokes
Person A At	doesn't smoke	+ 8	+ 12
Other Times	smokes	- 12	- 8

As with the littering problem if you perceive the situation narrowly apart from it's context from the perspective of Person A now (from the top of Table 1b), your "rational" choice is to smoke because given that you do not smoke at other times (top row) then your choice now is between +8 points for not smoking and +12 points for smoking; you should smoke. On the other hand if you do smoke at other times (bottom row) then your choice is between -12 points for not smoking and -8 points for smoking: you should still smoke.

But this "rational" defense of smoking *presumes* a narrow viewpoint. Just as the littering dilemma is solved (as it is in Japan) where people directly perceive their common interests so the smoking dilemma may be solved where a person perceives common interests across time—where the person's time window is wide—where this particular act is embedded in its temporal context. Then, like an ocean liner "ignores" small waves, the person ignores fluctuations of value at the present moment and chooses not between +8 and +12 points or between -12 and -8 points but simply between +8 and -8 points. The alternatives are to generally smoke and be healthy or to generally not smoke and be unhealthy.

The question, how can we bring about such global perceptions by ourselves and by others, in both social and interpersonal spheres, is I believe the most important psychological question there is. No possible avenue should be left unexplored. Mechanisms underlying global perception have been suggested by thinkers from Aristotle (who compared the process to the re-formation of soldiers in a rout in battle where first one soldier turns and makes a stand, then another and another, until an effective formation is created) to Ainslie, who suggests an internal marketplace where "interests" bargain with each other, make promises to each other, and look for loopholes in their promises. These are solutions organized from the right in Figure 1. Physiological mechanisms, and solutions for addiction belong to this same class.

Another class of solutions would focus directly on behavioral context—on long-term contingencies and complex behavioral patterns. Skinner's (1948) tentative suggestions for development of self-control in *Walden II*, Mazur and Logue's (1978) shaping methods for pigeons' choice of large-delayed over small-immediate reinforcers, my own current work with response-patterning, the study of behavioral economics generally (Lee, Tarpy & Webley, 1987) belong to this class, organized from the left in Figure 1. The original plans for this approach were laid out in Plato's *Republic* and Aristotle's theories of education. They were dropped when psychology became interested exclusively in *inner* causes of behavior, taken up again briefly with the rise of Skinnerian behaviorism and dropped again in the excesses of the "cognitive revolution." They deserve to be taken up once again.

References

Ainslie, G. (1974). Impulse control in pigeons. *Journal of the Experimental Analysis of Behavior, 21*, 485-489.

Ainslie, G. (1992). *Picoeconomics: The strategic interaction of successive motivational states within the person*. New York: Cambridge University Press.

Flaubert, G. (1856-7/1950). *Madame Bovary*. tr. by Alan Russell. New York: Penguin Books.

Fry, A., & Green, L. (1992). Discounting of delayed rewards by young and older adults and children. Paper presented at the Cognitive Aging Conference (April, 1992) Atlanta.

Lea, S. E. G., Tarpy, R. M., & Webley, P. (1987). *The individual in the economy*. Cambridge: Cambridge University Press.

March, J. G. (1978). Bounded rationality, ambiguity, and the engineering of choice. *Bell Journal of Economics, 9*, 587-610.

Mazur, J. E. (1986). Choice between single and multiple delayed reinforcers. *Journal* of the Experimental Analysis of Behavior, 46, 67-78.

Mazur, J. E. (1989). Theories of probabilistic reinforcement. Journal of the Experimental Analysis of Behavior, 51, 87-99.

Mazur, J. E.,& Logue, A. W. (1978). Choice in a "self-control" paradigm: Effects of a fading procedure. Journal of the Experimental Analysis of Behavior, 30, 11-17.

Mischel, W., Shoda, Y., & Rodriguez, M. (1989). Delay of gratification in children. Science, 244, 933-938.

Premack, D. (1965). Reinforcement theory. In D. Levine (Ed.), Nebraska symposium on motivation: 1965. Lincoln: University of Nebraska Press.

Rachlin, H. (1990). Why do people gamble and keep gambling despite heavy losses? Psychological Science, 1, 294-297.

Rachlin, H. (in press, a). Behavior and mind: Two psychologies. New York: Oxford University Press.

Rachlin, H. (in press, b). Teleological behaviorism. American Psychologist.

Rachlin, H., Battalio, R., Kagel, J., & Green, L. (1981). Maximization theory in behavioral psychology. The Behavioral and Brain Sciences, 4, 371-388.

Rachlin, H., Castrogiovanni, A., & Cross, D. V. (1987). Probability and delay in commitment. Journal of the Experimental Analysis of Behavior, 48, 347-354.

Rachlin, H., & Green, L. (1972). Commitment, choice and self-control. Journal of the Experimental Analysis of Behavior, 17, 15-22.

Rachlin, H., & Raineri, A. (in press). Irrationality, impulsiveness and selfishness as discount reversal effects. In G. F. Loewenstein and J. Elster (Eds.), Choice over time. New York: Russell Sage Foundation.

Rachlin, H., Raineri, A., & Cross, D. (1991). Subjective probability and delay. Journal of the Experimental Analysis of Behavior, 55, 233-244.

Raineri, A., & Rachlin, H. (in press). The effect of temporal constraints on the value of money and other commodities. Behavioral Decision Making.

Skinner, B. F. (1948). Walden two. New York: Macmillan.

Timberlake, W., & Allison, J. (1974). Response deprivation: An empirical approach to instrumental performance. Psychological Review, 81, 146-164.

Williams, B. A. (1988). Reinforcement, choice, and response strength. In R. C. Atkinson, R. J. Herrnstein, G. Lindzey, and R. D. Luce (Eds.), Stevens' handbook of experimental psychology: Vol. 2. Learning and cognition. New York: Wiley.

This article was written with the aid of a grant from the National Institute of Mental Health. Correspondence should be addressed to Howard Rachlin, Psychology Department, State University of New York, Stony Brook, NY 11794-2500.

Notes

1. How do we observe our own overt behavior? I can directly see my own fingers moving as I write but this view can never tell me about my behavior as a whole organism. We get a better view of our selves as our behavior is reflected in the environment—when I read my own writing, for instance, or when I interact with

other people.

2. The most common objection to this behavioral point of view is that a perfect actor might pretend to be in some mental state (pain, for instance) yet not really be in it. As I have argued elsewhere (Rachlin, in press a, b) the perfect-actor argument fails when it is extended over wide spans of time. An actor may pretend to be in pain on the stage but if he acts as if he were in pain off-stage for long periods of time he is in pain. Similarly, the man who on his death bed claims to have loved his wife "deep down" although he has consistently beaten her and been unfaithful to her cannot even possibly have loved her.

3. Equation 1 is hyperbolic in form but any non-exponential discount function may predict reversals. Reversals of discounted value are common not only in psychology, where they apply to memory (I remember what I had for breakfast today better than I remember what was served on my Bar Mitzvah party but as time passes todays breakfast will fade to oblivion while my Bar Mitzvah meal which, the reader may be assured, occurred many years ago., will dimly remain.) and to perception (With no distance cues a close small object may appear bigger than a far-away large object but as you withdraw from both of them the large object will again appear bigger.) but also to economics (A new VW costs more than a 2-year old BMW but 8 years hence the same BMW, now 10 years old, costs more than the 8-year old VW.) and even to physics (A low-intensity radiant energy source like a sound or light very close to an energy-measuring meter may read higher than a high-intensity source 10-ft distant from the meter. Now withdrawing the meter 100 ft away from both sources, so the high intensity source is 110 ft, and the low intensity source 100 ft from the meter, the measured intensities may reverse. The non-exponential inverse-square law of energy "discounting" predicts the reversal.) In the case of physics it has not been found necessary to postulate any internal unobserved discount processes (still less, Ainslie's internal "interests") to account for the one observed. It would seem equally unnecessary in psychology.

4. I am not advocating smoking, even occasionally. The problem with smoking is, perhaps, that a rate of smoking not injurious to one's health is not even pleasurable at all. One cigarette a week would taste harsh. You have to "invest" a little in smoking in order to enjoy it and that investment itself damages one's health. Perhaps the same is true for alcoholism for some people (see Raineri & Rachlin, in press for discussion of addiction as learning of rapid consumption). A better example than smoking might have been eating hot fudge sundaes (being thin, +10 points; being fat, -10 points; eating the sundae now, +2 points; not eating it, -2 points). Ainslie (1992) suggests that occasional use of a substance, harmful if used to excess, may be achieved through the search for "bright lines." A bright line is an environmental pattern (like an anniversary) vivid enough to bring behavior under its control. So having an ice cream sundae once a year on your birthday would allow you to eat ice cream sundaes and sill remain thin. For Ainslie the value of external patterns is wholly in their use to

control internal emotions. But I do not see why bright lines should not be conceived as directly controlling overt behavior. The pattern of one sundae per year (or per month, say) is I believe more valuable than either one sundae per day or none at all not because it makes us feel better inside but in itself. Otherwise we would have music and art and literary critics discussing not the works themselves but the emotions to which they give rise.

Other Books from CONTEXT PRESS

Ethical Issues in Developmental Disabilities
Linda J. Hayes, Gregory J. Hayes, Stephen L. Moore, and
Patrick M. Ghezzi (Eds.) (208 pp.)

Behavior Analysis of Social Behavior
Bernard Guerin (400 pp.)

Outline of J. R. Kantor's Psychological Linguistics
Sidney W. Bijou and Patrick M. Ghezzi (79 pp.)

Varieties of Scientific Contextualism
Steven C. Hayes, Linda J. Hayes, Hayne W. Reese,
Theodore R. Sarbin (Eds.) (320 pp.)

Behavior Analysis of Child Development (3rd edition)
Sidney W. Bijou (224 pp.)

Radical Behaviorism: Willard Day on Psychology and Philosophy
S. Leigland (Ed.) (208 pp.)

Understanding Verbal Relations
Steven C. Hayes and Linda J. Hayes (Eds.) (224 pp.)

Dialogues on Verbal Behavior
Linda J. Hayes and Philip N. Chase (Eds.) (349 pp.)

To order write to:

CONTEXT PRESS
933 Gear St.
Reno, NV 89502-2729